Currency Trading

FOR

DUMMIES®

A Wiley Brand

3rd Edition

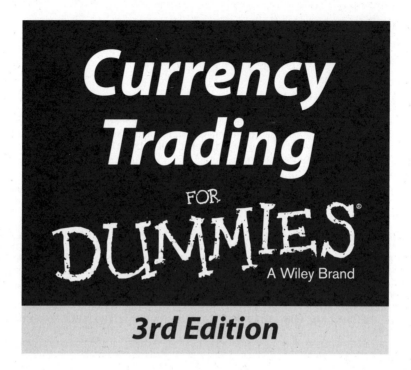

Currency Trading

FOR

DUMMIES®

A Wiley Brand

3rd Edition

by Kathleen Brooks and Brian Dolan

FOR

DUMMIES®

A Wiley Brand

Currency Trading For Dummies,® 3rd Edition

Published by: **John Wiley & Sons, Inc.,** 111 River Street, Hoboken, NJ 07030-5774, www.wiley.com

Copyright © 2015 by John Wiley & Sons, Inc., Hoboken, New Jersey

Published simultaneously in Canada

For general information on our other products and services, please contact our Customer Care Department within the U.S. at 877-762-2974, outside the U.S. at 317-572-3993, or fax 317-572-4002. For technical support, please visit www.wiley.com/techsupport.

Wiley publishes in a variety of print and electronic formats and by print-on-demand. Some material included with standard print versions of this book may not be included in e-books or in print-on-demand. If this book refers to media such as a CD or DVD that is not included in the version you purchased, you may download this material at http://booksupport.wiley.com. For more information about Wiley products, visit www.wiley.com.

Library of Congress Control Number: 2014950596

ISBN 978-1-118-98980-7 (pbk); ISBN 978-1-118-98981-4 (ebk); ISBN 978-1-118-98983-8 (ebk)

Manufactured in the United States of America

10 9 8 7

Contents at a Glance

Table of Contents

Introduction

*T*oday, millions of individual traders and investors all over the world are discovering the excitement and challenges of trading in the forex market. You don't even have to be at your desk to trade — these days, you can trade on the go using a smartphone or other handheld device.

No question about it, the forex market can be one of the fastest and most volatile financial markets to trade. Money can be made or lost in a matter of seconds or minutes. At the same time, currencies can display significant trends lasting several days to weeks and even years. Most important, forex markets are always moving, providing an accessible and target-rich trading environment.

In contrast to stock markets, which are more familiar and relatively intuitive to most investors, the forex market somehow remains more elusive and seemingly complicated to newcomers.

In this book, we show you how the forex market really works, what moves it, and how you can actively trade it. We also provide you with the tools you need to develop a structured game plan for trading in the forex market without losing your shirt. We cover the following:

- ✔ Getting a handle on the forces that drive currency movements
- ✔ Understanding forex market trading conventions and strategies
- ✔ Interpreting economic data and official statements
- ✔ Finding sources of data and market intelligence
- ✔ Gauging market psychology, sentiment, and positioning
- ✔ Identifying key traits of individual currency pairs
- ✔ Utilizing technical analysis to spot trade opportunities
- ✔ Developing a regimented and disciplined approach to trading currencies
- ✔ Focusing on risk management to minimize losses and keep more of your gains

About This Book

If you're an active trader looking for alternatives to trading stocks or futures, the forex market is hard to beat due to its sheer size (more than $5 trillion turnover per day at last count) and the depth of the market.

But as an individual trader, gaining access to the forex market is only the beginning. Just because you've got the keys to a Formula One race car doesn't mean you're ready to compete in a Grand Prix. First, you have to understand how the car works. Then you have to figure out some of the tactics and strategies the pros use. And *then* you have to get behind the wheel and practice, developing your skills, instincts, and tactics as you go.

To succeed in the forex market, you'll have to do the same. This book gives you the no-nonsense information you need, with the perspective, experience, and insight of two forex market veterans.

Whether you're an experienced trader in other markets looking to expand into currencies, or a total newcomer to trading looking to start out in currencies, this book has what you need. Best of all, it's presented in the easy-to-use *For Dummies* format. Divided into easy-to-follow parts, this book can serve as both your reference and troubleshooting guide.

Note: Trading foreign currencies is a challenging and potentially profitable opportunity for educated and experienced investors. However, before deciding to participate in the forex market, you should carefully consider your investment objectives, level of experience, and risk appetite. Most important, don't invest money you can't afford to lose. The leveraged nature of forex trading means that any market movement will have an equally proportional effect on your deposited funds; this may work against you as well as for you. (To manage exposure, employ risk-reducing strategies such as stop-loss or limit orders.) Any off-exchange foreign exchange transaction involves considerable exposure to risk, including, but not limited to, leverage, creditworthiness, limited regulatory protection, and market volatility that may substantially affect the price or liquidity of a currency or currency pair. Using the Internet to trade also involves its own risks, including, but not limited to, the failure of hardware, software, and Internet connection.

Finally, this book is a reference. You don't have to read it from beginning to end, in order; instead, you can use the table of contents and index to find the information you need right now. *Sidebars* (text in gray boxes) and anything marked with the Technical Stuff icon are skippable — they're interesting but not essential to your understanding of the topic at hand. Also, within this book, you may note that some web addresses break across two lines of text. If you're reading this book in print and you want to visit one of these web pages, simply key in the web address exactly as it's noted in the text, pretending as though the line break doesn't exist. If you're reading this as an e-book, you've got it easy — just click the web address to be taken directly to the web page.

Foolish Assumptions

Making assumptions is always a risky business, but knowing where we're coming from may help put you at ease. Obviously, not all these assumptions will apply to you, but at least we'll have it all out in the open. In writing this book, we assume the following:

- ✔ You've heard about currency trading, and you're looking to find out more about what's involved before you try it.
- ✔ You're intrigued by the international dimensions of the forex market, and you want to find out how to profit from currency movements.
- ✔ You're seeking to diversify your trading activities or hedge your investments.
- ✔ You want to discover more about technical analysis and how it can be used to improve trading results.
- ✔ You understand that trading currencies carries the risk of losses.
- ✔ You're prepared to devote the time and resources necessary to understand what's involved in currency trading.
- ✔ You have the financial resources to pursue margin trading, meaning that you'll never risk more than you can afford to lose without affecting your lifestyle.
- ✔ You aren't gullible enough to believe the infomercials that promise easy money by trading currencies.
- ✔ You understand that there is a big difference between gambling and speculating.

These assumptions should serve as a healthy reality check for you before you decide to jump into currency trading actively. A lot of it is similar to being a weekend golfer and being disappointed when your play doesn't reach pro-level scores. But when you think about it, why should it? The pros are out there practicing and playing all day, every day — it's their full-time job. Most people can only hope to get a round in on the weekend or get to the driving range for a few hours a week. Keep your perspective about what's realistic for you, and you'll be in a much better position to profit from actively trading.

Icons Used in This Book

Throughout this book, you see icons in the margins, highlighting certain paragraphs. Here are the icons we use and what they mean:

Theories are fine, but anything marked with a Tip icon tells you what currency traders *really* think and respond to. These are the tricks of the trade.

 Paragraphs marked with the Remember icon contain the key takeaways from this book and the essence of each subject's coverage.

 Achtung, baby! The Warning icon highlights potential errors and misconceptions that can cost you money, your sanity, or both.

 You can skip anything marked by the Technical Stuff icon without missing out on the main message, but you may find the information useful for a deeper understanding of the subject.

Beyond the Book

In addition to the material in the print or e-book you're reading right now, this product also comes with some access-anywhere goodies on the web. Check out the free Cheat Sheet at www.dummies.com/cheatsheet/ currencytrading for tips on choosing a broker for currency trading, the fundamentals of currency rates, and more.

You can find articles on trading forex with other asset classes, determining what kind of trader you are, and more at www.dummies.com/extras/ currencytrading.

Where to Go from Here

This book is set up so you can jump right into the topics that are of greatest interest to you. If you're an absolute newcomer to trading in general and currencies in particular, we recommend reading Parts I and II to build a foundation for the other topics. If you have more experience with trading, use the table of contents and index to find the subject you have questions about right now. This book is a reference — keep it by your computer, and turn to it whenever you have a question about currency trading.

Part I
Getting Started with Currency Trading

In this part . . .

- Get a comprehensive overview of the forex market and how it works.
- Find out what moves currencies.
- Get acquainted with the main players in the forex market.
- Understand the motivations behind trading decisions and simple strategies to get started.
- Find out why the world's biggest market is the most fascinating market.
- Get an introduction to trading plans.

Chapter 1

Currency Trading 101

. . . .

. . . .

The forex market has exploded onto the scene and is the hot new financial market. It's been around for years, but advances in electronic trading have now made it available to individual traders on a scale unimaginable just a few years ago.

We've spent our professional careers in the forex market and we can't think of a better traders' market. In our opinion, nothing quite compares to the speed and exhilaration of the forex market or the intellectual and psychological challenges of trading in it. We've always looked at our work as essentially doing the same thing every day, but no two days are ever the same in the forex market. Not many people can say that about their day jobs and we wouldn't trade it for the world, no pun intended.

What Is Currency Trading?

At its heart, currency trading is about speculating on the value of one currency versus another. The key words in that last sentence are *speculating* and *currency*. We think that looking at currency trading from those two angles — or two dimensions, if you allow us to get a little philosophical — is essential.

On the one hand, it's speculation, pure and simple, just like buying an individual stock, or any other financial security, in the hope that it will make a profitable return. On the other hand, the securities you're speculating with are the currencies of various countries. Viewed separately, that means that currency trading is both about the dynamics of market speculation, or trading, and the factors that affect the value of currencies. Put them together and you've got the largest, most dynamic and exciting financial market in the world.

Throughout this book, we approach currency trading from those two perspectives, looking at them separately and blending them together to give you the information you need to trade in the forex market.

Speculating as an enterprise

Speculating is all about taking on financial risk in the hope of making a profit. But it's not gambling and it's not investing. Gambling is about playing with money even when you know the odds are stacked against you. Investing is about minimizing risk and maximizing return, usually over a long time period. Speculating, or active trading, is about taking calculated financial risks to attempt to realize a profitable return, usually over a very short time horizon.

To be a successful trader in any market requires

- ✔ Dedication (in terms of both time and energy)
- ✔ Resources (technological and financial)
- ✔ Discipline (emotional and financial)
- ✔ Decisiveness
- ✔ Perseverance
- ✔ Knowledge

But even if you have all those traits, there's no substitute for developing a comprehensive trading plan (see Chapters 11, 12, and 13). You wouldn't open up a business enterprise without first developing a business plan (at least we hope not!). So you shouldn't expect any success in trading if you don't develop a realistic trading plan and stick to it. Think of trading as if it were your own business, and approach it as you would a business enterprise, because that's what it is.

Above all, try not to take your trading results too personally. Financial markets are prone to seemingly irrational movements on a regular basis, and the market doesn't know or care who you are and what your trade idea is.

Currencies as the trading vehicle

If you've heard anything at all about the forex market, it's probably that it's the largest financial market in the world, at least in terms of daily trading volumes. To be sure, the forex market is unique in many respects. The volumes are, indeed, huge, which means that liquidity is ever present. It also operates around the clock six days a week, giving traders access to the market any time they need it. (In Chapter 2, we give you a sense of the scale of the forex market and how it operates on a daily basis. In Chapter 3, we look at who the major forex players are.)

Few trading restrictions exist — no daily trading limits up or down, no restrictions on position sizes, and no requirements on selling a currency pair short. (We cover all the mechanics and conventions of currency trading in Chapter 4.)

Selling a currency pair short means you're expecting the price to decline. Because of the way currencies are quoted and because currency rates move up and down all the time, going short is as common as being long.

Most of the action takes place in the major currency pairs, which pit the U.S. dollar (USD) against the currencies of the *Eurozone* (the European countries that have adopted the euro as their currency), Japan, Great Britain, and Switzerland. There's also plenty of trading opportunities in the minor pairs, which see the U.S. dollar traded against the Canadian, Australian, and New Zealand dollars. On top of that, there's cross-currency trading, which directly pits two non-USD currencies against each other, such as the Swiss franc against the Japanese yen. Altogether, there are anywhere from 15 to 20 different major currency pairs, depending on which forex brokerage you deal with. (See Chapters 5 and 6 for a look at the fundamental and market factors that affect the most widely traded currency pairs.)

Most individual traders trade currencies via the Internet — on a desktop, tablet, or even smartphone — through a brokerage firm. Online currency trading is typically done on a margin basis, which allows individual traders to trade in larger amounts by leveraging the amount of margin on deposit.

One of the key features of the forex market is trading with leverage. The *leverage,* or margin trading ratios, can be very high, sometimes as much as 200:1 or greater, meaning a margin deposit of $1,000 could control a position size of $200,000. (***Note:*** Margin rules can vary by country.) Trading on margin is the backdrop against which all your trading will take place. It has benefits, but it carries its own rules and requirements as well. Leverage is a two-edged sword, amplifying gains and losses equally, which makes risk management the key to any successful trading strategy (see Chapter 13).

Before you ever start trading, in any market, make sure you're only risking money that you can afford to lose, what's commonly called *risk capital.* Risk management is the key to any successful trading plan. Without a risk-aware strategy, margin trading can be an extremely short-lived endeavor. With a proper risk plan in place, you stand a much better chance of surviving losing trades and making winning ones. (We incorporate risk management throughout this book, but especially in Chapters 11, 13, and 19.)

Downturns don't affect the forex market as they do other financial markets. Selling a currency pair is normal in the forex market. This is different from other markets — for example, stock markets, where retail investors rarely sell physical stocks due to the financial risks involved. Because selling is so common in the forex market, the forex market is fairly immune to downturns. You trade one currency against another, so something is always going up, even in times of financial crisis. (We talk more about risk on and risk off and what this means for currencies in Chapter 2.)

What Affects Currency Rates?

In a word — information. Information is what drives every financial market, but the forex market has its own unique roster of information inputs. Many different cross-currents are at play in the currency market at any given moment. After all, the forex market is setting the value of one currency relative to another, so at the minimum, you're looking at the themes affecting two major international economies. Add in half a dozen or more other national economies, and you've got a serious amount of information flowing through the market.

Fundamentals drive the currency market

Fundamentals are the broad grouping of news and information that reflects the macroeconomic and political fortunes of the countries whose currencies are traded. (We look at those inputs in depth in Chapters 7 and 9.) Most of the time, when you hear someone talking about the fundamentals of a currency, she's referring to the economic fundamentals. Economic fundamentals are based on:

- Economic data reports
- Interest rate levels
- Monetary policy·
- International trade flows
- International investment flows

There are also political and geopolitical fundamentals (see Chapter 7). An essential element of any currency's value is the faith or confidence that the market places in the value of the currency. If political events, such as an election, a war, or a scandal, are seen to be undermining the confidence in a nation's leadership, the value of its currency may be negatively affected.

Gathering and interpreting all this information is just part of a currency trader's daily routine, which is one reason why we put dedication at the top of our list of successful trader attributes (see "Speculating as an enterprise," earlier in this chapter).

Unless it's the technicals that are driving the currency market

The term *technicals* refers to *technical analysis,* a form of market analysis most commonly involving chart analysis, trend-line analysis, and mathematical studies of price behavior, such as momentum or moving averages, to mention just a couple (see Chapter 10).

We don't know of too many currency traders who don't follow some form of technical analysis in their trading. Even the stereotypical seat-of-the-pants, trade-your-gut traders are likely to at least be aware of technical price levels identified by others. If you've been an active trader in other financial markets, chances are, you've engaged in some technical analysis or at least heard of it.

If you're not aware of technical analysis, but you want to trade actively, we strongly recommend that you familiarize yourself with some of its basics (see Chapter 10). Don't be scared off by the name. Technical analysis is just a tool, like an electric saw — you don't need to know the circuitry of the saw to know how to use it. But you do need to know how to use it properly to avoid injury.

Technical analysis is especially important in the forex market because of the amount of fundamental information hitting the market at any given time. Currency traders regularly apply various forms of technical analysis to define and refine their trading strategies, with many people trading based on technical indicators alone. (See Chapters 14, 15, and 16 for how traders really use technicals.)

Or it may be something else

We're not trying to be funny here. Honest. What we are trying to do is get across the idea of the many cross-currents that are at play in the forex market at any given time. Earlier in this chapter, we note that currency trading is just one form of market speculation, and that speculative trading involves an inherent market dynamic (see "What Is Currency Trading?" earlier in this chapter).

Call it what you like — trader's instinct, market psychology, sentiment, position adjustment, or more buyers than sellers. The reality is that the forex market is made up of hundreds of thousands of different traders, each with a different view of the market and each expressing his view by buying or selling different currencies at various times and price levels.

That means that in addition to understanding the currency-specific fundamentals, and familiarizing yourself with technical analysis, you also need to have an appreciation of the market dynamic (see Chapter 8). And that's where trading with a plan comes in (see the following section).

Developing a Trading Plan

If your email inbox is anything like ours, you probably get inundated with random penny-stock tips or the next great Chinese stock initial public offering (IPO). (If you're not, please send us your spam filter.)

Those are about the only times you're going to get a message telling you how to trade. The rest of the time you're going to be on your own. But isn't that what speculative trading is all about, anyway?

Don't get us wrong, we're not trying to scare you off. We're just trying to make it clear that you're the only one who knows your risk appetite and your own trading style. And very likely, you may not have even settled on a trading style yet.

Finding your trading style

Before you can develop a trading plan, settling on a trading style is essential. (See Chapter 10 for more on trading styles.) Different trading styles generally call for variations on trading plans, though there are plenty of overarching trading rules that apply to all styles.

What do we mean by a *trading style?* Basically, it boils down to how you approach currency trading in terms of

> ✔ **Trade time frame:** How long will you hold a position? Are you looking at short-term trade opportunities (day trading), trying to capture more-significant shifts in currency prices over days or weeks, or something in between?

✔ **Currency pair selection:** Are you interested in trading in all the different currency pairs, or are you inclined to specialize in only one or two?

✔ **Trade rationale:** Are you fundamentally or technically inclined? Are you considering creating a systematic trading model? What strategy will you follow? Are you a trend follower or a breakout trader?

✔ **Risk appetite:** How much are you prepared to risk and what are your return expectations?

We don't expect you to have answers to any or all of those questions, and that's exactly the point. As you read this book, we hope you'll be thinking about what trading style you'd like to pursue. Feel free to experiment with different styles and strategies — that's what *practice accounts,* or demo accounts, are for. (See Chapter 2 for the best way to utilize practice accounts.)

At the end of the day, though, zeroing in on a trading style that you feel comfortable with and that you can pursue on a consistent basis helps. Your own individual circumstances (including work, family, free time, finances, temperament, and discipline) will be the key variables, and you're the only one who knows what they are.

Planning the trade

Whatever trading style you ultimately choose to follow, you won't get very far if you don't establish a concrete trading plan and stick to it (see Chapter 10). Trading plans are what keep small, bad trades from becoming big, bad trades and what can turn small winners into bigger winners. More than anything, though, they're your road map, helping you to navigate the market after the adrenaline and emotions start pumping, no matter what the market throws your way.

We're not telling you that currency trading is any easier than any other financial market speculation. But we can tell you that trading with a plan will greatly improve your chances of being successful in the forex market over time. Most important, we want to caution you that trading without a plan is a surefire recipe for disaster. You may survive a few close calls, but a day of reckoning comes for any trader without a plan — it's just what happens in markets.

The starting point of any trading plan is to identify a trading opportunity (see Chapter 12). No one is going to give you a call or shoot you an email telling you what and when to trade. You have to devote the effort and gray cells to spotting viable trading opportunities yourself.

Throughout this book, we offer our own observations on how the forex market behaves in various market conditions. We think there are plenty of kernels for spotting trade opportunities in those observations. (In Chapter 12, in particular, we show you a number of concrete ways to look at the market with a view to spotting trade opportunities.) Above all, be patient and wait for the market to show its hand, which it always does, one way or the other.

Executing the Trading Plan from Start to Finish

The start of any trade comes when you step into the market and open up a position. How you enter your position, how you execute the first step of your trading plan, can be as important as the trade opportunity itself. (More on getting into a position in Chapter 14.) After all, if you never enter the position, the trade opportunity will never be exploited. And probably nothing is more frustrating as a trader than having pinpointed a trade opportunity, having it go the way you expected, but having nothing to show for it because you never put the trade on.

The effort and resources you invest in researching, monitoring, and analyzing the market come to a concrete result when you open a trade. This process is made easier by formulating a personal trading system, with trigger points and setups to help you enter the trade. Placing the trade is just the beginning.

Just because you have a trading plan doesn't mean the market is necessarily going to play ball. You need to be actively engaged in managing your position to make the most of it if it's a winner and to minimize the damage if the market is not going in your favor (see Chapter 15).

Active trade management is also critical to keeping more of what you make in a trade. In our experience, making money in the forex market is not necessarily the hard part. More often than not, keeping what you've made is the *really* hard part.

You need to stay on your toes, and keep thinking about and monitoring the market while your trade is still active. The market will always be moving, sometimes faster than at other times, and new information will still be coming into the market. In Chapter 15, we look at several different ways you can monitor the market while your trade is open, as well as how and when you should adjust your trade strategy depending on events and time.

Exiting each trade is the culmination of the entire process and you're either going to be pleased with a profit or disappointed with a loss. Every trade ends in either a profit or a loss (unless you get out at the entry price); it's just the way the market works. While your trade is still active, however, you're still in control and you can choose to exit the trade at any time. In Chapter 16, we look at important tactical considerations to keep in mind when it's time to close out the trade.

Even after you've exited the position, your work is not done. If you're serious about currency trading as an enterprise, you need to review your prior trade for what it tells you about your overall trading style and trade execution. Keeping a record of your trading history is how you stay focused, learn from your mistakes, and avoid lapses in discipline that could hurt you on your next trade.

Only then is it time to move on to the next trading opportunity.

Chapter 2

What Is the Forex Market?

*W*e like to think of it as the Big Kahuna of financial markets. The foreign exchange market — most often called the forex market, or simply the FX market — is the largest and most liquid of all international financial markets. (See the "Getting liquid without getting soaked" section, later in this chapter, for our discussion of liquidity.)

The forex market is the crossroads for international capital, the intersection through which global commercial and investment flows have to move. International trade flows, such as when a Swiss electronics company purchases Japanese-made components, were the original basis for the development of the forex markets.

Today, however, global financial and investment flows dominate trade as the primary nonspeculative source of forex market volume. Whether it's an Australian pension fund investing in U.S. Treasury bonds, or a British insurer allocating assets to the Japanese equity market, or a German conglomerate purchasing a Canadian manufacturing facility, each cross-border transaction passes through the forex market at some stage.

The forex market is the ultimate traders' market. It's a market that's open around the clock six days a week, enabling traders to act on news and events as they happen. It's a market where half-billion-dollar trades can be executed in a matter of seconds and may not even move prices noticeably. That is what's unique about forex — try buying or selling a half-billion of anything in another market and see how prices react.

The rise of electronic currency trading

The forex markets have had a limited form of electronic trading since the mid-1980s. At that time, the primary means of electronic trading relied on an advanced communication system developed by Reuters, known as *Reuters Dealing*. It was a closed-network, real-time chat system well before the Internet ever hit the scene. The Reuters system enabled banks to contact each other electronically for price quotes in so-called *direct dealing*. This system functioned alongside a global network of brokerage firms that relied on telephone connections to currency trading desks and broadcast running price quotes, making them known as *voice brokers.*

The modern form of electronic currency trading debuted in the forex market in the early to mid-1990s, eventually supplanting much of the voice brokers' share of trading volume. The two main versions of electronic *matching systems* were developed by Reuters and EBS for the institutional "interbank" forex market. Both systems allowed banks to enter bids and offers into the system and trade on eligible prices from other banks, based on prescreened credit limits. The systems would match buyers and sellers, and the prices dealt in these systems became the benchmarks for currency price data, such as highs and lows.

Advances in trading software saw the development by major international banks of their own individualized trading platforms. These platforms allowed banks and their institutional clients, like corporations and hedge funds, to trade directly on live streaming prices fed over the banks' trading platforms. These systems function alongside the matching systems, which remain the primary sources of market liquidity.

At the same time, retail forex brokers introduced online trading platforms designed for individual traders. Online currency trading allows for smaller trade sizes instead of the 1 million *base currency units* that are standard in the interbank market, such as $1 million or £1 million. Forex markets trade in such large, notional amounts because the price fluctuations are in tiny increments, commonly known as *pips,* usually 0.0001.

Remember: When retail currency trading broke into the mainstream, most online currency platforms offered trade sizes in amounts commonly known as *lots,* with a standard-size lot equal to 100,000 base currency units and mini-lots equal to 10,000 base currency units. However, as the retail market has evolved, brokers have started to act on demand for the ability to place smaller trades. Most brokers now have an option to trade in micro 1,000 lots, which require a lot less capital than a mini or standard lot. This means that traders can enter the forex market with a lot less capital at risk.

In addition to multiple lot sizes, online brokerages offer generally high levels of margin, ranging from 50:1 to 200:1 and sometimes higher, depending on the regulations of the country that you trade in. This allows individual traders to make larger trades based on the amount of margin on deposit. For example, at 100:1 leverage, a $2,000 margin deposit would enable an individual trader to control a position as large as $200,000. Retail forex brokerages offer leverage to allow individual traders to trade in larger amounts relative to the small size of pips.

Firms such as FOREX.com, Saxo Bank, Oanada, CMC Markets, and IG Group have made the forex market accessible to individual traders and investors. You can now trade the same forex market as the big banks and hedge funds.

Getting Inside the Numbers

Average daily currency trading volumes exceed $5 trillion per day. That's a mind-boggling number, isn't it? $5,000,000,000,000 — that's a lot of zeros, no matter how you slice it. To give you some perspective on that size, it's about 10 to 15 times the size of daily trading volume on all the world's stock markets *combined*.

That $5-trillion-a-day number, which you may've seen in the financial press or other books on currency trading, actually overstates the size of what the forex market is all about — spot currency trading.

Trading for spot

Spot refers to the price where you can buy or sell currencies *now,* as in "on the spot." If you're familiar with stock trading, the price you can trade at is essentially a spot price. The term is primarily meant to differentiate spot, or cash, trading from futures trading, or trading for some future delivery date. The spot currency market is normally traded for settlement in two business days. Unless otherwise specified, the spot price is most likely to be what you buy and sell at with your currency broker.

Speculating in the currency market

While commercial and financial transactions in the currency markets represent huge nominal sums, they still pale in comparison to amounts based on speculation. By far the vast majority of currency trading volume is based on speculation — traders buying and selling for short-term gains based on minute-to-minute, hour-to-hour, and day-to-day price fluctuations.

Estimates are that upwards of 90 percent of daily trading volume is derived from speculation (meaning, commercial or investment-based FX trades account for less than 10 percent of daily global volume). The depth and breadth of the speculative market means that the liquidity of the overall forex market is unparalleled among global financial markets.

The bulk of spot currency trading, about 75 percent by volume, takes place in the so-called "major currencies," which represent the world's largest and most developed economies. Trading in the major currencies is largely free from government regulation and takes place outside the authority of any national or international body or exchange.

Additionally, activity in the forex market frequently functions on a regional "currency bloc" basis, where the bulk of trading takes place between the USD bloc, JPY bloc, and EUR bloc, representing the three largest global economic regions.

Trading in the currencies of smaller, less-developed economies, such as Thailand or Chile, is often referred to as *emerging market* or *exotic* currency trading. Although trading in emerging markets has grown significantly in recent years, in terms of volume it remains some way behind the developed currencies. Due to some internal factors (such as local restrictions on currency transactions by foreigners), and some external factors (such as geopolitical crises and the financial market crash, which can make emerging market currencies tricky to trade), the emerging-market forex space can be illiquid, which can be a turnoff for a small investor.

Getting liquid without getting soaked

Liquidity refers to the level of *market interest* — the level of buying and selling volume — available at any given moment for a particular asset or security. The higher the liquidity, or the *deeper* the market, the faster and easier it is to buy or sell a security.

From a trading perspective, liquidity is a critical consideration because it determines how quickly prices move between trades and over time. A highly liquid market like forex can see large trading volumes transacted with relatively minor price changes. An illiquid, or *thin,* market will tend to see prices move more rapidly on relatively lower trading volumes. A market that only trades during certain hours (futures contracts, for example) also represents a less liquid, thinner market.

We refer to liquidity, liquidity considerations, and market interest throughout this book because they're among the most important factors affecting how prices move, or *price action.*

It's important to understand that, although the forex market offers exceptionally high liquidity on an overall basis, liquidity levels vary throughout the trading day and across various currency pairs. For individual traders, though, variations in liquidity are more of a strategic consideration rather than a tactical issue. For example, if a large hedge fund needs to make a trade worth several hundred million dollars, it needs to be concerned about the tactical levels of liquidity, such as how much its trade is likely to move market prices depending on when the trade is executed. For individuals, who generally trade in smaller sizes, the amounts are not an issue, but the strategic levels of liquidity are an important factor in the timing of when and how prices are likely to move.

In the next section, we examine how liquidity and market interest changes throughout the global trading day with an eye to what it means for trading in particular currency pairs. (We look at individual currency pairs in greater detail in Chapters 8 and 9.)

Around the World in a Trading Day

The forex market is open and active 24 hours a day from the start of business hours on Monday morning in the Asia-Pacific time zone straight through to the Friday close of business hours in New York. At any given moment, depending on the time zone, dozens of global financial centers — such as Sydney, Tokyo, or London — are open, and currency trading desks in those financial centers are active in the market.

In addition to the major global financial centers, many financial institutions operate 24-hour-a-day currency trading desks, providing an ever-present source of market interest.

Currency trading doesn't even stop for holidays when other financial markets, like stocks or futures exchanges, may be closed. Even though it's a holiday in Japan, for example, Sydney, Singapore, and Hong Kong may still be open. It might be the Fourth of July in the United States, but if it's a business day, Tokyo, London, Toronto, and other financial centers will still be trading currencies. About the only holiday in common around the world is New Year's Day, and even that depends on what day of the week it falls on.

The opening of the trading week

There is no officially designated starting time to the trading day or week, but for all intents the market action kicks off when Wellington, New Zealand, the first financial center west of the international dateline, opens on Monday morning local time. Depending on whether daylight saving time is in effect in your own time zone, it roughly corresponds to early Sunday afternoon in North America, Sunday evening in Europe, and very early Monday morning in Asia.

The Sunday open represents the starting point where currency markets resume trading after the Friday close of trading in North America (5 p.m. eastern time [ET]). This is the first chance for the forex market to react to news and events that may have happened over the weekend. Prices may have closed New York trading at one level, but depending on the circumstances, they may start trading at different levels at the Sunday open. The risk that currency prices open at different levels on Sunday versus their close on Friday is referred to as the *weekend gap risk* or the *Sunday open gap risk*. A *gap* is a change in price levels where no prices are tradable in between.

As a strategic trading consideration, individual traders need to be aware of the weekend gap risk and know what events are scheduled over the weekend. There's no fixed set of potential events and there's never any way of ruling out what may transpire, such as a terror attack, a geopolitical conflict, or a natural disaster. You just need to be aware that the risk exists and factor it into your trading strategy.

Of typical scheduled weekend events, the most common are quarterly Group of Twenty (G20) meetings (see Chapter 3 for more on the G20) and national elections or referenda. Just be sure you're aware of any major events that are scheduled. During the height of the Eurozone sovereign debt crisis, a lot of last-minute bailout decisions were made over the course of a weekend, which had major implications for the markets when they opened.

On most Sunday opens, prices generally pick up where they left off on Friday afternoon. The opening price spreads in the interbank market will be much wider than normal, because only Wellington and 24-hour trading desks are active at the time. Opening price spreads of 10 to 30 points in the major currency pairs are not uncommon in the initial hours of trading. When banks in Sydney, Australia, and other early Asian centers enter the market over the next few hours, liquidity begins to improve and price spreads begin to narrow to more normal levels.

Because of the wider price spreads in the initial hours of the Sunday open, most online trading platforms do not begin trading until 5 p.m. ET on Sundays, when sufficient liquidity enables the platforms to offer their normal price quotes. Make sure you're aware of your broker's trading policies with regard to the Sunday open, especially in terms of order executions.

Trading in the Asia-Pacific session

Currency trading volumes in the Asia-Pacific session account for about 21 percent of total daily global volume, according to the 2004 BIS survey. The principal financial trading centers are Wellington, New Zealand; Sydney, Australia; Tokyo, Japan; Hong Kong, and Singapore.

News and data reports from New Zealand, Australia, and Japan are going to be hitting the market during this session. New Zealand and Australian data reports are typically released in the early morning local time, which corresponds to early evening hours in North America. Japanese data is typically released just before 9 a.m. Tokyo time, which equates to roughly 7 or 8 p.m. ET. Some Japanese data reports and events also take place in the Tokyo afternoon, which equates to roughly midnight to 4 a.m. ET.

The overall trading direction for the NZD, AUD, and JPY can be set for the entire session depending on what news and data reports are released and what they indicate.

In addition, news from China, such as economic data, interest rate changes and official comments or currency policy adjustments, may also be released. Occasionally as well, late speakers from the United States, such as Federal Reserve officials speaking on the West Coast of the United States, may offer remarks on the U.S. economy or the direction of U.S. interest rates that affect the value of the U.S. dollar against other major currencies.

Because of the size of the Japanese market and the importance of Japanese data to the market, much of the action during the Asia-Pacific session is focused on the Japanese yen currency pairs, such as USD/JPY and the JPY crosses, like EUR/JPY and AUD/JPY. Of course, Japanese financial institutions are also most active during this session, so you can frequently get a sense of what the Japanese market is doing based on price movements.

For individual traders, overall liquidity in the major currency pairs is more than sufficient, with generally orderly price movements. In some less liquid, non-regional currencies, like GBP/USD or USD/CAD, price movements may be more erratic or nonexistent, depending on the environment. With no Canadian news out for the next 12 hours, for example, there may be little reason or interest to move that pair. But if a large market participant needs to make a transaction in that pair, the price movement could be larger than normal.

Trading in the European/London session

About midway through the Asian trading day, European financial centers begin to open up and the market gets into its full swing. European financial centers and London account for over 50 percent of total daily global trading volume, with London alone accounting for about one-third of total daily global volume, according to the 2004 BIS survey.

The European session overlaps with half of the Asian trading day and half of the North American trading session, which means that market interest and liquidity is at its absolute peak during this session.

News and data events from the Eurozone (and individual countries like Germany and France), Switzerland, and the United Kingdom are typically released in the early-morning hours of the European session. As a result, some of the biggest moves and most active trading takes place in the European currencies (EUR, GBP, and CHF) and the euro cross-currency pairs (EUR/CHF and EUR/GBP).

Asian trading centers begin to wind down in the late-morning hours of the European session, and North American financial centers come in a few hours later, around 7 a.m. ET.

Trading in the North American session

Because of the overlap between North American and European trading sessions, the trading volumes are much more significant. Some of the biggest and most meaningful directional price movements take place during this crossover period. On its own, however, the North American trading session accounts for roughly the same share of global trading volume as the Asia-Pacific market, or about 22 percent of global daily trading volume.

The North American morning is when key U.S. economic data is released and the forex market makes many of its most significant decisions on the value of the U.S. dollar. Most U.S. data reports are released at 8:30 a.m. ET, with others coming out later (between 9 and 10 a.m. ET). Canadian data reports are also released in the morning, usually between 7 and 9 a.m. ET. There are also a few U.S. economic reports that variously come out at noon or 2 p.m. ET, livening up the New York afternoon market. (See Chapter 9 for more details on individual economic data reports.)

London and the European financial centers begin to wind down their daily trading operations around noon eastern time (ET) each day. The London, or European close, as it's known, can frequently generate volatile flurries of activity. A directional move that occurred earlier in European trading or the New York session may be reversed if enough traders decide to *take profit* (selling out or exiting long positions) or *cover shorts* (buying back short positions). Or the directional move may extend farther, as more traders jump onboard before the end of the trading day. There's no set recipe for how the European close plays out, but significant flurries of activity frequently occur around this time.

On most days, market liquidity and interest fall off significantly in the New York afternoon, which can make for challenging trading conditions. On quiet days, the generally lower market interest typically leads to stagnating price action. On more active days, where prices may have moved more significantly, the lower liquidity can spark additional outsized price movements, as fewer traders scramble to get similarly fewer prices and liquidity. Just as with the London close, there's never a set way in which a New York afternoon market move will play out, so traders just need to be aware that lower liquidity conditions tend to prevail, and adapt accordingly.

Lower liquidity and the potential for increased volatility is most evident in the least-liquid major-currency pairs, especially USD/CHF and GBP/USD.

North American trading interest and volume generally continue to wind down as the trading day moves toward the 5 p.m. New York close, which also sees the change in value dates take place. (See Chapter 4 for more on rollovers and value dates.) But during the late New York afternoon, Wellington and Sydney have reopened and a new trading day has begun.

As you can see, in terms of volume, London is the center of the forex world, but plenty of opportunities exist during the New York and Asia Pacific sessions. As a general rule, if you trade during the Asian session and no major data releases or events have taken place, the themes from the U.S. session the day before tend to prevail. When the European session comes around, there are usually a few meaty events to move the markets and create new themes; likewise during the U.S. trading session.

Key daily times and events

In addition to the ebb and flow of liquidity and market interest during the global currency trading day, you need to be aware of the following daily events, which tend to occur around the same times each day.

Expiring options

Currency options are typically set to expire either at the Tokyo expiry (3 p.m. Tokyo time) or the New York expiry (10 a.m. ET). The New York option expiry is the more significant one, because it tends to capture both European and North American option market interest. When an option expires, the underlying option ceases to exist. Any hedging in the spot market that was done based on the option being alive suddenly needs to be unwound, which can trigger significant price changes in the hours leading up to and just after the option expiry time.

The amount and variety of currency option interest is just too large to suggest any single way that spot prices will always react around the expiry (there may not even be any significant option interest expiring on many days), but if you do notice some volatility around 10 a.m. ET, it could be due to the expiry of some currency options.

Setting the rate at currency fixings

There are several daily currency fixings in various financial centers, but the two most important are the 8:55 a.m. Tokyo time and the 4 p.m. London time fixings. A *currency fixing* is a set time each day when the prices of currencies for commercial transactions are set, or fixed. (See Chapter 3 for more on fixings.)

From a trading standpoint, these fixings may see a flurry of trading in a particular currency pair in the run-up (generally 15 to 30 minutes) to the fixing time that abruptly ends exactly at the fixing time. A sharp rally in a specific currency pair on fixing-related buying, for example, may suddenly come to an end at the fixing time and see the price quickly drop back to where it was before.

The London forex fix is traditionally benchmarked to WM/Reuters fixing rates. At the time of writing, global financial market regulators were investigating potential manipulation of the forex fix. The outcome of this investigation could lead to changes to the fixing process in the future. (See Chapter 8 for more about forex-market regulation.)

Squaring up on the currency futures markets

The Chicago Mercantile Exchange (CME), one of the largest futures markets in the world, offers currency futures through its International Monetary Market (IMM) subsidiary exchange. A currency futures contract specifies the price at which a currency can be bought or sold at a future date. Daily currency futures trading closes each day on the IMM at 2 p.m. central time (CT), which is 3 p.m. ET. Many futures traders like to square up or close any open positions at the end of each trading session to limit their overnight exposure, or for margin requirements.

The 30 to 45 minutes leading up to the IMM closing occasionally generates a flurry of activity that spills over into the spot market. Because the amount of liquidity in the spot currency market is at its lowest in the New York afternoon, sharp movements in the futures markets can trigger volatility in the spot market around this time. There's no reliable way to tell if or how the IMM close will trigger a move in the New York afternoon spot market, so you just need to be aware of it and know that it can distort prices in the short term.

The U.S. dollar index

The U.S. dollar index is a futures contract listed on the New York Board of Trade (NYBOT) and Dublin-based Financial Instruments Exchange (FINEX) futures exchanges. The dollar index is an average of the value of the U.S. dollar against a basket of six other major currencies, but it's heavily weighted toward European currencies.

The rise of the Chinese renminbi

China has been climbing the global economic ranks. At the time of writing, it was the world's second-largest economy, but the same is not true for the Chinese currency, the renminbi (also known as the yuan). Although the role of the renminbi in global forex trading has surged, according to the 2013 BIS Triennial Central Bank Survey, the renminbi was the ninth most-traded currency in the world, with a share of 2.2 percent in global forex volumes. However, most of this trading activity is for trade purposes only.

The renminbi is a managed currency, which means that the Chinese government controls its value. This makes it very difficult to trade for speculative purposes. Either the currency doesn't move very much (because it can move only within a controlled band, which means there are few trading opportunities), or the

government intervenes out of the blue, creating a wave of volatility that could take you out of your position before you know it.

Most currency brokers allow you to trade the renminbi, but why would you want to? Some people believe that the Chinese government will eventually loosen its control over the renminbi and allow it to trade freely. Due to the importance of the Chinese economy, if the currency could trade freely, the renminbi might become a currency that would be liquid enough to rival the U.S. dollar. For now, though, it doesn't look like Beijing will embark on a liberal currency regime any time soon.

Warning: A managed currency like the renminbi can be fairly illiquid, so it can experience large price moves if the government suddenly chooses to intervene. Due to this, trading the renminbi is considered risky.

The exact weightings of other currencies in the U.S. dollar index are

- ✔ **Euro:** 57.6 percent
- ✔ **Japanese yen:** 13.6 percent
- ✔ **British pound:** 11.9 percent
- ✔ **Canadian dollar:** 9.1 percent
- ✔ **Swedish krona:** 4.2 percent
- ✔ **Swiss franc:** 3.6 percent

The European currency share of the basket — Eurozone, United Kingdom, Sweden, and Switzerland — totals 77.3 percent.

The U.S. dollar is the most important global currency, with the bulk of forex trading usually involving the dollar on one side of the transaction. Commodities are priced in dollars, and a vast amount of global currency reserves held by central banks are in dollars. This makes the dollar (also affectionately referred to as the greenback or the buck) the most liquid currency in the world. As a trader, you need to know if the dollar is strong or weak. The U.S. dollar index helps you do this because it gives you a broad-based view of how the dollar is performing in the G10 forex space. As a currency trader, be sure to follow the U.S. dollar index, especially its technical developments.

Currencies and Other Financial Markets

As much as we like to think of the forex market as the be all and end all of financial trading markets, it doesn't exist in a vacuum. You may even have heard of some these other markets: gold, oil, stocks, and bonds.

There's a fair amount of noise and misinformation about the supposed inter-relationship among these markets and currencies or individual currency pairs. To be sure, you can always find a correlation between two different markets over some period of time, even if it's only zero (meaning, the two markets aren't correlated at all).

Be very careful about getting caught up in the supposed correlations between the forex market and other financial markets. Even when a high degree of correlation is found (meaning, the two markets move in tandem or inversely to each other), it's probably over the long term (months or years) and offers little information about how the two markets will correlate in the short term (minutes, hours, and days).The other point to consider is that even if two markets have been correlated in the period, you have no guarantee that the correlation will continue to exist now or into the future. For example, depending on when you survey gold and the U.S. dollar, which supposedly have a strong negative correlation, you may find a correlation coefficient of as much as –0.8 (a solidly negative correlation) or as low as –0.2 (very close to a zero correlation, meaning that the two are virtually noncorrelated).

Always keep in mind that all the various financial markets are markets in their own right and function according to their own internal dynamics based on data, news, positioning, and sentiment. Will markets occasionally overlap and display varying degrees of correlation? Of course, and it's always important to be aware of what's going on in other financial markets. But it's also essential to view each market in its own perspective and to trade each market individually.

With that rather lengthy disclaimer in mind, let's look at some of the other key financial markets and see what conclusions we can draw for currency trading.

Gold

Gold is commonly viewed as a hedge against inflation, an alternative to the U.S. dollar, and as a store of value in times of economic or political uncertainty. Over the long term, the relationship is mostly inverse, with a weaker USD generally accompanying a higher gold price, and a stronger USD coming with a lower gold price. However, in the short run, each market has its own dynamics and liquidity, which makes short-term trading relationships generally tenuous.

Overall, the gold market is significantly smaller than the forex market, so if we were gold traders, we'd sooner keep an eye on what's happening to the dollar, rather than the other way around. With that noted, extreme movements in gold prices tend to attract currency traders' attention and usually influence the dollar in a mostly inverse fashion.

Oil

A lot of misinformation exists on the Internet about the supposed relationship between oil and the USD or other currencies, such as CAD, NOK, or JPY. The idea is that, because some countries are oil producers, their currencies are positively (or negatively) affected by increases (or decreases) in the price of oil. If the country is an importer of oil, the theory goes, its currency will be hurt (or helped) by higher (or lower) oil prices.

Correlation studies show no appreciable relationships to that effect, especially in the short run, which is where most currency trading is focused. When there is a long-term relationship, it's as evident against the USD as much as, or more than, any individual currency, whether an importer or exporter of black gold.

The best way to look at oil is as an inflation input and as a limiting factor on overall economic growth. The higher the price of oil, the higher inflation is likely to be and the slower an economy is likely to grow. The lower the price of oil, the lower inflationary pressures are likely (but not necessarily) to be. Because the United States is a heavily energy-dependent economy and also intensely consumer-driven, the United States typically stands to lose the most from higher oil prices and to gain the most from lower oil prices. We like to factor changes in the price of oil into our inflation and growth expectations, and then draw conclusions about the course of the USD from them (see more in Chapter 7). Above all, oil is just one input among many.

Stocks

Stocks are microeconomic securities, rising and falling in response to individual corporate results and prospects, while currencies are essentially macroeconomic securities, fluctuating in response to wider-ranging economic and political developments. As such, there is little intuitive reason that stock markets should be related to currencies. Long-term correlation studies bear this out, with correlation coefficients of essentially zero between the major USD pairs and U.S. equity markets over the last five years.

Risk on/risk off: Wax on, wax off

One of the first things new clients ask is what *risk on/risk off* means. This is a piece of financial market jargon that all traders should know, because it can determine the direction of a currency. *Risk on/risk off* refers to changes in investment behavior in response to global economic conditions. For example, when risk is perceived as being low, risk on/risk off states that investors tend to engage in higher-risk activities; in contrast, when the risks are perceived as high, investors tend to move toward lower-risk investments.

Risky currencies include emerging markets and some of the less liquid G10 currencies,

such as the Scandis (the Norwegian krone and Swedish krona), CAD, AUD, and NZD. Interestingly, most of the higher-risk currencies are also the currencies of commodity producers. According to risk on/risk off, these currencies should fall when risk is perceived as being high.

In contrast, the JPY, CHF, and, occasionally, the USD are considered safe havens and tend to be bought during periods when risk aversion is high. The JPY is probably the most-famous safe haven; it can rally when the risk is centered in Japan. For example, after the 2011 Japanese tsunami, the yen surged.

The two markets occasionally intersect, though this is usually only at the extremes and for very short periods. For example, when equity market volatility reaches extraordinary levels (say, the Standard & Poor's [S&P] loses 2+ percent in a day), the USD may experience more pressure than it otherwise would — but there's no guarantee of that. The U.S. stock market may have dropped on an unexpected hike in U.S. interest rates, while the USD may rally on the surprise move.

In another example, the Japanese stock market is more likely to be influenced by the value of the JPY, due to the importance of the export sector in the Japanese economy. A rapid rise in the value of the JPY, which would make Japanese exports more expensive and lower the value of foreign sales, may translate to a negative stock-market reaction on the expectation of lower corporate sales and profitability.

Bonds

Fixed income or bond markets have a more intuitive connection to the forex market because they're both heavily influenced by interest rate expectations. However, short-term market dynamics of supply and demand interrupt most attempts to establish a viable link between the two markets on a short-term basis. Sometimes the forex market reacts first and fastest depending on shifts in interest rate expectations. At other times, the bond market more accurately reflects changes in interest rate expectations, with the forex market later playing catch-up (because it takes longer to turn a bigger ship around).

Overall, as currency traders, you definitely need to keep an eye on the yields of the benchmark government bonds of the major-currency countries to better monitor the expectations of the interest rate market. Changes in relative interest rates exert a major influence on forex markets. (See Chapter 7 for more on interest rates and currencies.)

Getting Started with a Practice Account

For newcomers to currency trading, the best way to get a handle on what currency trading is all about is to open a *practice account* at any of the online forex brokers. Most online forex brokers offer practice accounts to allow you to experience the real-life price action of the forex market. Practice accounts are funded with "virtual" money, so you're able to make trades with no real money at stake and gain experience in how margin trading works.

Practice accounts give you a great chance to experience the minute-to-minute price movements of the forex market. You'll be able to see how prices change at different times of the day, as well as how various currency pairs may differ from each other. Be sure to check out the action when major news and economic data is released, so you can get a sense of how the forex market reacts to new information.

In addition to witnessing how the forex market really moves, you can

- ✔ Start trading in real market conditions without any fear of losing money.
- ✔ Experiment with different trading strategies to see how they work.
- ✔ Gain experience using different orders and managing open positions.
- ✔ Improve your understanding of how margin trading and leverage work.
- ✔ Start analyzing charts and following technical indicators.

We think using a practice account while you read this book is a great way to experience many of the ideas and concepts we introduce. If a picture is worth a thousand words, then a real-time currency trading platform with constantly changing prices, market updates, and charting tools has to be worth a book. We'd like to think we're pretty good at explaining how currency trading works, but nothing beats being able to see it for yourself.

Interpreting your results realistically

Trading in a practice account is the 21st-century form of paper trading. *Paper trading* is writing down trades on paper based on real-time market prices, but not having any real money at risk. Practice accounts are a souped-up version of paper trading — you only have to click and deal, and the trading platform does all the recording for you.

Whether you're trading in an online forex practice account or paper trading on stock quotes from the morning newspaper, be sure to keep in mind that your results aren't real, because you never had any real money at stake.

Think of it this way: If you make a handshake bet with a friend on a sports game, you're probably not going to be too concerned with whether you win or lose. You may not even watch the game. But if you bet $50 or $100 on the game, you're probably going to be watching the whole game and cheering and yelling while you do. The difference: Your emotions come alive when real money is on the line.

Practice accounts are a great way to experience the forex market up close and personal. They're also an excellent way to test-drive all the features and functionality of a broker's platform. However, the one thing you can't simulate is the emotions of trading with real money. To get the most out of your practice-account experience, you have to treat your practice account as if it were real money, as much as you can.

We recommend that you open practice accounts with a few different forex brokers, because each trading platform has varying capabilities and functionalities. In addition, different brokers have different trading policies, charting packages, and research offerings. Also, try to get a feel for the level of customer support you'll receive as a client. (You can find more information on choosing a forex broker on the Cheat Sheet.)

Chapter 3

Who Trades Currencies? Meet the Players

The forex market is regularly referred to as the largest financial market in the world based on trading volumes. But this massive market was unknown and unavailable to most individual traders and investors until the early 2000s.

That leaves a lot of people in the dark when it comes to exactly what the currency market is: how it's organized, who's trading it, and why. In this chapter, we take a look at how the FX market is structured and who the major players are. Along the way, we clue you in to how they go about their business and what it means for the market overall.

If you believe that information is the lifeblood of financial market trading, which we certainly do, we think you'll appreciate this guide to the movers and shakers of the currency market. When you have a better understanding of who's active in the FX market, you'll be able to make better sense of what you see and hear in the market.

The Interbank Market Is "The Market"

When people talk about the "currency market," they're referring to the *interbank market,* whether they realize it or not. The interbank market is where the really big money changes hands. Minimum trade sizes are one million of the base currency, such as €1 million of EUR/USD or $1 million of USD/JPY. Much larger trades (in the hundreds of millions) are routine and can go through the market in a matter of seconds. Even larger trades and orders are a regular feature of the market.

For the individual trading FX online, the prices you see on your trading platform are based on the prices being traded in the interbank market.

The sheer size of the interbank market is what helps make it such a great trading market, because investors of every size are able to act in the market, usually without significantly affecting prices. It's one market where we would say size really doesn't matter. We've seen spot traders be right with million-dollar bets, and sophisticated hedge funds be wrong with half-billion-dollar bets.

Daily trading volumes are enormous by any measure, dwarfing global stock trading volumes many times over. The most recent Bank of International Settlement (BIS) report, released in 2013, estimated daily FX trading volumes of over $5 trillion.

Getting inside the interbank market

So what is the interbank market and where did it come from? The forex market originally evolved to facilitate trade and commerce between nations. The leading international commercial banks, which financed international trade through letters of credit and bankers' acceptances, were the natural financial institutions to act as the currency exchange intermediary. They also had the foreign branch network on the ground in each country to facilitate the currency transfers needed to settle FX transactions.

The result over a number of years was the development of an informal interbank market for currency trading. As the prefix suggests, the *interbank* market is "between banks," with each trade representing an agreement between the banks to exchange the agreed amounts of currency at the specified rate on a fixed date. The interbank market is alternately referred to as the *cash market* or the *spot market* to differentiate it from the currency futures market, which is the only other organized market for currency trading.

Currency futures markets operate alongside the interbank market, but they are definitely the tail being wagged by the dog of the spot market. As a market, currency futures are generally limited by exchange-based trading hours and lower liquidity than is available in the spot market.

The interbank market developed without any significant governmental oversight and it remains largely unregulated to this day. In most cases, there is no regulatory authority for spot currency trading apart from local or national banking regulations. Interbank trading essentially evolved based on credit lines between international banks and trading conventions that developed over time.

The big commercial banks used to rule the roost when it came to currency trading, as investment banks remained focused more on stocks and bonds. But the financial industry has undergone a tremendous consolidation over the last 20 to 25 years, as bank merger after bank merger has seen famous names subsumed into massive financial conglomerates. Just 20 years ago, there were over 200 banks with FX trading desks in New York City alone. Today that number is well below a hundred. But overall trading volumes have steadily increased, testament to the power of electronic trading.

Currency trading today is largely concentrated in the hands of about a dozen major global financial firms, such as UBS, Deutsche Bank, Citibank, JPMorgan Chase, Barclays, and Goldman Sachs, to name just a few. Hundreds of other international banks and financial institutions trade alongside the top banks, and all contribute liquidity and market interest.

Bank to bank and beyond

The interbank market is a network of international banks operating in financial centers around the world. The banks maintain trading operations to facilitate speculation for their own accounts, called *proprietary trading* or just *prop trading* for short, and to provide currency trading services for their customers. Banks' customers can range from corporations and government agencies to hedge funds and wealthy private individuals.

Trading in the interbank market

The interbank market is an over-the-counter (OTC) market, which means that each trade is an agreement between the two counterparties to the trade. There are no exchanges or guarantors for the trades, just each bank's balance sheet and the promise to make payment.

The bulk of spot trading in the interbank market is transacted through electronic matching services, such as EBS and Reuters Dealing. Electronic matching services allow traders to enter their bids and offers into the market, *hit bids* (sell at the market), and *pay offers* (buy at the market). Price spreads vary by currency pair and change throughout the day depending on market interest and volatility.

The matching systems have prescreened credit limits and a bank will only see prices available to it from approved counterparties. Pricing is anonymous before a deal, meaning you can't tell which bank is offering or bidding, but the counterparties' names are made known immediately after a deal goes through.

The rest of interbank trading is done through currency brokers, referred to as *voice brokers* to differentiate them from the electronic ones. Traders can place bids and offers with these brokers the same as they do with the electronic matching services. Prior to the electronic matching services, voice brokers were the primary market intermediaries between the banks.

Stepping onto a currency trading floor

Although trading rooms in the large banks have shrunk since the 2008–2009 financial crisis, interbank trading rooms can still be lively and are staffed by a variety of different market professionals and each has a different role to play. The typical currency trading room has

- **Flow traders:** Sometimes called *execution traders,* these are the market-makers, showing two-way prices at which to buy and sell, for the bank's customers. If the customer makes a trade, the execution trader then has to cover the resulting deal in the interbank market, hopefully at a profit. These traders are also responsible for watching and executing customer orders in the market. These are the traders who are generating most of the electronic prices and price action.

- **Proprietary traders:** These traders are focused on speculative trading for the bank's own account. Their strategies can run the gamut from short-term day trading to longer-term macroeconomic bets. In the wake of the 2008–2009 financial crisis and changes to regulation such as the Volcker Rule, there has been a sharp decline in banks' trading for their own accounts, and many proprietary trading desks have closed down or moved to hedge funds.

- **Forward traders:** Forward traders are active in the *forward* currency market, which refers to trades made beyond the normal spot value date. The forward market is essentially an interest rate differential market, where the interest rates of the various currencies are traded. These traders provide the bank's customers with pricing for non-spot deals or currency swap agreements. They also manage the bank's interest rate exposure in the various currencies.

- **Options traders:** Options traders manage the bank's portfolio, or book, of outstanding currency options. They hedge the portfolio in the spot market, speculate for the bank's own account with option strategies, and provide pricing to the bank's customers on requested option strategies.

- **Sales staff:** The sales staff acts as the intermediary between the trading desk and the bank's customers. They advise the bank's customers on market flow, as well as who's buying and selling; recommend spot and option trading strategies; and execute trades between the bank and its customers.

Hedgers and Financial Investors

The forex market sits at the crossroads of global trade and international finance and investing. Whether it's a U.S. conglomerate managing its foreign affiliates' balance sheets or a German mutual fund launching an international stock fund, they all have to go through the forex market at some point.

Participants in the forex market generally fall into one of two categories: financial transactors and speculators. *Financial transactors* are active in the forex market as part of their overall business but not necessarily for currency reasons. *Speculators* are in it purely for the money.

The lion's share of forex market turnover comes from speculators. Market estimates suggest that upwards of 90 percent of daily FX trading volume is based solely on speculation. We look at the types and roles of speculators in the "Speculators" section of this chapter, but here we want to introduce the players who are active in the forex markets for nonspeculative reasons.

Financial transactors are important to the forex market for several reasons:

- ✔ Their transactions can be extremely sizeable, typically hundreds of million or billions.
- ✔ Their deals are frequently one-time events.
- ✔ They are generally not price sensitive or profit maximizing.

 Add up those reasons and you're looking at potentially very large, one-off trading flows that are not really concerned with where the current market is trading or which way it's headed. They enter the market to do their deal and then they're gone, which can introduce an element of market inefficiency that can allow traders to take advantage of counter-trend movements.

Hedging your bets

Hedgers come in all shapes and sizes, but don't confuse them with *hedge funds*. (Despite the name, a hedge fund is typically 100 percent speculative in its investments.)

Hedging is about eliminating or reducing risk. In financial markets, hedging refers to a transaction designed to insure against an adverse price move in some underlying asset. In the forex market, hedgers are looking to insure themselves against an adverse price movement in a specific currency rate.

Hedging for international trade purposes

One of the more traditional reasons for hedging in the forex market is to facilitate international trade. Let's say you're a widget maker in Germany and you just won a large order from a UK-based manufacturer to supply it with a large quantity of widgets. To make your bid more attractive, you agreed to be paid in British pounds (GBP).

But because your production cost base is denominated in euros (EUR), you face the exchange rate risk that GBP will weaken against the EUR. That would make the amount of GBP in the contract worth fewer EUR back home, reducing or even eliminating your profit margin on the deal. To insure, or *hedge*, against that possibility, you would seek to sell GBP against EUR in the forex market. If the pound weakened against the euro, the value of your market hedge would rise, compensating you for the lower value of the GBP you'll receive. If the pound strengthens against the euro, your loss on the hedge is offset by gains in the currency conversions. (Each pound would be worth more euros.)

Trade hedgers follow a variety of hedging strategies and can utilize several different currency hedging instruments. Currency *options* can be used to eliminate downside currency risk and sometimes allow the hedger to participate in advantageous price movements. Currency *forward* transactions essentially lock in a currency price for a future date, based on the current spot rate and the interest rate differentials between the two currencies.

Trade-related hedging regularly comes into the spot market in two main forms:

- ✔ **At several of the daily currency fixings:** The largest is the London afternoon fixing, which takes place each day at 4 p.m. local time, which corresponds to 11 a.m. eastern time (ET). The Tokyo fixing takes place each day at 8:55 a.m. Tokyo time, which corresponds to 6:55 p.m. eastern time (ET). A *fixing* is a process where commercial hedgers submit orders to buy or sell currencies in advance. The orders are then filled at the prevailing spot rate (the rate is fixed) at the time of the fixing.

The difference between the amount of buying and selling orders typically results in a net amount that needs to be bought or sold in the market prior to the fixing time. On some days, this can see large amounts (several billion dollars or more) being bought or sold in the hour or so leading up to the fixing time. After the fix, that market interest has been satisfied and disappears. Month-end and quarter-end fixings typically see the largest amounts of volume.

Short-term traders need to closely follow live market commentaries to see when there is a substantial buying or selling interest for a fixing. (See Chapter 2 for more on potential future changes to the fixing process.)

> ✔ **Mostly in USD/JPY, where Japanese exporters typically have large amounts of USD/JPY to sell:** Japanese exporters receive dollars for their exports, which must then be converted into JPY (sell USD/buy JPY). The Japanese export community tends to be closely knit and their orders are likely to appear together in large amounts at similar levels. Again, real-time market commentaries are the most likely source for individual traders to hear about Japanese exporter selling interest.

Hedging for currency options

The currency option market is a massive counterpart to the spot market and can heavily influence day-to-day spot trading. Currency option traders are typically trading a portfolio of option positions. To maximize their returns, options traders regularly engage in delta hedging and gamma trading. Without getting into a major options discussion here (we cover currency options in Chapter 6), option portfolios generate a synthetic, or hypothetical, spot position based on spot price movements.

To maximize the return on their options portfolios, they regularly trade the synthetic spot position as though it were a real spot position. Trading the synthetic positions generated by options is called *delta hedging* or *gamma trading*.

Option hedgers are frequently found selling at technical resistance levels or buying on support levels. When a currency pair stays in a range, it can do quite nicely. But when range breakouts occur, options traders frequently need to rush to cover those range bets, adding to the force of the directional breakout. Keep an eye out for reports of option-related buying and selling as technical levels are tested.

Another daily feature of the spot market is the 10 a.m. ET option expiry, when options due to expire that day that finish out of the money cease to exist. Any related hedging that was done for the option then needs to be unwound, though this is likely to have been done prior to the expiry if the option is well out of the money. Traders need to follow market commentaries to see if large option interest is set to expire on any given day and generally anticipate a flurry of option-related buying/selling that may suddenly reverse course after the 10 a.m. expiry.

Global investment flows

One of the reasons forex markets remain as lightly regulated as they are is that no developed nation wants to impose restrictions on the flow of global capital. International capital is the lifeblood of the developed economies and the principal factor behind the rapid rise of the BRIC economies (Brazil,

Russia, India, and China). The forex market is central to the smooth functioning of international debt and equity markets, allowing investors to easily obtain the currency of the nation they want to invest in.

Financial investors are the other main group of nonspeculative players in the forex market. As far as the forex market is concerned, financial investors are mostly just passing through on their way to another investment. More often than not, financial investors look at currencies as an afterthought, because they're more focused on the ultimate investment target, be it Japanese equities, German government bonds, or French real estate.

Crossing borders with mergers and acquisitions

Mergers and acquisitions (M&A) activity is often international and shows no sign of abating. International firms are now involved in a global race to gain and expand market share, and cross-border acquisitions are frequently the easiest and fastest way to do that.

When a company seeks to buy a foreign business, there can be a substantial foreign exchange implication from the trade. When large M&A deals are announced, note the answers to the following two questions:

- **Which countries and which currencies are involved?** If a French electrical utility buys an Austrian power company, there are no currency implications because both countries use the euro (EUR). But if a Swiss pharmaceutical company announces a takeover of a Dutch chemical firm, the Swiss company may need to buy EUR and sell Swiss francs (CHF) to pay for the deal.

- **How much of the transaction will be in cash?** Again, if it's an all stock deal, then there are no forex market implications. But if the cash portion is large, forex markets will take note and begin to speculate on the currency pair involved.

Speculators

Speculators are market participants who are involved in the market for one reason only: to make money. In contrast to hedgers, who have some form of existing currency market risk, speculators have no currency risk until they enter the market. Hedgers enter the market to neutralize or reduce risk. Speculators embrace risk taking as a means of profiting from long-term or short-term price movements.

Speculators (*specs* for short) are what really make a market efficient. They add liquidity to the market by bringing their views and, most important, their capital into the market. That liquidity is what smoothes out price movements, keeps trading spreads narrow, and allows a market to expand.

In the forex market, speculators are running the show. Conventional market estimates are that upwards of 90 percent of daily trading volume is speculative in nature. If you're trading currencies for your own account, welcome to the club. If you're trading currencies to hedge a financial risk, you can thank the specs for giving you a liquid market and reducing your transaction costs.

Speculators come in all types and sizes and pursue all different manner of trading strategies. In this section, we take a look at some of the main types of speculators to give you an idea of who they are and how they go about their business. Along the way, you may pick up some ideas to improve your own approach to the market. At the minimum, we hope this information will allow you to better understand market commentaries about who's buying and who's selling.

Hedge funds

Hedge funds are a type of *leveraged fund,* which refers to any number of different forms of speculative asset management funds that borrow money for speculation based on real assets under management. For instance, a hedge fund with $100 million under management can *leverage* those assets (through margin agreements with their trading counterparties) to give them trading limits of anywhere from $500 million to $2 billion. Hedge funds are subject to the same type of margin requirements as you or we are, just with a whole lot more zeroes involved.

The other main type of leveraged fund is known as a Commodity Trading Advisor (CTA). A CTA is principally active in the futures markets. But because the forex market operates around the clock, CTAs frequently trade spot FX as well.

The major difference between the two types of leveraged funds comes down to regulation and oversight. CTAs are regulated by the Commodity Futures Trading Commission (CFTC), the same governmental body that regulates retail FX firms. As a result, CTAs are subject to a raft of regulatory and reporting requirements. Hedge funds, on the other hand, remain largely unregulated. What's important is that they all pursue similarly aggressive trading strategies in the forex market, treating currencies as a separate asset class, like stock or commodities.

In the forex market, leveraged funds can hold positions anywhere from a few hours to days or weeks. When you hear that leveraged names are buying or selling, it's an indication of short-term speculative interest that can provide clues as to where prices are going in the near future.

Speculating with black boxes, models, and systems

Many leveraged funds have opted for a *quantitative* approach to trading financial markets. A quantitative approach is one that uses mathematical formulas and models to come up with buy and sell decisions. The *black box* refers to the proprietary quantitative formula used to generate the trading decisions. Data goes in, trading signals come out, and what's inside the black box, no one knows. Black box funds are also referred to as *models* or *system-based funds.*

Some models are based on complex statistical relationships between various currencies, commodities, and fixed income securities. Others are based on macroeconomic data, such as relative growth rates, inflation rates, and geopolitical risks. Still others are based on technical indicators and price studies of the underlying currency pair. These are frequently referred to as *rules-based trading systems,* because the system will employ defined rules to enter and exit trades.

If you're technically or statistically inclined, you can create your own model or rules-based trading system. Many online trading platforms offer application programming interface (API) access to their trading platforms, allowing you to draw price data from the platform, filter it through your trading system, and generate trading signals. Some even allow for automated trade execution without any further user action. Check with your online currency brokerage firm to see if it has an API and supports automated trade executions.

These days there are also ready-made automated trading systems available, called expert advisors (EAs). Most currency brokers offer these to retail clients. If you're happy to let someone else create a trading program, this could make your life easier, but all automated programs come with their own level of risk that you should be aware of. (See Chapter 10 for more information.)

Trading with discretion

The opposite of a black box trading system is a *discretionary* trading fund. The discretion, in this case, refers to the fund manager's judgment and overall market view. The fund manager may follow a technical or system-based approach but prefer to have a human make the final decision on whether a trade is initiated. A more refined version of this approach accepts the trade signals but leaves the execution up to the discretionary fund manager's trading staff, which tries to maximize position entry/exit based on short-term market dynamics.

Still another variation of discretionary funds is those that base their trading strategies on macroeconomic and political analysis, known as *global-macro funds.* This type of discretionary fund manager is typically playing with a longer-time horizon in mind. The fund may be betting on a peak in the interest rate cycle or the prospect that an economy will slip into recession. Shorter-term variations on this theme may take positions based on a specific event risk, such as the outcome of the next central bank meeting or national election.

High-frequency trading

High-frequency trading (HFT) is a type of algorithmic or black-box trading that has grown in significance in the last 10 to 15 years. It's a rapid way to trade currencies and other asset classes. High-frequency traders move in and out of short-term positions in seconds or even fractions of seconds, sometimes aiming to capture a fraction of a cent of profit on every trade.

HFT has exploded onto the scene and has grown rapidly since 2000. However, it isn't without its critics. Some people believe that HFT causes excessive market volatility — it was found to contribute to the 2010 "flash crash."

Today HFT is mostly centered in the institutional and hedge-fund space. Most retail brokers don't offer HFT and actively stop clients from using it, for a couple reasons:

✔ **Cost:** HFT execution happens in just a fraction of a second, so it requires top-notch Internet connections and hardware, which retail traders may not have. Any latency in your trading (for example, if there is a delay between placing your trade and execution because of a slow Internet connection) could leave you exposed to losses.

✔ **Regulation:** On balance, reputable retail brokers apply high standards to how they trade, and the reputational issues that currently surround HFT have been thus far been a turnoff.

Day traders, big and small

This is where you and we fit into the big picture of the forex market. If the vast majority of currency trading volume is speculative in nature, then most of that speculation is short-term in nature. Short-term can be minute-to-minute or hour-to-hour, but rarely is it longer than a day or two. From the interbank traders who are scalping EUR/USD (high frequency in-and-out trading for few pips) to the online trader looking for the next move in USD/JPY, short-term day traders are the backbone of the market.

Intraday trading was always the primary source of interbank market liquidity, providing fluid prices and an outlet for any institutional flows that hit the market. Day traders tend to be focused on the next 20 to 30 pips in the market, which makes them the source of most short-term price fluctuations.

When you're looking at the market, look in the mirror and imagine several thousand similar faces looking back, all trying to capture the same currency trading gains that you're shooting for. It helps to imagine this so you know you're not alone and also so you know whom you're up against.

The rise of online currency trading has thrust individual retail traders into the mainstream of the forex market. Online currency brokerage firms are referred to as *retail aggregators* by the institutional interbank market, because brokerage firms typically aggregate the net positions of their clients for hedging purposes. The online brokerages then transact with the interbank market to manage their market exposure.

Governments and Central Banks

National governments are routinely active in the forex market, but not for purposes of attempting to realign or shift the values of the major currencies. (We discuss those currency policies in greater depth in Chapter 7.)

Instead, national governments are active in the forex market for routine funding of government operations, making transfer payments, and managing foreign currency reserves. The first two functions have generally little impact on the day-to-day forex market, so we won't bore you with the details. But the last one has taken on increased prominence in recent years, and all indications are that it will continue to play a major role in the years ahead.

Currency reserve management

Currency reserve management refers to how national governments develop and invest their foreign currency reserves. Foreign currency reserves are accumulated through international trade. Countries with large trade surpluses will accumulate reserves of foreign currency over time. Trade surpluses arise when a nation exports more than it imports. Because it is receiving more foreign currency for its exports than it is spending to buy imports, foreign currency balances accumulate. China, one of the world's largest exporters, has many trillions of dollars as reserves.

The USD has historically been the primary currency for international reserve holdings of most countries. International Monetary Fund (IMF) data from June 2014 showed that the USD accounted for just over 60 percent of global currency reserve holdings, with EUR (25 percent) and JPY (4 percent) the next most widely held currencies.

In recent years, however, the United States has run up massive trade and current account deficits with the rest of the world. The flip side has been the accumulation of large trade surpluses in other countries, most clearly in Asia. The U.S. deficits essentially amount to the United States borrowing money from the countries with trade surpluses, while those other countries (think China) buy IOUs in the form of U.S. Treasury debt securities.

The problem is one of perception and also of prudent portfolio management:

- ✔ **The perception problem stems from the continuing growth of U.S. deficits, which equates to your continually borrowing money from a bank.** At a certain point, no matter how good your credit is, the bank will stop lending you money because you've already borrowed so much in the first place. In the case of the United States, no one is sure exactly where that point is, but let's just say we don't want to find out. In recent years, the U.S. Congress has had to raise its debt ceiling to accommodate its growing need to borrow. At the time of writing, the U.S. debt ceiling stood at more than $16 trillion.

- ✔ **The portfolio-management problem arises from the need to diversify assets in the name of prudence.** Due to the high proportion of U.S. dollars in global forex reserves, forex reserve managers need to be cognizant of the risks they face if there is a sharp drop in the U.S. dollar's value. This was particularly relevant after the financial crisis when the U.S. dollar started to weaken.

The result has been an effort by many national governments to begin to diversify their reserves away from the USD and into other major currencies. The euro, the Japanese yen, the British pound, and to a lesser extent the Australian dollar, have been the principal beneficiaries of this shift. But before you think the sky is falling, the USD remains the primary reserve currency globally.

In terms of daily forex market trading, national governments (or their operatives) have become regular market participants over the last few years. Generally speaking, they appear to be engaging in active currency reserve management, selling USD on rallies, and buying EUR on weakness. But they're also not averse to then selling EUR on subsequent strength and buying USD back on weakness.

Currency reserve management has taken on a market prominence in recent years that never existed before. Market talk of central bank buying or selling for reserve management purposes has become almost a daily occurrence. The impact of this in the market varies, but it can frequently lead to multiday highs and lows being maintained in the face of an otherwise compelling trend.

Traders need to closely follow real-time market commentaries for signs of central bank involvement.

The Bank for International Settlements

The Bank for International Settlements (BIS) is the central bank for central banks. Located in Basel, Switzerland, the BIS also acts as the quasigovernment regulator of the international banking system. It was the BIS that established the capital adequacy requirements for banks that today underpin the international banking system.

As the bank to national governments and central banks, the BIS frequently acts as the market intermediary of those nations seeking to diversify their currency reserves. By going through the BIS, those countries can remain relatively anonymous and prevent speculation from driving the market against them.

Market talk of the BIS being active in the market is frequently interpreted as significant reserve interest to buy or sell. Keep an eye out for market rumors of the BIS, but also keep in mind that the BIS performs more routine and smaller trade execution on behalf of its clients.

The Group of Twenty

The Group of Twenty, or G20, is a forum for the governments and central bank governors of the world's 20 largest economies. Members include the developed markets and the larger emerging markets, including Mexico, Brazil, China, and Korea, along with Saudi Arabia. The G20 superseded the G7 and the G8 as the global leaders' summit to keep an eye on. G20 summits take place each year, depending on the circumstances, currency values may be on the agenda for these meetings and the communiqué, the official statement issued at the end of each gathering, may contain an explicit indication for a desired shift among the major currencies. If currencies are not a hot-button topic, the G20 will include a standard boilerplate statement that currencies should reflect economic fundamentals and that excessive currency volatility is undesirable.

Forex markets closely follow the preparations leading up to the meetings for several weeks in advance. Traders are looking first to see if currencies will even be discussed, and then to see which currency or currencies will be on the agenda. The market will generally have a sense of whether currencies are an issue, and the general feeling of what the G20 would like to see done, well in advance. Still, comments from ministers and their deputies holding the preparatory consultations set the stage for the market's expectations and can provoke market reactions even before the G20 meets, although this can be rare.

Chapter 4

The Mechanics of Currency Trading

*T*he currency market has its own set of market trading conventions and related lingo, just like any other financial market. If you're new to currency trading, the mechanics and terminology may take some getting used to. But at the end of the day, you'll see that most currency trade conventions are pretty straightforward.

Buying and Selling Simultaneously

The biggest mental hurdle facing newcomers to currencies, especially traders familiar with other markets, is getting their head around the idea that each currency trade consists of a simultaneous purchase and sale. In the stock market, for instance, if you buy 100 shares of Google, it's pretty clear that you now own 100 shares and hope to see the price go up. When you want to exit that position, you simply sell what you bought earlier. Easy, right?

But in currencies, the purchase of one currency involves the simultaneous sale of another currency. This is the *exchange* in *foreign exchange*. To put it another way, if you're looking for the dollar to go higher, the question is "Higher against what?" The answer has to be another currency. In relative terms, if the dollar goes up against another currency, it also means that the other currency has gone down against the dollar. To think of it in stock-market terms, when you buy a stock, you're selling cash, and when you sell a stock, you're buying cash.

Currencies come in pairs

To make matters easier, forex markets refer to trading currencies by pairs, with names that combine the two different currencies being traded against each other, or exchanged for one another. Additionally, forex markets have given most currency pairs nicknames or abbreviations, which reference the pair and not necessarily the individual currencies involved.

The U.S. dollar is the central currency against which other currencies are traded. In its most recent triennial survey of the global foreign exchange market in 2013, the Bank for International Settlements (BIS) found that the U.S. dollar was on one side of 87 percent of all reported forex market transactions, and the dollar's position as the world's dominant currency has remained virtually unchallenged for decades.

The U.S. dollar's central role in the forex markets stems from a few basic factors:

- ✔ The U.S. economy is the largest national economy in the world.
- ✔ The U.S. dollar is the primary international reserve currency.
- ✔ The U.S. dollar is the medium of exchange for many cross-border transactions. For example, oil is priced in U.S. dollars. So even if you're a Japanese oil importer buying crude from Saudi Arabia, you're going to pay in U.S. dollars.
- ✔ The United States has the largest and most liquid financial markets in the world.
- ✔ The United States is a global military superpower, with a stable political system, even if we have seen a dysfunctional Congress in recent years!

Major currency pairs

The major currency pairs all involve the U.S. dollar on one side of the deal. The designations of the major currencies are expressed using International Standardization Organization (ISO) codes for each currency. Table 4-1 lists the most frequently traded currency pairs, what they're called in conventional terms, and what nicknames the market has given them.

Table 4-1	The Major U.S. Dollar Currency Pairs		
ISO Currency Pair	*Countries*	*Long Name*	*Nickname*
EUR/USD	Eurozone*/United States	Euro-dollar	N/A
USD/JPY	United States/Japan	Dollar-yen	N/A

ISO Currency Pair	Countries	Long Name	Nickname
GBP/USD	United Kingdom/United States	Pound-dollar	Sterling or Cable
USD/CHF	United States/ Switzerland	Dollar-Swiss	Swissy
USD/CAD	United States/Canada	Dollar-Canada	Loonie
AUD/USD	Australia/United States	Australian-dollar	Aussie or Oz
NZD/USD	New Zealand/United States	New Zealand-dollar	Kiwi

* The Eurozone is made up of all the countries in the European Union that have adopted the euro as their currency. As of this printing, the Eurozone countries are Austria, Belgium, Cyprus, Estonia, Finland, France, Germany, Greece, Ireland, Italy, Luxembourg, Malta, the Netherlands, Portugal, Slovakia, Slovenia, and Spain.

Currency names and nicknames can be confusing when you're following the forex market or reading commentary and research. Be sure you understand whether the writer or analyst is referring to the individual currency or the currency pair.

- ✔ If a bank or a brokerage is putting out research suggesting that the Swiss franc will weaken in the future, the comment refers to the *individual* currency, in this case CHF, suggesting that USD/CHF will move *higher* (USD stronger/CHF weaker).

- ✔ If the comment suggests that Swissy is likely to weaken going forward, it's referring to the currency *pair* and amounts to a forecast that USD/ CHF will move *lower* (USD weaker/CHF stronger).

Major cross-currency pairs

Although the vast majority of currency trading takes place in the dollar pairs, cross-currency pairs serve as an alternative to always trading the U.S. dollar. A cross-currency pair, or *cross* or *crosses* for short, is any currency pair that does not include the U.S. dollar. Cross rates are derived from the respective USD pairs but are quoted independently and usually with a narrower spread than you could get by trading in the dollar pairs directly. (The *spread* refers to the difference between the bid and offer, or the price at which you can sell and buy and spreads are applied in most financial markets.)

Crosses enable traders to more directly target trades to specific individual currencies to take advantage of news or events. For example, your analysis may suggest that the Japanese yen has the worst prospects of all the major currencies going forward, based on interest rates or the economic outlook. To take advantage of this, you'd be looking to sell JPY, but against which other currency? You consider the USD, potentially buying USD/JPY (buying USD/selling JPY), but then you conclude that the USD's prospects are not much better than the JPY's. Further research on your part may point to another currency that has a much better outlook (such as high or rising interest rates or signs of a strengthening economy), say the Australian dollar (AUD). In this example, you would then be looking to buy the AUD/JPY cross (buying AUD/selling JPY) to target your view that AUD has the best prospects among major currencies and the JPY the worst.

Cross trades can be especially effective when major cross-border mergers and acquisitions (M&A) are announced. If a UK conglomerate is buying a Canadian utility company, the UK company is going to need to sell GBP and buy CAD to fund the purchase. The key to trading on M&A activity is to note the cash portion of the deal. If the deal is all stock, then you don't need to exchange currencies to come up with the foreign cash.

The most actively traded crosses focus on the three major non-USD currencies (namely EUR, JPY, and GBP) and are referred to as euro crosses, yen crosses, and sterling crosses. The remaining currencies (CHF, AUD, CAD, and NZD) are also traded in cross pairs. Tables 4-2, 4-3, and 4-4 highlight the key cross pairs in the euro, yen, and sterling groupings, respectively, along with their market names. Table 4-5 lists other cross-currency pairs.

Table 4-2	Euro Crosses	
ISO Currency Pair	*Countries*	*Market Name*
EUR/CHF	Eurozone/Switzerland	Euro-Swiss
EUR/GBP	Eurozone/United Kingdom	Euro-sterling
EUR/CAD	Eurozone/Canada	Euro-Canada
EUR/AUD	Eurozone/Australia	Euro-Aussie
EUR/NZD	Eurozone/New Zealand	Euro-Kiwi

Table 4-3	Yen Crosses	
ISO Currency Pair	*Countries*	*Market Name*
EUR/JPY	Eurozone/Japan	Euro-yen
GBP/JPY	United Kingdom/Japan	Sterling-yen
CHF/JPY	Switzerland/Japan	Swiss-yen
AUD/JPY	Australia/Japan	Aussie-yen
NZD/JPY	New Zealand/Japan	Kiwi-yen
CAD/JPY	Canada/Japan	Canada-yen

Table 4-4	Sterling Crosses	
ISO Currency Pair	*Countries*	*Market Name*
GBP/CHF	United Kingdom/Switzerland	Sterling-Swiss
GBP/CAD	United Kingdom/Canada	Sterling-Canadian
GBP/AUD	United Kingdom/Australia	Sterling-Aussie
GBP/NZD	United Kingdom/New Zealand	Sterling-Kiwi

Table 4-5	Other Crosses	
ISO Currency Pair	*Countries*	*Market Name*
AUD/CHF	Australia/Switzerland	Aussie-Swiss
AUD/CAD	Australia/Canada	Aussie-Canada
AUD/NZD	Australia/New Zealand	Aussie-Kiwi
CAD/CHF	Canada/Switzerland	Canada-Swiss

Base currencies and counter currencies

When you look at currency pairs, you may notice that the currencies are combined in a seemingly strange order. For instance, if sterling-yen (GBP/JPY) is a yen cross, then why isn't it referred to as "yen-sterling" and written "JPY/GBP"? The answer is that these quoting conventions evolved over the years to reflect traditionally strong currencies versus traditionally weak currencies, with the strong currency coming first.

It also reflects the market quoting convention where the first currency in the pair is known as the *base currency*. The base currency is what you're buying or selling when you buy or sell the pair. It's also the *notional*, or *face*, amount of the trade. So if you buy 100,000 EUR/JPY, you've just bought 100,000 euros and sold the equivalent amount in Japanese yen. If you sell 100,000 GBP/CHF, you just sold 100,000 British pounds and bought the equivalent amount of Swiss francs.

The second currency in the pair is called the *counter currency*, or the *secondary currency*. Hey, who said this stuff isn't intuitive? Most important for you as an FX trader, the counter currency is the denomination of the price fluctuations and, ultimately, what your profit and losses will be denominated in. If you buy GBP/JPY, it goes up, and you take a profit, your gains are not in pounds, but in yen. (We run through the math of calculating profit and loss later in this chapter.)

The long and the short of it

Forex markets use the same terms to express market positioning as most other financial markets do. But because currency trading involves simultaneous buying and selling, being clear on the terms helps — especially if you're totally new to financial market trading.

Going long

No, we're not talking about running out deep for a football pass. A *long position,* or simply a *long,* refers to a market position in which you've bought a security. In FX, it refers to having bought a currency pair. When you're long, you're looking for prices to move higher, so you can sell at a higher price than where you bought. When you want to close a long position, you have to sell what you bought. If you're buying at multiple price levels, you're *adding to longs* and *getting longer.*

Getting short

A *short position,* or simply a *short,* refers to a market position in which you've sold a security that you never owned. In the stock market, selling a stock short requires borrowing the stock (and paying a fee to the lending brokerage) so you can sell it. In forex markets, it means you've sold a currency *pair,* meaning you've sold the base currency and bought the counter currency. So you're still making an exchange, just in the opposite order and according to currency-pair quoting terms. When you've sold a currency pair, it's called *going short* or *getting short* and it means you're looking for the pair's price to move lower so you can buy it back at a profit. If you sell at various price levels, you're *adding to shorts* and *getting shorter.*

In most other markets, *short selling* either comes with restrictions or is considered too risky for most individual traders. In currency trading, going short is as common as going long. "Selling high and buying low" is a standard currency trading strategy.

Currency pair rates reflect relative values between two currencies and not an absolute price of a single stock or commodity. Because currencies can fall or rise relative to each other, both in medium and long-term trends and minute-to-minute fluctuations, currency pair prices are as likely to be going down at any moment as they are up. To take advantage of such moves, forex traders routinely use short positions to exploit falling currency prices. Traders from other markets may feel uncomfortable with short selling, but it's just something you have to get your head around.

Squaring up

If you have no position in the market, it's called being *square* or *flat.* If you have an open position and you want to close it, it's called *squaring up.* If you're short, you need to buy to square up. If you're long, you need to sell to go flat. The only time you have no market exposure or financial risk is when you're square.

Profit and Loss

Profit and loss (P&L) is how traders measure success and failure. You don't want to be looking at the forex market as some academic or thrill-seeking exercise. Real money is made and lost every minute of every day. If you're going to trade currencies actively, you need to get up close and personal with P&L.

A clear understanding of how P&L works is especially critical to online margin trading, where your P&L directly affects the amount of margin you have to work with. (We introduce online margin trading in Chapter 2.) Changes in your margin balance will determine how much you can trade and for how long you can trade if prices move against you.

Margin balances and liquidations

As we mention in Chapter 2, one of the benefits of forex trading is that you can use leverage, which allows you to gain a large exposure to a financial market while only tying up a small amount of your capital. The initial capital that you have to post to your account in order to open a trade is called *margin*.

That initial margin deposit becomes your opening *margin balance* and is the basis on which all your subsequent trades are collateralized. Think of this as a bit like the collateral a bank will ask for if you apply for a loan. Unlike futures markets or margin-based equity trading, online forex brokerages do not issue *margin calls* (requests for more collateral to support open positions). Instead, they establish ratios of margin balances to open positions that must be maintained at all times.

If your account's margin balance falls below the required ratio, even for just a few seconds, your broker probably has the right to close out your positions without any notice to you. In most cases, that only happens when an account has losing positions. If your broker liquidates your positions, that usually means your losses are locked in and your margin balance just got smaller.

Be sure you completely understand your broker's margin requirements and liquidation policies. Requirements may differ depending on account size and whether you're trading standard lot sizes (100,000 currency units), mini lot sizes (10,000 currency units), or micro lots (1,000 currency units). Some brokers' liquidation policies allow for all positions to be liquidated if you fall below margin requirements. Others close out the biggest losing positions or portions of losing positions until the required ratio is satisfied again. You can find the details in the fine print of the account opening contract that you sign. Always read the fine print to be sure you understand your broker's margin and trading policies.

Unrealized and realized profit and loss

Most online forex brokers provide real-time mark-to-market calculations showing your margin balance. *Mark-to-market* is the calculation that shows your unrealized P&L based on where you could close your open positions in the market at that instant. Depending on your broker's trading platform, if you're long, the calculation will typically be based on where you could sell at that moment. If you're short, the price used will be where you can buy at that moment. Your margin balance is the sum of your initial margin deposit, your unrealized P&L, and your realized P&L.

Realized P&L is what you get when you close out a trade position, or a portion of a trade position. If you close out the full position and go flat, whatever you made or lost leaves the unrealized P&L calculation and goes into your margin balance. If you only close a portion of your open positions, only that part of the trade's P&L is realized and goes into the margin balance. Your unrealized P&L will continue to fluctuate based on the remaining open positions and so will your total margin balance.

If you've got a winning position open, your unrealized P&L will be positive and your margin balance will increase. If the market is moving against your positions, your unrealized P&L will be negative and your margin balance will be reduced. FX prices are constantly changing, so your mark-to-market unrealized P&L and total margin balance will also be constantly changing.

Calculating profit and loss with pips

Profit-and-loss calculations are pretty straightforward in terms of math — it's all based on position size and the number of pips you make or lose. A *pip* is the smallest increment of price fluctuation in currency prices. Pips can also be referred to as *points;* we use the two terms interchangeably.

We're not sure where the term *pip* came from. Some say it's an abbreviation for *percentage in point,* but it could also be the FX answer to bond traders' *bips,* which refers to *bps,* or *basis points* (meaning 1/100 of 1 percent).

Even the venerable pip is in the process of being updated as electronic trading continues to advance. Just a couple paragraphs earlier, we tell you that the pip is the smallest increment of currency price fluctuations. Not so fast. The online market is rapidly advancing to decimalizing pips (trading in 1/10 pips) and half-pip prices have been the norm in certain currency pairs in the interbank market for many years.

But for now, to get a handle on P&L calculations you're better off sticking with pips. Let's look at a few currency pairs to get an idea of what a pip is. Most currency pairs are quoted using five digits. The placement of the decimal point depends on whether it's a JPY currency pair — if it is, there are two digits behind the decimal point. For all other currency pairs, there are four digits behind the decimal point. In all cases, that last itty-bitty digit is the pip.

Here are some major currency pairs and crosses, with the pip underlined:

- **EUR/USD:** 1.353<u>5</u>
- **USD/CHF:** 0.907<u>4</u>
- **USD/JPY:** 101.4<u>3</u>
- **GBP/USD:** 1.614<u>2</u>
- **EUR/JPY:** 138.0<u>1</u>

Focus on the EUR/USD price first. Looking at EUR/USD, if the price moves from 1.3535 to 1.3555, it's just gone up by 20 pips. If it goes from 1.3535 down to 1.3515, it's just gone down by 20 pips. Pips provide an easy way to calculate the P&L. To turn that pip movement into a P&L calculation, all you need to know is the size of the position. For a 100,000 EUR/USD position, the 20-pip move equates to $200 (EUR 100,000 × 0.0020 = $200).

Whether the amounts are positive or negative depends on whether you were long or short for each move. If you were short for the move higher, that's a – in front of the $200, if you were long, it's a +. EUR/USD is easy to calculate, especially for USD-based traders, because the P&L accrues in dollars.

If you take USD/CHF, you've got another calculation to make before you can make sense of it. That's because the P&L is going to be denominated in Swiss francs (CHF) because CHF is the counter currency. If USD/CHF drops from 0.9074 to 0.9040 and you're short USD 100,000 for the move lower, you've just caught a 34-pip decline. That's a profit worth CHF 340 (USD 100,000 × 0.0034 = CHF 340). Yeah, but how much is that in real money? To convert it into USD, you need to divide the CHF 340 by the USD/CHF rate. Use the closing rate of the trade (0.9032), because that's where the market was last, and you get USD 376.43.

Factoring profit and loss into margin calculations

The good news is that online FX trading platforms calculate the P&L for you automatically, both unrealized while the trade is open and realized when the trade is closed. So why did we just drag you through the math of calculating P&L using pips? Because online brokerages will only start calculating your P&L for you *after* you enter a trade.

To structure your trade and manage your risk effectively (How big a position? How much margin to risk?), you're going to need to calculate your P&L outcomes *before* you enter the trade. Understanding the P&L implications of a trade strategy you're considering is critical to maintaining your margin balance and staying in control of your trading. This simple exercise can help prevent you from costly mistakes, like putting on a trade that's too large, or putting *stop-loss orders* beyond prices where your account falls below the margin requirement. At the minimum, you need to calculate the price point at which your position will be liquidated when your margin balance falls below the required ratio. (We cover this subject more extensively in Chapter 13.)

Understanding Rollovers and Interest Rates

One market convention unique to currencies is *rollovers*. A rollover is a transaction where an open position from one *value date* (settlement date) is rolled over into the next value date. Rollovers represent the intersection of interest-rate markets and forex markets.

Currency is money, after all

Rollover rates are based on the difference in interest rates of the two currencies in the pair you're trading. That's because what you're actually trading is good old-fashioned cash. That's right: Currency is cold, hard cash with a fancy name. When you're long a currency (cash), it's like having a deposit in the bank. If you're short a currency (cash), it's like having borrowed a loan. Just as you would expect to earn interest on a bank deposit or pay interest on a loan, you should expect an interest gain/expense for holding a currency position over the change in value.

The catch in currency trading is that if you carry over an open position from one value date to the next, you have two bank accounts involved. Think of it as one account with a positive balance (the currency you're long) and one with a negative balance (the currency you're short). But because your accounts are in two different currencies, the two interest rates of the different countries will apply.

The difference between the interest rates in the two countries is called the *interest-rate differential.* The larger the interest-rate differential, the larger the impact from rollovers. The narrower the interest-rate differential, the smaller the effect from rollovers. You can find relevant interest-rate levels of the major currencies from any number of financial-market websites, but www. marketwatch.com and www.fxstreet.com have especially good resources. Look for the base or benchmark lending rates in each country.

Rollover rates have a bigger impact on you, depending on the size of your position. They have a bigger impact on someone trading in the millions than they do on someone trading in the tens. However, regardless of your size, it's still handy to know how a rollover affects you.

So how do interest rates get turned into currency rates? After all, interest rates are in percent and currency rates are, well, *not* in percent. The answer is that deposit rates yield actual cash returns, which are netted, producing a net cash return. That net cash return is then divided by the position size, which gives you the currency pips, which is rollover rate.

The following calculation illustrates how this works. We've simplified matters by using just one interest rate for each currency. In the real world, each currency would have a slightly different interest rate depending on whether you're borrowing or lending (depositing).

> *Position:* Long EUR/USD 100,000 at 1.3000 (long EUR/short USD 130,000)
>
> EUR interest rate: 3.50 percent per annum → 1 day = 0.035 × (1 ÷ 365) = 0.009589 percent
>
> Euro deposit earns: 100,000 × 0.00009589 = EUR +9.59
>
> USD interest rate: 5.25 percent per annum → 1 day = 0.0525 × (1 ÷ 365) = 0.01438 percent
>
> USD loan costs: 130,000 × 0.0001438 = USD −18.70
>
> Because EUR/USD pips are denominated in USD, convert the EUR to USD: EUR 9.59 × 1.3000 = USD 12.47.
>
> Net the USD amounts 12.47–18.70 = USD −6.23 ÷ 100,000 = 0.0000623
>
> On a long EUR 100,000 position, the rollover costs 0.0000623, or −0.623 pips.

Value dates and trade settlement

When we talk about currency trading, we're implicitly referring to trading the spot forex market. A *spot market* is one that's trading for immediate delivery of whatever security is being traded. But in the real world, *immediate* means a few business days, to allow banks and financial firms time to settle a trade (make payment, deliver/receive a security).

In forex markets, *spot* refers to trade settlement in *two* business days, which is called the *value date*. That time is needed to allow for trade processing across global time zones and for currency payments to be wired around the world.

The forex market operates on a 24-hour trade date basis beginning at 5 p.m. eastern time (ET) and ending the next day at 5 p.m. ET. So if it's a Monday, spot currencies are trading for value on Wednesday (assuming no holidays). At 5 p.m. ET on Monday, the trade date becomes Tuesday and the value date is shifted to Thursday. If you have an open position on Monday at 5 p.m. ET closing, your position will be rolled over to the next value date, in this case from Wednesday to Thursday, or a *one-day rollover*.

If you close your position the next day (Tuesday) and finish the trade date square, there are no rollovers because you have no position. The same is true if you never carry a position through the daily 5 p.m. ET close.

On Wednesday trade dates, spot currencies are normally trading for a Friday value date. At 5 p.m. ET on Wednesday, the value date changes from Friday to Monday, a *weekend rollover*. In rollover calculations, that's a *three-day rollover* (Saturday, Sunday, and Monday), which means the rollover costs/gains are going to be three times as much as any other day.

The one exception to the two-day spot convention in FX are trades in USD/CAD. And that's because the main financial centers in the United States and Canada share the same time zone, so communications and wire transfers can be made more quickly. USD/CAD trades settle in one business day. The weekend rollover for USD/CAD takes place on Thursday after the 5 p.m. ET close, when the value date shifts from Friday to Monday. This only applies to USD/CAD and not to other pairs involving CAD, such as CAD/JPY or EUR/CAD.

Market holidays and value dates

Value dates are based on individual currency pairs to account for banking holidays in respective countries. Rollover periods can be longer if there is a banking holiday in one of the countries whose currency is part of the trade. For example, if it's Wednesday and you're trading GBP/USD, the normal spot value date would be Friday. But if there's a banking holiday in the United Kingdom on Friday, UK banks are not open to settle the trade. So the value date is shifted to the next valid banking day common to the United Kingdom and the United States, typically the following Monday. In this case, the weekend rollover would take place at the close on Tuesday at 5 p.m. ET, when the value date would change from Thursday to Monday, skipping Friday's holiday. That's a *four-day rollover* (Friday, Saturday, Sunday, and Monday).

So what happens at the change in value date at Wednesday's 5 p.m. ET close? No rollovers in GBP/USD, that's what. Because the value date for trades made on Wednesday is already Monday, no rollover is needed because trades made on Thursday are also for value on Monday. That's called a *double value date,* meaning two trade dates (Wednesday and Thursday) are settling for the same value date (Monday).

A few times each year (mostly around Christmas, New Year's, and Golden Week spring holidays in Japan) when multiple banking holidays in various countries coincide over several days, rollover periods can be as long as seven or eight days. So you may earn or pay rollovers of seven or eight times normal on one day, but then not face any rollovers for the rest of the holiday period.

Applying rollovers

Rollover transactions are usually carried out automatically by your forex broker if you hold an open position past the change in value date.

Rollovers are applied to your open position by two offsetting trades that result in the same open position. Some online forex brokers apply the roll-over rates by adjusting the average rate of your open position. Other forex brokers apply rollover rates by applying the rollover credit or debit directly to your margin balance. In terms of the math, it's six of one, half a dozen of the other.

Here's an example of how the rollover of an open position would work under each model:

Position: Long 100,000 AUD/JPY at a rate of 90.15 for a value date of January 10

At 5 p.m. ET, the rollover takes place and the following rollover trades hit your account. (**Remember:** This is done automatically by most online brokers.)

You sell 100,000 AUD/JPY at 90.22 for a value date of January 10. (This trade closes the open position for the same value date.)

You buy 100,000 AUD/JPY at 90.206 for a value date of January 11. (This trade reopens the same position for the new value date.)

The difference in the rates represents the rollover points. (90.22 − 90.206 = 0.014, which is expressed as 1.4 points.)

If the rollover is applied to your average rate on the open position, your new average rate on the position is 90.136. (Here's the math: 90.15 – 0.014 = 90.136.) Because you're now long from a lower average price, you earned money on the rollover.

If the rollover is applied directly to your margin balance, the rollover points are multiplied by the position size (100,000 × 0.014 = JPY 1,400 earned) and converted into USD (JPY 1,400 ÷ 116.00 [the USD/JPY rate] = $12.07) and added to your margin balance.

Here's what you need to remember about rollovers:

- ✔ Rollovers are applied to open positions after the 5 p.m. ET change in value date, or trade settlement date.

- ✔ Rollovers are not applied if you don't carry a position over the change in value date. So if you're square at the close of each trading day, you'll never have to worry about rollovers.

- ✔ Rollovers reflect the interest rate return or cost of holding an open position.

- ✔ Rollovers represent the difference in interest rates between the two currencies in your open position, but they're applied in currency-rate terms.

- ✔ Rollovers constitute net interest earned or paid by you, depending on the direction of your position.

- ✔ Rollovers can earn you money if you're long the currency with the higher interest rate and short the currency with the lower interest rate.

- ✔ Rollovers will cost you money if you're short the currency with the higher interest rate and long the currency with the lower interest rates.

- ✔ Rollovers can have spreads applied to them by some forex brokers, which can reduce any interest earned by your position.

- ✔ Rollover costs/credits are based on position size — the larger the position, the larger the cost or gain to you.

- ✔ Rollovers should be considered a cost of doing business and rarely influence overall trading decisions.

If you're going to be trading a relatively large account with an online forex broker (say, over $25,000 in margin deposited), you'll probably be able to negotiate a tighter rollover spread with your broker. This will enable you to capture more of the gains if you're positioned the right way, or to reduce your cost of carry if you're not.

Understanding Currency Prices

Now we're getting down to the brass tacks of actually making trades in the forex market. Before we get ahead of ourselves, though, it's critical to understand exactly how currency prices work and what they mean to you as a trader. Earlier in this chapter, we show you that *buying* means "buying the *currency pair*" and *selling* means "selling the *currency pair*."

Here, we look at how online brokerages display currency prices and what they mean for trade and order execution. Keep in mind that different online forex brokers use different formats to display prices on their trading platforms. A thorough picture of what the prices mean will allow you to navigate different brokers' platforms and know what you're looking at.

Bids and offers

When you're in front of your screen and looking at an online forex broker's trading platform, you'll see two prices for each currency pair. The price on the left-hand side is called the *bid* and the price on the right-hand side is called the *offer* (some call this the *ask*). Some brokers display the prices above and below each other, with the bid on the bottom and the offer on top. The easy way to tell the difference is that the bid price will always be lower than the offer price.

The price quotation of each bid and offer you see will have two components: the big figure and the dealing price. The *big figure* refers to the first three digits of the overall currency rate and is usually shown in a smaller font size or even in shadow. The *dealing price* refers to the last two digits of the overall currency price and is brightly displayed in a larger font size.

For example, in Figure 4-1 the full EUR/USD price quotation is 1.40225/1.40246. The 1.40 is the big figure and is there to show you the full price level (or big figure) that the market is currently trading at. The 225/246 portion of the price is the bid/offer dealing price.

Figure 4-1:
A dealing box from the FOREX. com trading platform for EUR/USD.

Spreads

A *spread* is the difference between the bid price and the offer price. Most online forex brokers utilize spread-based trading platforms for individual traders. In one sense, you can look at the spread as the commission that the online brokers charge for executing your trades. So even if they *say* they're commission free, they may be earning the difference when one trader sells at the bid price and another trader buys at the offer price. Another way to look at the spread is that it's the compensation the broker receives for being the market-maker and providing a regular two-way market.

Spreads will vary from broker to broker and by currency pairs at each broker as well. Generally, the more liquid the currency pair, the narrower the spread; the less liquid the currency pair, the wider the spread. This is especially the case for some of the less-traded crosses.

Executing a Trade

It's trigger-pulling time, pardner. In this section, we assume you've signed up for a practice account at an online forex broker and you're ready to start executing some practice trades. Getting a feel for executing deals now, before you're ready to commit any real money to a trade, will be very helpful. (See Chapters 2 and 11 for more on using a practice account.)

There are two main ways of executing trades in the FX market: live trades and orders. If you're an adrenaline junkie, don't focus only on the "Trading online" section — the "Orders" section gives you plenty of juice to keep you going, too.

Trading online

Live dealing is how you access the market to buy or sell at current market rates. Knowing exactly what you want to do is important, because when you make a live deal, it's a *done* deal. If you make a mistake, you'll have to make another trade to correct your erroneous trade, and that is very likely going to cost you real money.

There are a few different avenues to get to the market depending on how your broker is set up. In the following sections, we cover all the bases.

Clicking and dealing

Most forex brokers provide live streaming prices that you can deal on with a simple click of your computer mouse. On those platforms, to execute a trade:

1. **Specify the amount of the trade you want to make.**

2. **Click the Buy or Sell button to execute the trade you want.**

   The forex trading platform will respond back, usually within a second or two, to let you know whether the trade went through:

   - If the trade went through, you'll see the trade and your new position appear in your platform's list of trades.

   - If the trade failed because of a price change, you need to start again from the top.

   - If the trade failed because the trade was too large based on your margin, you need to reduce the size of the trade.

   When the trade goes through, you have a position in the market and you'll see your unrealized P&L begin updating according to market price fluctuations.

Click-and-deal platforms usually have a number of shortcuts to enable more rapid trading. Some of these are for more advanced or active traders, so be sure you know what they are before you engage them. Here are the parameters that you can usually set up in advance:

- ✔ **Preset trade amounts:** These are so you don't have to specify the amount each time you make a deal.

- ✔ **Automatic stop-loss orders at a predetermined distance from the trade-entry price:** These automatic stop-loss functions can be turned on or off, and you define the number of pips away for the stop loss. These functions are good for providing fail-safe stop-loss protection until you can enter a more detailed order for your trade strategy. *Remember:* You never know when a headline will roil the market, and you don't want to get caught with your pants down.

- ✔ **Close buttons:** These will appear next to all open positions. By clicking them, you'll automatically square up (close) the open position you've selected (assuming the position size is within the maximum per-trade deal size).

Some online brokers advertise narrower trading spreads as a way to attract traders. If your click-and-deal trade attempts frequently fail, and the platform then asks if you'd like to make the trade at a worse price, you're probably being re-quoted. *Re-quoting* is when brokers offer you a worse price to make your trade, meaning you end up paying a larger spread than you bargained for.

Trading using smartphones

As much as 50 percent of FOREX.com's trading volume is now conducted using a smartphone. In the past, people traded using devices that were constantly plugged into a power source (such as your desktop computer) or over the phone.

The evolution of trading apps that allow individuals to trade on their phones or tablets has many benefits — you can trade when you're in line at a store or at a football game — but this new way of trading comes with new risks. For example, if your phone has an unreliable battery, it could die when you're in the middle of placing a trade, potentially leaving you exposed to losses.

Here are a few tips for trading on a smartphone:

✔ Make sure your battery is well charged before you attempt to place a new trade or change an existing trade.

✔ Close other apps while you're trading on your smartphone. You need the best possible Internet connection when you're trading to ensure you get constant price updates. If you have multiple apps open at once, this can slow your connection and interfere with your trading.

✔ Make sure you have an uninterrupted Internet signal when you're trading. Don't trade if you're on a train and about to go through a tunnel that will cut your signal. This could also cost you money.

✔ If your phone is unreliable, don't trade on it. Get a new device or trade on a desktop. Using a high-quality device can save you money and protect your profits.

Phone dealing

Placing live trades over the phone is available from most online forex brokers (although it's probably the least popular form of trading). You need to find out from your broker whether it offers this service and exactly what its procedures are before you can be ready to use it.

The capability to make trades over the phone is critical if you're frequently trading while away from your computer or tablet or in cases of technological disruptions. At the minimum, you need to have the dealing phone number in your contact list and a reliable phone connection in case something goes wrong with your Internet connection. If your dog chews through your mouse cable or your kid spills a sippy cup of juice on your tablet, you'll need a fallback plan to protect your market exposure. (We discuss more such risk considerations in Chapter 13.)

To place a trade over the phone, you'll need to:

1. **Call the telephone number at your broker for placing a trade.**

2. **When you're connected to a representative, identify yourself by name and give your trading account number.**

   Be ready to provide whatever account password is needed. (Knowing what's required *before* you call to place the trade is a good idea.)

   Know what your position is. If you're not sure, your broker will be able to give you this info, but be prepared for time delays.

3. **Ask what the current price is for the currency pair you're trading.** The broker's representative will quote you a two-way bid/offer price, such as "EUR/USD is trading at 1.3213/15."

4. **If you don't want the price, say, "No, thank you."**

5. **If you want the price, specify *exactly* what trade you would like to make.**

   Don't just say "Close my position" or "Square me up." Note the direction (buy or sell), the amount (don't use lots — use the real amounts), and the currency pair. For example, "I would like to sell 140,000 EUR/USD."

   The broker should then say, "Done" or "That's agreed."

6. **Confirm with your broker exactly what trade you just made.**

   For example, say, "To confirm, I just sold 140,000 EUR/USD at 1.3213."

   Be sure the broker confirms the trade. You can double-check that the trade was correct by asking the broker to input the trade and update your position.

7. **Get the name of the broker's representative you just made the trade with in case you have to call back.**

Orders

Currency traders use orders to catch market movements when they're not in front of their screens. *Remember:* The forex market is open 24 hours a day. A market move is just as likely to happen while you're asleep or in the shower as it is while you're watching your screen. If you're not a full-time trader, then you've probably got a full-time job that requires your attention when you're at work — at least your boss *hopes* she has your attention. Orders are how you can act in the market without being there.

Experienced currency traders also routinely use orders to:

- ✔ Implement a trade strategy from entry to exit
- ✔ Capture sharp, short-term price fluctuations
- ✔ Limit risk in volatile or uncertain markets

✔ Preserve trading capital from unwanted losses

✔ Maintain trading discipline

✔ Protect profits and minimize losses

We can't stress enough the importance of using orders in currency trading. forex markets can be notoriously volatile and difficult to predict. Using orders will help you capitalize on short-term market movements, as well as limit the impact of any adverse price moves. A disciplined use of orders will also help you to quantify the risk you're taking and, with any luck, give you peace of mind in your trading. ***Bottom line:*** If you don't use orders, you probably don't have a well-thought-out trading strategy — and that's a recipe for pain.

Types of orders

In this section, we introduce you to all the types of orders available in the forex market. Bear in mind that not all order types are available at all online brokers. So add order types to your list of questions to ask your prospective forex broker. (For more in-depth information, we look at tactical considerations for placing orders in Chapter 13 and offer practical tips for entering orders in Chapter 14.)

Take-profit orders

Don't you just love that name? There's an old market saying that goes, "You can't go broke taking profit." You'll use *take-profit orders* to lock in gains when you have an open position in the market. If you're short USD/JPY at 107.20, your take-profit order will be to buy back the position and be placed somewhere below that price, say at 106.80 for instance. If you're long GBP/USD at 1.6640, your take-profit order will be to sell the position somewhere higher, maybe 1.6675.

Partial take-profit orders are take-profit orders that only close a portion of your open position. Let's say you bought 200,000 EUR/USD at 1.2950 expecting it to move higher — and it does. But to take some money off the table and lock in some gains, you decide to sell half the position (100,000 EUR/USD) at 1.3000 and to allow the market to see how high it wants to go with the rest. Or you can place two partial take-profit orders to close the whole position at two different levels.

Limit orders

Technically speaking, a take-profit order is a type of *limit order*. The key difference is that take-profit orders close or reduce open positions and limit orders open new positions or add to existing positions in the same direction.

A limit order is any order that triggers a trade at more favorable levels than the *current* market price. Think "Buy low, sell high." If the limit order is to buy, it must be entered at a price below the current market price. If the limit order is to sell, it must be placed at a price higher than the current market price.

Stop-loss orders

Boo! Sound's bad doesn't it? Actually, stop-loss orders are critical to trading survival. The traditional *stop-loss order* does just that: It stops losses by closing out an open position that is losing money. You'll use stop-loss orders to limit your losses if the market moves against your position. If you don't, you're leaving it up to the market, and that's always a dangerous proposition.

Stop-loss orders are on the other side of the current price from take-profit orders, but in the same direction (in terms of buying or selling). If you're long, your stop-loss order will be to sell, but at a lower price than the current market price. If you're short, your stop-loss order will be to buy, but at a higher price than the current market.

Trailing stop-loss orders

A trailing stop is a beautiful little tool, especially when you've got a winning trade going. You may have heard that one of the keys to successful trading is to cut losing positions quickly, and let winning positions run. A trailing stop-loss order allows you to do just that. The idea is that when you have a winning trade on, you wait for the market to stage a reversal and take you out, instead of trying to pick the right level to exit on your own.

A trailing stop-loss order is a stop-loss order that you set at a fixed number of pips from your entry rate. The trailing stop adjusts the order rate as the market price moves, *but only in the direction of your trade.* For example, if you're long EUR/CHF at 1.2350 and you set the trailing stop at 30 pips, the stop will initially become active at 1.2320 (1.5750 – 30 pips).

When stops don't lose, and take profits don't profit

Sometimes the roles of take-profit orders and stop-loss orders reverse. This can happen if you adjust your order levels after you've entered a position and the market has already moved away from your entry price.

With both take-profit orders and stop-loss orders, the important price is not your entry price, but the current market price. For example, you may be short USD/JPY at 108.00 and the market is trading higher at 108.30. You originally had your take-profit order below to buy back at 107.60, but now you're having second thoughts. You decide to raise your take-profit order to 108.15 to try to close the position on a dip. The order is still a take profit because it is below the current market price (118.30), even though it will result in a loss if it's filled.

The same can apply to stop losses. If you bought AUD/USD at 0.7640 and the price has since moved higher to 0.7670, you may decide to raise your stop-loss sell order from its original level (0.7610) to lock in some of the gains. So you raise your stop-loss order to 0.7655. If your stop-loss sell order is triggered, you'll actually be taking profit.

If the EUR/CHF price moves higher to 1.2360, the stop adjusts higher, pip for pip, with the price and will then be active at 1.2330. The trailing stop will continue to adjust higher as long as the market continues to move higher. When the market puts in a top, your trailing stop will be 30 pips (or whatever distance you specify) below that top, wherever it may be.

If the market ever goes down by 30 pips, as in this example, your stop will be triggered and your position closed. So in this case, if you're long at 1.2350 and you set a 30-pip trailing stop, it will initially become active at 1.2320. If the market never ticks up and goes straight down, you'll be stopped out at 1.2320. If the price first rises to 1.2375 and then declines by 60 points, your trailing stop will have risen to 1.2345 (1.2375 – 30 pips) and that's where you'll be stopped out.

Pretty cool, huh? The only catch is that not every online trading platform offers trailing stops. If you find a platform you like and it doesn't offer trailing stops, you can mimic a trailing stop by frequently manually changing the rate on your regular stop-loss order. But this is an imperfect solution unless you can monitor your position constantly.

One-cancels-the-other orders

A *one-cancels-the-other order* (more commonly referred to as an OCO order) is a stop-loss order paired with a take-profit order. It's the ultimate insurance policy for any open position. Your position will stay open until one of the order levels is reached by the market and closes your position. When one order level is reached and triggered, the other order automatically cancels.

Let's say you're short USD/JPY at 101.00. You think if it goes up beyond 101.50, it's going to keep going higher, so that's where you decide to place your stop-loss buying order. At the same time, you believe that USD/JPY has downside potential to 100.25, so that's where you set your take-profit buying order. You now have two orders bracketing the market and your risk is clearly defined.

As long as the market trades between 100.26 and 101.49, your position will remain open. If 100.25 is reached first, your take profit will trigger and you'll buy back at a profit. If 101.50 is hit first, then your position is stopped out at a loss.

OCO orders are highly recommended for every open position.

Contingent orders

A *contingent order* is a fancy term for combining several types of orders to create a complete currency trade strategy. You'll use contingent orders to put on a trade while you're asleep, or otherwise indisposed, knowing that you're contingent order has all the bases covered and your risks are defined. Contingent orders are also referred to as *if/then orders*. If/then orders require the *If* order to be *done* first, and *then* the second part of the order becomes active, so they're sometimes called *If done/then* orders.

Let's look at a trade idea and see how a contingent order works. Say NZD/USD has been trading in a range between 0.6700 and 0.6800 and is currently sitting in the middle at 0.6750/54. You think it's going to go higher, but you don't want to jump in at the middle of the range and risk watching it go down before it goes up. So you use a contingent order to implement your strategy, even if you're not watching the market.

Because you're ultimately looking to buy on a dip toward 0.6700 to get long, you would place an if/then limit order to buy at 0.6710, the *if* part of the order. The contingent, or *then,* part of the order only becomes active if the *if* part is triggered and you enter a position.

The *then* part consists of either a stop-loss order or a take-profit order, or both in the form of an OCO order.

Continuing with this example, your contingent order may be to place a stop-loss order below 0.6700, in case the range breaks and you're wrong. So you may place your stop-loss order at 0.6690 to sell what you bought in the *if* part. This type of contingent order is called an *if/then stop loss.* You may opt for only an *if/then stop-loss order* if you want to limit your downside risk, but let your upside gains run.

If you think the upside is limited to the range highs at 0.6800, you may want to add a contingent take-profit order at 0.6790 to sell what you bought at 0.6710, in addition to your stop-loss order. Now if your position is opened at 0.6710, you have an OCO order to stop sell at 0.6690 or take profit at 0.6790. Now you have a complete trade strategy with defined risk parameters.

If the market continues to trade in the range, it may drop from the level you saw (0.6750/55) before you went to bed. If it hits 0.6710, then your long position is established and your OCO orders are activated. If the range holds and the price moves back up to the range highs, your take profit at 0.6790 might be triggered. If the range fails to hold, your stop-loss order will limit your losses and close out your trade for you.

Be careful about using if/then orders with only a contingent take-profit order. Not using a stop loss to protect your downside is always very risky. At the minimum, always use an if/then stop loss to limit your risks.

If you use an if/then OCO order and the market behaves as you expect, you could awaken to find that you bought at 0.6710 and took profit (sold) at 0.6790, all while you slumbered through the night. Or you could awaken to find that your if order to buy was done, but the market has not yet hit either your stop-loss or take-profit levels. But at least your open position is protected by the activated OCO order. Worst-case scenario in this example: You wake up and find that your *if* limit order was filled and your stop was triggered on a break through the bottom of the range, giving you a loss. The key is that you effectively managed your risk.

Spreads and orders in online currency trading

Now that we've covered the different order types, we think it's important for you to be aware of how online trading platforms typically handle traders' orders. We spent some time earlier in this chapter discussing forex market spreads and the role of the market-maker. There was a good reason for that: Online forex brokers accept your orders according to their trading policies, which are spelled out in detail in the fine print in the contract you'll have to sign to open up an online trading account. Make sure you read that section to be absolutely certain what your broker's order execution policies are.

The key feature of most brokers' order policies is that your orders will be executed based on the *price spread* of the trading platform. That means that your limit order to buy will only be filled if the trading platform's offer price reaches your buy rate. A limit order to sell will only be triggered if the trading platform's bid price reaches your sell rate.

In practical terms, let's say you have an order to buy EUR/USD at 1.2855 and the broker's EUR/USD spread is 3 pips. Your buy order will only be filled if the platform's price deals 1.2852/55. If the lowest price is 1.2853/56, no cigar, because the broker's lowest offer of 56 never reached your buying rate of 55. The same thing happens with limit orders to sell.

Stop-loss execution policies are slightly different than in equity trading because most online forex brokers guarantee that your stop-loss order will be executed at the order rate. To be able to guarantee that, brokers rely on the spread.

✔ Stop-loss orders to sell are triggered if the broker's *bid* price reaches your stop-loss order rate. In concrete terms, if your stop-loss order to sell is at 1.2820 and the broker's lowest price quote is 1.2820/23, your stop will be filled at 1.2820.

✔ Stop-loss orders to buy are triggered if the platform's *offer* price reaches your stop-loss rate. If your stop order to buy is at 1.2875 and the broker's high quote is 1.2872/75, your stop will be filled at 1.2875.

The benefit of this practice is that some firms will guarantee against slippage on your stop-loss orders in normal trading conditions. (Rarely, if ever, will a broker guarantee stop losses around the release of economic reports.) The downside is that your order will likely be triggered earlier than stop-loss orders in other markets, so you'll need to add in some extra cushion when placing them on your forex platform.

We explore in more detail the nuances and strategies of trading with orders in Chapter 13.

Part II
Driving Forces behind Currencies

Source: Bloomberg, FOREX.com

Get tips on trading forex with other asset classes in a free article at www.dummies.com/extras/currencytrading.

In this part . . .

- ✔ Get to know the main drivers of currency rates.

- ✔ Find out the economic and structural forces that cause currencies to move.

- ✔ Develop a framework for understanding market data and eliminating market noise.

- ✔ Understand central bank decisions and how changes in monetary policy are crucial for the forex market.

- ✔ See how to gauge risk sentiment and why it matters for the markets.

Chapter 5

Looking at the Big Picture

. . . .

In This Chapter

▶ Getting to know the main drivers of currency rates

▶ Monitoring monetary policy and interest rates

▶ Understanding official currency policies and intervention

▶ Gauging risk sentiment and financial stability

. . . .

*T*he forex market is inherently a big-picture market. FX traders focus on

✔ Interest rates and monetary policy developments.

✔ Economic growth and inflation data.

✔ Political elections and economic policies in major economies.

✔ Geopolitical risks, trade conflicts, and terror attacks.

✔ Major movements in other financial markets.

On a daily basis, currency traders have to sort through myriad economic reports, interpret the comments of political and financial officials from around the world, take stock of geopolitical developments, and assess movements in other financial markets. They do all this to help them determine what direction major currencies are likely to move.

Unfortunately, there is no set recipe for absorbing the daily flow of data and news to produce a clear-cut answer. Even if there were, many different market actors are pursuing their own interests, which may not be profit maximizing (see Chapter 3). Throw in market sentiment and future expectations, and you're looking at market participants interpreting the same data and reaching different conclusions, or maybe reaching the same conclusions but at different times. In this chapter, we lay the foundation for building the framework to make sense of the many policy, data, and news inputs that affect the forex markets every day.

The first step in laying the foundation is to get a handle on interest rates and monetary policy, because they're the final product of most of the other inputs. Unless you're an economist or banker, following monetary policy developments probably is not one of your favorite hobbies. But if you're going to actively trade in the forex market, you need to get a handle on monetary policy and interest rates. We're not trying to turn you into an economist or an interest-rate analyst — we just want to give you the lowdown on how interest rates affect currencies.

In this chapter, we lay it all out so you can make sense of how it works, what goes into it, and how it's communicated to the market. Later in the chapter, we get into the key elements of official currency policies and what happens when governments intervene in forex markets. Lastly, we take a look at the Great Financial Crisis of 2008–2009 (GFC) to see what lessons it holds for currency traders.

Currencies and Interest Rates

If the guiding principle in real estate is "location, location, location," in currency trading it's "interest rates, interest rates, interest rates." The most significant overall determinant of a currency's value relative to other currencies is the nature and direction of monetary policy set by a country's central bank.

When we say "monetary policy," we mean policy changes by a country's central bank, such as changing interest rates and introducing quantitative easing, among other things.

Perhaps the most important thing that a central bank does in relation to the forex market is set domestic interest rates, which also influence overall economic activity. Lower interest rates typically stimulate borrowing, investment, and consumption, while higher interest rates tend to reduce borrowing and increase saving over consumption.

Interest rates are important to currencies because they influence the direction of global capital flows and serve as benchmarks for what investors expect to earn investing in a particular country. This situation applies most directly to fixed income investing (bonds), which comprise the lion's share of investments, but it also influences equity and other investment flows. All other things being equal, if you could invest in a government-backed bond that yields 6 percent or one that yields 2 percent, which would you choose? The one with the higher yield, of course. And that's exactly what happens with currencies. Currencies with higher yields (higher interest rates) tend to go up, and currencies with lower yields (lower interest rates) tend to weaken.

Although we stress interest rates as one of the primary drivers of currency rates, interest rates are not the only determinant of currency values. Plenty of other elements come into play, affecting currency rates both in short-term trading and in long-term trends. To use an analogy, think of the stage in a theater. Now think of interest rates as being the backdrop and the lighting on that stage. Various actors come and go; sets and props are changed between acts; but all the action on the stage takes place against the backdrop and under the lights. Interest rates provide the backdrop and set the lighting for most major currency movements, even if they're not always the center of attention.

The future is now: Interest rate expectations

It's not just the current level of interest rates that matter. Markets are always adjusting to changing circumstances and anticipating future developments. When it comes to currencies and interest rates, forex markets are focused more on the direction of future interest rate moves (higher or lower) than they are on the current levels because they're already priced in by the market. So even though a currency may have a low interest rate, market expectations of higher interest rates in the future frequently will cause the currency to appreciate.

And what drives interest rate expectations? The evolving economic outlook based on incoming data (we look at understanding and interpreting economic data in Chapters 6 and 7), economic assessments and guidance by monetary policymakers (see "Watching the central bankers" section later in this chapter), and a host of other economic, fiscal, and political developments (some of which we look at later in this chapter).

Keep an eye on various interest rate futures markets, such as the Fed Funds futures contract for U.S. rates, to see what expectations markets are pricing in. These can be found on financial websites like Bloomberg.com, Reuters.com, and Marketwatch.com. The commentary will usually note that markets have priced in, say, 18 bps of tightening by the next FOMC meeting, meaning the market is expecting a 72 percent chance of a 25 bp rate hike (18 bps/25 bps= 72 percent).

The *outlook period,* or the time frame in which markets are expecting interest rates to change, can span several months or quarters into the future. Depending on the economic circumstances and the outlook, markets may price-in interest rate changes a full year in advance, driving short term yields and currency levels in the process. Subsequent currency and yield fluctuations are based on incoming data and official guidance relative to the expectations markets have priced-in.

Relative interest rates

It's important to remember that currencies always come in pairs. Rather than focusing solely on a particular currency's interest rate level or outlook, forex markets tend to focus on the potential difference between two currencies' prospective interest rate changes. If two major currencies' central banks are both expected to be raising rates by the same amount in the future, there's little reason for one to outperform the other. But if one is expected to raise rates higher or faster, there are grounds for one currency to strengthen relative to the other.

Forex market volatility sunk to record lows in 2014 after the major global central banks all kept interest rates at close to record low levels. At the time of writing, the market was waiting for some divergence in interest rate policies to trigger a bout of volatility in the forex market. This is a good reminder of the fact that interest rates are one of the key drivers of the forex market.

Interest-rate differentials

The difference between the interest rates of the two currencies, known as the *interest-rate differential* or *spread,* is the key rate to watch. An increasing or widening interest-rate differential will generally favor the higher-yielding currency, whereas a falling or narrowing interest-rate differential will tend to favor the lower-yielding currency.

Some of the largest currency swings occur when two countries' interest rate cycles are moving, or are thought to be set to move, in opposite directions. And they don't necessarily have to both be moving — one currency could see expectations of higher/lower rates, whereas the other's rates are set to stay on hold. By focusing on the interest-rate differential, you can detect such changes more readily than by focusing on the rates of any individual currency.

Traders should monitor the interest-rate differentials among the major currencies by looking at the spreads between short-term government debt yields to spot shifts that may not otherwise be evident. Worth noting: The government bond market tends to price-in expected changes to interest rates, so it can give a more up-to-date view of what the market is thinking about rates compared to, say, the actual level of interest rates announced by a central bank. For example, U.S. 2-year yields may decline by 5 bps (basis points, or a hundredth of 1 percent) — not an unusual daily development. Around the same time, Australian 2-year yields may move 5 bps higher — again, nothing earth shattering there viewed on its own. But add the two together, and you're looking at a 10 bps move between the two, and that's something to pay attention to. If the same thing happens again the following day, now you're looking at a 20 bps change in the differential, which is nearly equivalent to a typical 25 bps interest rate change from a central bank. You can be sure that if the Reserve

Bank of Australia (RBA) unexpectedly raised interest rates by ¼ percent, or the Fed surprised everyone by cutting rates by ¼ percent, there would be some sharp swings in AUD/USD. The same holds true for changes in the interest-rate differentials, and they occur on a daily basis rather than the monthly meetings of most central banks.

Nominal and real interest rates

The interest rate to focus on is not always just the *nominal interest rate* (the base interest rates you see, such as the yield on a bond). Markets focus on *real interest rates* (inflation-adjusted rates, which is the nominal interest rate minus the rate of inflation [usually consumer price index]). So even though a bond may carry a nominal yield of, say, 8.5 percent, if the annual rate of inflation in the country is 4.5 percent, the real yield on the bond is closer to 4 percent.

This phenomenon is most evident in emerging market economies facing hyperinflation. Even though nominal interest rates may be 20 percent, if the annual rate of inflation is 25 percent, the real yield is –5 percent. Hyperinflation and negative yields lead to capital flight. The result is extreme weakness in the domestic currency, even though nominal interest rates may be extremely high.

The same can be true with very low interest rates and *deflation* (negative inflation), such as what happened in Japan from 2000 to 2013. With interest rates at very low levels, eventually zero, and facing deflation, real Japanese yields were significantly higher than the nominal zero rates on offer. (***Remember:*** If you subtract a negative number, it's the same as adding that positive number.) As a result, the JPY experienced overall appreciation in this period despite very low nominal rates and abysmal economic prospects.

In the following sections, we introduce the key objectives of monetary policy, take you through the tool kits of monetary policymakers, and show you how to stay on top of the evolving interest rate picture.

Monetary Policy 101

Monetary policy is the set of policy actions that central banks use to achieve their legal mandates. Most central banks function under legislative mandates that focus on two basic objectives:

- ✔ Promoting price stability (a.k.a. restraining inflation)
- ✔ Promoting sustainable economic growth, sometimes with an explicit goal of promoting maximum employment

Although it's a no-brainer that promoting economic growth is more important to those of us who work for a living, central bankers like to focus primarily on inflation. Low inflation fosters stable business and investment environments, so central bankers see it as the best way to promote long-run economic growth. Low inflation is also an end in itself because high inflation erodes asset values and undermines capital accumulation. Some central banks, like the U.S. Federal Reserve, have a joint mandate of price stability and promoting maximum employment. Other central banks, such as the European Central Bank (ECB), have only one mandate — to ensure price stability — with other policy objectives (growth and employment) explicitly relegated to secondary status. Still other central banks — the Swiss National Bank, for example — have a mandate to ensure a stable currency, though most countries have delegated that responsibility to the national finance ministry/treasury department.

Looking at benchmark interest rates

The primary lever of monetary policy is changes to benchmark interest rates, such as the federal funds rate in the United States or the refinance rate in the Eurozone. Changes in interest rates effectively amount to changes in the cost of money, where higher interest rates increase the cost of borrowing and lower interest rates reduce the cost of borrowing. The benchmark rates set by central banks apply to the nation's banking system and determine the cost of borrowing between banks. Banks in turn adjust the interest rates they charge to firms and individual borrowers based on these benchmark rates, affecting domestic retail borrowing costs. Other tools in the monetary policy toolkit used by central bankers are

- **Quantitative easing (QE):** An unconventional monetary policy used by central banks, where they buy financial assets from commercial banks and private institutions to raise the price of assets and lower their yields, while simultaneously increasing the monetary base. In the aftermath of the financial crisis, major central banks embarked on programs of QE to try to boost their economies. This included buying government and some corporate bonds to lower bond yields and try to boost lending.

- **Reserve requirements:** The amount of capital required to be set aside by the banking system; money that cannot be used for lending.

Easy money, tight money

The main thrust (or *bias,* as markets call it) of monetary policy generally falls into two categories: expansionary or restrictive. An expansionary monetary policy aims to expand or stimulate economic growth, while a restrictive bias aims to slow economic growth, usually to fight off inflation.

Expansionary monetary policy

Expansionary monetary policy (also known as accommodative or stimulative monetary policy) is typically achieved through lowering interest rates (that is, reducing the costs of borrowing in the hope of spurring investment and consumer spending). Cutting interest rates is also known as *easing* interest rates and is frequently summed up in the term *easy monetary policy.* Central banks can also increase the money supply — the overall quantity of money in the economy — which also works to lower borrowing costs. A reduction in the reserve requirement of banks frees up capital for lending, adding to the money supply and reducing borrowing costs as well.

An expansionary monetary policy is typically employed when economic growth is low, stagnant, or contracting, and unemployment is rising. Central banks of the major economies reacted to the fallout from the GFC and the global recession by slashing interest rates to historically low levels, near zero in the case of the United States, Switzerland, and Japan.

Restrictive monetary policy

Restrictive monetary policy (also known as contractionary or *tighter monetary policy*) is achieved by raising, or "tightening," interest rates. Higher interest rates increase the cost of borrowing, and work to reduce spending and investment with the aim of slowing economic growth and lowering inflation.

Central banks typically employ a tighter monetary policy when an economy is believed to be expanding too rapidly. The fear from the central banker's perspective is that heightened demand coupled with the low cost of borrowing may lead to inflation beyond levels considered acceptable to the long-run health of an economy. With too much money chasing the same or too few goods, prices begin to rise, and inflation rears its ugly head. Rapid wage gains, for example, may lead to increased personal consumption, driving up the cost of all manner of retail products.

Changing rates incrementally

Changes in monetary policy usually involve many small shifts in interest rates, because central bankers are generally reluctant to shock an economy by adjusting interest rates too drastically. Even the *potential* for large interest rate changes could contribute to uncertainty among investors and businesses, potentially disrupting or delaying well-laid business plans, thereby harming the overall economy in the process and potentially boosting unemployment. Typical interest rate changes among the major central banks center on ¼ percent or 25 basis points (a basis point is 1/100th of 1 percent, or 0.01 percent), with 50 bps (or ½ percent) as the next most frequent rate adjustment.

The GFC and the accompanying global recession caused key central banks to slash rates rapidly, with cuts of 75 to 100 bps coming in rapid succession in some cases. Having cut benchmark rates to near zero, several major central banks felt compelled to undertake additional *unconventional easing* measures, such as QE, to support their economies.

Unconventional easing

Central banks can only directly influence the level of short term interest rates. Longer-term interest rates, the ones used by markets to set business and consumer lending rates, are determined by bond investors and are based on their views of growth, inflation, and creditworthiness. For example, the 10-year U.S. Treasury rate is the benchmark for U.S. mortgage rates.

When central banks cut their benchmark rates to near-zero levels, they were faced with the zero-lower bound of interest rates. To further support their economies, they sought to drive down longer-term lending rates through unconventional means, typically large-scale asset purchase programs where the central bank buys longer-term government bonds. (Remember, bond prices move inversely to bond yields — it's just bond math. Buying longer-maturity bonds theoretically pushes bond prices higher and yields lower, hopefully sending consumer and business lending rates down in the process.)

Such large-scale asset purchase programs are frequently referred to as QE because the central bank is increasing the money supply, the quantity, by creating money to buy the bonds. In the United States, the Federal Reserve initiated two rounds of quantitative easing, while in the UK and Japan, the Bank of England and the Bank of Japan also undertook large-scale asset purchase programs. (Japan had also pursued QE repeatedly in the prior decade, well before the GFC.)

Currencies of countries pursuing such unconventional easing typically tend to weaken because such measures may drive down interest rates relative to other countries' rates, at least while the program is in place. Some investors also view an increasing money supply as a currency negative (the greater the supply, the lower the value). But that doesn't always hold true, especially if the extra money seeps out of the economy and into other markets, as it did in the United States in 2009.

A good example of this is when the U.S. Federal Reserve indicated in August 2010 it was considering undertaking a second round of QE, known as QE2. Initially, the USD weakened as the Fed was seen to be trying to lower rates further. But when the actual program was announced, the USD began to strengthen and U.S. yields moved higher. It might look like a case of "sell the rumor, buy the fact," but it was more in response to U.S. data and the immediate outlook: The Fed was looking at QE2 in response to a slowdown in the summer of 2010, but by the time QE2 started in November 2010, U.S. data and the outlook had rebounded. And all that money the Fed was supposedly printing? It mostly ended up back at the Fed in the form of excess reserves held by the banking system, meaning it never entered the real economy.

Watching the central bankers

If you've read this chapter from the beginning, you've probably gotten the impression that determining monetary policy is mostly an exercise in shades of gray rather than a simple black-and-white equation — and you'd be exactly right. But given the significance of monetary policy to currencies, currency traders devote a great deal of attention trying to divine the intentions of central bankers. This has not always been an easy task, but recent trends among central banks to improve the openness of communications with markets, frequently referred to as *transparency,* have made the process less of a guessing game.

Central bankers communicate with the markets in a number of ways, and their comments can provoke market reactions similar to major economic data releases — by that, we mean sharp initial price movements followed by continued volatility or a potential change in direction.

- ✔ **Rate decisions:** Interest-rate setting committees of central banks meet at regularly scheduled times. At the conclusion of a meeting, they issue a formal announcement of the policy decisions made at the meeting. They can raise, lower, or hold interest rates steady. They can also make changes to reserve requirements or liquidity operations.

- ✔ **Policy statements or guidance:** Along with the interest rate decision, central banks frequently issue an accompanying statement that explains the basis for their policy action. These statements are also used to provide guidance to markets on the future course of monetary policy. The statements are carefully parsed by markets intent on discovering what the central bank is thinking, which way it's leaning, and what the timing may be for future changes. In recent years, rate announcements are often preceded by a press conference by the head of the central bank. The Federal Reserve and the European Central Bank both hold press conferences after some of their meetings. Rate announcements and accompanying policy statements are included on economic data/event calendars.

- ✔ **Public speeches:** Central bankers frequently appear before community and business groups, and address subjects ranging from trends in the financial industry (such as the rise of hedge funds or the use of derivatives) to relatively mundane governance issues (such as financial reporting requirements). But when a central banker gives a speech that assesses the economic outlook or the future course of monetary policy, forex markets are all ears.

Appearances by central bank officials typically are included on most economic event/data calendars, and you need to be aware of them to avoid being taken by surprise. Sometimes, the topic of the speech is given in advance; other times, it's not. The most important speeches are those that focus on the economic outlook or the current monetary policy assessment.

In most cases, a prepared text is released by financial newswires at the scheduled start time of the speech. Accredited news agencies receive copies of speeches in advance to allow their reporters to prepare stories and headlines, but the release of the information is embargoed until the designated time. The remarks are then encapsulated into a series of headlines that capture the main points of the speech; this is the news that markets receive at the appointed time. When these headlines hit traders' screens, market prices start to react. If a question-and-answer session follows, the central banker's comments will be posted by the newswires as they're delivered live. This setup can make for some exciting headline-driven trading.

Currency traders need to be aware of and constantly follow the current market thinking on the direction of interest rates because of the strong relationship between interest rates and currency values. The best way to do this is to follow market commentaries in print and online news media, always keeping in mind that such outlets (especially print) are usually one step behind the current market. This makes online news commentaries that much more relevant. Some of the best sites for timely insights and market reporting are Bloomberg. com, Reuters.com, and MarketWatch.com. Twitter is a great resource for getting the latest central bank headlines. Best of all, for now, most of these sites are free.

Look for currency brokers that offer real-time market analysis and news updates.

In the next section, we delve a bit deeper into how monetary policy is presented to financial markets by central bank officials. We also look at currency-specific policies and rhetoric. Sometimes, how a message is delivered or who delivers it is more important than the message itself. This is certainly true of monetary or currency policy comments from central bank or government finance officials.

Interpreting monetary policy communications

Earlier in this chapter, we cover the various ways in which central bankers communicate their thinking to market participants (see the preceding section). But the process is far more nuanced and evolved than relying simply on official policy statements or speeches before the Rotary Club of Indianapolis. Central bankers are keenly aware that their comments have the ability to move, and potentially disrupt, financial markets all over the world. So they choose their words very carefully, leaving traders to act as interpreters. Before you start interpreting monetary policy statements and commentary, it'll help to know the following.

Not all central bankers are created equal

The interest rate setting committees of central banks, frequently known as Monetary Policy Committees (MPCs) — the Fed's FOMC is one of these — typically operate under a one-member/one-vote rule. But when it comes to delivering a message to the markets, the chairman or president of the central bank and its deputies hold far more sway than any other individual member. This is partly in deference to the central bank chief's role as first among equals, but also because that person is frequently viewed as expressing the thinking of the entire committee. Central bankers strive for consensus in reaching their decisions, and who better to represent and present this view than the chairman or president?

When the head of the central bank gives an update on the economy or the outlook for interest rates, listen up. A scheduled speech by the chair of the Fed, for instance, is likely to be preceded by market speculation similar to that of a major economic data report. And the reaction to his comments can be equally sharp.

In the case of the Fed, the FOMC is composed of 12 voting members consisting of the board of governors and a *rotating* slate of regional Federal Reserve Bank presidents each year. So when a Federal Reserve Bank president is set to speak, make sure you know whether she's a voting member in the current year before acting on her comments.

Remarks by nonvoting FOMC members are frequently discounted or ignored by traders because the speaker is not going to be casting a vote at the next meeting. But this is a bit of an oversimplification and can be risky. Before downplaying a nonvoter's comments, you need to consider her comments in the context of the FOMC consensus. Is she expressing her own views or elaborating on a shift in consensus thinking?

Birds of a feather: Hawks and doves

Central bank officials are frequently a known commodity to market analysts and traders, either from past policy statements or from their academic or policy writings prior to becoming central bankers. Markets typically refer to central bankers in terms of being hawks or doves. A *hawk* is someone who generally favors an aggressive approach to fighting inflation and is not averse to raising rates even if it will hurt economic growth. A *dove,* on the other hand, is a central banker who tends to favor pro-growth and employment monetary policy, and is generally reluctant to tighten rates if it will hurt the economy. In short, hawks tend to be fixated on fighting inflation, and doves tend to stress growth and employment.

Don't get us wrong: There are plenty of central bankers in the middle who can wear both hats (or feathers, in this instance). In those cases, the middle-of-the-roaders tend to reveal their hawkish or dovish leanings only at the extremes of the policy cycles.

So if a hawk is slated to speak on the outlook for monetary policy, and he cites the risks from inflation or the need to prevent any increase in inflationary pressures, guess what? You're not going to see much of a reaction from the markets because he's a known quantity speaking true to form. You get a much sharper reaction when a hawk downplays the threats from inflation or suggests that inflationary pressures may be starting to recede. Markets will jump all over dovish comments coming from a hawk, and vice versa with hawkish comments made by a dove.

Official Currency Policies and Rhetoric

Another major influence on currency values is government policies or official stances regarding the value of individual currencies. Some of the largest changes in currency values in recent decades have been brought on by official policies and multilateral agreements among the major industrialized economies. For instance, the Plaza Accord of 1985 stands out as a watershed in forex market history, ultimately resulting in a roughly 50 percent *devaluation* of the U.S. dollar over the course of the next two years.

National governments have a great deal at stake when it comes to the value of their currencies. After all, in a sense, a nation's currency is the front door to its economy and financial markets. If the currency is viewed as unstable or too volatile, it's tantamount to slamming the front door shut. And no major economy can afford to do that today.

In this section, we look at the major objectives of national currency policies, who sets them, and how they're implemented.

Currency policy or currency stance?

Referring to official government thinking on currencies as a *currency policy* may be a mischaracterization. Instead, you may do better to think of it as a *stance* on particular currency values at a particular point in time.

Daily trading volumes in the forex market dwarf most national central bank currency reserve holdings. (*Currency reserves* are the accumulated stocks of international currencies held by central banks for use in market interventions and overall central bank reserve management.) Japan and China together have more than $2 trillion in central bank currency reserves. That may seem like a lot, but average currency trading volume in the global forex market is over $4 trillion *per day.* This means that even if national governments *wanted* to routinely manage the value of their national currency, they would be hard-pressed to overcome market forces if they were at odds with the official policy.

To summarize why governments are generally reluctant to get involved in trying to influence currency values, it comes down to the following:

- ✔ **They can't because they're too small.** Forex markets are much bigger than any one nation's foreign currency reserves.

- ✔ **They can't because of market structure.** Forex markets operate outside national jurisdictions.

- ✔ **They can't agree on what to do.** Currencies always have another country or countries on the other side of the pair. You may want your currency to weaken, but do others want their currencies to strengthen? Not everyone can have a weak currency.

- ✔ **They don't want to meddle in the free market.** Tampering with international capital flows is a recipe for economic disaster and, in some cases, diplomatic discontent.

Generally speaking, then, governments prefer to refrain from getting involved in setting currency rates or trying to influence overall currency direction. They recognize that their power is extremely limited and that it must be used sparingly, usually only when extreme circumstances demand action from the national government or collective action from several governments. Moreover, the global economic superpowers are believers in the power of free markets to best allocate capital and maximize long-run economic potential. It simply would not do for them to openly reject free-market policies by regularly seeking to influence currency rates. You have to practice what you preach, or you start losing your following. For governments, that translates to credibility — and that's a trait most governments seek to cultivate and protect.

But — and this is a big *but* — governments *do* seek to influence currency rates from time to time. And when they do, it's usually a key long-term turning point in currency values.

In the next section, we look at the principal actors in each country or currency zone and what their recent actions on currencies suggest for their currency policy goals.

Calling the shots on currencies

In the "Currency policy or currency stance?" section, earlier in this chapter, we list a number of reasons why national governments are reluctant to get involved in trying to influence the value of their currencies. Chief among these are the size and extent of the global forex market and the need for nations to reach agreement on whether adjustments are even needed. The Group of Seven (G7) used to be the main body where currency issues would be handled, but globalization has brought more economies to the table in the form of the Group of Twenty (G20). (We list the membership of the G7 and G20 at the end of Chapter 3.) With an even larger collection of competing national interests in the bigger G20, collective action on currencies seems less likely.

If governments had their way, they would probably prefer to see fixed exchange rates replace floating rates and avoid the subject entirely, but that's not a realistic option for the foreseeable future. Confronted with the realities of forex markets, most government currency officials go to great lengths to avoid discussing currency values out of fear that their comments will be misinterpreted and lead to sharp exchange rate shifts. That fear was born out of experience, and today's top currency officials are much more discreet than their predecessors just a few decades ago.

Responsibility for currency matters typically falls to the finance ministry or the central bank in the nations of the most heavily traded currencies. In the following sections, we take a look at who has responsibility for setting and implementing currency policies in the five major currencies and what their major motivations are.

The United States

The Department of the Treasury has the legal mandate for all currency matters, from printing the notes and minting the coins to ensuring the soundness of the U.S. dollar in international markets. The secretary of the Treasury is the primary spokesman for the U.S. dollar. The deputy Treasury secretary for international affairs is the hands-on Treasury official responsible for day-to-day currency matters.

When the U.S. Treasury secretary speaks on the value of the dollar, or any other currency for that matter, FX markets listen.

The Eurozone

The European Central Bank (ECB) is responsible for both monetary policy and currency matters under the agreement that created the single-currency Euro in 1999. The ECB's governing council is the primary decision-making body; it's composed of the presidents of the central banks of the participating nations, with the ECB president as the group's chief policy maker and spokesman.

When the ECB needs to intervene in the market, it can do so by itself, along with the central banks of the member states on its behalf. In the EUR's early years, global central banks intervened to prop up the newly formed currency; however, in recent years, there has been no official intervention in the EUR.

However, individual European countries continue to exert influence over currency policy through their finance ministers, who had responsibility for currencies prior to the introduction of the euro and the creation of the ECB. The Eurozone finance ministers meet regularly as a group and frequently weigh in on forex market developments. There still appears to be great consideration given to the member states' governments by markets with regard to currency values, with the two largest European economies — Germany and France — wielding the greatest influence. But consensus appears to be the key element in deciding if the euro is too strong or too weak, and a clear majority of member states needs to be on board in opposing market movements before the market will pay attention.

The ECB is primarily concerned with fighting inflation and seeks to achieve currency stability as a means of fostering long-term economic growth. Although Europe remains heavily export oriented, so extreme euro strength is a risk factor for the Eurozone economy, the ECB has been reluctant to intervene in the forex market so far.

Japan

The Ministry of Finance (MOF) is responsible for currency matters in Japan. The MOF is the most powerful government ministry in Japan and can wield more influence over economic affairs than even the Bank of Japan (BOJ), the central bank. The MOF devotes a great deal of attention to the value of the JPY. The primary day-to-day currency spokesman for the MOF is the vice minister for international affairs, but during periods of volatility the finance minister will frequently issue statements. It is not at all uncommon for the MOF to issue daily comments on the forex markets, particularly when JPY volatility increases. The MOF last ordered an intervention (see the next section) in September 2010 as the JPY was strengthening and USD/JPY was threatening to drop under the key 80.00 level as the Fed geared up for a second round of quantitative easing. The Japanese authorities, along with the major global central banks, also intervened in the JPY in the aftermath of the 2011 tsunami. The yen surged on the back of safe-haven flows, but the intervention was necessary to limit JPY strength and help rebuild the Japanese economy on the back of this tragic event.

Japan's economy remains highly export oriented, so the value of the JPY is important to export competitiveness and corporate profitability. Excessive JPY strength, which makes exports more expensive abroad and lowers the profit from foreign sales, is usually the trigger point for the MOF to express concern and possibly take action in the market.

Great Britain

The Chancellor of the Exchequer (treasury secretary or finance minister) is the individual responsible for the British pound's fate. The governor of the Bank of England (BOE) also shares responsibility for the pound in a bit of a holdover arrangement from when the BOE became independent from the government in 1997.

The chancellor/BOE generally stays out of currency matters and appears most concerned with the pound's exchange rate versus the euro, because the bulk of UK trade is conducted with the Eurozone.

The United Kingdom is closely aligned with European economies and would be a candidate to join the Eurozone single currency, but nationalism runs deep when it comes to getting rid of the pound. The standing government line is that no decision on joining the euro would be made without conducting a national referendum.

Switzerland

The Swiss National Bank (SNB) is charged with responsibility for the Swiss franc along with setting monetary policy. The SNB is most concerned with the Swiss franc's exchange rate versus the euro, because nearly 80 percent of Swiss trade is conducted with Eurozone nations. The SNB has been known to speak up in opposition to CHF strength or weakness whenever the EUR/CHF exchange rate approaches extreme levels. During the Eurozone debt crisis in late 2009–2010, EUR weakened sharply against the CHF and prompted the SNB to intervene repeatedly to stem CHF strength, but without any success.

However, in 2011, the SNB took the unusual step of imposing a 1.20 peg on the EUR/CHF rate. At the time of writing, the SNB remains fully committed to this peg. Whenever the EUR/CHF rate approaches 1.20, the SNB is ready to intervene to stop it from falling below this level and limiting CHF strength. The market has taken the SNB at its word, and there have been only a handful of occasions since 2011 when the EUR/CHF rate has fallen below 1.20. This is an unusual situation — usually, intervention occurs only for a temporary period or in response to an economic crisis or national disaster.

Taking a closer look at currency market intervention

In every big-bank currency trading room in major financial centers, there is a direct line to the open market trading desk of the central bank. When that line lights up, the whole dealing room erupts. That line is reserved for open market intervention by the central bank, and when it rings, it usually means only one thing: The central bank is intervening in the market.

Intervention refers to central banks buying or selling currencies in the open market to drive currency rates in a desired direction. Direct intervention in the market is usually taken only as a last resort. It also may be a stopgap measure to stabilize markets upset by extreme events, such as a stock market collapse or a natural disaster. When it's not necessitated by emergency circumstances, markets are generally aware of the increasing risks of intervention.

Open market intervention is usually preceded by several less-blunt forms of official intervention. The idea from the government's point of view is to get as much bang for the buck as possible before committing real money. *Remember:* Central banks have limited firepower in relation to the overall market, so they have to pick their spots well. Sometimes, the government's objective is simply to slow a market move to restore financial market stability, and less drastic forms of intervention are not yet necessary. Some of the more subtle forms of intervention are

- ✔ **Verbal intervention or jawboning:** These are efforts by finance ministry or central bank officials to publicly suggest that current market directions are undesirable. Basically, it amounts to trying to talk up or talk down a particular currency's value. For example, if the Japanese MOF is intent on preventing further JPY strength to protect its export sector, but the USD/JPY rate keeps moving lower, senior MOF officials may indicate that "excessive exchange rate movements are undesirable." This message is a warning for currency traders to reduce their USD selling/JPY buying or risk the potential consequences. If the market ignores the warning, the MOF may take it up a notch and indicate that it is "closely monitoring exchange rates," which is language typically used before actual open market intervention.

- ✔ **Checking rates:** This is the central bank's open market desk ringing in on the direct line to major currency banks' trading desks. The traders don't know if it's going to be a real intervention or not, but they still react instinctively based on previously indicated preferences. Even rumors of a central bank checking rates are enough to trigger a significant market reaction.

In terms of actual open market intervention, there are several different forms it can take, all depending on which and how many central banks are participating. The more the merrier; better still, there's strength in numbers.

- ✔ **Unilateral intervention:** This is intervention by a single central bank to buy or sell its own currency, such as the SNB. Unilateral intervention is generally the least effective form of intervention, because the government is perceived (usually correctly) to be acting alone and without the support of other major governments. Markets will typically revert to the earlier direction after the intervention has run its course to test the central bank's resolve and to see if it's intent on stopping the move or simply slowing it. The MOF/BOJ intervention in fall 2010 was a unilateral intervention and had little success stemming the tide of JPY strength. However, as we mention earlier, the Swiss authorities have been successful at pegging the EUR/CHF rate at 1.20, even though it's acting alone. There is always an exception to every rule.

- ✔ **Joint intervention:** This is when two central banks intervene together to shift the direction of their shared currency pair. For example, if the ECB and the Federal Reserve are concerned about EUR strength versus the USD, they may decide to intervene jointly to sell EUR/USD. This is a clear sign to markets that the two governments are prepared to work together to alter the direction of that pair's exchange rate. Joint intervention is very rare, and this example is, so far, only hypothetical.

✓ **Concerted or multilateral intervention:** This is when multiple central banks join together to intervene in the market simultaneously, also referred to as *coordinated intervention*. This is the most powerful and effective type of intervention, because it suggests unity of purpose by multiple governments. Concerted intervention is not done lightly by major central banks — and markets don't take it lightly either. It's the equivalent of a sledgehammer to the head. Concerted intervention frequently results in major long-term trend changes. This is considered a last resort, and it's typically used only in response to natural disasters such as the 2011 tsunami in Japan.

In terms of the impact of intervention, different governments are given different degrees of respect by the market. Due to the frequency of past interventions and constant threats of it, the Japanese tend to get the least respect. The BOE, the SNB, and the ECB are treated with considerably more respect by markets, with the ECB being the linchpin of credibility for the Eurozone. Finally, when the U.S. Treasury (via the Fed) formally intervenes, which is a rare occurrence, it's considered a major event, and the market usually respects the intervention.

There is a difference between a central bank intervening for its own account and a central bank intervening on behalf of another foreign central bank. For example, during the MOF/BOJ intervention campaign in 2003 and 2004, there were several instances where the U.S. Fed bought USD/JPY during the New York trading day. The first reaction was that the U.S. Treasury was joining in and supporting the intervention by the MOF/BOJ, and this amplified the effect of the intervention. But the U.S. Treasury later denied that it had ordered the intervention. What happened was that the BOJ asked the New York Fed to intervene on its behalf during the New York trading session. Central banks have standing agreements to act as each other's representatives in their local markets. So even though the New York Fed bought dollars, it bought them for the BOJ.

Does intervention work? That is a question that frequently comes up when central banks get involved. The simple answer is an unequivocal "Yes, but . . . ." Intervention is most effective when it's backed by monetary policy moving in the same direction, such as expected higher interest rates to support a weak currency or easier monetary policy to weaken a strong one. Even then, interest rate changes are no guarantee that the intervention will be successful.

In the short run, the intervention may seem fruitless and counterproductive. This is especially the case with unilateral intervention. The market typically rejects the unilateral intervention and reverts to pushing the market in the direction opposed by the intervention. This situation can go on for weeks and months or — in the SNB's case in 2010 — years, which can lead central banks to take even more dramatic action, such as imposing a currency peg. When it's a joint or concerted intervention, the results are usually more immediate and successful.

Financial stability

The Great Financial Crisis of 2008–2009 triggered a massive global recession, the likes of which not seen since the Great Depression of the 1930s. As a result, major governments' finances were thrown into disarray, as tax revenues plunged and spending was maintained or increased through fiscal stimulus. Suddenly the creditworthiness and financial stability of major national governments were being questioned by global markets.

A currency's perceived value is intrinsically linked to the faith investors have in the financial stability of the nation(s) standing behind it. If investors fear a *sovereign debt default,* meaning government bonds won't be paid back, they're likely to sell both those bonds and the country's currency. The result can be a market frenzy in which government bond prices crash, sending yields soaring and increasing the government's borrowing costs, effectively forcing the government out of global capital markets and leading to a default.

The Eurozone debt crisis of 2009–2012 is the most obvious recent example, where bond investors fled Greek, Irish, Portuguese, and Cypriot government debt, raising borrowing costs to unaffordable levels and forcing those governments to seek a bailout from wealthier Eurozone members. From the start of the Greek debt crisis in November 2009 until a temporary bailout mechanism was established in May 2010, the euro weakened against the USD by more than 20 percent, and fell even more against other currencies.

And the fallout from the GFC is not confined to government debt. Major global banks lost trillions in the crisis, and some didn't survive. In the aftermath of the financial crisis and the Eurozone debt crisis, some global banks remain extremely fragile and on government life support. In the case of European banks in particular, they hold around half of outstanding Eurozone government debt, meaning sovereign defaults or *restructurings* (a euphemism meaning investors don't get back the full amount or payments are delayed) have the potential to cause additional massive losses to the banking sector, imperiling the Eurozone economy even further.

Debts, deficits, and growth

In the aftermath of the GFC, highly indebted European countries are certainly not alone in having investors question their financial stability. Debt levels in the United Kingdom, United States, and Japan are routinely cited as potential negatives, weighing on sentiment for those currencies from time to time. For the USD, its standing as the global reserve currency of choice is increasingly being called into question. And then there are the outliers, like Hungary, Iceland, and Dubai, small economies overall, but credit fears over their financial stability have a way of reverberating throughout global markets and sending risk sentiment (which we discuss later in this chapter) into a tailspin.

As part of your analysis of individual currencies, you need to be aware of the financial stability of the key currency countries. The metrics to keep in mind are

- ✓ **Debt to GDP ratio.** A measure of the total amount of government debt relative to the size of the economy. Debt/GDP ratios over 90 percent of GDP tend to put countries under the credit-risk microscope.

- ✓ **Deficits as a percent of GDP.** Current and projected deficits add to the total amount of government debt, which can increase the debt/GDP ratio, potentially destabilizing a country's credit outlook. As a general rule, anything over 6 percent is usually considered danger level, and a deficit in the region of 3 percent is considered stable.

- ✓ **Growth rates (GDP).** Low or negative growth can undermine a nation's GDP relative to its debt service obligations, increasing the burdens of debt service and raising the risk of default. The imposition of *austerity measures* (budget cuts and tax increases) in the most beleaguered Eurozone countries during the sovereign debt crisis threatened to lock those countries into a cycle of underperformance, which weighed heavily on their debt loads.

For the economics novice, this may all seem overwhelming. Don't worry if you couldn't imagine finding out a debt-to-GDP level on your own. Read the business pages in the paper or on the web — they usually flag countries with debt problems well in advance.

Gauging credit risk

Just as with monetary policy and interest rate developments, financial stability evolves over a long time period. But there are day-to-day developments that impact the markets' views of individual countries' financial stability.

How can you monitor the current state of the markets' views of a nation's creditworthiness? Keep an eye on the following credit risk measures through markets' news reports and economic commentaries:

- ✓ **Credit ratings.** Although often late to the game in the GFC, the sovereign debt ratings issued by Moody's, Standard & Poor's (S&P), and Fitch still carry a lot of weight. A ratings downgrade can make government debt issues ineligible for certain institutional investors, forcing them to sell those government bonds. Prior to a ratings change (they can be upgrades as well as downgrades), the credit rating agencies will typically issue an announcement that a country's debt ratings are under review and offer a bias to that review, such as "Portugal sovereign debt placed on review; outlook negative." Such announcements can have a significant impact on the currency involved.

✔ **Yield spreads.** These are the difference between the yields (interest rates) of one government's bonds relative to an ostensibly safer country's bonds. In the Eurozone debt crisis of 2009–2013, for example, markets fixated on the spread between yields of peripheral countries like Greece and Portugal and those of stalwart Germany. A widening spread indicates increasing credit concerns, as the bonds of the weak country are sold, sending yields higher, and bonds of the safe country are bought, sending those yields lower, widening the spread. Yield spreads fluctuate on a daily and intra-day basis, with widening spreads indicating deteriorating credit risk and narrowing spreads indicating greater relief.

✔ **Credit default swaps (CDS).** These derivatives are basically an insurance policy in the event of a default, where the buyer pays a premium and the seller is obligated to make good on the bond in the event of a default. CDS are an active speculative counterpart to the underlying bonds themselves, and may often lead bond market moves. Rising CDS indicate increasing credit risk and falling CDS rates, expressed in basis points (bps), signal lesser concern.

✔ **Debt auction results.** Governments borrow money through regularly scheduled auctions or *issuances,* where the government offers its debt for sale to global investors. The extent of demand and the price investors are willing pay (the yield) are the key measures here. Demand is gauged according to the *bid/cover ratio,* meaning how much is bid, or sought, relative to the amount being offered. The higher the bid/cover ratio, the greater the demand and supposed security. A *failed auction,* one where the government is not able to sell, or borrow, the full amount it seeks is "not a good thing," as Martha Stewart might say. But some investors are usually willing to buy anything if the price is right, and that's where the yield comes in. If investors demand a higher yield (bid a lower price) relative to current rates, it's an indication of concern. For U.S. Treasury debt, there's yet another indicator, supposedly attesting to the international appetite for U.S. debt, with implications for the value of the USD. The amount bought by *indirect bidders* is viewed as a proxy for foreign central bank and reserve managers' demand. A low turnout by indirect bidders could be interpreted as a vote of no confidence for U.S. debt and/or the USD by other major governments. The bid/cover ratio, yield results, and amount of indirect bids measures are all interpreted relative to prior auction results for similar issuances.

Geopolitical Risks and Events

Geopolitics is nothing more than a fancy word used to describe what's going on in the world at large. As it's applied to the currency markets, geopolitics tends to focus on political, military/security, or natural disruptions to the global economy or individual regions or nations. Because currency markets are the conduits for international capital flows, they're usually the first to react to international events, as global investors shift assets in response to geopolitical developments.

Currency markets have no national or patriotic allegiances when it comes to favoring one currency over another. The forex market simply calculates the likely economic fallout from an international event and its ultimate currency impact. A recent example is the popular uprisings in the Middle East and North Africa in early 2011. Egypt is a relatively small economy, meaning that the turmoil there did not threaten the global economic outlook, and forex and other financial markets were not seriously affected. But as the unrest spread to Libya, a major oil producer, oil prices spiked on supply disruptions, and concerns grew that other oil producers could be affected. Stock markets started to wobble, and the USD weakened as oil and gold soared. Likewise, geopolitical tensions between the Ukraine and Russia in 2014 had very little influence on markets because the Ukraine economy is fairly small and the market took the view that the tensions wouldn't escalate or threaten European oil and gas supplies from Russia. You have to interpret each international event dispassionately, with an eye on the short- and long-term economic impact to determine its significance for individual currencies.

The United States tends to wield more influence on the world's stage because it's the largest national economy and the primary military superpower. In addition, the U.S. dollar is the largest global reserve currency and the de facto currency in many developing economies. Finally, with increasing globalization of trade and markets, the U.S. dollar frequently functions as a global risk barometer (see the next section for more on risk). For these reasons, the U.S. dollar tends to experience the greatest reaction in times of global turmoil or uncertainty, and the market tends to think in USD-positive and USD-negative terms, viewing all other currencies in contrast to the U.S. dollar. When geopolitical events are looking problematic, the USD tends to suffer, especially against safe havens like the yen. If the risks or tensions come down, the dollar may go up.

Elections in individual countries, including by-elections and legislative referenda, also fall under the geopolitical risk umbrella, especially when the outcome may lead to a change in government or economic policies. *By-elections* (ad hoc elections to fill individual legislative seats made vacant by death or resignation, for example) are typically seen as interim votes of confidence on the governing party. Depending on how near the next general election is, and on other economic factors, by-elections may have a greater effect on political sentiment.

As important as geopolitical issues are to the market's overall assessment of a currency's value, they tend to have relatively short-run implications and must be interpreted in light of other prevailing economic fundamentals. For instance, if the USD is weakening based on a weak economic outlook, for example, and there's a disruption to oil supplies from political unrest or a natural disaster, sending oil prices higher, it's just another reason to sell USD. In contrast, if the USD is strengthening based on a more positive economic trajectory and higher rate expectations, a spike in oil prices may see the usual inverse relationship break down, and both oil and the USD move higher.

Gauging risk sentiment

In recent years, the concept of *risk sentiment* has taken hold as a way of expressing overall conditions across financial markets, including forex. Risk sentiment refers to investor behavior and whether investors are actively seeking returns by embracing riskier assets (*risk seeking* or *risk appetite*), or whether they're seeking the safety of supposed more secure assets (*risk averse* or *risk aversion*). These two behavioral modes are frequently referred to as *risk-on* and *risk-off,* or *risk-positive* and *risk-negative.*

For currency traders, the risk environment can be a critical factor in driving currency rate movements. Part of the reason has to do with the interest rates of various major currencies. Hedge funds, commodity trading advisors (CTAs), and other leveraged speculators (see Chapter 3 for more on these guys) borrow funds (the leverage) on a short-term basis at the lowest cost available, meaning currencies with the lowest interest rates are used as *funding currencies*. In a risk-on environment, they then sell those currencies and use the proceeds to buy risk assets with greater price appreciation potential. In a risk-off environment, they're compelled to sell their risk assets and buy back those funding currencies that they previously sold.

Risk on or risk off?

So what determines whether risk is on or off? In a word, volatility. *Volatility* refers to the size and speed of price movements over a short time frame, meaning hours or days. But volatility is the symptom and not the cause of those price changes. News and events are what dictate market reactions. In the simplest sense, when news and economic data are positive and everyone's feeling good about the outlook, risk is on and risk assets tend to appreciate (see the following section for what constitutes risk assets). When the news or data turns negative or outright catastrophic in the case of the GFC, investors turn more cautious and may exit risk trades, potentially triggering widespread selling that may force prices lower and force other investors to bail out as well, amplifying the sell-off.

We have little doubt that much of the increase in the risk-on/risk-off trading dynamic in recent years is the result of algorithmic, or model-based, trading, which has taken on increased prominence in all markets. If the computer is told that an X percent change in one asset or indicator means it should exit an existing position, it will literally not "think" twice about selling out.

Gauges of risk sentiment

To follow the evolution of risk sentiment, it helps to have a good handle on the current state of market affairs and expectations (see Chapter 10 for how to get up to speed on these). For more empirical indications of risk sentiment, pay attention to the following:

- ✔ **VIX index:** This is the options volatility on the S&P 500 U.S. stock index, frequently referred to as the *fear index*. A rising VIX indicates increased risk aversion (stocks are being sold), and a falling VIX signals the outlook is calming.

- ✔ **Government bond yields:** Major government bonds, such as U.S. Treasuries, German bunds, UK Gilts, or Japanese JGBs, are considered safe assets (for now at least). Rising yields typically mean those bonds are being sold and investors are embracing risk. But sometimes those bonds are being sold on credit concerns, which is risk-negative. Falling yields suggest risk aversion, as investors are fleeing risk assets and buying the safety of government bonds.

- ✔ **Emerging-market stock performance:** Investors have become increasingly international in their perspective and buying shares in Shanghai or Rio is no longer considered exotic. Such emerging market economies have led the way out of the GFC, and their stock markets can be the canary in the coal mine — prices down, risk-off; prices up, risk-on.

Risky versus safe assets

The low interest rate environment of recent years has forced investors and speculators alike to chase returns by investing in so-called *risk assets* that offer higher potential returns. The clearest example of risk assets are stocks and commodities: A more positive outlook (risk-on) may see stocks gain as corporate profits increase, and commodities may benefit on stronger demand for raw materials and natural resources, like oil. In forex, the risk-on currencies are those linked to commodities (AUD, CAD, and NZD, in particular) and major alternatives to the USD, like EUR and GBP. A risk-on environment may also see carry trades bought, where higher yielding currencies such as those just mentioned are bought and lower yielding currencies like the JPY, USD and CHF are sold (funding currencies). For example, a positive risk environment may see AUD/JPY move higher.

On the other side of the risk equation (risk-off) are the supposedly safe assets, such as U.S. Treasury bonds, the USD, CHF, and JPY. When bad news and events hit markets (think the Great Financial Crisis or Eurozone debt bailouts), investors typically flee risk assets, selling stocks and commodities and buying the safety of government bonds and safer currencies like CHF, JPY, and the USD. Price moves in a risk-off environment can be extremely volatile because it's a one-two punch where traders exit (sell) risk-on positions and also buy safer, risk-off assets.

Pay attention to the news when potentially disruptive events threaten the economic outlook, and be aware of the risk-on/risk-off dynamic. Depending on the nature of events, especially whether they're short-term like a natural disaster, or more enduring like a debt crisis in Europe, they can offer potential opportunities to reenter a longer-term trend from lower price levels.

Sometimes there is no such unifying theme such as risk on/risk off and individual currencies tend to walk to the beat of their own drums. As major global central banks take steps to unwind enormous stimulus programs and normalize monetary policy in the coming months and years, risk on/risk off could be replaced with a greater focus on the economic fundamentals (see Chapter 6).

Chapter 6

Understanding and Applying Market News and Information

- -

In This Chapter

▶ Getting up to speed on market developments

▶ Finding the news, information, and data

▶ Making sense of it all with themes

▶ Anticipating data and market reactions

- -

*A*s Roseanne Roseannadanna used to say, "It just goes to show you. It's always something. If it's not one thing, it's another." Okay, maybe we're dating ourselves with a reference to the classic *Saturday Night Live* "Weekend Update" commentator, played by Gilda Radner way back in the 1970s, but her tagline fits the forex market nicely.

Any number of real-world forces are at work in the forex market at a given moment — economic data, interest rate decisions, and geopolitical events, to name just a few. And they all get filtered through the market's collective consciousness and translated into price movements.

As currency traders, we're focused on trying to make money based on those price movements, but we're not alone. A whole raft of participants is active in the currency market, and they're all analyzing the same news and data, and drawing differing conclusions. To add yet another dimension, they're making trades based on those conclusions, which is what ultimately moves currency prices.

Which brings us back to the observation: If it's not one thing, it's another. The "other" in this case boils down to how markets process information — and there's a lot of it. We've spent years in the forex market as traders, analysts, and strategists, and just when we think we've seen it all, something new and unexpected comes along. So you're not alone when it comes to having to sift through the mountain of information and make trading decisions.

Your aim is to avoid paralysis by analysis and to absorb and understand as much as you can about what's driving the market, all with the goal of making successful currency trades. *Our* aim is to give you a better understanding of the types of information that move the market and a solid foundation to interpret and apply that information.

Sourcing Market Information

The jumping-off point for the discussion of market information has to be getting the market information in the first place. Institutional traders have teams of economists, analysts, and strategists providing them with up-to-the-minute observations and interpretations. Does this give them an advantage? Not necessarily. In the big picture, most of the information they're getting is available to individual traders, but you have to make the effort to find it, read it, and understand it.

The art of boarding a moving train

Anyone who's ever tried to jump on a moving train knows you have to start running alongside it before you reach out and try to grab hold. If you're standing flat-footed and you try to grab on, you're likely to get your arm ripped off. The forex market is no different, and any trader who tries to jump in without first getting up to speed is asking for trouble.

Getting up to speed in the forex market means learning what current themes are driving the market. To do that, you're going to need to know where to find market information and how to interpret it.

But getting up to speed takes time, so don't be in a rush to start trading based on a few days or hours of research. We recommend spending a month following the various currency pairs and familiarizing yourself with what's going on before you consider yourself up to speed. Using a practice account at an online forex broker is a great way to get up to speed. Over the course of a month, you'll be exposed to a full cycle of economic data indicators and most market events, like central bank meetings, which will give you a firsthand sense of how the market behaves and adjusts to new information.

Part of the excitement of currency trading is that there's always something going on — a train is leaving the station every few minutes. So don't worry about missing the next train, because there's always another one right behind it.

Taking the pulse of the market

As online currency trading has grown in popularity in recent years, there's been a proliferation of currency-specific websites targeted at individual traders. We can't possibly begin to review them all here, but you'd do well to start out with FXstreet.com (`www.fxstreet.com`), a comprehensive site featuring diverse sources of market analysis, many from big-name institutional contributors, all for free. Twitter is another good source of information, especially around major data releases and breaking news events.

When you're looking at forex research from various information sources, be mindful of who is providing the analysis. If you don't know the identities or backgrounds of the analysts, you may be reading the work of someone with just a few months or a year of market experience — not exactly the most sophisticated insight. When in doubt, focus on the reports made available by major financial institutions or market analysts that you trust.

Most online currency trading platforms also offer various types of market research and analysis, so when you're deciding which broker you should open your account with, look at the quality of its research offerings.

News sources

In the past, we tended to focus on the mainstream financial press, which provide continuous coverage of the major financial markets. Their websites provide frequent intraday updates that cover data releases and announcements, usually with some institutional commentary as well, so you can better understand how and why the market is reacting. In alphabetical order, our favorites are

- ✔ Bloomberg (`www.bloomberg.com`)
- ✔ MarketWatch.com (`www.marketwatch.com`)
- ✔ Reuters (`www.reuters.com`)

That said, it's always worth following trusted sources on Twitter. Some of the most respected analysts tweet throughout the day, and you can also follow most of the major news outlets to get a quick view of what's going on. It's also worth looking at some blogs, which can provide useful information, including Forex Factory (`www.forexfactory.com`) and Baby Pips (`www.babypips.com`). As with anything, quantity doesn't always mean quality when it comes to analysis, so check out a few sources and then narrow them down to the ones that work for you.

When you're reading a market news report, always use a critical eye. Keep in mind that what's being reported has already happened, and the market has digested the information and adjusted prices accordingly.

When interpreting news and information, always ask yourself:

- ✔ **What is the source of the information?** You need to differentiate fact from opinion or rumor.

- ✔ **How old is the information?** You need to gauge the timeliness of the information and the extent to which the market has already acted on it.

Real-time market news sources

The forex market moves on news quickly, and the institutional players generally have multiple live feeds from the major accredited newswires, such as Dow Jones, Bloomberg, and Reuters. These days, one of the quickest ways to get real-time news, especially data releases, is from Twitter, which gives you access to hundreds of thousands of news sources and can be an effective way to get real-time market information. We're prolific tweeters here at FOREX. com, and you can follow us at @forexcom. Everyone on our global research team tweets throughout the day, so you can get 24-hour coverage no matter where you are.

At FOREX.com, we provide a real-time market commentary (known as Forex Insider) directly on our trading platform. The updates are provided by our research team and senior traders based on our years of experience trading in the interbank forex market. Forex Insider offers instant analysis of data releases and other news events, as well as short-term tactical trading considerations such as institutional buying and selling flows, currency option interest, and technical support and resistance levels. We think it's a great resource for individual traders and about as close as you can get to the institutional market.

Economic data and event calendars

The forex market revolves around economic data and events, and you're going to need to find a reliable market calendar to see what's coming down the road next. The best market calendars contain all the major upcoming economic releases, showing the time of the report, what the market is forecasting, and the prior report indicated.

Perhaps even more important than data reports are economic events like central bank rate-setting meetings, the release of the minutes of those meetings, speeches by central bankers, and important meetings such as monthly gatherings of Eurozone finance ministers. Comments from these events frequently move the market in the short term, and if you're not aware of them, you risk getting blindsided.

Later in this chapter, we look at how markets anticipate data and events, and how this anticipation can affect currency prices. But you can't anticipate if you don't know what's scheduled.

Currency forecasts

Most of the financial media are keen on institutional forecasts of where currency rates are headed, and you'll likely encounter a lot of one-month, quarterly, and year-ahead currency-rate forecasts in your market research. However, treat these as an indication of overall market sentiment and outlook instead of as a concrete trading recommendation. Most forecasts are heavily skewed to current circumstances and are a much better guide to what the market is thinking at the moment than to where rates will actually be in a month or a year.

Rumors: Where there's smoke, there's fire

As if there weren't enough legitimate news and information to contend with in the 24-hour-a-day forex market, rumors have the nasty habit of popping up at unpredictable times. All financial markets love rumors. Here is a pair of the forex market's favorites:

- **Whisper numbers:** These are rumors of economic data anywhere from a few minutes to a few hours before the scheduled release time. They tend to roil short-term positions opened in anticipation of a report, and they also influence the market's subsequent reaction to the report. For example, a whisper number suggesting a much-worse-than-expected U.S. data report, which was originally forecast to be weak anyway, may see the USD come under more intense pressure prior to the release time. When the real number comes out, and it's weak but in line with forecasts, and not as weak as the whisper number, the USD may actually rebound because the worst fears were not realized.

- **Large market orders:** These are rumors that frequently do hold water, but like everything else, not always. They're typically associated with central banks or large institutional players buying or selling, and they usually mention a price level. Pay attention to the price level as a potential source of support or resistance. If the price level is broken, the order either wasn't real or has been filled. Either way, the price level has given way, potentially triggering a further directional move.

These days, rumors spread rapidly, and you may have to contend with them multiple times every day, which, over time, can reduce their impact on the market. The trouble with rumors is that you have no easy way to determine whether they're true, and even if you can, you have no way of being certain of the price reaction, which is ultimately the key to dealing with rumors. Rumors have the uncanny habit of coming out after relatively extensive directional moves or attempts to break through important technical levels, attempts that subsequently fail and see prices reverse direction.

The key is to be aware that an intraday move or test of a technical level is under way and to have a relatively tight exit strategy if the market turns tail. If there is a rumor behind a sudden reversal, you'll usually find out only after the fact anyway, but a tight exit plan will save you from getting left behind in the reversal.

Putting Market Information into Perspective: Focusing on Themes

At any given moment in the forex market, several *themes* dominate the market's attention. Market themes are the essence of the real-world forces currently holding sway in the market. Themes are what market commentators and analysts are talking about when they explain what's happening in the market. But most important, themes are the filters through which new information and data are absorbed by the market.

Market themes come in all shapes and sizes, and have differing impacts on the market over time. Some are long-term themes that can color the market's direction for months and years, such as the persistent U.S. trade deficit. Others may hold sway for only a few hours, days, or weeks, such as unexpectedly hawkish comments from a central banker.

Market themes come in two main forms that coexist in parallel universes but that also frequently overlap. The two types of themes that we like to focus on are fundamental themes and technical themes.

Driving fundamental themes

Each currency has its own set of fundamental circumstances in which it's being evaluated by the market. The basic fundamental environment is ever-present, but it's also subject to change over time, just as economic conditions will change in the course of business cycles. Fundamental themes will also shift in relative importance to one another, with certain themes being pushed to the side for a period when news or events focus the market's attention on other, more pressing themes.

As you read the following sections, keep in mind that each theme applies to each and every currency but in varying degrees at any given moment. We include some examples of what's likely to happen to a currency based on what incoming information means for each theme; we go into more detail on how the market processes fresh data at the end of this chapter.

Rising or falling interest rates

Interest rates are usually the single most important determinant of a currency's value. (We go into greater detail on the significance of monetary policy and interest rates in Chapter 5.) But it's not just about where interest rate levels are now, though that's still important (higher interest-rate currencies tend to do better against lower-yielding currencies). What matters most is their overall direction (whether they're going up or down), their future level (how high or low they're likely to go), and the timing of any changes (how fast rates are likely to change).

Markets are constantly speculating about the direction of interest rates, even though interest rate changes are relatively infrequent. For example, as of this writing, the Bank of England hasn't changed the level of interest rates since 2009. Speculation over the direction and timing of interest rate changes is one of the primary drivers of a currency's value on a daily basis as well as over longer time frames.

The information inputs that drive the interest rate outlook are centered on economic growth data and inflation reports, which we cover in detail in Chapter 7. The stronger the growth picture is, or the higher inflation pressures are, the more likely interest rates are to move higher, normally improving a currency's outlook. The weaker the growth outlook or the lower the inflation readings, the more likely interest rates are to remain steady or move lower, typically hurting a currency in the process.

Bond markets also have a lot to say about the direction of interest rates and are the best real-time barometer of the market's interest rate expectations. Central banks can really only influence short-term interest rates, which are driven by the central bank's target interest rate. But longer-term bond yields, with the ten-year maturity as the benchmark, reflect the market's long-term view of an economy's outlook and the direction of likely future interest rate moves. (Central bankers can really only impact long-term yields by embarking on expensive quantitative easing [QE] programs, which central bankers do not do lightly. This approach only came into vogue in the aftermath of the financial crisis.) Falling long-term bond yields (lower interest rates) point to a weaker economic outlook and the probability of lower interest rates ahead, typically denting that currency, while higher bond yields point to economic optimism and likely higher rates, usually supporting that currency.

The effect of interest rate themes is most powerful when the interest rates of two currencies are seen to be diverging — when one currency's interest rate is expected to move higher and the other either at the same level or lower. Keep an eye on the three-month *yield spreads* — the difference between yields of two government bonds — for relative changes that can favor one currency over another. Rates don't necessarily have to diverge to affect currencies. One currency's yields may simply move higher faster than another, and the widening spread between the two will reveal this.

When you're looking at economic data or monetary policy rhetoric, always assess the incoming information first in terms of what it means for the interest rates of the nation's currency — the interest rate theme. A currency that is expected to see lower rates in the near future, for example, is likely to stop declining and may even rebound if an economic growth report or an inflation reading comes in higher than expected. The market will pause to consider whether its outlook for lower rates is correct. By the same token, a currency facing the prospect of lower interest rates ahead, when hit with weaker economic data or lower inflation readings, is likely to weaken further. We say "weaken further" because it was probably already under pressure and moving lower before the latest batch of data hit the market.

Looking for growth

Economic growth prospects are the linchpin to a host of currency value determinants, from the interest rate outlook to the attractiveness of a nation's investment climate (stocks and bonds). Not surprisingly, the stronger the outlook for growth, the better a particular currency is likely to perform relative to currencies of countries with weaker growth outlooks. Strong economic growth increases the likelihood of higher interest rates down the road, as central bank officials typically seek to restrain too rapid growth to head off inflationary pressures. Weaker growth data increases the prospect of potentially lower interest rates, as well as dampening the outlook for the investment environment.

Many growth data reports reflect only a particular sector of a nation's larger economy, such as the manufacturing sector or the housing market. Depending on how significant that sector is to the larger national economy, those reports will tend to be interpreted as correspondingly more or less significant. Industrial production data in Japan, for example, is more significant to the Japanese outlook than it is to the U.S. outlook because of the more prominent role manufacturing plays in Japan.

There's no set recipe for how growth data will impact a currency's value, but when the interest rate outlook is generally neutral, as in no solid conviction on the direction of two countries' rates, the growth theme becomes more important.

Fighting inflation

Inflation is the bogeyman that all central bankers have nightmares about. Even when inflation is low, they still worry about it — it's just part of the job. When inflation is running too high for their comfort, fuhgeddaboutit. As a currency trader attuned to monetary policy developments, you need to monitor inflation readings as well. (We look at the key inflation reports in greater detail in Chapter 7.)

The inflation theme is far more nuanced than the growth theme in what it implies for a currency's value. Depending on the bigger picture, it can produce starkly different outcomes for a currency. In general, if growth is good, and inflation is too high, it's a currency plus. If growth is low or weakening, and inflation is too high, it's a currency negative. Come again? Both scenarios point to steady-to-higher interest rates, which should typically be a currency plus, right? The rub is that the low-/slow-growth scenario coupled with high/ higher interest rates increases the risks of an economy dropping into recession, which would ultimately result in interest rate cuts farther down the road. In this sense, currencies are a bit fickle in that they like higher interest rates some of the time, but not all of the time.

The same phenomenon can happen when a central bank holds rates too high for too long, usually based on fighting inflation, and the market begins to speculate that an economic downturn is ahead. The response is actually not that bizarre if you consider that the forex market is, first and foremost, always anticipating future interest rates.

When factoring inflation data into the interest rate theme, be aware of how the overall growth theme is holding up. If growth is good, and inflation is high because of economic strength, higher inflation readings will be currency supportive. If growth is slowing, and inflation is still too high, the currency impact will be decidedly less positive and very likely downright negative.

Seeking stability

The Great Financial Crisis of 2008–2009 (GFC) along with the Eurozone debt crisis of 2009–2013 exposed financial stability as another overarching theme. In the initial phases of the crisis, the financial sector (banks and insurers) was shaken to its core and required massive government intervention to prevent a system-wide failure. The subsequent economic downturn later exposed excessive government debt levels and budget deficits as a threat to sovereign debt and economic growth. The road to recovery in the developed economies remains a tough haul, and government debt levels and the risk of a sovereign default may continue as a theme for years to come.

Whether it's high debt levels in Europe or quantitative easing in the United States, financial stability and perceptions of creditworthiness can exert a significant impact on national currencies, usually for the worse. Keep an eye on government bond yields as an indication of market fears. Higher yields may mean investors are selling a country's bonds over fears of a default and not because of positive growth expectations. If so, the currency of the at-risk country is going to suffer alongside its bonds. (See Chapter 5 for more on this topic.)

Gauging the strength of structural themes

Beyond interest rates, growth, inflation and, stability, several other prominent themes regularly assert themselves, mostly in the structural sphere (the big-picture elements of how an economy is performing).

Structural themes can be fleeting — they can be in full force one day or for several weeks or months and then drop from the radar screen altogether. These themes are also usually secondary to those we outline in the preceding sections (interest rates, growth, inflation, and stability), but structural themes can still exert significant influence on a currency on their own. Most important, they can amplify the impact of the primary themes, like throwing gas on a fire. Following are frequently recurring structural themes:

- **Employment:** Employment is the key to an economy's long-run performance and a primary driver of interest rates. As long as employment is rising, the longer-term economic outlook is supported. But if job growth begins to falter, as reflected in incoming labor market reports, economic prospects will tend to be marked down. Sharp increases in unemployment are among the fastest triggers to interest rate cuts by central bankers, going back to the primary interest rate theme.

- **Deficits:** Both fiscal and trade deficits are typically currency negatives. During times of low/slow growth, the impact of deficits can be magnified, as the very credibility of a currency can be questioned, as was recently the case with the euro. During times of steady/high growth, deficits may have less impact but are still a negative hanging over the outlook.

- **Geopolitical issues:** It seems like a fact of life now, but geopolitical tensions weren't always ever-present, as they seem to be today, from North Korean nuclear tests to political upheaval in the Middle East or trade disputes with China. During periods of geopolitical tension, safe-haven currencies like the Japanese yen and the Swiss franc tend to outperform the riskier currencies like the Aussie and Kiwi dollars. The USD is also vulnerable to geopolitical issues, given the size of the U.S. economy and potential military involvement. After geopolitical tensions subside, the market is quick to revert to preexisting themes.

- **Political elections or uncertainty:** Changes of government and political uncertainty in the major-currency countries can certainly dent the market's sentiment toward the currency concerned. But shortly after the political situation is resolved, political issues tend to fade quickly into the background.

Analyzing technical themes

Technical themes are perhaps a little harder to grasp than fundamental themes (see the preceding section), especially if you're not familiar with technical analysis (see Chapter 11). But to make a long story short, sometimes currency prices move simply because currency prices are moving.

The fundamental economic or political themes may not have changed dramatically, but price levels have, and that is frequently enough to bring major market interest out of the woodwork.

In most cases, breaks of major technical or price levels will be in the direction suggested by the prevailing fundamental themes, but the timing is often suspect and can leave traders scratching their heads, asking what just happened. But sizeable price movements have a way of taking on a life of their own, forcing market participants to take action based on price adjustments alone.

In addition, the prevalence of technical analysis as the basis for many trading decisions can add weight to existing fundamental-driven moves, generating yet another theme to propel the move — the technical theme. It may be a trending market movement that attracts trend-following traders who don't give a hoot about the underlying fundamentals. As long as the technical trend is in place, they keep pushing the market in the direction it's going, perhaps far beyond what the fundamentals would dictate.

When a currency pair has broken through important technical levels, it's also going to attract breakout traders — speculators who focus on jumping in on breaks of key price levels, looking to get in on the move for an easy trade. (But nothing is ever quite that easy, and breakout traders can suffer when the breaks are false and the ranges survive.) The additional interest entering the market in the direction of the move again propels the price farther and faster than it may ordinarily go.

Having a sense of where a currency pair stands from a technical perspective is always important, even if you're not basing your trades on technical analysis.

The technical-theme phenomenon also stems from several real-life considerations that all relate back to the relative level of currency prices.

- ✔ **Option interest:** The currency options market is massive and is one of the reasons that the spot currency market is as large as it is. Option-related hedging is one of the biggest sources of spot market activity outside short-term spot speculation. When spot prices have been trading in well-worn territory (a relatively narrow price range, for example), option interest tends to accumulate around the recent range. If the ranges are broken, sizeable option-related interest is frequently forced to come into the market and trade in the direction of the price breakout, either to unwind hedges or to cover new exposures created by the price break, and usually some combination of both. The amounts can be staggering, propelling the directional move in an extreme way.

- ✔ **Systematic models:** We look at so-called black box or algorithmic trading in Chapter 3. Algorithmic trading has dramatically increased in scale in recent years, with some estimates suggesting 30 to 35 percent of daily volume is from algorithmic systems. In many cases, systematic models trading decisions are generated based solely on price movements. They may be short a currency pair until a certain price level on the upside is traded, for example, which triggers a signal to exit the short and go long, no questions asked.

✔ **Hedgers:** Large-scale hedgers may be forced to come into the market if a rapid and unexpected price movement develops. Many firms identify an internal hedging rate for corporate and financial management purposes. As long as they're able to sell above or buy below that rate, they're looking good. If the market moves sharply on them, they may be forced to jump in on the direction of the move for fear of not ever seeing the internal hedging rate again.

Reality Check: Expectations versus Actual

When it comes to reacting to data reports and market events, the forex market typically displays two responses. The first reaction is a short-term price response to the data report or news itself, which is where most of the intraday fireworks in the forex market go off. The second reaction, usually more important in the bigger picture, comes in later trading, when the underlying themes (outlined earlier in this chapter) are updated to reflect the latest piece of news or data.

In one case, the data or news may be in line with the dominant themes of the moment, and the initial directional price reaction may be extended even further in subsequent trading action. The market may be anticipating lower U.S. interest rates, for example, and a weak U.S. consumer confidence report is released, sending the USD initially lower against other currencies. Because the weaker confidence reading supports the theme that the U.S. economy may be weakening, additional selling interest may materialize and lead to further price declines in the USD.

In other cases, the data report may fly in the face of the prevailing market themes, leading to an initial reaction in the opposite direction of the recent theme. The market may be trading on the theme that Eurozone interest rates are going higher and that the Eurozone economic outlook is improving. A subsequent Eurozone retail sales report may come in on the weak side, potentially leading to an initial market reaction that sees the euro weaken. Whether the euro's move lower will be sustained depends largely on what the market decides the latest retail sales report means in terms of the larger theme of stronger European growth and higher Eurozone interest rates.

The data report may have been influenced by bad weather keeping shoppers at home, for example, and may be interpreted as just a bump in the road on the way to higher Eurozone interest rates. In such a case, initial euro weakness may be short lived and eventually reverse course higher. On the other hand, the weak retail sales report may cause the market to reconsider that higher European Central Bank (ECB) rates are a sure thing and keep on selling euros.

Of course, there's never a set recipe for how data and news are ultimately going to be acted on by the market. The potential data and event outcomes and subsequent market reactions are myriad, to say the least. That's one reason the market reaction to the data is always more important than the data itself.

But as currency traders, we still have to understand what the data means to make sense of what the subsequent market response suggests for the bigger picture. The starting point is to understand the initial market response to the data/news in terms of what the market was expecting and what it actually got. We need a baseline from which to interpret subsequent price movements.

The role of consensus expectations

Data reports and news events don't happen in a vacuum. Forex markets evaluate incoming data reports relative to market forecasts, commonly referred to as *consensus expectations* or simply the *consensus*. Consensus expectations are the average of economic forecasts made by economists from the leading financial institutions, and private firms or academia. News agencies like Bloomberg and Reuters survey economists for their estimates of upcoming data and collate the results. The resulting average forecast is what appears on market calendars, indicating what is expected for any given data report.

The consensus becomes the baseline against which incoming data will be evaluated by the market. In the case of economic data, the market will compare the *actual* result — the economic figure that's actually reported — with what was expected (the consensus). The actual data is typically interpreted by the market in the following terms:

- ✔ **As expected or in line with expectations:** The actual data report was at or very close to the consensus forecast.

- ✔ **Better than expected:** The report was generally stronger than the consensus forecast. For inflation reports, a better-than-expected reading means inflation was lower than expected, or more *benign*.

- ✔ **Worse than expected:** The data is weaker than the consensus forecast. For inflation reports, a worse-than-expected reading means inflation was higher than forecast, or more inflationary.

Additionally, the degree to which a data report is better or worse than expected is important. The farther off the mark the data report is, the greater the likelihood and degree of a subsequent price shift following the data release.

When evaluating central bank statements and comments from monetary policymakers, the market evaluates the language used in terms of *hawkish* (leaning toward raising interest rates) and *dovish* (leaning toward steady to lower interest rates). (We look at interpreting central bank rhetoric in greater detail in Chapter 5.)

Pricing in and pricing out forecasts

But financial markets don't typically wait for news to actually be released before they start trading on it, and the currency market is no different. Currency traders begin to price consensus expectations into the market anywhere from several days to several hours before a report is scheduled. *Pricing in* is the practice of trading as though the data were already released and, usually, as though it has come out as expected. The more significant the report, the sooner markets are likely to start pricing in expectations.

Unfortunately, there's no clear way to always tell whether or how much the market has priced in consensus expectations, so you need to follow market commentaries and price action in the hours and days before a scheduled report to get a sense of how much the market has priced in any forecast. And it's not always a case of the market pricing in an as-expected result. Market sentiment may have soured (or improved) in the run-up to the release, leading the market to price in a worse-than-expected (or better-than-expected) report. Stay on top of the market reports to get a handle on the mood.

Consensus estimates can also sometimes change in the days leading up to the report, based on other interim reports. For example, Institute for Supply Management (ISM) manufacturing forecasts may be downgraded (or upgraded) if the regional Chicago purchasing managers' index, which comes out a few days before the ISM index, is weaker (or stronger) than expected. This can lead to *pricing out* of consensus expectations, depending to what degree the consensus was priced in.

When good expectations go bad

Data miss is the market euphemism for when a data report comes in outside expectations. If the consensus was for an improvement in a particular indicator, and the actual report is worse than expected or disappointing, the result may be a sharp reversal in price direction. If core U.S. durable goods orders are expected to rise, for example, but they end up falling, we may be looking at a sharp drop in the USD. If the USD has gained prior to the release on the basis of pricing in the positive consensus, those who went long are going to be dumping their positions alongside traders selling the USD on the weak result. The same thing can happen in reverse if negative expectations are met by a surprisingly positive data report.

With as-expected data reports, it's frequently a case of "buy the rumor, sell the fact" (meaning, traders have already priced in a strong report, and if it meets expectations and sometimes even exceeds them, traders who bought in advance will be looking to take profit and sell on any subsequent gains).

This market phenomenon can also happen in the other direction — as in "sell the rumor, buy the fact" — depending on the currency pair involved and the nature of the consensus forecast.

Anticipating alternative outcome scenarios

We've found that it frequently helps to think through the likely reactions to major data releases to prepare for how the market may react in the very likely case that the data surprises one way or the other. It's a thoroughly academic exercise, and it won't cost you anything, but it may just give you a significant leg up on the rest of the market, if you're inclined to trade around data reports. Considering various "what if" scenarios helps us focus our attention and our trading strategies on the major themes currently operative.

For example, if the market is expecting an increase in the upcoming U.S. ISM manufacturing index, we like to ask ourselves what's the likely reaction if the ISM disappoints those expectations, and also what happens if it surprises to the upside and is even stronger. This makes us focus on the most recent price action, and perhaps we note that the USD has declined slightly in advance of the report based on better Eurozone data overnight.

If the ISM comes in below expectations, we're now thinking about how many pips lower the USD is likely to fall. We pinpoint key support levels and use those as our benchmarks to gauge the subsequent market reaction. If the report should surprise to the upside, we've also identified key resistance levels above that may come into play and where the next resistance levels are after them.

When the data does come out, we have a fairly rational baseline to judge the subsequent market reaction. If ISM rises as expected, we've identified which USD resistance levels may be tested. If they're not being tested, we're starting to think that maybe the market is more intent on buying EUR than buying the greenback, and it may not be wise to fight the near-term trend. If the ISM surprises on the weak side, we've also identified downside USD support levels (EUR/USD resistance levels), breaks of which may see further USD weakness/EUR strength.

Think ahead about what the market is expecting based on consensus expectations and how much has been priced in. Be prepared to factor various data outcomes in the larger themes you've already identified. Think through how the market is likely to react based on those scenarios, and you're likely to be several steps ahead of the crowd. (See the "Anticipating and trading on market reactions" sidebar for a real-world look at how we prepare for market reactions to data and events.)

Anticipating and trading on market reactions

For major U.S. releases like the nonfarm payrolls (NFP) report, retail sales, or Federal Open Market Committee (FOMC) minutes, for example, we like to construct various concrete outcome scenarios in terms of pips. Using the NFP report as an example, let's say the consensus forecast is for an increase of 100,000 jobs. In the days prior to the release, the market will likely have gravitated to a level that reflects that consensus. Using that level as a pivot, we establish our own expectations. For example, if the NFP number comes in at +125,000 jobs, we may expect EUR/USD to drop 30 pips. If the NFP registers +150,000 jobs, we may look for EUR/USD to drop 60 pips. Then we do the same for weaker-than-expected reports. If the number comes in at only +50,000 jobs, EUR/USD may rally 50 pips, and so on.

When the number actually comes out, and prices start to react, we've got a firm sense of where prices should move based on various data readings. The real trading information comes when prices don't react as we expected them to. For example, if the NFP number comes out at +180,000, (say we expected a 90-pip drop or so), and EUR/USD drops only 40 pips and begins to stabilize, we're thinking there's something wrong with the market's reaction to the data and something else is going on. In many cases, we're not alone — the rest of the market is likely drawing the same conclusion. The message is clear: Cover EUR/USD shorts, and start thinking about maybe even getting long. If EUR/USD trades back up through the pre-NFP price level within the next few hours (possibly minutes), it's a clear sign the market has other ideas about where EUR/USD should be, and it's a stronger signal to get long EUR/USD.

Getting a sense of how markets should react to data comes with experience, which you gain over time and by using a practice account. But you can also get a sense of how markets should react to data by studying past data outcomes and subsequent market reactions.

Chapter 7

Getting Down and Dirty with Fundamental Data

In This Chapter

▶ Building a model to put the data in perspective

▶ Getting to know data-reporting conventions

▶ Understanding the key U.S. data reports

▶ Looking at major international economic reports

*F*undamental economic data reports are among the most significant information inputs because policy makers and market participants alike use them to gauge the state of the economy, set monetary policy, and make investment decisions. From a trader's perspective, data reports are the routine catalysts that stir up markets and get things moving.

We run through a lot of economic information in this chapter, but you don't need to understand it like an economist — you're mainly interested in what it means for the market reaction. (If you're interested in understanding data like an economist, we recommend reading *The Secrets of Economic Indicators: Hidden Clues to Future Economic Trends and Investment Opportunities,* 2nd Edition, by Bernard Baumohl.)

As we note in Chapter 6, the significance of individual reports varies depending on the economic environment, the market's current focus, and a host of other factors. Always keep in mind that markets interpret incoming data based on what it means for the big picture outlook. If a country's economic outlook is generally viewed as promising, data pointing to stronger growth will reinforce that view, while data that disappoints may suggest a more negative reaction. Most important, the market's reaction to data is more important than the data itself.

In the first half of this chapter, we look at how to absorb the various data reports and factor them into a broader view of the economic outlook for each particular country, with its attendant implications for interest rates and currency values. In the second half of this chapter, we run through the major data reports to give you an idea of what they cover and how the market interprets them.

Finding the Data

Before you can start processing all the economic data, you need to know where to find it. In Chapter 6, we look in greater detail at where to find data info, but here's a quick overview.

The starting point is the economic calendars typically provided by online forex brokerages. Be aware that some calendars are not as comprehensive as others, so be sure to look for calendars that show events and speakers and not just data. Also, look for a broker that provides data and event previews, and real-time data and market analysis; this type of commentary will help you get a sense of what the market is expecting, how it may be positioned for the news, and how it's likely to react.

Cable TV business channels such as Bloomberg TV, CNBC, and Fox Business News typically carry U.S. data releases live on air. In our opinion, Bloomberg TV does the best job of covering non-U.S. data releases, and CNBC World is another option. But your best bet for seeing U.S. and global data releases immediately can be Twitter.

In addition, www.bloomberg.com, www.marketwatch.com, and www.reuters.com provide excellent data coverage, both before and after it's released, along with event calendars. Read the economic data news stories on these sites to get the inside story of the data reports, such as any subcomponent readings or significant revisions.

Also, many calendars may include some designations of market significance for each data series, like some are *high impact* or *low impact*. Remember it's the big picture that counts and even a so-called low impact report could have a big impact if it's big enough of a surprise.

In the next section, we sketch out a model for understanding where the types of data fit into the big picture. It should help you determine which categories of data are most significant, depending on the particular economic environment at any given time.

Economics 101 for Currency Traders: Making Sense of Economic Data

If you're like most people, you probably have a decent idea of what certain economic reports mean, like the unemployment rate or the consumer price index (CPI). But like lots of people, you probably don't have a strong idea of how to put the data together to make sense of it all. Having a fundamental model to put the data in perspective is critical to understanding what the data means and how the market is likely to react to the data. The sooner you're able to make sense of what a specific report means and factor it into the bigger picture, the sooner you'll be able to react in the market.

In the next few sections, we suggest a basic model to interpret the deluge of economic indicators you'll encounter in the forex market. By no means is this model the be-all and end-all of economic theory, but we do think it's a solid framework on which to hang the economic indicators and see how they fit together.

The labor market

We place the employment picture first for the simple reason that jobs and job creation are the keys to the medium- and long-term economic outlook for any country or economic bloc. No matter what else is going on, always have a picture of the labor market in the back of your mind.

If jobs are being created, more wages are being paid, consumers are consuming more, and economic activity expands. If job growth is stagnant or weak, long-run economic growth will typically be constrained. Signs of broader economic growth will be seen as tentative or suspect unless job growth is also present. Both scenarios have major implications for interest rates moves and investment themes, which are key currency drivers.

From the currency-market point of view, labor-market strength is typically seen as a currency positive, because it indicates positive growth prospects going forward, along with the potential for higher interest rates based on stronger growth or wage-driven inflation. Needless to say, labor-market weakness is typically viewed as a currency negative.

The employment indicator that gets the most attention is the monthly U.S. non-farm payrolls (NFP) report. The NFP report triggers loads of attention and speculation for a few days before and after it's released, but then the market seems to stop talking about jobs. Keep an eye on the job-specific reports outlined in the "Other labor-market indicators" sidebar, later in this chapter.

To illustrate the importance that markets place on jobs, Figure 7-1 shows changes in U.S. private payrolls overlaid with the S&P 500 stock index. As you can see, major turning points in the stock market (but not necessarily the economy) are closely associated with peaks and troughs in job markets.

Figure 7-1:
Job market trends coincide very closely with stock market performance, which reflects the economic outlook (but not necessarily the current state of the economy), as seen in U.S. private payroll changes and the S&P 500.

Source: Bloomberg, FOREX.com

The consumer

If it weren't for the overarching importance of jobs to long-run economic growth, the consumer would certainly rank first in any model seeking to understand economic data. The economies of the major currencies are driven overwhelmingly by *personal consumption,* accounting for 60 to 70 percent or more of overall economic activity in developed economies.

Personal consumption (also known as *private consumption, personal spending,* and similar impersonal terms) refers to how people spend their money. In a nutshell, are they spending more, or are they spending less? Also, what's the outlook for their spending — to increase, decrease, or stay the same? If you want to gauge the short-run outlook of an economy, look no further than how the individual consumer is faring.

The business sector

Businesses and firms make up the other third of overall economic activity after personal spending. (We're leaving government out of our model to simplify matters.) Firms contribute directly to economic activity through *capital expenditures* (for example, building factories, stores, and offices; buying software and telecommunications equipment) and indirectly through growth (by hiring, meaning there are jobs again), expanding production, and producing investment opportunities.

Look at the data reports coming from the corporate sector for what they suggest about overall sentiment, capital spending, hiring, inventory management, and production going forward.

Keep in mind that the manufacturing and export sectors are more significant in many non-U.S. economies than they are in the United States. For instance, manufacturing activity in the United States accounts for only about 10 to 15 percent of overall activity versus shares of 30 to 40 percent and higher in other major-currency economies, such as Japan or Germany. So Japanese industrial production data tends to have a bigger impact on the yen than U.S. industrial production has on the dollar.

The structural

Structural indicators are data reports that cover the overall economic environment. Structural indicators frequently form the basis for currency trends and tend to be most important to medium- and long-term traders. The main structural reports focus on

- ✔ **Inflation:** Whether prices are rising or falling, and how fast. Inflation readings can be an important indicator for the direction of interest rates, which is a key determinant of currency values.

- ✔ **Growth:** Indicators of growth and overall economic activity, typically in the form of gross domestic product (GDP) reports. Structural growth reports tell you whether the economy is expanding or contracting, and how fast, which is another key input to monetary policy and the interest rate outlook. Growth forecasts from economists are important benchmarks for evaluating subsequent economic data on growth.

- ✔ **Trade balance:** Whether a country is importing more or less than it exports. The currency of a country with a *trade deficit* (the country imports more than it exports; the country loses from trade) tends to weaken because more of its currency is being sold to buy foreign goods (imports). A currency with a *trade surplus* (the country exports more than it imports; the country gains from trade) tends to appreciate because more of it is being bought to purchase that country's exports. This is just a rule of thumb — it doesn't always hold true. For example, between 2013 and 2014, the British pound appreciated by more than 11 percent, yet the U.K.'s trade balance continued to deteriorate.

✔ **Fiscal balance:** The overall level of government borrowing and the market's perception of financial stability. Countries with high debt levels run the risks of a weakening currency if economic conditions take a turn for the worse and markets fear financial instability. Debts and deficits became a major theme for currency markets in the wake of the Great Financial Crisis of 2008–2009 (GFC) and the Eurozone debt crisis of 2009–2013, but they were always in the background.

Assessing Economic Data Reports from a Trading Perspective

The data that you find in economic textbooks is very neat and clean — but the data as it actually arrives in the market can be anything *but* neat and clean. We're talking here not only about the imperfections of economic data gathering, but also about how markets interpret individual data reports.

In Chapter 6, we introduce the idea of consensus expectations as one of the keys to understanding how markets interpret economic news and data. In the following sections, we look at important data-reporting conventions and how they can also affect market reactions. When currencies don't react to the headlines of a data report as you would expect, odds are that one of the following elements is responsible, and you need to look more closely at the report to get the true picture.

Understanding and revising data history

Economic data reports don't originate in a vacuum — they have a history. Another popular market adage expressing this thought is "One report does not make a trend." However, that saying is mostly directed at data reports that come in far out of line with market estimates or vastly different from recent readings in the data series. To be sure, the market will react strongly when data comes in surprisingly better or worse than expected, but the sustainability of the reaction will vary greatly depending on the circumstances. If retail sales are generally increasing, for instance, does a one-month drop in retail sales indicate that the trend is over, or was it a one-off decline due to bad weather keeping shoppers at home?

When you're looking at upcoming economic data events, not only do you need to be aware of what's expected, but it also helps to know what, if any, trends are evident in the data series. The more pronounced or lengthy the trend is, the more likely the reactions to out-of-line economic reports will prove short lived. The more uneven the recent data has been, the more likely the reaction to the new data will be sustained.

The other important element to keep in mind when interpreting incoming economic data is to see whether the data from the prior period has been revised. Unfortunately, there is no rule preventing earlier economic data from being changed. It's just one of those odd facts of life in financial markets that what the market thought it knew one day (and actually traded for several weeks based on that understanding) can be substantially changed later.

When prior-period data is revised, the market will tend to net out the older, revised report with the newly released data, essentially looking at the two reports together for what they suggest about the data trend. For example, if a current report comes out worse than expected, and the prior report is revised lower as well, the two together are likely to be interpreted as more disappointing. If a current report comes out better than expected, but the prior period's revision is negative, the positive reaction to the current report will tend to be restrained by the downgrade to the earlier data.

As you can imagine, there are many different ways and degrees in which current/revised data scenarios can play out. A general rule is that the larger the revision to the prior report, the more significance it will carry into the interpretation of the current release. The key is to first be aware of prior-period revisions and to then view them relative to the incoming data. In general, current data reports tend to receive a higher weighting by the market if only because the data is the freshest available, and markets are always looking ahead.

Getting to the core

A number of important economic indicators are issued on a headline basis and a core basis. The *headline* reading is the complete result of the indicator, while the *core* reading is the headline reading minus certain categories or excluding certain items. Most inflation reports and measures of consumer spending use this convention.

In the case of inflation reports, many reporting agencies strip out or exclude highly volatile components, such as food and energy. In the United States, for instance, the consumer price index (CPI) is reported on a core basis excluding food and energy, commonly cited as *CPI ex-F&E.* (Whenever you see a data report "ex-something," it's short for "excluding" that something.) The rationale for ignoring those items is that they're prone to market, seasonal, or weather-related disruptions. For example, food prices may change rapidly due to drought, floods, or unseasonably hot or cold weather. By excluding those items, the core reading is believed to paint a more accurate picture of structural, long-term price pressures, which is what concerns monetary policymakers the most.

Looking at consumer spending reports, the retail sales report in the United States is reported on a core basis excluding autos (retail sales ex-autos), which are heavily influenced by seasonal discounting and sales promotions, as well as being relatively large-ticket items in relation to other retail expenditures. The durable goods report is also issued on a core basis excluding transportation (durable goods ex-transportation), which mostly reflects aircraft sales, which are also highly variable on a month-to-month basis as well as extremely big-ticket items that can distort the overall data picture.

Markets tend to focus on the core reading over the headline reading in most cases, especially where a known preference for the core reading exists on the part of monetary-policy makers. The result can be large discrepancies between headline data and the core readings, such as headline retail sales falling 1 percent on a month-to-month basis but rising 0.5 percent on a core ex-autos basis. Needless to say, market reactions will be similarly disjointed, with an initial reaction based on the headline reading frequently followed by a different reaction to the core.

Market-Moving Economic Data Reports from the United States

Now let's get down to the nitty-gritty data. In this section, we run through the major economic data reports that come out of the United States. (We list the data reports according to the model we outline earlier in this chapter.) Our intention here is not necessarily to magnify the importance of U.S. economic data, even though the United States is the world's largest national economy and the U.S. dollar is on one side of 80 percent of currency trades.

Nope, our aim here is to kill two birds with one stone:

- Introduce you to the major economic reports issued by every major currency country, using U.S. data as the example
- Let you in on the finer points of how the market views the important data reports

At the end of this chapter, we take you through a country-by-country look at major non-U.S. data reports that don't fall into the main report categories or are too important to be ignored.

Labor-market reports

We put the job market at the top of our economic model because job creation/destruction is the single-most important driver of overall economic growth. Every major economy issues updates on its labor market by reporting the number of jobs added/lost, the unemployment rate, or some variation of those. United States employment data holds special significance because it reflects on the world's largest economy and the primary global reserve currency. The following are the key U.S. employment reports.

U.S. monthly employment report

Typically released on the first Friday of each month and covering the prior month, the U.S. jobs report is considered among the timeliest of economic indicators. But it's also subject to large revisions to prior periods and significant statistical volatility. The main components of the report include:

- ✔ **Change in non-farm payrolls (NFP):** This is the big number everyone focuses on. The NFP change is derived from the *establishment survey* (because it's based on responses from companies), and shows the number of jobs gained or lost in the prior month. The going wisdom among economists is that the United States needs to add around 200,000 jobs each month just to offset population growth and keep the unemployment rate steady. The market's initial reaction is based on the difference between the actual and the forecast change in NFP. The prior two months' NFP changes are also revised, and those revisions will color the market's interpretation of the current report.

- ✔ **Unemployment rate:** Measures unemployed individuals seeking work as a percentage of the civilian labor force. The unemployment rate is derived from a separate survey (the *household survey* because it surveys real households), which also includes a jobs change number that may be at odds with the change in NFP. Increases in the unemployment rate are typically interpreted as a sign of weakness in the labor market and the economy overall, while declines in the rate are considered a positive sign for the job market and the overall economy.

- ✔ **Change in manufacturing payrolls:** Measures the number of jobs added or lost in manufacturing industries and is looked at as a gauge of near-term production activity.

- ✔ **Average hourly earnings:** Measures the change in employee wages and is looked as an indicator of whether incomes are rising or falling and the implications for consumer spending.

- ✔ **Average weekly hours:** Measures the average number of hours worked each week and is looked at as a rough gauge of the demand for labor, with increasing weekly hours seen as a positive for the labor market.

ADP national employment report

The ADP national employment report is put together by the payroll processing company of the same name (www.adp.com) and works in close collaboration with Moody's Analytics. It comes out on Wednesdays at 8:15 a.m. ET, two days before the government's NFP report (see the preceding section). ADP measures only private jobs and excludes government hiring. The ADP report is intended to serve as an alternative measurement of the labor market, but it's got a spotty track record of predicting the NFP with any accuracy. Because of that uncertainty, market reaction to the ADP is typically minor and short-lived, but economists may adjust their forecasts for the NFP depending on what the ADP indicates.

Weekly initial unemployment claims

Initial jobless claims are reported every Thursday at 8:30 a.m. ET for the week ending the prior Saturday and represent first-time filings for unemployment insurance. Initial claims are looked at as interim updates on the overall labor market between monthly NFP reports. The changes in initial claims can be volatile on a week-to-week basis — there are a fair number of hiccups caused by weather, strikes, and seasonal labor patterns — so analysts look at a four-week moving average of initial claims to factor out one-off events. Still, sharp increases or declines in initial claims data will get the market's attention, producing a market reaction on their own, as well as causing estimates of upcoming monthly NFP reports to be downgraded or upgraded.

A second part of the weekly claims report is *continuing claims,* which is a measure of the total number of people receiving unemployment benefits, excluding first-time filers. The market looks at continuing claims as another gauge of labor-market conditions. Increases in continuing claims typically suggest deterioration in the job market, because unemployed individuals are finding it difficult to get work and staying on unemployment insurance longer. Declines in continuing claims are similarly viewed as an improvement in the job market, because workers are presumably finding jobs more easily.

Other labor-market indicators

On top of the reports listed in the "Labor-market reports" section of this chapter, a number of other employment indicators come out inside other economic reports. These employment measures don't trigger market reactions in their own right, but they're used to update the overall understanding of the employment outlook. These include

✔ **Consumer confidence index (CCI):** Within the monthly consumer confidence report by the Conference Board (www.conference-board.org), respondents are asked whether "jobs are hard to get" and also whether "jobs are plentiful." The difference between the two is known as the *labor differential* and serves as another barometer of conditions in labor-markets.

✔ **Institute for Supply Management (ISM) employment indices:** The national ISM purchasing manager indices contain a subcategory asking managers to rate the employment situation at their companies, with responses over 50 indicating plans to hire and expand, and readings below 50 indicating contraction.

✔ **Regional Federal Reserve indices:** Surveys of manufacturing businesses, like the Philadelphia Fed survey, also include questions on the outlook for hiring. Readings above zero indicate plans to add employees; levels below zero suggest layoffs ahead.

Consumer-level data reports

Personal consumption accounts for two-thirds or more of most developed nations' economies, so how consumers are doing has a big impact on the economic outlook and the direction of interest rates, which are both key drivers of forex rates. Here are the main U.S. data reports focusing on personal consumption.

Consumer sentiment

Consumer psychology is at the heart of the market's attempts to interpret future consumer activity and, with it, the overall direction of the economy. The theory is that if you feel good, you'll spend more, and if you feel uncertain, you'll cut back spending. The market likes to pay attention to consumer confidence indicators even though there is little correlation between how consumers tell you they feel and how they'll actually go on to spend.

In fact, consumer sentiment is frequently the result of changes in gasoline prices, how the stock market is faring, or what recent employment indicators suggested. More reliable indicators of consumer spending are money-in-the-pocket gauges like average weekly earnings, personal income and spending, and retail sales reports. Still, the market likes to react to the main sentiment gauges, if only in the short run, with improving sentiment generally supporting the domestic currency and softer sentiment hurting it. The key confidence gauges are

- **Consumer confidence index:** A monthly report issued by the Conference Board comprised of the expectations index (looking six months ahead) and the present-situation index. The surveys ask households about their outlooks for overall economic conditions, employment, and incomes.

- **University of Michigan consumer sentiment index:** Comes out twice a month: a preliminary reading in the middle of the month and a final reading at the start of the next month.

- **ABC Consumer Confidence:** A weekly consumer-sentiment report issued each Tuesday evening. The weekly ABC confidence report can be used to update your expectations of upcoming monthly consumer confidence and University of Michigan reports.

If market forecasts envision an increase in the Michigan or Conference Board's consumer confidence index, for example, but the prior two or three weeks of the ABC survey suggest confidence is waning, you've got a pretty good indication that the monthly surveys may disappoint.

Personal income and personal spending

These two monthly reports always come out together and provide as close an indication as we can get of how much money is going into and out of consumers' pockets. The market looks at these reports to get an update on the health of the U.S. consumer and the outlook for personal consumption going forward. *Personal income* includes all wages and salaries, along with transfer payments (such as Social Security or unemployment insurance) and dividends. *Personal spending* is based on personal consumption expenditures for all types of individual outlays.

Personal income is watched as a leading indicator of personal spending on the basis that future spending is highly correlated with income. The greater the increases in personal income, the more optimistic the consumption outlook will be, and vice versa. But it's important to note that inflation-adjusted incomes are the key. If incomes are just keeping pace with inflation, the outlook for spending is less positive.

Retail sales

The monthly advance retail sales report is the primary indicator of personal spending in the United States, covering most every purchase Americans make, from gas-station fill-ups to dinner and a movie. Retail sales are reported on a headline basis as well as on a core basis (which excludes automobile purchases). The market focuses mainly on the core number to get a handle on how the consumer is behaving, but substantial strength or weakness in the auto industry doesn't go unnoticed. The advance retail sales report is a preliminary estimate based on survey samples and can be revised substantially based on later data.

Retail sales reports are subject to a variety of distorting effects, most commonly from weather. Stretches of bad weather, such as major storms or bouts of unseasonable cold or heat, can impair consumer mobility or alter shopping patterns, reducing retail sales in the affected period. Sharp swings in gasoline prices can also create illusory effects, such as price spikes leading to an apparent increase in retail sales due to the higher per-gallon price, while overall non-gas retail sales are reduced or displaced by the higher outlays at the pump.

Durable goods orders

Durable goods orders are another major monthly indicator of consumption, both by individuals and businesses. Durable goods measure the amount of orders received by manufacturers that produce items made to last at least three years. As a data series, durable goods is one of the most volatile of them all, with multiple percentage swings (as opposed to 0.1 percent or 0.3 percent changes) between months a norm rather than an exception. Durable goods are reported on a headline basis and on a core basis, excluding transportation, or ex-transportation (mostly aircraft).

Durables are generally bigger-ticket purchases, such as washing machines and furniture, so they're also looked at as a leading indicator of overall consumer spending. If consumers are feeling flush with cash and confidence, big-ticket spending is more common. If consumers are uncertain, or times are tight, high-cost purchases are the first to be postponed. Also, businesses tend to concentrate their spending in the final month of each quarter, which can distort prior months and exaggerate the last.

Housing-market indicators

The real estate or housing market is a major factor behind consumer spending since homes typically represent the largest asset on a household's balance sheet. Rising home prices are seen to support consumption through the *wealth effect* (the richer you feel, the more likely you are to spend), whereas falling house prices can be a major drag on personal spending. The U.S. real estate bubble burst in 2006–2007 and triggered the GFC and recession of 2008–2009, turning U.S. housing data into a major drag on U.S consumption. One of the hangovers from the financial crisis is that the markets continue to look closely at the U.S. housing market as a gauge of economic strength. If you see a weak housing market, it can send a chill through the U.S. dollar market and the U.S. stock markets.

There's a raft of monthly housing market reports to monitor the sector, based on whether the homes are new or existing.

- **Existing-home sales** data is reported by the National Association of Realtors (NAR). Sales of preexisting homes (condos included) account for the lion's share of residential real-estate activity — about 85 percent of total home sales. Existing-home sales are reported on an annualized rate, and the market looks at the monthly change in that rate. Median home prices and the inventory of unsold homes are important clues to how the housing market is evolving. Existing-home sales are counted after a closing. Pending home sales are a separate report viewed as a leading indicator of existing-home sales. Pending home sales are counted when a contract is signed to buy an existing home.

- **New-home sales** are just that, brand-new homes and condos built for sale, reported on an annualized basis. New-home sales account for about 15 percent of residential home sales, but the sector was the fastest growing during the recent real-estate boom and has since seen activity decline steeply. New-home sales are counted when a contract is signed to purchase the new home, which means that contract cancellations (not reported) may result in lower actual sales than originally reported.

- **Housing starts** measure the number of new-home construction starts that took place in each month, reported on an annualized rate. Housing starts are considered a leading indicator of new-home sales but more recently have been looked at as an indication of home builder sentiment, as builders try to reduce inventories of unsold new homes.

- **Building permits** are the starting point of the whole new-housing cycle and are reported alongside housing starts each month. Building permits are required before construction can begin on new homes, so they're viewed as another leading indicator of housing starts and new-home sales.

Business-level data reports

Getting a handle on how businesses are faring is an important clue to the strength of the economy, which in turn drives the outlook for interest rates and the overall investment environment. The following series of data reports offer insights into how companies are responding at the enterprise level.

Institute for Supply Management and Purchasing Managers Index

The Institute for Supply Management (ISM) calculates several regional and national indices of current business conditions and future outlooks based on surveys of purchasing managers. ISM readings are based on a boom/bust scale, with 50 as the tipping point — a reading above 50 indicates expansion, whereas a reading below 50 signals contraction.

The main ISM reports to keep an eye on are

- **Chicago Purchasing Managers Index (PMI):** The Chicago PMI remains the key regional manufacturing activity index because the Chicago area and the Midwest region are still significant hubs of manufacturing activity in the United States. The Chicago PMI is also the first of the national PMIs to be reported, and the market frequently views it as a leading indicator of the larger national ISM manufacturing report, which is typically released a day after the Chicago PMI.

- **ISM manufacturing report:** The ISM manufacturing report is the monthly national survey of manufacturing activity and is one of the key indicators of the overall manufacturing sector. The ISM manufacturing report also includes a prices-paid index, which is viewed as an interim inflation reading, along with other key subsector measurements, like the employment situation. The market tends to react pretty strongly to sharp changes in the report or if the ISM is moving above or below 50, but keep in mind that the manufacturing sector accounts for a relatively small portion of overall U.S. economic activity, so the importance of the ISM manufacturing gauge tends to be exaggerated.

- **ISM nonmanufacturing report:** The ISM nonmanufacturing report is the monthly ISM report that covers the other 80 percent of the U.S. economy, namely the service sector. The ISM manufacturing report may get more attention, but the ISM non-manufacturing report is the one to focus on.

The equivalent of the ISM reports in Europe and China are the PMI reports that are put together by a data collection company called Markit. Since 2011, Markit has produced an index for the U.S., which is released at the end of each month. Although not as popular as the ISM survey, the fact that it's released before the ISM survey has seen its popularity start to rise, although it has some way to go before it overtakes the ISM as the business survey of choice for the markets.

Regional Federal Reserve indices

A number of the Federal Reserve district banks issue monthly surveys of business sentiment in their regions, usually concentrated on the manufacturing sector. The regional Fed indices are looked at on their own as well as for what they suggest about subsequent national sentiment surveys, like the ISM index. The main index reading is a subjective response on general business conditions, with responses above zero indicating that conditions are improving and readings below zero indicating deterioration. The main regional Fed indices to watch are

- ✔ **Philadelphia Fed index:** Usually the first of the major Fed indices to be reported each month, covering the manufacturing sector in Pennsylvania, New Jersey, and Delaware. The Philly Fed index includes subindices focusing on new orders, employment, inventories, and prices, among others.
- ✔ **New York Empire State index:** Assesses New York state manufacturers' current and six-month outlooks.
- ✔ **Richmond Fed manufacturing index:** A composite index based on new orders, production, and employment, covering the Middle Atlantic states.

Industrial production and capacity utilization

Industrial production measures the amount of output generated by the nation's factories, mines, and utilities on a monthly basis and is viewed as an indication of changes in the broader economy. The manufacturing sector is still viewed as a leading indicator for overall business cycles, so changes here could signal a larger swing in the economic outlook. The capacity utilization report measures actual output versus a theoretical maximum capacity and is looked at for what it suggests about inflationary pressures. High levels of capacity utilization above 80 percent may indicate price pressures are building and send a warning sign to policy makers. Lower levels of capacity utilization may signal the absence of inflationary pressures and allow monetary policy makers to keep interest rates lower.

The Fed's Beige Book

The Beige Book, named for the color of its cover, is a compilation of regional economic assessments from the Fed's 12 district banks, issued about two weeks before every Federal Open Market Committee (FOMC) policy-setting meeting. The regional Fed banks develop their summaries based on surveys and anecdotal reporting of local business leaders and economists, and the report is then summarized by one of the Fed district banks, all of which take turns issuing the report. The Beige Book is designed to serve as the basis of economic discussions at the upcoming FOMC meeting.

Markets look at the Beige Book's main findings to get a handle on how the economy is developing as well as what issues the FOMC might focus on. A typical Beige Book report may include generalized observations along the following lines: Most districts reported retail sales activity that was steady or moderately expanding; a few districts reported declines in manufacturing activity; some districts noted increased labor-market tightness and rising wage demands; all districts noted a sharp slowing in real-estate activity.

The key for the market is to assess the main themes of the report, such as:

✔ Is the economy expanding or contracting? How fast, and how widespread?

✔ Which sectors are strongest, and which sectors are weakest?

✔ Are there any signs of inflation?

✔ How does the labor market look?

The Beige Book is released in the afternoon (New York time), when liquidity is thinner, so it can generate a larger-than-normal response if its tone or conclusions are significantly different from what markets had been expecting.

Structural data reports

Structural data reports are the big picture, macroeconomic data that depict the longer-term economic outlook. What is the structure of the economy? Is it growing or contracting? If so, how fast? Is inflation under control or are prices rising too fast? Is the economy gaining or losing from trade? These reports can be some of the most significant drivers of central bank monetary policy.

Inflation gauges

Inflation reports are used to monitor overall changes in price levels of goods and services and as key inputs into setting interest rate expectations. Increases in inflation are likely to be met with higher interest rates by central-bank policy makers seeking to stamp out inflation, while moderating or declining inflation readings suggest generally lower interest-rate expectations.

There are a number of different inflation reports, with each focused on a different source of inflation or stage of the economy where the price changes are appearing. In the United States and other countries, inflation reports come out on a headline (total) basis and a core basis (which excludes food and energy to minimize distortions from these volatile inputs). Inflation indexes report changes on a month-to-month basis (abbreviated MoM, for month-over-month) to monitor short-term changes, as well as changes over the prior year's levels (YoY, for year-over-year) to gauge the longer-term rate of inflation. The main inflation reports to keep an eye on are

✔ **Consumer price index (CPI):** The CPI is what most people are familiar with when they think of inflation. The CPI measures the cost of a basket of goods and services at the consumer or retail level — the prices that we're paying. The CPI is looked at as the final stage of inflation.

✔ **Producer price index (PPI):** The PPI measures the change in prices at the producer or wholesale level, or what firms are charging one another for goods and services. The PPI looks at upstream inflation by stage of processing and may serve as a leading indicator of overall inflation.

✔ **Personal consumption expenditure (PCE):** The PCE is roughly equivalent to the CPI in that it measures the changes in price of a basket of goods and services at the consumer level. But the PCE has the distinction of being preferred by the Federal Reserve as its main inflation gauge because the composition of items in the PCE basket changes more frequently than in the CPI, reflecting evolving consumer tastes and behavior. If the Fed thinks the more-dynamic basket is the one to watch, who are we to disagree? When the Fed refers to an inflation target or tolerable level of inflation, it's typically referring to core PCE readings.

✔ **Institute for Supply Management (ISM) prices paid index:** The national and regional purchasing managers indices have subcategories reporting on the level of prices paid and the level of prices received by firms. The prices-paid component usually gets the most attention as another producer-level indication of price pressures, likely to be mirrored by the PPI.

Gross domestic product

Gross domestic product (GDP) measures the total amount of economic activity in an economy over a specified period, usually quarterly and adjusted for inflation. The percentage change in GDP from one period to the next is looked at as the primary growth rate of an economy. If GDP in the first quarter of a year is reported as +0.5 percent, it means the economy expanded by 0.5 percent in the first quarter relative to the prior fourth quarter's output. GDP is frequently calculated on a quarterly basis but reported in *annualized* terms. That means a 0.5 percent quarterly GDP increase would be reported as a 2 percent annualized rate of growth for the quarter (0.5 percent × 4 quarters = 2 percent). The use of annualized rates is helpful for comparing relative growth among economies.

In most countries, GDP is reported on a quarterly basis, so it's taken as a big-picture reality check on overall economic growth. The market's economic outlook will be heavily influenced by what the GDP reports indicate. Better-than-expected growth may spur talk of the need for higher interest rates, while steady or slower GDP growth may suggest easier monetary policy ahead. At the same time, though, GDP reports cover a relatively distant economic past — a quarter's GDP report typically comes out almost midway through the next quarter and is looking back at economic activity three to four months ago. As a result, market expectations continue to evolve based on incoming data reports, so don't get too caught up in GDP for too long after its initial release.

Trade and current account balances

Two of the most important reports for the forex markets, because there are direct and potentially long-term currency implications, are trade and current account balances:

- ✔ **Trade balance** measures the difference between a nation's exports and its imports. If a nation imports more than it exports, it's said to have a *trade deficit;* if a nation exports more than it imports, it's said to have a *trade surplus.* Trade balances are reported on a monthly basis; prior periods are subject to revision.

- ✔ **Current account balance** is a broader measure of international trade, and includes financial transfers as well as trade in goods and services. Current accounts are also either in deficit or surplus, reflecting whether a country is a net borrower or lender to the rest of the world. Nations with current account deficits are net borrowers from the rest of the world, and those with current account surpluses are net lenders to the world. Current account reports are issued quarterly, and because the monthly trade balance comprises the bulk of the current account balance, markets tend to have a good handle on what to expect in current account data.

Countries with persistently large trade or current account deficits tend to see their currencies weaken relative to other currencies, whereas currencies of countries running trade surpluses tend to appreciate. The basic idea is that the currency of a deficit nation is in less demand (it's being sold to buy more foreign goods) than the currency of a surplus nation (it's being bought to pay for domestically produced goods).

For example, the U.S. dollar was under pressure for several years before the GFC, owing to its widening (increasing) trade and current account deficits. In late 2006, however, the size of the deficit stopped increasing, which removed some of the pressure on the dollar. But because the deficit remains high in absolute and historical terms, the U.S. trade deficit is still a major U.S. dollar negative, although the U.S.'s increased oil production in recent years could cause the trade deficit to shrink sharply in the future and could be a dollar positive in the future.

Government debt and budget deficits

The aftermath of the GFC has exposed high debt and deficit levels in many major economies, especially in the United States, Europe, the U.K., and Japan. Fears of a debt *restructuring* (where terms of a bond are altered) or default can seriously undermine confidence in a national currency, leading to an extended bout of weakness, as was seen with the euro in the 2010 European debt crisis.

There's no single data release that adequately covers the debt situations in major economies, though most national governments typically release a monthly budget statement. Instead, monitoring the debt/deficit picture of key countries depends on a series of news and data flows:

✔ **Budget and deficit forecasts:** Issued by individual governments and the IMF, these are the best way to stay on top of evolving fiscal changes.

✔ **Government bond yields, spreads, and CDS (credit default swaps):** As investors' fears increase over the creditworthiness of governments, they sell those countries' bonds, driving yields higher. *Yield spreads* are another measure of risk, noting the difference between the yields of an embattled nation and a safer alternative. Credit default swaps are a form of insurance that pays investors in the event of a default — the higher they are, the greater the perceived risk.

✔ **Government debt auctions:** When governments seek to borrow in capital markets, lack of demand or too high a price can shut them out and possibly trigger a default. Watch for indicators of demand, like the *bid/cover ratio,* which measures the amount of bids submitted relative to the issuance amount (the higher the better) and pricing (the higher the yield demanded, the greater the risk).

✔ **Sovereign credit ratings:** Major credit rating agencies, like Moody's, S&P and Fitch, may announce periodic credit reviews of sovereign debt, possibly suggesting a downgrade. Actual credit rating downgrades can send investors fleeing, driving up a country's borrowing costs and increasing the risks of default.

Major International Data Reports

In the preceding sections, we cover the main economic reports using U.S. data as the basis for explaining what each report measures and how the market views them. The main data reports of other major national economies essentially mirror the U.S. data reports, but with some minor differences in calculation methods or reporting. In other words, the CPI report out of the United Kingdom is looked at the same way as the CPI report is viewed in the United States — as a measure of consumer-level inflation.

But plenty of national data reports don't have an equivalent in the United States, and others are followed more closely in local markets and require extra attention. In the next few sections, we highlight the main data reports of other national economies beyond what we cover earlier.

Eurozone

The main data reports out of the Eurozone are remarkably similar to those of the United States. The key difference is that individual European countries report national economic data, which comes out alongside Eurozone-wide reports from Eurostat or the European Central Bank (ECB).

Because the Eurozone has a common currency and central bank, the forex market focuses primarily on indicators that cover the entire region, such as Eurozone industrial production and CPI, for example. Among individual national reports, the market concentrates on data from the largest Eurozone economies, mainly Germany and France. Keep an eye on all the major reports coming out of those countries. They can generate sizeable reactions based on the idea that they're leading indicators of Eurozone-wide data. If German industrial production slumps, for instance, it may suggest that overall Eurozone industrial production is set to decline, too. Since the Eurozone sovereign debt crisis, the market has also tended to concentrate on how countries that received bailouts (Greece, Ireland, and Portugal) are faring. Believe it or not, a Greek unemployment report has been known to move the market!

The only European reports that may escape your attention due to unusual names are the principal European confidence indicators. These reports can generate sizeable reactions depending on how they compare to forecasts:

- ✔ **ZEW survey:** This survey measures growth expectations over the next six months by institutional investors and analysts. The survey is done for Germany and the whole Eurozone.

- ✔ **IFO and GfK surveys:** IFO is a corporate sentiment survey that queries businesses across Germany on current sentiment and how business is expected to develop over the next six months. The GfK survey is a monthly measure of consumer confidence

- ✔ **Purchasing Manager Indexes (PMIs):** A data firm called Markit produces monthly PMIs for the manufacturing and service sectors for Germany, France, and the whole Eurozone, similar to the Chicago PMI in the United States. The reports come out on a preliminary and final basis.

- ✔ **Eurozone Confidence:** The European Commission (EC) produces monthly confidence surveys for a variety of sectors: consumer, services, industrial, and overall economic sentiment.

Japan

When looking at Japanese data, keep in mind that the Japanese economy is still heavily export oriented. In addition to following all the usual reports, pay special attention to industrial production and manufacturing data because of their large role in the economy. Since 2012, the Bank of Japan has tried to fight off the threat of deflation, which means that CPI reports have also taken on a special significance in recent years. Outside the standard reports to watch, keep an eye on the following:

- ✔ **Tankan index:** The Tankan survey is a quarterly survey of business outlooks produced by the Bank of Japan (BOJ). The survey produces four readings — current conditions and future outlook from both large manufacturers and large non-manufacturers. The large all-industry capital expenditures survey is an important gauge of capital spending and is often the focus of the entire Tankan survey.

✓ **Trade balance:** Japan's monthly trade balance is nearly always in surplus. The size of that surplus carries indications for the health of the export sector as well as potential political repercussions against excessive JPY weakness when the trade surplus is seen to be too large.

✓ **All-industry and tertiary industry (services) indices:** Monthly sentiment gauges of industrial and service-sector firms.

United Kingdom

In addition to the usual major government-issued data reports, be alert for the following reports that can frequently trigger sharp reactions in GBP:

✓ **Bank of England (BOE) Minutes:** Released two weeks after each Monetary Policy Committee (MPC) meeting, they show the voting results for the most recent decision. Market expectations and GBP are frequently upended when the policy discussion or vote shows a split leaning in the direction of an interest rate change.

✓ **BOE Quarterly Inflation Report:** Although it only comes out quarterly, the BOE's forecasts for growth and inflation over the next two years can have a significant impact on the interest rate outlook and GBP. It also includes a press conference, which is watched closely by the markets.

✓ **Purchasing Manager Indexes (PMIs):** A data firm called Markit produces monthly PMIs for the manufacturing, construction, and service sectors.

✓ **GfK consumer confidence and Nationwide consumer confidence:** Two separate, monthly, consumer-sentiment gauges put out by GfK, a U.K./European marketing agency, and the Nationwide Building Society, a U.K. mortgage lender.

✓ **CBI distributive trades survey and industrial trends survey:** Two monthly reports put out by the Confederation of British Industry, a private trade group. The distributive trades survey is a measure of retail and wholesale sales, and the industrial trends survey is a survey of manufacturers' current and future outlook.

✓ **British Retail Consortium (BRC) retail sales monitor and shop price index:** Two monthly reports put out by the British Retail Consortium, a private trade organization. The retail sales monitor is another measure of retail sales, and the shop price index measures inflation at the retail level.

TIP

European Central Bank press briefings

The European Central Bank (ECB) was the first of the major central banks to hold press conferences after each policy meeting. The Federal Reserve has followed suit, as has the Bank of Japan; however, the Bank of England is still holding out, and releases nothing after a policy meeting unless it has changed policy, in which case it releases a brief statement explaining its action. The ECB president reads a statement that surveys the economic landscape and provides a future outlook. The most important element of the ECB statement is the inflation outlook because the ECB has only a single mandate — to maintain price stability, such as fight inflation or deflation. The ECB president then takes questions from the press and frequently addresses market expectations on ECB policy. The president's comments in the Q&A session can significantly alter market perceptions, potentially triggering sharp moves in the euro. The ECB may have held rates steady and indicated inflation risks are contained, for example, but if the ECB president suggests that inflation risks have shifted lower, markets may take it as a signal the ECB is prepared to loosen monetary policy soon and the euro could weaken. From the start of 2015, the ECB will also release the minutes of its meetings, which will include individual members' voting decisions. Up until 2015, it had not done this, which is different to other central banks, which usually release minutes a couple weeks after a policy meeting.

Canada

Canadian data mirrors U.S. data in many respects, but here are a few other important Canadian indicators to watch:

- **International securities transactions:** Roughly the equivalent of the U.S. Treasury's TIC report (see "Trade and current account balances," earlier in this chapter), showing net investment flows into and out of Canada on a monthly basis. High inflows typically support the CAD, and outflows tend to hurt it.

- **Ivey Purchasing Manager index:** A key monthly gauge of Canadian business outlooks issued by the Richard Ivey School of Business. The report covers purchases, employment, inventories, deliveries, and prices.

Australia

Australian data reports exert a strong influence on Aussie, similar in many respects to how U.K. data affects the pound. In particular, keep an eye on

- **RBA rate decisions and RBA Minutes:** The RBA's statement following a rate decision, and the subsequent release of the minutes two weeks later, can drive interest rate expectations and AUD big time.

✔ **Westpac consumer confidence and National Australia Bank (NAB) business confidence:** Two separate monthly sentiment gauges put out by two of Australia's leading banks.

New Zealand

New Zealand data is similarly provocative for the Kiwi. In addition to the main data reports and Reserve Bank of New Zealand (RBNZ) statements, keep an eye on the following Kiwi-specific data:

✔ **NZ Card Spending:** This monthly report covers purchases using credit, debit, and store cards, and gives another view of retail sales.

✔ **ANZ Consumer Confidence:** This monthly survey of consumer sentiment is conducted by ANZ Bank.

China

In early 2011, China surpassed Japan as the world's second largest national economy after the United States. Chinese growth over the last decade has been nothing short of astronomical and played a major role in supporting the global recovery after the GFC. Data out of China has taken on increased prominence as a result, with global markets frequently reeling on weaker China data or surging on stronger reports.

The Chinese growth outlook affects global markets through a number of different channels. Stronger Chinese growth is good for global trade and tends to positively influence stock markets around the world. Chinese demand for commodities is also influenced by its growth trajectory, with consequent implications for individual commodity markets (China also recently surpassed the U.S. as the largest oil consumer) and commodity producing countries such as Australia and South Africa. As a result, financial markets around the world are increasingly driven by Chinese growth prospects.

In terms of economic reports, Chinese data that reflects growth are the most significant, and we would highlight the trade surplus, industrial production, manufacturing PMIs, and quarterly GDP as the key data releases to watch. Chinese consumers are also increasingly seen to be key to developed nations' economic outlooks and signs of rising imports and gains in retail sales are viewed as supportive of global growth.

The Chinese still manage their currency and it's not accessible to individual traders. But Chinese data can have an impact far beyond its borders due to its newfound prominence in the global economy. This is especially relevant for the Aussie dollar, because China is Australia's main trading partner.

Chapter 8

Getting to Know the Major Currency Pairs

The vast majority of trading volume takes place in the *major* currency pairs: EUR/USD, USD/JPY, GBP/USD, and USD/CHF. These currency pairs account for about two-thirds of daily trading volume in the market and are the most watched barometers of the overall forex market. When you hear about the dollar rising or falling, it's usually referring to the dollar against these other currencies.

Even though these four pairs are routinely grouped together as the major currency pairs, each currency pair represents an individual economic and political relationship. In this chapter, we look at the fundamental drivers of each currency pair to see what moves them. We also look at the market's quoting conventions and what they mean for margin-based trading.

Although it's important to understand *why* a currency rate moves, we think it's also essential to have an understanding of *how* different pairs' rates move. Most currency trading is very short-term in nature, typically from a few minutes to a few days. This makes understanding a currency pair's *price action* (how a currency pair's price moves in the very short term) a key component of any trading strategy.

When you're reading this chapter, keep in mind that our observations are not hard and fast rules. As far as we know, there are no hard and fast rules in any market, anywhere, any time. Think of them as rules of thumb that apply more often than not. When it comes to applying our insights into real-life trading, you'll have to evaluate the overall circumstances each time to see if our insights make sense. The idea is that with a baseline of currency pair behavior, you'll be in a better position to anticipate, interpret, and react to market developments.

The flip side of this coin is that there is information content when our insights don't hold water. If the market usually reacts to certain events in a regular fashion, but it's not doing so this time, it's a clue that something else is at work (usually bigger). And that can be even more valuable trading information.

The Big Dollar: EUR/USD

EUR/USD is by far the most actively traded currency pair in the global forex market. Everyone and his brother, sister, and cousin trades EUR/USD. This will come as no surprise to anyone who has traded in the forex market, because if you have, more likely than not you traded EUR/USD at some point.

The same goes for the big banks. Every major trading desk has at least one, and probably several, EUR/USD traders to deal with the volume in this currency pair. This is in contrast to less liquid currency pairs such as USD/CAD or AUD/USD, for which trading desks may not have a dedicated trader. All those EUR/USD traders add up to vast amounts of market interest, which increases overall trading liquidity.

Trading fundamentals of EUR/USD

EUR/USD is the currency pair that pits the U.S. dollar against the single currency of the Eurozone, the euro. The *Eurozone* refers to a grouping of countries in the European Union (EU) that in 1999 retired their own national currencies and adopted a unified single currency. In one fell swoop, at midnight on January 1, 1999, the Deutsche mark, Italian lira, French franc, and nine other European currencies disappeared and the euro came into being.

The move to a single currency was the culmination of financial unification efforts by the founding members of the European Union. In adopting the single currency, the nations agreed to abide by fiscal policy constraints that limited the ratio of national budget deficits to gross domestic product (GDP), among other requirements. (Some people would say that the 2010 sovereign debt crisis made a mockery of these rules.) The nations also delegated monetary policy (setting interest rates) to the newly founded European Central Bank (ECB).

As of this printing, the countries that use the euro are: Austria, Belgium, Cyprus, Estonia, Finland, France, Germany, Greece, Ireland, Italy, Latvia, Luxembourg, Malta, the Netherlands, Portugal, Slovakia, Slovenia, and Spain.

In 2010, the Eurozone underwent its first major challenge, known as the *sovereign debt crisis.* Some states had built up unsustainable debt loads and ended up needing bailouts. Greece was the first member state to topple, with Ireland, Portugal, and Cyprus also requiring financial bailouts in recent years.

At the time of writing, the situation had stabilized, although the road to recovery for some of the countries involved is a long one. The sovereign debt crisis has been the defining event of the Eurozone this decade.

On a brighter note, even with the sovereign debt crisis, the Eurozone has continued to expand in recent years, boosting the size of the monetary union's population to more than 300 million. Although its economy has taken a knock due to the sovereign debt crisis, its total GDP is still about equal to the GDP of the United States.

Trading EUR/USD by the numbers

Standard market convention is to quote EUR/USD in terms of the number of USD per EUR. For example, a EUR/USD rate of 1.3000 means that it takes $1.30 to buy €1.00.

EUR/USD trades inversely to the overall value of the USD, which means when EUR/USD goes up, the euro is getting stronger and the dollar weaker. When EUR/USD goes down, the euro is getting weaker and the dollar stronger. If you believed the U.S. dollar was going to move higher, you'd be looking to sell EUR/USD. If you thought the dollar was going to weaken, you'd be looking to buy EUR/USD.

EUR/USD has the euro as the base currency and the U.S. dollar as the secondary or counter currency. That means

- ✔ **EUR/USD is traded in amounts denominated in euros.** In online currency trading platforms, standard lot sizes are €100,000, mini lot sizes are €10,000, and micro lots are €1,000.

- ✔ **The pip value, or minimum price fluctuation, is denominated in USD.**

- ✔ **Profit and loss accrue in USD.** For one standard lot position size, each pip is worth $10; for one mini lot position size, each pip is worth $1. For each micro lot, each pip is worth $0.10.

- ✔ **Margin calculations in online trading platforms are typically based in USD.** At a EUR/USD rate of 1.3000, to trade a one-lot position worth €100,000, it'll take $1,300 in available margin (based on 100:1 leverage). That calculation will change over time, of course, based on the level of the EUR/USD exchange rate. A higher EUR/USD rate will require more USD in available margin collateral, and a lower EUR/USD rate will need less USD in margin.

Swimming in deep liquidity

Liquidity in EUR/USD is unmatched by other major currency pairs. This is why you tend to get narrower trading spreads in EUR/USD. Normal market spreads for EUR/USD are typically less than 1 pip, although this can vary. Over the years, spreads have narrowed sharply, and you can typically trade most of the major currency pairs for a 1 pip spread, or even less.

In terms of concrete numbers, EUR/USD accounted for 33 percent of global daily trading volume, according to the 2013 Bank for International Settlements (BIS) survey of the foreign exchange markets. This has fallen in recent years because the legacy of the sovereign debt crisis has caused some investors to diversify away from the single currency. One of the beneficiaries has been the yen. In 2013, trading USD/JPY rose some 4 percent to 23 percent.

Liquidity in EUR/USD is based on a variety of fundamental sources, such as

- **Global trade and asset allocation:** The Eurozone constitutes the second largest economic bloc after the United States. Not only does this create tremendous commercial trade flows, but it also makes Eurozone financial markets, and the euro, the destination for massive amounts of international investment flows. In April 2007, overall European stock-market valuations surpassed the value of U.S. equity markets for the first time ever.

- **Central bank credibility:** The ECB has established itself in the eyes of global investors as an effective institution in fighting inflation and maintaining currency stability. It has also been given credit for stabilizing the currency bloc during the sovereign debt crisis, which has enhanced its reputation in recent years.

- **Enhanced status as a reserve currency:** Central banks around the world hold foreign currency reserves to support their own currencies and improve market stability. The euro is increasing in importance as an alternative global reserve currency to the U.S. dollar, although this has stalled in recent years due to the onset of the sovereign debt crisis.

The euro also serves as the primary foil to the U.S. dollar when it comes to speculating on the overall direction of the U.S. dollar in response to U.S. news or economic data. If weak U.S. economic data is reported, traders are typically going to sell the dollar, which begs the question, "Against what?" The euro is the first choice for many, simply because it's there. It also helps that it's the most liquid alternative, allowing for easy entry and exit.

This is not to say that EUR/USD only reacts to U.S. economic data or news. On the contrary, Eurozone news, politics, and data can move EUR/USD as much as U.S. data moves the pair and sometimes more so, as during the sovereign debt crisis.

Drivers of the EUR/USD can be cyclical. On any given day, traders will respond to European news and data and adjust prices accordingly for several hours until U.S. data is released.

Watching the data reports

Country-specific economic reports, such as Dutch retail sales or Italian industrial production, are increasingly disregarded by the forex market in favor of Eurozone aggregate economic data. However, German and French national economic reports can still register with markets as they represent the two largest Eurozone economies. Here's a list of the major European data reports and events to keep an eye on:

- **European Central Bank (ECB) interest rate decisions and press conferences after ECB Central Council meetings.** This is when the ECB president explains the ECB's thinking and offers guidance on the future course of interest rates. It includes a press conference by the ECB president.

- **Speeches by ECB officials and individual European finance ministers.**

- **EU-harmonized Consumer Price Index (CPI), as well as national CPI and Producer Price Index (PPI) reports.**

- **EU Commission economic sector confidence indicators.**

- **Consumer and investor sentiment surveys separately issued by three private economic research firms known by their acronyms: Ifo, ZEW and GfK.** The Markit sentiment surveys are also closely watched because they give a timely view of confidence across all sectors of the economy.

- **Industrial production.**

- **Retail sales.**

- **Unemployment rate.**

- **Sovereign debt sales.** These are now closely watched, especially in Europe's smaller, financially fragile states, such as Greece. Although the sovereign debt crisis has calmed down in recent years, a failed bond auction could trigger more sovereign fears and weigh on the EUR.

Trading behavior of EUR/USD

The deep liquidity and tight trading spreads in EUR/USD make the pair ideal for both shorter-term and longer-term traders. The price action behavior in EUR/USD regularly exhibits a number of traits that traders should be aware of.

Trading tick by tick

In normal market conditions, EUR/USD tends to trade tick by tick, as opposed to other currency pairs, which routinely display sharper short-term price movements of several pips. In trading terms, if EUR/USD is trading at 1.2910/13, there are going to be traders looking to sell at 13, 14, and 15 and higher, while buyers are waiting to buy at 9, 8, 7, and lower.

In contrast, other less-liquid currency pairs, like AUD/USD and USD/CAD, typically fluctuate in a far jumpier fashion, which is reflected by the wider price spread in those pairs.

Fewer price jumps and smaller price gaps

The depth of liquidity in EUR/USD also reduces the number of *price jumps* or *price gaps* in short-term trading. A price *jump* refers to a quick movement in prices over a relatively small time frame (roughly 50 pips or more) in the course of normal trading. A price *gap* means prices have instantaneously adjusted over a larger price distance, typically in response to a news event or data release.

Don't get us wrong, price jumps/gaps do occur in EUR/USD, as anyone who has traded around data reports or other news events can attest. But price jumps/gaps in EUR/USD tend to be generated primarily by news/data releases and breaks of significant technical levels, events which can usually be identified in advance. As a caveat, there were large price gaps during the sovereign debt crisis, as uncertainty about the future of the Eurozone hung in the balance. At the time of writing, trading conditions had mostly returned to normal.

This is in contrast to other major currency pairs where short-term price gaps can develop from a one-off market flow, such as a portfolio manager selling a large amount of AUD/USD or a USD/CAD stop-loss order being triggered. When price gaps do occur in EUR/USD, they tend to be smaller relative to gaps in other pairs.

Backing and filling

When prices move rapidly in one direction, they tend to reach a short-term stopping point when opposite interest enters the market. For instance, let's say EUR/USD just traded higher from 1.2910/13 to 1.2922/25 in relatively orderly fashion, tick by tick over two minutes, meaning no price gaps. When the price move higher pauses, short-term traders who were long for the quick 12-pip move higher will look to exit and sell.

As selling interest begins to enter the market and prices stop rising, other not-so-fast longs will also start *hitting bids* (selling), pushing prices lower. From the other side, traders who missed the quick run up, or who were not as long as they wanted to be, will enter their buying interest in the market. Other buyers, sensing selling interest, may wait and place their buying interest at slightly lower levels. This back-and-forth consolidation after a short-term price movement is referred to as *backing and filling*. The price *backs up* and *fills* the short-term movement, though it can happen in both up and down price movements.

When it comes to EUR/USD price action, backing and filling is quite common and tends to be more substantial than in most currency pairs, meaning a greater amount of the directional move is retraced. Look at Figure 8-1 to get a visual idea of what backing and filling looks like. When EUR/USD is not backing and filling the way you would expect, it means the directional move is stronger and with greater interest behind it.

Figure 8-1:
A one-minute EUR/USD chart showing periods of backing and filling price action after short-term directional moves. Backing and filling occurs in price declines, too.

Source: eSignal (www.esignal.com)

Prolonged tests of technical levels

When it comes to trading around technical support and resistance levels, EUR/USD can try the patience of even the most disciplined traders. We say this because EUR/USD can spend hours (an eternity in forex markets) or even several days undergoing tests of technical levels. (See Chapter 10 for a primer on technical analysis.)

This goes back to the tremendous amount of interest and liquidity that defines the EUR/USD market. All those viewpoints come together in the form of market interest (bids and offers) when technical levels come into play. The result is a tremendous amount of market interest that has to be absorbed at technical levels, which can take time.

Looking at GBP/USD and USD/CHF as leading indicators

Given the tremendous two-way interest in EUR/USD, it can be very difficult to gauge whether a test of a technical level is going to lead to breakout or a rejection. To get an idea of whether a test of a technical level in EUR/USD is going to lead to a break, professional EUR/USD traders always keep an eye on GBP/USD and USD/CHF, as they tend to be leading indicators for the bigger EUR/USD and dollar moves in general.

If GBP/USD and USD/CHF are aggressively testing (trading at or through the technical level with very little pullback) similar technical levels to EUR/USD (for example, daily highs or equivalent trend-line resistance), then EUR/USD is likely to test that same level. If GBP/USD and USD/CHF break through their technical levels, the chances of EUR/USD following suit increases. By the same token, if GBP/USD and USD/CHF are not aggressively testing the key technical level, EUR/USD is likely to see its similar technical level hold.

GBP/USD and USD/CHF lead times can be anywhere from a few seconds or minutes to several hours and even days. Just make sure you're looking at the equivalent technical levels in each pair.

Tactical trading considerations in EUR/USD

We've looked at the major trading attributes of EUR/USD and now its time to look at how those elements translate into real-life trading tactics. After all, that's where the real money is made and lost.

Deciding whether it's a U.S. dollar move or a euro move

Earlier in this chapter, we note that EUR/USD routinely acts as the primary vehicle for forex markets to express their view on the USD. At the same time, we also indicated that EUR/USD will also react to euro-centric news and data. So for traders approaching EUR/USD on any given day, it helps to understand whether the driving force at work is dollar-based or euro-based. Are they bearish on the USD, or are they bullish on the EUR? Or is it some combination of the two?

Having a sense of which currency is driving EUR/USD at any given moment is important so you can better adapt to incoming data and news. If it's a EUR-based move higher, for instance, and surprisingly positive USD news or data is released later in the day, guess what? We've got countertrend information hitting the market, which could spark a reversal lower in EUR/USD (in favor of the dollar). By the same token, if that U.S. data comes out weaker than expected, it's likely to spur further EUR/USD gains, because EUR-buying interest is now combined with USD-selling interest.

Being patient in EUR/USD

Earlier in this chapter, we explore why EUR/USD can spend hours trading in relatively narrow ranges or testing technical levels. The key in such markets is to remain patient based on your directional view and your technical analysis. You should be able to identify short-term support that keeps an upside test alive or resistance that keeps a down-move going. If those levels fail, the move is stalling at the minimum and may even be reversing.

Taking advantage of backing and filling

Because EUR/USD tends to retrace more of its short-term movements, you can usually enter a position in your desired direction by leaving an order to buy or sell at slightly better rates than current market prices may allow. If the post–08:30 ET U.S. data price action sees EUR/USD move lower, and you think getting short is the way to go, you can leave an offer slightly (roughly 5 to 10 pips) above the current market level and use it to get short, instead of reaching out and hitting the bid on a downtick.

If your order is executed, you've got your desired position at a better rate than if you went to market, and you're probably in a better position rhythm-wise with the market (having sold on an uptick). Alternatively, you can take advantage of routine backing and filling by dealing at the market by selling on upticks and buying on downticks.

Allowing for a margin of error on technical levels

When it comes to determining whether EUR/USD has broken a technical level, we like to use a 10- to 15-pip margin of error. (Shorter-term traders may want to use a smaller margin of error.) Some very short-term traders and technical purists like to pinpoint an exact price level as support or resistance. If the market trades above or below their level, they'll call it a break and that's that. But the spot forex market rarely trades with such respect for technical levels to make such a clear and pinpointed distinction. And given the amount of interest in EUR/USD, it's especially prone to hazy technical lines in the sand.

The key point to take away from this is that all sorts of interest emerges around technical levels, and it's still going through the market even though the pinpointed level might have been breached. And this is where our margin of error comes in. Again, it's not a hard and fast rule, but generally speaking, EUR/USD will have chewed through most of the market interest around a technical level within about 10 to 15 points beyond the level.

East Meets West: USD/JPY

USD/JPY is one of the more challenging currency pairs among the majors and trading in it requires a higher degree of discipline and patience. Where other currency pairs typically display routine market fluctuations and relatively steady, active trading interest, USD/JPY seems to have an on/off switch. It can spend hours and even days in relatively narrow ranges and then march off on a mission to a new price level.

USD/JPY can offer some of the clearest trade setups among the major pairs. When you're right in USD/JPY, the returns can be astonishingly quick. When you're wrong in USD/JPY, you'll also know it pretty quickly. The key to developing a successful trading game plan in USD/JPY is to understand what drives the pair and the how price action behaves.

Trading fundamentals of USD/JPY

The Japanese yen is the third major international currency after the U.S. dollar and the European single currency, the euro. USD/JPY accounts for more than 20 percent of global trading volume, according to the 2013 BIS survey of foreign exchange markets. Japan stands as the third largest national economy after the United States and China in terms of GDP, and the JPY represents the third major currency group after the USD and the EUR groupings.

Trading USD/JPY by the numbers

Standard market convention is to quote USD/JPY in terms of the number of JPY per USD. For example, a USD/JPY rate of 115.35 means that it takes ¥115.35 to buy $1.

USD/JPY trades in the same direction as the overall value of the USD, and inversely to the value of the JPY. If the USD is strengthening and the JPY is weakening, the USD/JPY rate will move higher. If the USD is weakening and the JPY is strengthening, the USD/JPY rate will move lower.

USD/JPY has the U.S. dollar as the base currency and the JPY as the secondary or counter currency. This means

- ✓ **USD/JPY is traded in amounts denominated in USD.** In online currency trading platforms, standard lot sizes are $100,000, mini lot sizes are $10,000, and micro lot sizes are $1,000.

- ✓ **The pip value, or minimum price fluctuation, is denominated in JPY.**

- ✓ **Profit and loss accrue in JPY.** For one standard lot position size, each pip is worth ¥1000; for one mini lot position size, each pip is worth ¥100; and for each micro lot, each pip is worth ¥10. To convert those amounts to USD, divide the JPY amount by the USD/JPY rate. Using 115.00 as the rate, ¥1,000 = $8.70 and ¥100 = $0.87.

- ✓ **Margin calculations are typically calculated in USD.** So it's a straightforward calculation using the leverage rate to see how much margin is required to hold a position in USD/JPY. At 100:1 leverage, $1,000 of available margin is needed to open a standard-size position of 100,000 USD/JPY.

USD/JPY is heavily influenced by U.S. interest rates

If we had to identify the main driver of USD/JPY, it would easily be the movements in U.S. interest rates. The main reason for this is the massive amount of U.S. government debt held by the Japanese government and Japanese investors. The Bank of Japan (BOJ) alone holds nearly $900 billion worth of U.S. Treasury debt. If U.S. interest rates begin to fall, the prices of U.S. government bonds rise, increasing the USD-value of Japan's U.S. debt holdings. To offset, or hedge, their larger USD-long currency exposure, Japanese reserve managers need to sell more USD. This causes USD/JPY to closely track U.S. Treasury yields, as seen in Figure 8-2, which shows the USD/JPY rate and the yield on two-year U.S. Treasury notes on a monthly basis over ten years.

Figure 8-2:
USD/JPY exchange rate and yields on two-year U.S. Treasury notes over ten years on a monthly basis. USD/JPY closely follows the track of U.S. Treasury yields due to asset manager hedging operations.

Source: Bloomberg, FOREX.com

USD/JPY (lhs) — — U.S. 2yr Treasury yield (rhs)

Source: Bloomberg, FOREX.com

Long-term traders can take advantage of U.S. interest rate cycles via USD/JPY, buying the pair when U.S. rates are set to rise and selling when rates have peaked and begin to decline.

It's politically sensitive to trade

USD/JPY is the most politically sensitive currency pair among the majors. Japan remains a heavily export-oriented economy, accounting for more than 40 percent of overall economic activity. This means the JPY is a critical policy lever for Japanese officials to stimulate and manage the Japanese economy — and they aren't afraid to get involved in the market to keep the JPY from strengthening beyond desired levels.

A weak currency makes a nation's exports cheaper to foreigners and, all other things being equal, creates a competitive advantage to gain market share. The flip side of a weak currency is that it makes imports from abroad more expensive, putting foreign exporters at a disadvantage in the domestic market.

In the past, this has led to accusations of currency manipulation by trade partners and efforts to force the JPY to strengthen. But with China's incredible growth in this decade, lil' ol' Japan and the yen seem to have dropped from the radar screen as the primary target of free-market advocates. But this is more a function of China's vast current and future potential rather than any change to how the Japanese effectively manage the JPY.

The Ministry of Finance is routinely involved in the forex market

Currency intervention is usually a last resort for most major national governments. Instead, the Japanese Ministry of Finance (MOF) engages in routine verbal intervention in not-so-subtle attempts to influence the level of the JPY. The chief spokesman on currencies is, of course, the Minister of Finance, but the Vice Finance Minister for International Affairs is the more frequent commentator on forex market developments. Also watch comments from the Bank of Japan (see Chapter 5).

The Japanese financial press devotes a tremendous amount of attention to the value of the JPY, similar to how the U.S. financial media cover the Dow or S&P 500. Press briefings by MOF officials are routine. During times of forex market volatility, expect near-daily official comments. These statements move USD/JPY on a regular basis.

Beyond such jawboning, known as verbal intervention, the MOF has been known to utilize covert intervention through the use of sizeable market orders by the pension fund of the Japanese Postal Savings Bank, known as Kampo. After the 2011 tsunami, the yen surged in value, as its safe-haven status kicked in. To limit the damage to the Japanese economy, a multilateral effort was made by major global central banks to sell the yen and bring down its value.

In 2012, the new prime minister, Shinzo Abe, announced a radical economic program to try to boost the economy. One side effect of this was a weaker yen, which was supported by an extremely loose monetary policy from the Bank of Japan. As you can see, there are many ways that politics can get in the way of the yen.

Japanese asset managers tend to move together

If Americans are the ultimate consumers, then the Japanese are the consummate savers. The Japanese *savings rate* (the percentage of disposable income that's not spent) is around 15 percent. (Compare that with the U.S. savings rate at around 5 percent!) As a result, Japanese financial institutions control trillions of dollars in assets, many of which find their way to investments outside of Japan. The bulk of assets are invested in fixed income securities and this means Japanese asset managers are on a continual hunt for the best yielding returns.

This theme has taken on added prominence in recent years due to extremely low domestic yields in Japan At the time of writing, the Bank of Japan had yields of close to 0 percent, and a massive QE program to keep interest rates low for the long term. These low yields tend to weigh on the yen's value, so Japanese investors and asset managers tend to sell the yen and buy higher-yielding currencies that are stronger than the yen. This makes domestic interest-rate yields in Japan a key long-term determinant of the JPY's value.

Japanese financial institutions also tend to pursue a highly collegial approach to investment strategies. The result for forex markets is that Japanese asset managers tend to pursue similar investment strategies at the same time, resulting in tremendous asset flows hitting the market over a relatively short period of time. This situation has important implications for USD/JPY price action (see the next section).

Important Japanese data reports

Keep in mind that politics and government officials' (MOF) comments are quite frequent and can shift market sentiment and direction as much as, or more than, the fundamental data. The key data reports to focus on coming out of Japan are

- Bank of Japan (BOJ) policy decisions, monthly economic assessments, and Monetary Policy Committee (MPC) member speeches
- Tankan Report (a quarterly sentiment survey of Japanese firms by the BOJ — the key is often planned capital expenditures)
- Industrial production
- Machine orders
- Trade balance and current account
- Retail trade
- Bank lending
- Domestic Corporate Goods Price Index (CGPI)
- National CPI and Tokyo-area CPI
- All-Industry Activity Index and Tertiary Industry (service sector) Activity Index

The ultimate safe haven

JPY is considered a safe haven, which means that it tends to rally when there is panic in the markets. For example, in the three months after the collapse of investment bank Lehman Brothers in 2008, the yen rallied more than 20 percent against the U.S. dollar. So, if there are periods of panic in the market, be wary of taking a short position in the yen.

The CPI data is extremely important these days, because the Bank of Japan has pledged to keep monetary policy low until inflation moves to a 2 percent target. Given that Japan has traditionally been mired in deflation, this is no small feat.

Price action behavior of USD/JPY

Earlier in this chapter, we note that USD/JPY seems to have an on/off switch when compared to the other major currency pairs. Add to that the fact that USD/JPY liquidity can be similarly fickle. Sometimes, hundreds of millions of USD/JPY can be bought or sold without moving the market noticeably; other times, liquidity can be extremely scarce.

This phenomenon is particularly acute in USD/JPY owing to the large presence of Japanese asset managers. As we mention earlier, the Japanese investment community tends to move en masse into and out of positions. Of course, they're not the only ones involved in USD/JPY, but they do tend to play the fox while the rest of the market is busy playing the hounds.

Prone to short-term trends, followed by sideways consolidations

The result of this concentration of Japanese corporate interest is a strong tendency for USD/JPY to display short-term trends (several hours to several days) in price movements, as investors pile in on the prevailing directional move. This tendency is amplified by the use of standing market orders from Japanese asset managers.

For example, if a Japanese pension fund manager is looking to establish a long position in USD/JPY, he's likely to leave orders at several fixed levels below the current market to try to buy dollars on dips. If the current market is at 102.00, he may buy a piece of the total position there, but then leave orders to buy the remaining amounts at staggered levels below, such as 101.75, 101.50, 101.25, and 101.00. If other investors are of the same view, then they'll be bidding below the market as well.

If the market begins to move higher, the asset managers may become nervous that they won't be able to buy on weakness and raise their orders to higher levels, or buy at the market. Either way, buying interest is moving up with the price action, creating a potentially accelerating price movement. Any countertrend move is met by solid buying interest and quickly reversed.

Such price shifts tend to reach their conclusion when everyone is onboard — most of the buyers who wanted to buy are now long. At this point, no more fresh buying is coming into the market, and the directional move begins to stall and move sideways. The early buyers may be capping the market with profit-taking orders to sell above, while laggard buyers are still buying on dips. This leads to the development of a consolidation range, which can be as wide as ¥1 or ¥2, or as narrow as 40 to 50 pips.

Short-term traders can usually find trading opportunities in such consolidation ranges, but medium and longer-term traders may want to step back and wait for a fresh directional movement. In summer 2014, USD/JPY experienced a prolonged period of sideways movement, which made *volatility* (a measure of variation of price movement over time) fall to its lowest-ever level. During that time, USD/JPY was a yawn to trade.

Technical levels are critical in USD/JPY

So if you're a regular trader or investor and you don't work at a Japanese bank, how can you know where the orders are? Simple: Focus on the technical levels.

Perhaps no other currency pair is as beholden to technical support and resistance as USD/JPY. In large part, this has to do with the prevalence of substantial orders, where the order level is based on technical analysis. USD/JPY displays a number of other important trading characteristics when it comes to technical trading levels:

- **USD/JPY tends to respect technical levels with far fewer false breaks.** This situation is typically due to the presence of substantial order interest at the technical level. If trend-line analysis or daily price lows indicate major support at 101.20, for example, sizeable buying orders are likely to be located there. The bank traders watching the order may buy in front of it, preventing the level from ever being touched, or tested. If the selling interest is not sufficient to fill the buying order, the level will hold. On the other hand, if the technical level is breached, it's a clear indication the selling interest is far greater and is likely to continue.

- **USD/JPY's price action is usually highly directional (one-way traffic) on breaks of technical support and resistance.** When technical support or resistance is overcome, price movements tend to be sharp and one-sided, with minimal pullbacks or backing and filling (prices coming back to test the breakout level). This situation is the result of strong market interest overcoming any standing orders, as well as likely stop-loss orders beyond the technical level. For example, after USD/JPY broke above 80.00 back in September 2012, USD/JPY went on to rally (the yen lost value) more than 30 percent over the next nine months.

- *Spike reversals* **(sharp — 20- to 50-pip — price movements in the opposite direction of the prior move) from technical levels are relatively common.** Spike reversals are evidence of a significant amount of market interest in the opposite direction and frequently define significant highs and lows. They're also evidence that the directional move that was reversed was probably false, which suggests greater potential in the direction of the reversal.

- **Orders frequently define intraday highs and lows and reversal points.** Japanese institutional orders also tend to be left at round-number prices, such as 84.00, 84.25, 84.50, and so on. When you look at charts involving JPY, always note tops/bottoms close to round-number price levels because there could be significant orders there.

Tactical trading considerations in USD/JPY

Earlier, we note USD/JPY's tendency to either be active directionally or consolidating — the on/off switch. As such, we like to approach USD/JPY on a more strategic, hit-and-run basis — getting in when we think a directional move is happening and standing aside when we don't. We look for breaks of trend lines, spike reversals, and candlestick patterns, as our primary clues for spotting a pending directional move (see Chapter 11).

On the tactical level, USD/JPY is generally a cleaner trading market than most of the other majors, so we like to approach it with generally tighter trading rules. The idea is that if we're right, we'll be along for the ride. But if we're wrong, we jump off the bus at the next stop.

Actively trading trend-line and price-level breakouts

One of our trigger points for jumping into USD/JPY is breaks of trend lines and key price levels, such as daily or weekly highs/lows. We note earlier that it usually takes a significant amount of market interest to break key technical levels. We look at the actual breaks as concrete evidence of sizeable interest, rather than normal back-and-forth price action.

Jumping on spike reversals

After USD/JPY has seen a relatively quick (usually within two to three hours) move of more than 70 to 80 pips in one direction, we're on alert for any sharp reversals in price. Spike reversals of 30 to 40 pips that occur in very short time frames (5 to 20 minutes) are relatively common in USD/JPY. We look at them as an indication that the prior move has ended and it's now time to exit. Spike reversals are short-term phenomena and, if you can't be in front of your trading screen, using a 30 to 40 point trailing stop-loss order is one way to guard against rapid reversals. Take a look at Figure 8-3 to see how spike reversals can frequently indicate significant turning points.

Monitoring EUR/JPY and other JPY crosses

USD/JPY is heavily influenced by cross flows and can frequently take a back seat to them on any given day. In evaluating USD/JPY, we always keep an eye on the JPY crosses and their technical levels as well. A break of important support in GBP/JPY, for instance, could unleash a flood of short-term USD/JPY selling, because GBP/JPY is mostly traded through the dollar pairs.

EUR/JPY is the most actively traded JPY cross and its movements routinely drive USD/JPY on an intraday basis. Be alert for when significant technical levels in the two pairs coincide, such as when both USD/JPY and EUR/JPY are testing a series of recent daily highs or lows. A break by either can easily spill into the other and provoke follow-through buying/selling in both.

Figure 8-3:
Hourly USD/
JPY chart
highlighting
spike rever-
sals (circled
areas).
Quick 20
to 30 point
reversals
can be an
important
signal that a
directional
move has
ended and
may be
reversing.

Source: eSignal (www.esignal.com)

The Other Majors: Sterling and Aussie

The other two major currency pairs are GBP/USD (otherwise known as sterling or cable) and AUD/USD. The pound is counted as a major currency pair, but its trading volume and liquidity are significantly less than EUR/USD or USD/JPY. In recent years, there has been a big shift in the most actively traded currencies, with the Aussie and Kiwi dollars overtaking the likes of the Swissy (Swiss franc) and the CAD. The Aussie in particular has seen its star rise, which is why we're including it in this section.

The British pound: GBP/USD

Trading in cable presents its own set of challenges, because the pair is prone to sharp price movements and seemingly chaotic price action. But it's exactly this type of price behavior that keeps the speculators coming back — when you're right, you'll know very quickly, and the short-term results can be significant.

Trading fundamentals of GBP/USD

The U.K. economy is the third largest national economy in Europe, after Germany and France, according to the 2013 GDP data, and the pound is heavily influenced by cross-border trade and mergers and acquisitions (M&A) activity between the United Kingdom and continental Europe. Upwards of two-thirds of U.K. foreign trade is conducted with EU member states, making the EUR/GBP cross one of the most important trade-driven cross rates.

The 2013 BIS survey of foreign exchange turnover showed that GBP/USD accounted for 8 percent of global daily trading volume, making cable the third most active pairing in the majors. But you may not believe that when you start trading cable, where liquidity seems always to be at a premium. These days, you can trade GBP/USD fairly cheaply and most brokers offer a spread of 1 pip or below.

Trading sterling by the numbers

GBP/USD is quoted in terms of the number of dollars it takes to buy a pound, so a rate of 1.6015 means it costs $1.6015 to buy £1. The GBP is the primary currency in the pair and the USD is the secondary currency. That means

- **GBP/USD is traded in amounts denominated in GBP.** In online currency trading platforms, standard lot sizes are £100,000, mini lot sizes are £10,000, and micro lots are GBP 1,000.

- **The pip value, or minimum price fluctuation, is denominated in USD.**

- **Profit and loss accrue in USD.** For one standard lot position size, each pip is worth $10; for one mini lot position size, each pip is worth $1; and for a micro lot, it is $0.10.

- **Margin calculations are typically calculated in USD in online trading platforms.** Because of its high relative value to the USD, trading in GBP pairs requires the greatest amount of margin on a per-lot basis. At a GBP/USD rate of 1.9000, to trade a one-lot position worth £100,000, it'll take $1,900 in available margin (based on 100:1 leverage). That calculation will change over time, of course, based on the level of the GBP/USD exchange rate. A higher GBP/USD rate will require more USD in available margin collateral, and a lower GBP/USD rate will need less USD in margin.

Trading alongside EUR/USD, but with a lot more zip!

Cable is similar to the EUR/USD in that it trades inversely to the overall USD. But while EUR/USD frequently gets bogged down in tremendous two-way liquidity, cable exhibits much more abrupt volatility and more extreme overall price movements. If U.S. economic news disappoints, for instance, both sterling and EUR/USD will move higher. But if EUR/USD sees a 60-point rally on the day, cable may see a 100+ point rally.

This goes back to liquidity and a generally lower level of market interest in cable. In terms of daily global trading sessions, cable volume is at its peak during the U.K./European trading day, but that level of liquidity shrinks considerably in the New York afternoon and Asian trading sessions. During those off-peak times, cable can see significant short-term price moves simply on the basis of position-adjustments (for example, shorts getting squeezed out).

Another important difference between cable and EUR/USD comes in their different reactions to domestic economic/news developments. Cable tends to display more explosive reactions to unexpected U.K. news/data than EUR/USD does to similar Eurozone news/data. For example, if better than expected Eurozone data comes out, EUR/USD may only politely acknowledge the data and move marginally higher. But if surprisingly strong U.K. data is reported, GBP/USD can take off on a moonshot.

Important U.K. data reports

Cable tends to react sharply to U.K. economic reports, especially when the data is in the opposite direction of expectations, or when the data is contrary to current monetary policy speculation. For example, if the market is expecting that the next rate move by the Bank of England (BOE) will be higher, and a monthly inflation report is released indicating a drop in price pressures, then GBP/USD is likely to drop quickly as interest rate bets are unwound.

Key U.K. data reports to watch for are

- BOE Monetary Policy Committed (MPC) rate decisions, as well as speeches by MPC members and the BOE governor and BOE Inflation Reports, which are released four times a year

- BOE MPC minutes (released two weeks after each MPC meeting)

- Inflation gauges, such as CPI, PPI, and the British Retailers Consortium (BRC) shop price index

- Retail sales and the BRC retail sales monitor

- Royal Institution of Chartered Surveyors (RICS) house price balance

- Industrial and manufacturing production

- Trade balance

- GfK (a private market research firm) U.K. consumer confidence survey

The new kid in town: Trading the Aussie

The Aussie dollar has overtaken some of the other major currencies in recent years to become the fourth most commonly traded USD pair, according to the 2013 BIS Triennial survey on foreign exchange turnover. This was triggered by a few developments:

- The Australian economy weathered the 2008 financial crisis extremely well, and was the only one of the major economies not to fall into recession.

- The Aussie is often traded as a proxy for China. It has extremely close trade links to China, so its currency often reflects Chinese economic fundamentals.

Trading fundamentals of AUD/USD

The Aussie is the fourth most widely traded currency in the world, according to the 2013 BIS survey. It can be traded as a proxy for China, so its fortunes are closely linked to the performance of the Chinese economy. So, when you trade the Aussie, you need to be aware of Chinese data releases.

Australia is also one of the world's major commodity producers, which influence it in two ways:

- ✓ **It can be sensitive to changes in commodity prices.** When commodity prices fall, this can be bad news for the Aussie because it reduces the value of Australian exports and can impact the economy. The reverse is also true.

- ✓ **Big exports tend to favor a weaker currency to boost the attractiveness of their exports.** This means that the Aussie can be at risk from verbal intervention from its central bank, the Reserve Bank of Australia (RBA), although the RBA rarely intervenes physically in the market, unlike the Bank of Japan or the Swiss National Bank.

Trading Aussie by the numbers

AUD/USD is quoted in terms of the number of dollars it takes to buy an Aussie dollar, so a rate of 0.9550 means it costs $0.9550 to buy AU$1. The AUD is the primary currency in the pair and the USD is the secondary currency. That means

- ✓ **AUD/USD is traded in amounts denominated in AUD.** In online currency trading platforms, standard lot sizes are AU$100,000, mini lot sizes are AU$10,000, and micro lots are AU$1,000.

- ✓ **The pip value, or minimum price fluctuation, is denominated in USD.**

- ✓ **Profit and loss accrue in USD.** For one standard lot position size, each pip is worth $10; for one mini lot position size, each pip is worth $1; and for a micro lot, it is $0.10.

- ✓ **Margin calculations are typically calculated in USD in online trading platforms.** At a AUD/USD rate of 0.9000, to trade a one-lot position worth £100,000, it'll take $900 in available margin (based on 100:1 leverage). That calculation will change over time, of course, based on the level of the AUD/USD exchange rate. A higher AUD/USD rate will require more USD in available margin collateral, and a lower AUD/USD rate will need less USD in margin.

Important Australian data reports

The Aussie can be sensitive to interest rates. Australia tends to have higher levels of interest rates than elsewhere. For example, the RBA did not embark on QE or negative interest rates in the aftermath of the financial crisis. This makes it attractive as a carry trade (see Chapter 12). Changes in interest rates and speeches from the head of the RBA can trigger volatility in the Aussie.

Key Australian data reports to watch for are

- ✔ RBA rate decisions, as well as speeches by RBA members and in particular the RBA governor
- ✔ RBA MPC minutes (released two weeks after each RBA meeting)
- ✔ Inflation gauges, such as CPI and PPI
- ✔ Retail sales
- ✔ House prices
- ✔ Industrial and manufacturing production
- ✔ Trade balance
- ✔ Employment data
- ✔ Chinese data, including manufacturing PMI survey data, trade data, and interest rate changes

Understanding Forex Positioning Data

Forex is not traded on an exchange, so how can you know which currencies people are buying and which ones people are selling? Never fear — there are many sources of forex positioning data. Because the forex market is so big, the best you can hope for is a snapshot of trading activity, based on a certain segment of the market. For example, the Commodities Futures Trading Commission (CFTC) releases data each week (at 3:30 p.m. Eastern time on Friday) that measures the net noncommercial (speculative) futures positions for the major currencies versus the U.S. dollar. This gives you a good idea of whether the market is *long* (buying a currency) or *short* (selling a currency) on a weekly basis.

This data is useful because it can be interpreted as an indicator of current trading activity in the forex market.

How to interpret the data

The data shows you the number of open positions in dollar pairs. They can be *positive* (people are buying the dollar pair) or *negative* (people are selling the dollar pair). Often, if a currency is trending higher against the USD, you see CFTC positioning data also moving higher. This data can be used to confirm the strength of a trend. For example, if a large segment of the forex community — the futures community — is buying the pound, then GBP/USD is likely to be in an uptrend. However, it can also be used as a contrarian indicator: If the market has been buying sterling for a while, some traders may use that as a sell signal. Because, by definition, trends don't go on forever, the contrarian trader may look at CFTC data to see if the market is too stretched to the upside in one currency pair (say, GBP/USD), and if he thinks that it is, he may choose to go short on GBP/USD.

Positioning data can be a useful resource, although we don't recommend that you trade only using CFTC positioning data, because it can be a lagging indicator and doesn't reflect news events or economic data that could impact a currency pair on a more frequent basis.

The FX fix

When you read about foreign exchange in the business press or if you go into a forex dealing room, you're likely to hear the term the *FX fix*. So, what is it? The FX fix is essentially a 60-second window at which major exchange rates are set. The forex market isn't controlled by any central exchange, so the fix is used to form benchmark forex rates.

The most popular fix times take place at 4 p.m. and 8 p.m. London time. The 4 p.m. London FX fix is a particularly popular benchmark, primarily because it was the first one introduced by the WM Company (it's now a joint venture with Thomson Reuters). These prices are mostly used by the investment community, which uses these FX rates to compare their portfolios against benchmarks and other portfolios, without concern for changes in exchange rates.

Trading at a fixing time is an example of point-in-time (PIT) trading. This involves buying or selling currencies at particular times each day. But retail traders should be wary of trading any of the major FX pairs during fixing times because it can trigger a spike in volatility. This trading strategy involves trading at times when the currency markets are transitioning from one global region to another. During this time, liquidity can start to fade, which can increase volatility.

At the time of writing, the FX fix is also under scrutiny from global market regulators over fears that it could be manipulated. The investigation is ongoing, so there could be changes to the fix in the future, like increasing the 60-second window, but so far nothing has been confirmed.

Forex and regulation

Despite being the largest market in the world, the forex market has largely escaped official regulation. This means that traders can set prices on their own, without getting an official body involved in the process.

Because there are no formal rules or regulation in the forex market, trust is of the utmost importance. The forex market works because both sides of a transaction trust each other. However, in the aftermath of the 2008 financial crisis, there has been a push for more formal regulation. As we mention earlier, changes are afoot to make the FX fix less susceptible to manipulation.

In the coming years, we expect big changes in the forex regulatory space. There is a push to impose more electronic trading and new codes of conduct. Although retail traders nearly always trade on an electronic platform, codes of conduct could impact how you trade.

Here at FOREX.com, we believe that any push toward greater transparency is good for the market and good for the retail trader.

Make sure that your broker is regulated before you start trading with it.

Chapter 9

Minor Currency Pairs and Cross-Currency Trading

In This Chapter

▶ Branching out beyond the majors

▶ Getting to know the minor dollar pairs and the Scandies

▶ Finding opportunities in cross-currency trading

▶ Understanding how cross-currency trading affects the overall market

*T*rading in the major currency pairs accounts for the lion's share of overall currency market volume, but speculative trading opportunities extend well beyond just the four major *dollar pairs* (currency pairs that include the USD). For starters, three other currency pairs — commonly known as the *minor* or *small* dollar pairs — round out the primary trading pairs that include the U.S. dollar. Still more trading options are available in the currencies of Scandinavian nations that haven't adopted the EUR, referred to as the *Scandies*. Then there are the *cross-currency* pairs, or *crosses* for short, which pit two non-USD currencies against each other.

In this chapter, we take a closer look at the minor currency pairs, Scandies, and cross-currency pairs to see how they fit into the overall market and offer an additional array of speculative trading opportunities. Although the USD is frequently the focus of the currency market, you're going to want to know where the opportunities are when the spotlight isn't on the greenback.

Trading the Minor Pairs

The minor dollar pairs are USD/CAD (the U.S. dollar versus the Canadian dollar) and NZD/USD (the New Zealand dollar versus the U.S. dollar). In the past, the AUD/USD (Australian dollar) was a minor currency, but trading volumes in the AUD have surged in recent years, so we include it in Chapter 8. Technically speaking, the Swissie should take the place of the AUD, but it rests somewhere between the majors and minors, so we haven't included it here. Worth noting: The minor currency pairs are also commonly referred to as *commodity currencies;* the Aussie is still a commodity currency because Australia is still a major commodity producer.

The (not just) commodity currencies

We don't want to leave you with the impression that the so-called commodity currencies' trading behavior is strictly a function of what's happening to commodity prices. To be sure, recent years' price movements in those pairs are generally highly correlated to movements in underlying commodities, like gold, silver, and oil. But correlation is not causation. What that means is that just because two assets may move together in a statistically significant relationship, the movement of one is not necessarily causing movement in the other.

More typically, they may both be responding to broader fundamental developments that affect each similarly, such as the strength of global demand as seen in Chinese growth data. China is a tremendous consumer of raw materials, and Australia is a leading exporter of metals, coal, and grains. Market perceptions of strong demand could see prices move higher for such commodities. Gains in commodity prices may improve profitability at Australian mining and agricultural firms, attracting global investors who need AUD to buy such Australian stocks. In this scenario, it would not be surprising to see the AUD gain alongside commodity prices.

But there are also plenty of scenarios that could see such relationships break down, especially in the short run, and see prices diverge. Carrying on with the previously mentioned China/Australia relationship, strong growth and commodity demand could see the Reserve Bank of Australia (RBA), the Australian central bank, indicate that interest rates may need to be raised, reinforcing the positive correlation and tending to support AUD. But if the RBA later postpones raising rates due to unforeseen events, such as happened after massive floods

in early 2011, currency market expectations may be disappointed and the AUD could weaken, even as commodity prices maintain gains, but now on production disruptions. We hope you get the idea that correlations between currencies and commodities are not carved in stone.

To give you a more concrete picture, the following tables show the historical correlations *(correlation coefficients)* between these currencies and individual commodities over a two-year and ten-year period ending in February 2011, respectively, based on weekly data and percentage changes. A *correlation coefficient* is a statistical measure of how closely two securities values change relative to each other. Coefficients can range from +1.00 to –1.00, with a coefficient of +1.00, meaning the two assets are perfectly positively correlated (meaning, a 1 percent gain in one would see a 1 percent gain in the other). A coefficient of –1.00 would mean the two are perfectly negatively correlated (meaning, a rise of 1 percent in the first would see a decline of 1 percent in the second). A coefficient of zero means there is no statistically identifiable relationship, and the two are said to be non-correlated. As a rough benchmark, a correlation of +0.7/–0.7 or more is considered a pretty strong relationship. But remember, correlations exist over time. What's closely correlated today may not be so closely correlated tomorrow, or next month. Medium and longer-term traders may find such correlations more useful than short-term, intraday traders, where individual market news is more likely to cause a breakdown in the observed relationship.

The following chart shows quarterly correlations between the commodity currencies and the commodities.

Two-Year Correlations					Ten-Year Correlations				
	CRB	**OIL**	**GOLD**	**SILVER**		**CRB**	**OIL**	**GOLD**	**SILVER**
AUD/USD	0.60	0.95	0.89	0.60	AUD/USD	0.93	0.70	0.77	0.74
NZD/USD	0.60	0.96	0.92	0.64	NZD/USD	0.87	0.40	0.603	0.80
CAD/USD	−0.86	−0.51	−0.62	−0.43	CAD/USD	−0.83	−0.61	−0.60	−0.91

Note the higher level of correlations over the more recent two-year period compared to the longer ten-year time frame. So instead of thinking of these currencies as strictly commodity-price driven, think of commodity price movements as just one factor affecting these currencies.

The *commodity currencies* reference stems from the key role that oil, metals, agricultural, and mining industries play in the national economies of Canada, Australia, and New Zealand. See the nearby sidebar "The (not just) commodity currencies" for important qualifications about the commodity relationship. AUD/USD and USD/CAD account for 7 percent and 4 percent of global daily trading volume, respectively, according to the 2013 Bank for International Settlements (BIS) survey of forex market volumes. NZD/USD accounts for less than 2 percent each of spot trading volume. But these three pairs offer more than ample liquidity to be actively traded and can offer significant trading opportunities, both for short-term traders and medium- to longer-term speculators.

Trading fundamentals of USD/CAD

The Canadian dollar (nicknamed the *Loonie* after the local bird pictured on the dollar coins) trades according to the same macroeconomic fundamentals as most other major currencies. That means you'll need to closely follow Bank of Canada (BOC) monetary-policy developments, current economic data, inflation readings, and political goings-on, just as you would any of the other majors.

A key element to keep in mind when looking at USD/CAD is that the trajectory of the Canadian economy is closely linked to the overall direction of the U.S. economy. The United States and Canada are still each other's largest commercial trading partners, and the vast majority of Canadians live within 100 miles of the U.S./Canadian border. Even the BOC regularly refers to the U.S. economic outlook in its own economic outlooks. So we don't think it's an overgeneralization to say that as goes the U.S. economy, so goes the Canadian economy. But it's a long-term dynamic, making for plenty of short-term trading opportunities, especially when U.S. and Canadian outlooks diverge.

The sharp rise in commodity demand from China and other rapidly developing economies in recent years has heightened the sensitivity of CAD to overall commodity price developments, although as China slowed in 2013–2014 and commodity prices seemed to have peaked, the relationship between CAD and commodities has also declined. However, it's still worth factoring in the global economic outlook when evaluating the Canadian outlook.

Geography also plays a role when it comes to U.S. and Canadian economic data, because both countries issue economic data reports around the same time each morning or only a few hours apart. At one extreme, the result can be a negative USD report paired with strong Canadian data, leading to a sharp drop in USD/CAD (selling USD and buying CAD). At the other end, strong U.S. data and weak Canadian numbers can see USD/CAD rally sharply. Mixed readings can see a stalemate, but it always depends on the bigger picture.

Trading USD/CAD by the numbers

The standard market convention is to quote USD/CAD in terms of the number of Canadian dollars per USD. A USD/CAD rate of 1.0200, for instance, means it takes CAD 1.02 to buy USD 1. The market convention means that USD/CAD trades in the same overall direction of the USD, with a higher USD/CAD rate reflecting a stronger USD/weaker CAD and a lower rate showing a weaker USD/stronger CAD.

USD/CAD has the USD as the primary currency and the CAD as the counter currency. This means

✔ **USD/CAD is traded in amounts denominated in USD.** For online currency trading platforms, standard lot sizes are USD 100,000, and mini lot sizes are USD 10,000.

✔ **The *pip value*, or minimum price fluctuation, is denominated in CAD.**

✔ **Profit and loss registers in CAD.** For a standard lot position size, each pip is worth CAD 10, and each pip in a mini lot position is worth CAD 1. Using a USD/CAD rate of 1.0200 (which will change over time, of course), that equates to a pip value of USD 9.80 for each standard lot and USD 0.98 for each mini lot.

✔ **Margin calculations are typically based in USD, so to see how much margin is required to hold a position in USD/CAD, it's a simple calculation using the leverage ratio.** At 50:1 leverage, for instance, $2,000 of available margin is needed to trade 100,000 USD/CAD, and $200 is needed to trade 10,000 USD/CAD.

USD/CAD is unique among currency pairs in that it trades for spot settlement only one day beyond the trade date, as opposed to the normal two days for all other currency pairs. The difference is due to the fact that New York and Toronto, the two nations' financial centers, are in the same time zone, allowing for faster trade confirmations and settlement transfers. For spot traders, the difference means that USD/CAD undergoes the extended weekend (three-day) rollover after the close of trading on Thursdays, instead of on Wednesdays like all other pairs, assuming no holidays are involved. However, if you trade spot FX in the short term or with your FX broker, you usually don't even notice these details about settlement dates (although understanding what's going on is handy).

Canadian events and data reports to watch

On top of following U.S. economic data to maintain an outlook for the larger economy to the south, you'll need to pay close attention to individual Canadian economic data and official commentaries. CAD can react explosively when data or events come in out of line with expectations. In particular, keep an eye on the following Canadian economic events and reports:

- Bank of Canada speakers, rate decisions, and economic forecasts
- Employment report
- Gross domestic product (GDP) reported monthly
- International securities transactions
- International merchandise trade
- Wholesale and retail sales
- Consumer price index (CPI) and BOC CPI
- Manufacturing shipments
- Ivey Purchasing Managers Index

Trading fundamentals of NZD/USD

The New Zealand dollar is nicknamed the *Kiwi,* as are most things New Zealand, after the indigenous bird of the same name; the term *Kiwi* refers to both the NZD and the NZD/USD pair. (What is it with birds and currency nicknames, anyway?) Given the relatively small size of the New Zealand economy, Kiwi is among the most interest-rate sensitive of all currencies.

The New Zealand economy has undergone a major transformation over the past two decades, moving from a mostly agricultural export orientation to a domestically driven service and manufacturing base. The rapid growth has seen disposable incomes soar; with higher disposable incomes have come generally high levels of inflation. As a result, the Reserve Bank of New Zealand (RBNZ), the central bank, has frequently been among the more hawkish central banks.

We put Kiwi in the commodity currency grouping, but there is an important distinction to note. New Zealand is primarily an agricultural-commodity-producing economy (dairy products and meat in particular), as opposed to the metals and energy commodities of Canada and Australia. As such, Kiwi displays a weaker relationship than CAD and AUD to the prices of gold, silver, and oil, as seen in the two tables in the previous sidebar.

In addition to all the standard New Zealand economic data and official pronouncements you'll need to monitor, Kiwi trading is closely tied to Australian data and prospects, due to a strong trade and regional relationship.

No set formula exists to describe the currencies' relationship, but a general rule is that when it's a USD-based move, Aussie and Kiwi will tend to trade in the same direction as each other relative to the USD. But when Kiwi or Aussie news comes in, the AUD/NZD (Aussie/Kiwi) cross will exert a larger influence. For example, disappointing Aussie data may see AUD/USD move lower, which will tend to drag down NZD/USD as well. But Aussie/Kiwi cross selling (selling AUD/USD on the weaker data and buying NZD/USD for the cross trade) will typically reduce the extent of NZD/USD declines relative to AUD/USD losses. A similar effect will play out when New Zealand data or news is the catalyst.

New Zealand events and data reports to watch

RBNZ commentary and rate decisions are pivotal to the value of Kiwi, given the significance of interest rates to the currency. Finance ministry comments are secondary to the rhetoric of the independent RBNZ but can still upset the Kiwi cart from time to time. Additionally, keep an eye on the following:

- Consumer prices, housing prices, and food prices
- Retail sales and electronic-card spending (debit and credit)
- Westpac and ANZ consumer confidence indices
- Quarterly GDP and monthly trade balance
- National Bank of New Zealand (NBNZ) business confidence survey

Trading Aussie and Kiwi by the numbers

You can find out more about AUD in Chapter 8, but it's worth looking at the numbers for AUD and NZD together as AUD/USD and NZD/USD are both quoted in the same way. AUD/USD and NZD/USD rates reflect the number of USD per AUD or NZD. For example, a NZD/USD rate of 0.7000 means it costs USD 0.70 (or 70¢) to buy NZD 1. Aussie and Kiwi trade in the opposite direction of the overall value of the USD, so a weaker USD means a higher Aussie or Kiwi rate, and a lower Aussie or Kiwi rate represents a stronger USD.

AUD and NZD are the primary currencies in the pairs, and the USD is the counter currency, which means

✔ **AUD/USD and NZD/USD are traded in position sizes denominated in AUD or NZD.**

✔ **The pip values are denominated in USD.**

✔ **Profit and loss accrues in USD.** On a 100,000 NZD/USD position, each pip is worth USD 10; on a 10,000 Aussie position size, each pip is worth USD 1.

✔ **Margin calculations are typically based in USD on margin trading platforms.**

Using an NZD/USD rate of 0.7000 and a leverage ratio of 50:1, a 100,000 Kiwi position requires USD 1,400 in margin, while a 10,000 NZD/USD position would need only USD 140 in margin.

Tactical trading considerations in USD/CAD, AUD/USD, and NZD/USD

We group these three currency pairs together because they share many of the same trading traits and even travel as a pack sometimes — especially Aussie and Kiwi, given their regional proximity and close economic ties. Whether they're being grouped as the commodity currencies or just smaller regional currencies versus the U.S. dollar, they can frequently serve as a leading indicator of overall USD market direction.

Liquidity and market interest are lower

One of the reasons these pairs tend to exhibit leading characteristics is due to the lower relative liquidity of the pairs, which amplifies the speculative effect on them. If sentiment is shifting in favor of the U.S. dollar, for example, the effect of speculative interest — the fast money — is going to be most evident in lower-volume currency pairs.

When a hedge fund or other large speculator turns around a directional bet on the U.S. dollar (for example, from short to long), it's going to start buying U.S. dollars across the board (meaning against most all other currencies). A half-billion EUR/USD selling order (650 million USD equivalent at 1.3000 EUR/USD) is relatively easily absorbed in the high-volume, liquid EUR/USD market and may move it only a few points (say, 10 to 20 pips, depending on the circumstances). However, a proportionately smaller order to sell Aussie, sell Kiwi, or buy USD/CAD (large speculators will typically allocate smaller position sizes to less-liquid currency pairs), amounting to only 100 million or 200 million in notional terms, may generate a 20- to 40-pip movement in these currency pairs, depending on the time of day and overall environment.

In general, you need to be aware that overall liquidity and market interest in these pairs is significantly lower than in the majors, although Aussie has caught up with the majors in recent years and has overtaken the CHF as the fifth most traded currency in the world. On a daily basis, liquidity in these pairs is at its peak when the local centers (Toronto, Sydney, and Wellington) are open. London market makers provide a solid liquidity base to bridge the gap outside the local markets, but you can largely forget about USD/CAD during the Asia/Pacific session, and the Aussie and Kiwi markets are problematic after the London/European session close until their financial centers reopen a few hours later. The net result is a concentration of market interest in these currency pairs among the major banks of the currency countries, which has implications of its own (see the "Technical levels can be blurry" section, later in this chapter).

Price action is highly event driven

As a result of the overall lower level of liquidity in these currency pairs, in concert with relatively high levels of speculative positioning (at times), you've got the ultimate mix for explosive reactions after currency-specific news or data comes out. A dovish statement from a previously hawkish Bank of Canada governor can trigger a sea change in sentiment against the CAD. If expectations are running high for an NZD interest-rate hike, and a key inflation report contradicts that outlook (it's lower than expected), we've got a relatively small market, probably overpositioned in one direction (long NZD/USD), that's all heading for the exit (selling) at the same time.

The bottom line in these currency pairs is that significant data or news surprises, especially when contrary to expectations and likely market positioning, tends to have an outsized impact on the market. Traders positioning in these currencies need to be especially aware of this and to recognize the greater degree of volatility and risk they're facing if events don't transpire as expected. It's one thing if Eurozone CPI comes in higher than expected, but it's another thing entirely if Australian CPI surprises to the upside.

A data or event surprise typically leads to a price gap when the news is first announced. If the news is sufficiently at odds with market expectations and positioning, subsequent price action tends to be mostly one-way traffic, as the market reacts to the surprise news and exits earlier positions. If you're caught on the wrong side after unexpected news in these pairs, you're likely better off getting out as soon as possible than waiting for a correction to exit at a better level. The lower liquidity and interest in these currency pairs mean you're probably not alone in being caught wrong-sided, which tends to see steady, one-way interest, punctuated by accelerations when additional stop-loss order levels are hit.

All politics (and economic data) is local

Most of our discussion of market drivers centers on economic data and monetary policy, but domestic political developments in these smaller-currency countries can provoke significant movements in the local currencies. National elections, political scandals, and abrupt policy changes can all lead to upheavals in the value of the local currency. The effect tends to be most pronounced on the downside of the currency's value (meaning, bad news tends to hurt a currency more than good news — if there ever is any in politics — helps it). Of course, every situation is different, but the spillover effect between politics and currencies is greatest in these pairs, which means you need to be aware of domestic political events if you're trading them.

In terms of economic data, these currency pairs tend to participate in overall directional moves relative to the U.S. dollar until a local news or data event triggers more concentrated interest on the local currency. If the USD is under pressure across the board, for instance, USD/CAD is likely to move lower in concert with other dollar pairs. But if negative Canadian news or data emerges, USD/CAD is likely to pare its losses and may even start to move higher if the news was bad enough. If the Canadian news was CAD-positive (say, a higher CPI reading pointing to a potential rate hike), USD/CAD is likely to accelerate to the downside, because USD selling interest is now amplified by CAD buying interest.

Technical levels can be blurry

The relatively lower level of liquidity and market interest in these currency pairs makes for sometimes-difficult technical trading conditions. Trend lines and retracement levels in particular are subject to regular overshoots. Prices may move beyond the technical level — sometimes only 5 to 10 pips, other times for extensive distances or for prolonged periods — only to reverse course and reestablish the technical level later.

The basic reason behind this tendency to overshoot technical levels is that market interest is concentrated in fewer market-makers for these pairs — usually the local banks of the currency country. The result is a concentration of market interest in fewer hands, which can result in order levels being triggered when they may not be otherwise. For example, if you're an interbank market-maker watching a stop-loss order for 5 million AUD/USD, it's not a big deal, because 5 million Aussie is transacted easily. But if you have a stop loss for 50 million or 100 million AUD/USD, you're going to need to be fast (and, likely, preemptive) to fill the order at a reasonable execution rate.

If the price break of a technical level is quickly reversed, it's a good sign that it was just a position-related movement. If fresh news is out, however, you may be seeing the initial wave of a larger directional move.

It's worth noting that things are changing, however, as the commodities currencies (the AUD and CAD, in particular) gain more of the FX market share of volume.

Trading the Scandies: SEK, NOK, and DKK

A few of the Scandinavian, or Nordic, countries chose not to join the monetary union that led to the euro, namely Sweden, Norway, and Denmark. Trading volumes in the Scandies are generally light, but sufficient enough to offer additional speculative trading opportunities depending on the circumstances. Most of the trading in the Scandies is done versus EUR, driven by intra-European divergences in either growth or interest rate outlooks. Generally speaking, trading the USD versus the Scandies tends to mimic EUR/USD, but in mirror image due to quoting conventions.

Swedish krona — "Stocky"

The Swedish krona is affectionately referred to as Stocky after the capital Stockholm, and its currency code is SEK. Trading volumes in USD/SEK (dollar/Stocky) and EUR/SEK (euro/Stocky) amounted to 2 percent and 1 percent, respectively, of daily global volume, according to the 2013 BIS survey of forex markets. Compared to the 2010 survey, trading volume in the SEK was down slightly in 2013, potentially due to the rising popularity of trading emerging market currencies and other majors like the Aussie dollar. The Swedish central bank, *Sveriges Riksbank* in Swedish, is independent and is the key actor in setting interest rates and maintaining currency stability.

In addition to following the economic data coming out of Sweden, pay close attention to comments from the governor and other Riksbank officials. The Riksbank follows an *inflation target*, a desired level of inflation, so CPI reports are also critical inputs to the outlook for interest rates and SEK. The Swedish central bank also has a history of speaking out on the value of the krona itself, especially when it's either too strong or weak relative to EUR, where most of Swedish trade is conducted. EUR/SEK can become especially active when the Riksbank and the ECB are seen to be on divergent interest rate paths.

Technically speaking, after joining the European Union in 1995, Sweden is obliged to adopt the euro at some point in the future, but has effectively opted out and shows no signs of joining the euro.

Norwegian krone — "Nokkie"

The Norwegian krone (NOK) is nicknamed Nokkie after its currency code and in symphony with Stocky. USD/NOK and EUR/NOK trading volumes didn't get broken out on the 2013 BIS survey, so they're likely sub-1 percent of daily global volume. Still, liquidity in NOK is more than sufficient, especially during European trading hours. Norway's central bank, *Norges Bank*, is independent and pursues a traditional policy of maintaining price stability. Keep an eye out for guidance from the governor and other central bank officials, as Norges Bank policy may frequently diverge from ECB policy.

Norway is exceptionally wealthy owing to its large energy reserves, mainly North Sea oil, which has given it a large sovereign wealth fund, making it an important global asset manager. More importantly for day-to-day trading, Norway is the world's tenth largest oil producer, and NOK tends to trade as a petro-currency, similar to CAD, strengthening as oil prices rise and vice versa. Norway is not a member of the EU and so is unlikely to ever adopt the euro.

Danish krone — "Copey"

The Danish krone (DKK) is sometimes called Copey in reference to the capital of Copenhagen. Rather than pursuing currency independence like Sweden and Norway, Denmark opted to enter into a cooperative exchange rate agreement with Eurozone members, and the Danish krone is linked to the euro at a fixed exchange rate of 7.46038 +/-2.25%. Within this arrangement, the Danish central bank (Danmarks Nationalbank) effectively sets interest rates according to ECB decisions. The result is that the USD/DKK pair trades in mirror opposite fashion to EUR/USD and that the EUR/DKK pair trades in a very narrow band, typically about 0.25 percent, around the fixed rate. As such, there is little incentive for trading DKK, as EUR/USD offers better liquidity and EUR/DKK doesn't move. In the aftermath of the Eurozone sovereign debt crisis, the Danish government has backed away from holding a referendum on Euro membership. However, the government seems happy to stick with the EUR/DKK peg for now.

Cross-Currency Pairs

A *cross-currency pair* (or *cross*, for short) is any currency pair that does not have the U.S. dollar as one of the currencies in the pairing. (Turn to Chapter 4 for a list of all the different cross pairs.) But the catch is that cross rates are derived from the prices of the underlying USD pairs. For example, one of the most active crosses is EUR/JPY, pitting the two largest currencies outside the U.S. dollar directly against each other. But the EUR/JPY rate at any given instant is a function (the product) of the current EUR/USD and USD/JPY rates.

The most popular cross pairs involve the most actively traded major currencies, like EUR/JPY and EUR/GBP. (In the past, EUR/CHF would have been in the mix, but since the 2011 peg, EUR/CHF has become less attractive to trade.) According to the 2013 BIS survey of foreign-exchange market activity, direct cross trading accounted for a relatively small percentage of global daily volume — around 7 percent for the major crosses combined, and this level has fallen since the 2010 survey.

But that figure significantly understates the amount of interest that is actually flowing through the crosses, because large interbank cross trades are typically executed through the USD pairs instead of directly in the cross markets. If a Japanese corporation needs to buy half a billion EUR/JPY (*half a yard,* in market parlance), for example, the interbank traders executing the order will alternately buy EUR/USD and buy USD/JPY to fill the order. Going directly through the EUR/JPY market would likely tip off too many in the market and drive the rate away from them. (We look at how large cross flows can drive the dollar pairs in the "Stretching the legs" section, later in this chapter.)

For individual traders dealing online, however, the direct cross pairs offer more than ample liquidity and narrower spreads than can be realized by trading through the dollar pairs. Additionally, most online platforms do not net out positions based on overall dollar exposure, so you'd end up using roughly twice the amount of margin to enter a position through the dollar pairs to create the same position you'd have if you'd gone through the direct cross market. The advances in electronic trading technology even make relatively obscure crosses like NZD/JPY and GBP/CHF easily accessible to individual online traders.

Why trade the crosses?

Cross pairs represent entirely new sets of routinely fluctuating currency pairs that offer another universe of trading opportunities beyond the primary USD pairs. Developments in the currency market are not always a simple bet on what's happening to the U.S. dollar. Crosses are the other half of the story, and their significance has increased as a result of electronic trading. Years ago, if you wanted a price in a cross pair, a human would have to push the buttons on a calculator to come up with the cross quote. Today's streaming price technology means that cross rates are as fluid as the dollar pairs, making them as accessible and tradable as USD/JPY or EUR/USD.

In particular, cross trading offers the following advantages:

- ✔ **You can pinpoint trade opportunities based on news or fundamental trends.** If the outlook and data for the UK is steadily deteriorating, you may be looking to sell GBP. But against what? If the USD is also weakening, buying USD and selling GBP may not yield any results. Selling GBP against another currency with better immediate prospects (such as selling GBP/CAD or GBP/NOK) may yield a more appreciable return.

- ✔ **You can take advantage of interest-rate differentials.** Selling low-yielding currencies against higher-yielding currencies is known as a *carry trade* (see Chapter 10). Carry trades seek to profit from both interest-rate differentials and spot price appreciation, and can form the basis of significant trends.

- ✔ **You can exploit technical trading opportunities.** The majors may be range bound or showing no actionable technical signals, but a cross rate may be extremely volatile and could provide a nice price breakout. Survey charts of cross rates to spot additional technical trading setups.

- ✔ **You can expand the horizon of trading opportunities.** Instead of looking at only four to seven dollar pairs, cross rates offer another dozen currency pairs that you can look to for trading opportunities.

> ✔ **You can go with the flow.** Speculative flows are ever-present in the currency market, but they don't always involve the dollar pairs. Today's speculative flow may be focused on the JPY crosses or selling CAD across the board on the back of surprisingly weak CAD data. The more attuned you are to cross-currency pairs, the more likely you are to identify and capitalize on the speculative move du jour.

Stretching the legs

A lot of interbank cross-trading volume does not go through the direct cross market, because institutional traders have a vested interest in hiding their operations from the rest of the market. In many cases, too, standing liquidity is simply not available in less-liquid crosses (GBP/JPY or NZD/JPY, for example). So they have to go through the legs, as the dollar pairs are called with respect to cross trading, to get the trade done. They also have an interest in maximizing the prices at which they're dealing — to sell as high as possible and to buy as low as possible.

One of the ways they're able to do that is to alternate their trading in the dollar legs. For instance, if you have to sell a large amount of EUR/JPY, you can alternate selling EUR/USD, which may tend to drive down EUR/USD but also push USD/JPY higher (because U.S. dollars overall are being bought). You now (you hope) have a higher rate at which to sell the USD/JPY leg of the order. But selling USD/JPY may push USD/JPY lower or cap its rise, leading EUR/USD to stop declining and recover higher, because U.S. dollars are now being sold. Now you have a slightly better EUR/USD rate to keep selling the EUR/USD leg of the order. By alternating the timing of which U.S. dollar leg you're selling, you have (you hope) executed the order at better rates than you could have directly in the cross and likely managed to obscure your market activity in the more active dollar pairs.

Of course, it doesn't always work out as neat and clean as what we just described. The net result in the market is a steady directional move in the cross rate, while the USD pairs remain relatively stagnant or within recent ranges. Be alert for such dollar-based movement, and consider that it may be a cross-driven move and a potential trading opportunity.

Cross-rate movements can also have a pronounced effect on how individual dollar pairs move in an otherwise dollar-based market reaction. Let's say some very USD-positive news or data has just been released, and the market starts buying USD across the board. (We focus on buying USD/JPY and selling EUR/USD in this example.) If USD/JPY happens to break a key technical resistance level, it may accelerate higher and prompt EUR/JPY to break a similarly significant resistance level, bringing in EUR/JPY buyers. The net effect in this case is that EUR/USD will not fall as much or as rapidly as USD/JPY will rally, because of the EUR/JPY cross buying. If you went short EUR/USD on the positive U.S.

news, you may not get as much joy. But the legs also tend to move in phases, and continued EUR/USD selling may eventually break through support, sending EUR/JPY lower and capping USD/JPY in the process.

As you can see, crosses can affect the market in virtually limitless ways, and there's no set way these things play out. Luckily, with the onset of online trading, you don't have to work out cross trading in the same way the guys did in the olden days! However, it's still interesting to find out how it was done and see how the dynamics of the market actually work.

When the U.S. dollar is not the primary focus of the market's attention, or if major U.S. news is approaching (like a nonfarm payrolls [NFP] report or a Federal Open Market Committee [FOMC] decision in a few days), sending market interest to the sidelines, speculative interest frequently shifts to the crosses. Always consider that the market's focus may be cross-driven rather than centered on the USD or any other single currency. Some days it's a dollar market, and other days it's a cross market. GBP may be weakening across the board on weak U.K. data, but if the USD is similarly out of favor, the pound's weakness is likely to be most evident on the crosses.

When looking at cross-trade opportunities, you may be tempted to translate the cross idea into a USD-based trade. You may think that AUD/JPY is forming a top, for example. If you're right, you may be thinking that one of two moves is likely — USD/JPY will move lower or AUD/USD will move lower — and you may be tempted into selling one of the legs (AUD/USD or USD/JPY) because you don't want to get involved in a cross. But there's another possibility: One leg may go down precipitously while the other moves higher, still sending the cross lower as you expected. But if you went short the wrong leg, you missed the boat.

When you spot a trade opportunity in a cross, trade the cross. Don't try to outguess the market and pick which component will make the cross move. Trust that if your trade analysis is correct, the cross will move the way you expect. And with the onset of electronic trading, it has never been easier to trade the crosses.

Trading the JPY crosses

The JPY crosses constitute one of the primary cross families and basically pit the JPY against the other major currencies. EUR/JPY is the highest volume of the JPY crosses, but the prominence of the carry trade, where the low-yielding JPY is sold and higher-yielding currencies are bought, has seen significant increases in AUD/JPY and NZD/JPY trading volume. Those currencies offer the highest interest-rate differentials against the JPY.

JPY crosses have their pip values denominated in JPY, meaning profit and loss will accrue in JPY. The margin requirement will vary greatly depending on which primary currency is involved, with GBP/JPY requiring the greatest margin and NZD/JPY requiring the least.

In terms of JPY-cross fundamentals, risk sentiment (see Chapter 5) and overall volatility tend to have the greatest impact, but as we caution earlier, trying to pin down which leg is going to cause the JPY crosses to move is a risky game. When trading in the JPY crosses, you need to keep an eye on USD/JPY in particular, due to its relatively explosive tendencies and its key place as an outlet for overall carry trade buying or selling. Be alert for similar technical levels between USD/JPY and the JPY crosses, as a break in either could spill over into the other.

Trading the EUR crosses

Outside of EUR/JPY, EUR cross action tends to be concentrated in EUR/GBP and EUR/CHF, where the cross direction is largely determined by changing outlooks between the Eurozone economy relative to the UK and Swiss economies. Reactions to Eurozone and Swiss news or data are most likely to be felt in the EUR crosses as opposed to EUR/USD or USD/CHF, whereas UK news/data is going to explode all over GBP/USD and EUR/GBP. Trading in EUR/SEK and EUR/NOK offers yet another way to exploit divergent economic or interest rate trajectories between continental Europe and the Scandinavian countries.

Sharp USD-driven moves will also affect these crosses, with the brunt of the USD move being felt in GBP/USD and USD/CHF, frequently biasing those legs to drive their EUR cross in the short run. That means frequently (but not always) that a sharp move higher in the USD will tend to see a higher EUR/CHF and EUR/GBP, while a rapid USD move lower will tend to see lower EUR/CHF and EUR/GBP.

The pip values of these EUR crosses will be denominated in either GBP or AUD. (EUR/CHF used to be a popular EUR cross, but since the 2011 peg was introduced by the Swiss National Bank, it has seen a dip in volume to 1.3 percent of daily trading volume, according to the 2013 BIS FX survey, down from 1.8 percent in 2010.) Typical daily ranges in the EUR crosses are relatively small on a pip basis — roughly 20 to 40 pips on average — but they're still substantial on a pip-value basis and roughly equivalent to daily EUR/USD ranges.

Part III

Developing a Trading Plan

Take a quiz to find out what kind of trader you are in an article at www.dummies.com/extras/currencytrading.

In this part . . .

✔ Understand the most common trading styles in the forex market.

✔ Find out how to determine which trading strategy fits you best.

✔ Spot trading opportunities early.

✔ Develop trading discipline and stay sane in the world's biggest market.

✔ Overcome psychological difficulties to boost your trading.

Chapter 10

Training and Preparing for Battle

*B*efore you get involved in actively trading the forex market, it's important to take a step back and think about how you want to approach the market. There is more to this than meets the eye, and we think it's one of the most important determinants of overall trading success.

Looking at the title of this chapter, you may think we're exaggerating a bit with the reference to training and preparing for battle, but we're really not. The Chinese military philosopher Sun Tzu famously observed that every battle is won or lost before it is ever fought. We can think of no better analogy when it comes to trading in financial markets in general or forex markets in particular.

In this chapter, we take you through the main points to consider as you seek to define your own approach to trading currencies. We review the characteristics of some of the most commonly applied trading styles and discuss what they mean in concrete terms. We also look at what constitutes trading discipline and some of the psychological and emotional hazards you're likely to experience. Last, and probably most important, we run you through the essential elements of developing and sticking to a trading plan.

Finding the Right Trading Style for You

We're frequently asked, "What's the best way to trade the forex market?" For starters, that's a loaded question that suggests there's a right way and a wrong way to trade currencies. It also implies that there's some magic formula out there, and if you can just find out what it is, you'll be guaranteed trading success. Unfortunately, there is no easy answer. Better put, there is no *standard* answer — one that applies to everyone.

The forex market's trading characteristics have something to offer every trading style (long-term, medium-term, or short-term) and approach (technical, fundamental, or a blend). So in terms of deciding what style or approach is best suited to currencies, the starting point is not the forex market itself, but your own individual circumstances and way of thinking.

Real-world and lifestyle considerations

Before you can begin to identify a trading style and approach that works best for you, you need to give some serious thought to what resources you have available to support your trading. As with many of life's endeavors, when it comes to financial-market trading, there are two main resources that people never seem to have enough of: time and money. Deciding how much of each you can devote to currency trading will help to establish how you pursue your trading goals.

 If you're a full-time trader, you have lots of time to devote to market analysis and actually trading the market. But because currencies trade around the clock, you still have to be mindful of which session you're trading, and of the daily peaks and troughs of activity and liquidity. (See Chapter 2 for trading-session specifics.) Just because the market is always open doesn't mean it's necessarily always a good time to trade.

If you have a full-time job, your boss may not appreciate you taking time to catch up on the charts or economic data reports while you're at work. That means you'll have to use your free time to do your market research. Be realistic when you think about how much time you'll be able to devote on a regular basis, keeping in mind family obligations and other personal circumstances.

 When it comes to money, we can't stress enough that trading capital has to be risk capital and that you should never risk any money that you can't afford to lose. The standard definition of *risk capital* is money that, if lost, will not materially affect your standard of living. It goes without saying that borrowed money is *not* risk capital — you should never use borrowed money for speculative trading.

When you determine how much risk capital you have available for trading, you'll have a better idea of what size account you can trade and what position size you can handle. Most online trading platforms typically offer generous leverage ratios that allow you to control a larger position with less required margin. But just because they offer high leverage doesn't mean you have to fully utilize it. (We look at the risk and reward components of leverage in greater detail in Chapter 13.)

Making time for market analysis

In other chapters, we talk about the amount of data and news that flows through the forex market on a daily basis — and it can be truly overwhelming. That's one reason the major banks that are active in the forex market employ teams of economists, strategists, technical analysts, and traders. So how can an individual trader possibly keep up with all the data and news?

The key is to develop an efficient daily routine of market analysis. Thanks to the Internet and online currency brokerages, independent traders can access a variety of daily and intraday market reports, covering both technical and fundamental perspectives. Your daily regimen of market analysis should focus on

- ✔ **Overnight forex market developments:** Who said what, which data came out, and how the currency pairs reacted.

- ✔ **Daily updates of other major market movements over the prior 24 hours and the stories behind them:** If oil prices or U.S. Treasury yields rose or fell substantially, find out why.

- ✔ **Data releases and market events (for example, the retail sales report, Fed speeches, central bank rate announcements) expected for that day:** Ideally, you'll monitor data and event calendars one week in advance, so you can anticipate the outcomes along with the rest of the market.

- ✔ **Multiple-time-frame technical analysis of major currency pairs:** There is nothing like the visual image of price action to fill in the blanks of how data and news affected individual currency pairs.

- ✔ **Current events and geopolitical themes:** Stay abreast on issues of major elections, political scandals, military conflicts, and policy initiatives in the major currency nations.

Establishing a research routine will take some time at first. You'll have to read many different news stories and analysts' reports before you get a handle on which sources provide the best overnight summaries, which fundamental analysts are most focused on the forex market, which technical analysts are focused on actionable trading strategies, and whom to follow on Twitter. We tend to focus on the mainstream financial news media, such as Bloomberg.com, Reuters.com, and MarketWatch.com.

Technical versus fundamental analysis

We look at fundamental analysis and technical analysis in greater depth in Chapters 7 and 11. We include them here as elements to consider as you develop your overall approach to the market. Ask yourself on what basis you'll make your trading decisions — fundamental analysis or technical analysis?

Followers of each discipline have always debated which approach works better. Rather than take sides, we suggest following an approach that *blends* the two disciplines. In our experience, macroeconomic factors, such as interest rates, relative growth rates, and market sentiment, determine the big-picture direction of currency rates. But currencies rarely move in a straight line, which means there are plenty of short-term price fluctuations to take advantage of — and some of them can be substantial.

Technical analysis can provide the guideposts along the route of the bigger price move, allowing traders to more accurately predict the direction and scope of future price changes. Most important, technical analysis is the key to constructing a well-defined trading strategy. For example, your fundamental analysis, data expectations, or plain old gut instinct may lead you to conclude that EUR/USD is going lower. But where exactly do you get short? Where do you take profit, and where do you cut your losses? We like to use technical analysis to refine trade entry and exit points, and to decide whether and where to add to positions or reduce them.

Sometimes forex markets seem to be more driven by fundamental factors, such as current economic data or comments from a central bank official. In those times, fundamentals provide the catalysts for technical breakouts and reversals. At other times, technical developments seem to be leading the charge — a break of trend-line support or recent daily lows may trigger stop-loss selling by market longs and bring in model systems that are selling based on the break of support. Subsequent economic reports may run counter to the directional breakout, but data be damned — the technical support is gone, and the market is selling.

Fundamental data and events are only one piece of the puzzle. Be aware that forex markets frequently ignore individual reports and do their own thing based on some larger theme or adjustment. That's why we always stress that the market reaction to data is more important than the data itself.

Approaching the market with a blend of fundamental and technical analysis will improve your chances of both spotting trade opportunities and managing your trades more effectively. You'll also be better prepared to handle markets that are alternately reacting to fundamental and technical developments or some combination of the two.

Different Strokes for Different Folks

After you've given some thought to the time and resources you're able to devote to currency trading and which approach you favor (technical, fundamental, or a blend), the next step is to settle on a trading style that best fits those choices.

There are as many different trading styles and market approaches in FX as there are individuals in the market. But most of them can be grouped into three main categories that boil down to varying degrees of exposure to market risk. The two main elements of market risk are time and relative price movements. The longer you hold a position, the more risk you're exposed to. The more of a price change you're anticipating, the more risk you're exposed to.

In the next few sections, we detail the main trading styles and what they really mean for individual traders. Our aim here is not to advocate for any particular trading style. (Styles frequently overlap, and you can adopt different styles for different trade opportunities or different market conditions.) Instead, our goal is to give you an idea of the various approaches used by forex market professionals so you can understand the basis of each style. We think this information will help you settle on a style that best fits your personality and individual circumstances. Equally important, you'll be able to recognize whether your style is drifting and generally maintain a more disciplined approach to the market.

Short-term, high-frequency day trading

Short-term trading in currencies is unlike short-term trading in most other markets. A short-term trade in stocks or commodities usually means holding a position for a day to several days at least. But because of the liquidity and narrow bid/offer spreads in currencies, prices are constantly fluctuating in small increments. The steady and fluid price action in currencies allows for extremely short-term trading by speculators intent on capturing just a few pips on each trade.

Short-term trading in forex typically involves holding a position for only a few seconds or minutes and rarely longer than an hour. But the time element is not the defining feature of short-term currency trading. Instead, the pip fluctuations are what's important. Traders who follow a short-term trading style are seeking to profit by repeatedly opening and closing positions after gaining just a few pips, typically 5 to 10 pips but also as little as 1 or 2 pips. For more information on high-frequency trading, check out Chapter 3.

Jobbing the market pip by pip

In the interbank market, extremely short-term, in-and-out trading is referred to as *jobbing the market;* online currency traders call it *scalping.* (We use the terms interchangeably.) Traders who follow this style have to be among the fastest and most disciplined of traders because they're out to capture only a few pips on each trade. In terms of speed, rapid reaction and instantaneous decision-making are essential to successfully jobbing the market.

When it comes to discipline, scalpers must be absolutely ruthless in both taking profits and losses. If you're in it to make only a few pips on each trade, you can't afford to lose much more than a few pips on each trade. The overall strategy is obviously based on being right more often than being wrong, but the key is not risking more than a few pips on each trade. The essential motto is "Take the money and run" — repeated a few dozen times a day.

Jobbing the market requires an intuitive feel for the market. (Some practitioners refer to it as *rhythm trading*.) Scalpers don't worry about the fundamentals too much. If you were to ask a scalper for her opinion of a particular currency pair, she would likely respond along the lines of "It feels *bid*" or "It feels *offered*" (meaning, she senses an underlying buying or selling bias in the market — but only at that moment). If you ask her again a few minutes later, she may respond in the opposite direction.

Successful scalpers have absolutely no allegiance to any single position. They couldn't care less if the currency pair goes up or down. They're strictly focused on the next few pips. Their position is either working for them, or they're out of it faster than you can blink an eye. All they need is volatility and liquidity. You can find out if you're a scalper and get some actionable trade ideas for this trading style in the appendix.

Adapting jobbing to online currency trading

Retail spreads have narrowed sharply in recent years. Some pairs have spreads that are lower than 1 pip, while other pairs have wider spreads. If you trade pairs or crosses with wider spread, this can make jobbing slightly more difficult; it doesn't mean you can't still engage in short-term trading — it just means you'll need to adjust the risk parameters of the style. Instead of looking to make 1 to 2 pips on each trade, you need to aim for a pip gain at least as large as the spread you're dealing with in each currency pair. The other basic rules of taking only minimal losses and not hanging on to a position for too long still apply.

Here are some other important guidelines to keep in mind when following a short-term trading strategy:

- ✔ **Trade only the most liquid currency pairs, such as EUR/USD, USD/JPY, EUR/GBP, EUR/JPY, and AUD/USD.** The most liquid pairs will have the tightest trading spreads and will be subject to fewer sudden price jumps.

- ✔ **Trade only during times of peak liquidity and market interest.** Consistent liquidity and fluid market interest are essential to short-term trading strategies. Market liquidity is deepest during the European session when Asian and North American trading centers overlap with European time zones — about 2 a.m. to noon Eastern time (ET). Trading in other sessions can leave you with far fewer and less predictable short-term price movements to take advantage of.

- ✔ **Focus your trading on only one pair at a time.** If you're aiming to capture second-by-second or minute-by-minute price movements, you'll need to fully concentrate on one pair at a time. It'll also improve your feel for the pair if that pair is all you're watching.

✔ **Preset your default trade size so you don't have to keep specifying it on each deal.**

✔ **Look for a brokerage firm that offers click-and-deal trading so you're not subject to execution delays or re-quotes.** (See Chapter 13 for more on broker executions.)

✔ **Adjust your risk and reward expectations to reflect the dealing spread of the currency pair you're trading.** With 1- to 4-pip spreads on most major pairs, you probably need to capture 3 to 10 pips per trade to offset losses if the market moves against you.

✔ **Avoid trading around data releases.** Carrying a short-term position into a data release can be risky because prices may gap sharply after the release, blowing a short-term strategy out of the water. Markets are also prone to quick price adjustments in the 15 to 30 minutes ahead of major data releases as nearby orders are triggered. This can lead to a quick shift against your position that may not be resolved before the data comes out.

Keeping sight of the forest while you're in the trees

Trading a short-term strategy online also requires individual traders to invest more time and effort in analyzing the overall market, especially from the technical perspective.

If you pursue a short-term trading strategy online, where dealing spreads can equal profit targets, you need to be right by a larger margin. To give yourself a better chance of capturing slightly larger short-term moves, always know where you stand in longer charting time frames. By all means, use tick, one-minute, and five-minute charts to refine your trade timing, entry, and exit. But be aware of the larger picture suggested by hourly, multihour, and daily charts because they're going to hold the keys to the larger directional movements.

Medium-term directional trading

If you thought short-term time frames were exceptionally brief, medium-term time frames aren't much longer. Medium-term positions are typically held for periods ranging anywhere from a few hours to a day or two, but usually not much longer. Just as with short-term trading, the key distinction for medium-term trading is not the length of time the position is open, but the amount of pips you're seeking/risking.

Where short-term trading looks to profit from the routine noise of minor price fluctuations, almost without regard for the overall direction of the market, medium-term trading seeks to get the overall direction right and profit from more significant currency rate moves. By the same token, medium-term traders recognize that markets rarely move in one direction for too long, so they approach the market with well-defined trade entry and exit strategies.

Almost as many currency speculators fall into the medium-term category (sometimes referred to as *momentum trading* and *swing trading*) as fall into the short-term trading category. Medium-term trading requires many of the same skills as short-term trading, especially when it comes to entering/exiting positions, but it also demands a broader perspective, greater analytical effort, and a lot more patience. Find out if you're a medium-term trader in the appendix.

Capturing intraday price moves for maximum effect

The essence of medium-term trading is determining where a currency pair is likely to go over the next several hours or days and constructing a trading strategy to exploit that view. Medium-term traders typically pursue one of the following overall approaches, but there's also plenty of room to combine strategies:

- **Trading a view:** Having a fundamental-based opinion on which way a currency pair is likely to move. View trades are typically based on prevailing market themes, like interest rate expectations or economic growth trends. View traders still need to be aware of technical levels as part of an overall trading plan.

- **Trading the technicals:** Basing your market outlook on chart patterns, trend lines, support and resistance levels, and momentum studies. Technical traders typically spot a trade opportunity on their charts, but they still need to be aware of fundamental events, because they're the catalysts for many breaks of technical levels.

- **Trading events and data:** Basing positions on expected outcomes of events, like a central bank rate decision or individual data reports. Event/data traders typically open positions well in advance of events and close them when the outcome is known (also known as buy the rumor/sell the fact, or vice versa).

- **Trading with the flow:** Trading based on overall market direction (trend) or information of major buying and selling (flows). To trade on flow information, look for a broker that offers market flow commentary, like that found in FOREX.com's *Forex Insider* (www.forex.com/forex_research.html).

When is a trend not a trend?

When it's a range. A *trading range* or a *range-bound market* is a market that remains confined within a relatively narrow range of prices. In currency pairs, a short-term (over the next few hours) trading range may be 20 to 50 pips wide, whereas a longer-term (over the next few days to weeks) range can be 200 to 400 pips wide.

For all the hype that trends get in various market literature, the reality is that most markets trend no more than a third of the time. The bulk of the time they're bouncing around in ranges, consolidating, and trading sideways.

If markets reflect all the currently known information that's available, they're going to experience major trends or shifts only when truly new and unexpected information hits the market. On a day-to-day basis, incoming economic data and events usually result in an adjustment of prices only within a prevailing range, rather than a breakout, but that's enough for medium-term traders to take advantage of the opportunity.

Taking what you get from the market

Medium-term traders recognize that sizeable price movements and trends are more the exception than the rule. So rather than selling and holding in the case of a downtrend, for example, they're looking to capitalize on the 50- to 150-point price declines that make up the overall downtrend. The key here is that medium-term traders will take profit frequently and step back to reassess market conditions before getting back in.

Although medium-term traders are normally looking to capture larger relative price movements — say, 50 to 100 pips or more — they're also quick to take smaller profits on the basis of short-term price behavior. For instance, if a break of a technical resistance level suggests a targeted price move of 80 pips higher to the next resistance level, the medium-term trader is going to be more than happy capturing 70 to 80 percent of the expected price move. They're not going to hold on to the position looking for the exact price target to be hit. It goes without saying that it's better to catch 75 percent of *something* than 100 percent of *nothing*.

Long-term macroeconomic trading

Long-term trading in currencies is generally reserved for hedge funds and other institutional types with deep pockets. Long-term trading in currencies can involve holding positions for weeks, months, and potentially years at a time. Holding positions for that long necessarily involves being exposed to significant short-term volatility that can quickly overwhelm margin trading accounts.

With proper risk management, individual margin traders can seek to capture longer-term trends. The key is to hold a small enough position relative to your margin that you can withstand volatility of as much as 5 percent or more. Mini accounts, which trade in lot sizes of 10,000 currency units, are a good vehicle to take advantage of longer-term price trends.

For example, let's say you're of the view that the euro is going to weaken due to the high debt levels of some of the member countries and the potential for a sovereign bond default. EUR/USD is trading around 1.3500, for this example, and you think it's heading to 1.1000 or even lower. But if EUR/USD strengthens above 1.4500, you think the debt crisis will have been resolved and you'd want to exit the trade. In this case, you're risking 1,000 pips to gain 2,500 pips. For a

10,000 EUR trade size, that works out to a risk of losing $1,000 (10,000 × 0.1000 [1,000 EUR pips] = USD 1,000) or gaining $2,500 (10,000 × 0.2500 [2,500 EUR pips] = USD 2,500).

Identifying the macro elements that lead to long-term trends

Long-term trading seeks to capitalize on major price trends, which are in turn the result of long-term macroeconomic factors. Before you embark on long-term speculation, you want to see how some of the following macroeconomic chips stack up:

- ✔ **Interest rate cycles:** Where are the two currencies' relative interest rates, and where are they likely to go in the coming months? Narrower interest-rate differentials will tend to help the lower-yielding currency and hurt the higher-yielding currency; wider interest-rate differentials will help the higher-yielding currency and hurt the lower-yielding one.

- ✔ **Economic growth cycles:** What's the outlook for relative growth over the next several months? An economy that is in an expansionary phase of growth is likely to see higher interest rates in the future, which would support that currency. An economy that is showing signs of slowing may see interest rate expectations lowered, hurting the currency in the process.

- ✔ **Currency policies:** Are the currencies considered to be excessively overvalued or undervalued by the major global trading powers? Is the G20 or national government/central bank agitating for changes in a currency's value?

- ✔ **Structural deficits or surpluses:** Do the currencies have any major structural issues that tend to see currencies weaken or strengthen, such as fiscal deficits/surpluses or trade deficits/surpluses?

Trading around a core position

Just because you're trading with a long-term view doesn't mean you can't take advantage of significant price changes when they're in your favor in the medium term. Trading around a core position refers to taking profit on a portion of your overall position after favorable price changes. You continue to hold a portion of your original position — the core position — and look to reestablish the full position on subsequent market corrections. *Remember:* It never hurts to take some money off the table when you're winning.

Taking partial profit on a long-term position works best when the currency pair you're trading is reaching significant technical levels, such as multiday or multiweek highs. If the trend of the currency pair you're holding is displaying a channel on the charts, taking partial profit near the top of the channel in an uptrend or near the channel bottom in a downtrend is one way of judging when to take partial profit.

The risk with trading around a core position is that the trend may not correct after you've taken partial profit, never giving you the chance to reestablish your desired full position. But you're still holding the core of your position, and because the market hasn't corrected, it means your core position is doing just fine.

Carry trade strategies

A *carry trade* happens when you buy a high-yielding currency and sell a relatively lower-yielding currency. The strategy profits in two ways:

- ✔ **By being long the higher-yielding currency and short the lower-yielding currency, you can earn the interest-rate differential between the two currencies, known as the *carry.*** If you have the opposite position — long the low-yielder and short the high-yielder — the interest-rate differential is against you, and it is known as the *cost of carry.*

- ✔ **Spot prices appreciate in the direction of the interest-rate differential.** Currency pairs with significant interest-rate differentials tend to move in favor of the higher-yielding currency as traders who are long the high yielder are rewarded, increasing buying interest, and traders who are short the high yielder are penalized, reducing selling interest.

So let me get this straight, you may be thinking: All I have to do is buy the higher-yielding currency/sell the lower-yielding currency, sit back, earn the carry, and watch the spot price move higher? What's the catch?

Right you are. There is a catch, and the catch is that downside spot price volatility can quickly swamp any gains from the carry trade's interest-rate differential. The risk can be compounded by excessive market positioning in favor of the carry trade, meaning a carry trade has become so popular that everyone gets in on it. When everyone who wants to buy has bought, why should the price continue to move higher? Even more daunting, if the price begins to reverse against the carry trade, it may trigger a panic exodus out of the trade, accelerating the price plunge. Take a look at Figure 10-1 to get an idea of the trends that can develop around carry trades as well as the sharp setbacks that can happen along the way.

Carry trades usually work best in low-volatility environments, meaning when financial markets are relatively stable and investors are forced to chase yield. Keep in mind that carry trades need to have a significant interest-rate differential between the two currencies (typically more than 2 percent) to make them attractive. And carry trades are definitely a long-term strategy, because depending on when you get in, you may get caught in a downdraft that could take several days or weeks to unwind before the trade becomes profitable again.

In the wake of the Great Financial Crisis of 2008–2009, major central banks slashed their benchmark interest rates to zero or nearly zero, and many of them are still around that level, or lower in some cases, as of this writing. Near-zero interest rates have eliminated much of the appeal of the carry trade in recent years, and it looks to be several years until interest rates are normalized and attractive differentials put carry trades back in vogue.

Figure 10-1:
AUD/JPY
trends
higher in line
with carry
trade fun-
damentals
(Australia's
interest
rates are
much
higher than
Japan's),
but it meets
sharp set-
backs along
the way.

Source: eSignal (www.esignal.com)

Trading on Auto-Pilot

In Chapter 3, we refer to algorithmic trading systems and indicate these were mainly the tools of hedge funds and other institutional players. The rapid growth of the online forex market has spawned a diverse array of automated trading systems for individual traders, known as *Expert Advisors,* or EAs for short. EAs represent yet another trading approach and one that can blend many of those we outlined earlier.

EAs come in all shapes and sizes with varying complexity or number of rules. (EAs are also known as *rules-based trading systems,* meaning whenever the systems' rules are satisfied, a trade signal is generated.) Some are fully auto-mated (nondiscretionary), firing off trades whenever the rules of the program are met by market movements. Others generate trade alerts and require a manual confirmation by the user before executing a trade (discretionary). Some EAs can be bought off the shelf in a ready-to-go, black-box format, meaning you're using a trading model designed by someone else that usually doesn't allow for modifications. Other EAs come in a build-it-yourself format, allowing you to select the rules you'd like to apply to your trading.

Potential inputs to drive an EA system

There are literally unlimited inputs that can be combined to form the set of rules that go into an EA, but most of them are usually based on technical indi-cators or price developments. Here are some of the more popular inputs:

- ✔ **Crossovers:** These could be crossovers of anything from moving averages (like a 5 minute and 15 minute for a short-term EA, or 9 day and 21 day for a medium-term EA) to momentum oscillators (like stochastics or MACD, again of any time frame).

- ✔ **New price highs or lows:** Some trend-following models generate trade signals when new highs or lows are made, usually based on the close of a defined time period, like a new high on an hourly closing basis.

- ✔ **Time periods:** Some EAs will function only during specified time periods, say during peak liquidity hours in the London afternoon/NY morning. Still others will function only around specified data releases, when a directional move may be more likely.

- ✔ **Daily or weekly closes:** Longer-term systems may look for a daily close above/below a daily moving average, Ichimoku lines, or some other technical approach.

Because many EAs are based on a combination of rules, there's virtually a limitless number of possibilities. Here's an example of one possibility for the long side of a short-term EA: Buy EUR/USD (specify amount) on a new high 5 minute close, if 5 minute MACD is positive, and GBP/USD is also making new high 5 minute close, and 5 minute RSI is <80, and time is between 0600ET-1200ET, and day is between Tuesday and Thursday. The EA would also include something similar for the sell side and also a set of rules for exiting the trade. Note these rules are untested; we just wanted to give you an idea of how an EA might look.

Caveat emptor on models

EAs carry their own set of risks and limitations. Just as you wouldn't put on a blindfold and go for a Sunday drive, you shouldn't expect an EA to deliver a smooth ride all the time. EAs are all based on historical relationships between the various parameters, or rules. And as the ultimate risk disclaimer goes, "past performance is no guarantee of future results."

EAs rely on *back-testing* to evaluate their potential future trading results. Back-testing is a process where a set of rules is applied to historical price data to see how the system *would have* performed. The results are by definition hypothetical, and don't reflect real-world trading conditions (for example, execution slippage, re-quoting, or price gaps, to mention just a few). To be sure, there is much to commend historical relationships, and we certainly employ them in our own mental models for forex trading. You need to be aware that they can break down, and factor that into your trading plan.

One important result of using an EA is that if you go with a nondiscretionary system, you're taking emotion out of the picture, and that may improve your trading discipline, which we look at next.

Using social media for trading: The power of the crowd

The arrival of social media has taken online currency trading by storm. Not only are sites like Twitter a great source of news for forex traders, but they can also be used to make trading decisions. In this section, we take a look at three of the most popular ways to use social media to help you with your trading decisions.

Crowd surfing

Some brokers have developed algorithms that trawl through Twitter, blogs, and other sites in an attempt to grasp bullish and bearish sentiment in the market. For example, these systems would be able to let you know if the majority of the social media it trawled is bearish about the EUR, which could then be a sell signal. Although limited, some academic studies have shown that these systems can have a predictive element that may be useful to your trading.

However, there are drawbacks — for example, not all sentiment is the same. A random person mouthing off about the EUR on Twitter may not be as accurate as a major currency analyst or fund manager who uses social media to explain why she thinks the EUR will fall over the next week. It's also worth remembering that you shouldn't use a sentiment indicator in isolation. It's far more effective when combined with other things, like fundamental or technical analysis.

If you're interested in using a sentiment indicator, ask your broker if it provides one. Keep in mind that extra charges may be involved if you want to access this type of system.

Net positions long/short

This is another form of sentiment indicator where brokers look at their own universe of users or clients and post whether their clients are long or short a selection of currencies, commodities, or equities. You can choose to either follow or ignore the crowd.

A popular way of using sentiment data is to use it as a contrarian indicator. Statistically, you may find that your fellow traders are wrong more often then they're right, so if the data shows that the "market" is long on the USD, you may choose to go short on the USD.

One of the drawbacks is the universe of users who have been polled to find out what positions they're taking. A low number of users, or a user with a very large position, can skew this data, so use it at your own risk.

Copy the leader

Some currency brokers offer a service whereby they publish the trades of their most successful clients, and you can then follow their every move. For example, these trade leaders may put on a long EUR/USD trade; if you wanted to follow them, you would get an alert to place the same trade, or in some cases you could request that trades be executed automatically for you.

This is every lazy trader's dream. You literally do nothing — you just follow someone whom you believe to be better at this than you, and reap the profits with him or her. But there's no such thing as a free lunch. When you're copying trade leaders, keep in mind the following:

✔ The charges for this service can be huge for followers, so make sure it's worth it before you dive in.

✔ Make sure that you understand how the trade leaders' performances are calculated. For example, trade leaders can run losses and still be top of the pile based on historical performance.

Do your research and don't think that following a trade leader is the answer to all your trading woes. Trade leaders have bad positions, too.

Developing Trading Discipline

No matter which trading style you decide to pursue, you need an organized trading plan, or you won't get very far. The difference between making money and losing money in the forex market can be as simple as trading with a plan or trading without one. A *trading plan* is an organized approach to executing a trade strategy that you've developed based on your market analysis and outlook.

Here are the key components of any trading plan:

✔ **Determining position size:** How large a position will you take for each trade strategy? Position size is half the equation for determining how much money is at stake in each trade.

✔ **Deciding where to enter the position:** Exactly where will you try to open the desired position? What happens if your entry level is not reached?

✔ **Setting stop-loss and take-profit levels:** Exactly where will you exit the position, both if it's a winning position (take profit) and if it's a losing position (stop loss)? Stop-loss and take-profit levels are the second half of the equation that determines how much money is at stake in each trade.

That's it — just three simple components. But it's amazing how many traders, experienced and beginner alike, open positions without ever having fully thought through exactly what their game plan is. Of course, you need to consider numerous finer points when constructing a trading plan, and we focus on them later in this chapter. But for now, we just want to drive home the point that trading without an organized plan is like flying an airplane blindfolded — you may be able to get off the ground, but how will you land?

Taking the emotion out of trading

If the key to successful trading is a disciplined approach — developing a trading plan and sticking to it — why is it so hard for many traders to practice trading discipline? The answer is complex, but it usually boils down to a simple case of human emotions getting the better of them. When it comes to trading in any market, don't underestimate the power of emotions to distract and disrupt.

So exactly how do you take the emotion out of trading? The simple answer is: You can't. As long as your heart is pumping and your synapses are firing, emotions are going to be flowing. And truth be told, the emotional highs of trading are one of the reasons people are drawn to it in the first place. There's no rush quite like putting on a successful trade and taking some money out of the market. So just accept that you're going to be experiencing some pretty intense emotions when you're trading.

The longer answer is that because you can't block out the emotions, the best you can hope to achieve is an understanding of where the emotions are coming from, recognizing them when they hit, and limiting their impact on your trading. It's a lot easier said than done, but keep in mind some of the following, and you may find you're better able to keep your emotions in check:

- **Focus on the pips and not the dollars and cents.** Don't be distracted by the exact amount of money won or lost in a trade. Instead, focus on where prices are and how they're behaving. The market has no idea what your trade size is and how much you're making or losing, but it does know where the current price is.

- **It's not about being right or wrong; it's about making money.** At the end of the day, the market doesn't care if you were right or wrong, and neither should you. The only true measure of trading success is dollars and cents.

- **You're going to lose in a fair number of trades.** No trader is right 100 percent of the time. Taking losses is as much a part of the routine as taking profits. You can still be successful over time with a solid risk-management plan.

- **The market is not out to get you.** The market is going to do what it does whether you're involved in it or not, so don't take your trading results personally. Interpret them professionally, just as you would the results of any other business venture.

Managing your expectations

Currency trading is a relatively new opportunity for individual traders, and a lot of people have no frame of reference about what to expect when it comes to price movements. A frequent question asked by newcomers is "How much can I expect to make on this trade?" Whoa, Nelly. Talk about a loaded question.

Financial markets are not bank ATMs, and the forex market is certainly no exception. There are a lot of people speculating on which way various currency pairs are going to move; some of those people are going to be right, and some are going to be wrong. Some may also be right for a moment but suddenly end up on the wrong side of equation.

Before you get involved with trading currencies, you need to have a healthy sense of what to expect when it comes to trading outcomes. Many people choose to focus only on the upside prospects of currency trading, like the view expressed in that loaded question earlier. But losses are part of trading, too. Even the biggest and best traders have losing trades on a regular basis.

One of the keys to establishing trading discipline is to first accept that losses are inevitable. The second step is to dedicate yourself to keeping those losses as small as possible. Most experienced traders will tell you the hardest part of trading is keeping the money you've made and not giving it back to the market.

Imagining realistic profit-and-loss scenarios

The trading style that you decide to pursue will dictate the relative size of profits and losses that you can expect to experience. If you're trading on a short- to medium-term basis, look at average daily trading ranges to get a good idea of what to expect.

The *average daily trading range* is a mathematical average of each day's trading range (high to low) over a specified period. Keep in mind that this figure is just a statistical average — there will be days with larger ranges and days with narrower ranges. Also, average daily ranges will vary significantly by currency pair.

But the average daily trading range covers a full 24-hour trading session and tends to overstate what short- and medium-term traders can expect from intraday trading ranges. Generally speaking, you're better off anticipating more modest price movements of 30 to 80 pips rather than aiming for the home-run ball.

And no matter what any infomercial tells you, you're not going to retire based on any single trade. The key is to hit singles and stay in the game.

Balancing risk versus reward

Trading is all about taking on risk to generate profits. So one question is frequently posed: "How much should I risk in any given trade?" There is no easy answer to that question. Some trading books advise people to use a risk/reward ratio, like 2:1, meaning that if you risk $100 on a trade, you should aim to make $200 to justify the risk. Others counsel to never risk more than a fixed percentage of your trading account on any single trade. It's all a bit formulaic, if you ask us, and it also has no relation to the reality of the markets.

A better way to think about risk and reward is to look at each trade opportunity on its own and assess the outcomes based on technical analysis. This approach has the virtue of being as dynamic as the market, allowing you to exploit trade opportunities according to prevailing market conditions.

Another factor to consider in balancing risk and reward is the use of leverage (see Chapter 13). In online currency trading, generous leverage ratios of 50:1 or 100:1 are typically available. The higher the leverage ratio, the larger position you can trade based on your margin. But leverage is a double-edged sword because it amplifies profits *and* losses.

The key here is to limit your overall leverage utilization so you're not putting all your eggs in one basket. If you open the largest position available based on your margin, you'll have very little cushion left in case of adverse price movements. It may seem sexy to trade as large a position as possible, but whoever said prudent, risk-aware trading was supposed to be sexy? Keep your feet on the ground, and don't lose your head in the clouds of leverage.

Keeping your ammunition dry

The margin you're required to post with your forex broker is the basis for all your trading. The amount of margin you put up will determine how large a position you can hold and for how long (in pips) if the market moves against you. Unless you just won the lottery, your margin collateral is a precious, finite resource, so you have to use it sparingly.

If Hamlet were alive today and trading currencies, his famous soliloquy might begin "To trade or not to trade?" One of the biggest mistakes traders make is known as overtrading. *Overtrading* typically refers to trading too often in the market or trading too many positions at once. Both forms suggest a lack of discipline, and sound more like throwing darts at a board and hoping something sticks.

Keeping your ammunition dry refers to staying out of the market, watching and waiting, and picking your trades more selectively.

Opportunity lost or opportunity cost?

One of the more popular market aphorisms is "You've got to be in it to win it." Though it's obviously a truism, we would counter that trading discretion is the better part of trading valor. Holding open positions not only exposes you to market risk, but can also cost you market opportunities.

After you enter a position, your available margin is reduced, which in turn lowers the amount of new positions you can establish. If you're routinely involved in the market because you don't want to miss out on the next big move, you actually run the risk of missing out on the next big move because you may not have enough available margin to support a new position for the big move.

Don't be afraid about missing out on some trade opportunities. No one ever catches all the moves. Instead, focus on your market analysis and pinpoint the next well-defined trading opportunity. (We look at spotting trade setups in Chapter 12.)

Thinking clearly while you still can

Another virtue of trading less frequently is that your market outlook is not skewed by any of the emotional entanglements that come with open positions. If you ask a trader who's long EUR/USD what he thinks of EUR/USD, surprise, surprise — he's going to tell you he thinks it's going up. That's called *talking your book*.

But being out of the market, or being square, allows you to step back and analyze market developments with a clear perspective. That's when you can spot opportunities more clearly and develop an effective trade strategy to exploit them. All too soon, you'll be on to your next trade, and the emotional roller coaster will start all over again.

Chapter 11

Cutting the Fog with Technical Analysis

Saying that there is a lot of information to absorb in the forex market is an understatement of major proportions. To help make sense of all the information, a lot of which can be just noise — the fog of the market — professional traders focus on the one piece of information that is not subject to dispute or opinion: price.

The field of technical analysis is huge, and there's no way we can cover it in its entirety in this single chapter. Literally hundreds of books have been written on technical analysis in general, as well as on specific approaches (such as the Elliott wave principle or candlestick analysis). In Chapter 19, we suggest several of our favorite books on technical analysis as additional reading. We strongly urge you to supplement the material in this chapter with further in-depth study.

In this chapter, we give you as rich a slice of the technical cake as possible, covering the main elements of technical analysis as they apply to the forex market. What's more, we approach it from a trader's perspective, focusing on the technical tools and approaches that we've found most useful in our own currency trading, as well as what it means for trade strategies and spotting trade setups. That approach may get us in trouble with some technical purists out there, but, hey, that's what makes a market — a difference of opinion.

The Philosophy of Technical Analysis

Calling technical analysis a philosophy is probably a bit of a stretch, but plenty of technical traders are almost cultish in their devotion to it. More than anything, technical analysis is a subjective approach aimed at bringing a sense of order to seemingly random price movements.

Traders use technical analysis to identify trade opportunities, refine their trading strategies (entry and exit levels), and manage their market risk.

Personally, we like to use fundamentals to guide our overall view of market direction, and refine that with technical analysis to identify entry and exit points for specific trades. But not infrequently, technical analysis will suggest a trade opportunity all by itself, even though it may be counter to our fundamental outlook (see the Tips in the "Candlestick patterns" section later in this chapter for more).

What is technical analysis?

In a nutshell, *technical analysis* is the study of historical price movements to predict future price movements. You're probably familiar with the standard disclaimer that "past performance is no guarantee of future results," a statement that tends to call into question the validity of using past price data to forecast future price developments.

But technical analysis is able to get *beyond* those concerns based on two main considerations:

- **Markets are made up of humans.** Human psychology and investing behavior haven't changed very much over the years, whether it's the Dutch tulip frenzy of the 1600s, the dot-com bubble of the 1990s, or the real estate bubbles of the last decade. The emotional forces that dictate buying and selling decisions are reflected in historical price patterns that appear over and over in all manner of financial markets. As long as humans are still making the decisions (or are writing the programs for the computers that make the decisions), you'll be able to look at past behavior as a guide to what is likely to happen in the future.

- **Technical analysis is widely practiced in all markets.** This is the self-fulfilling-prophecy aspect of technical analysis. The greater the number of traders who focus on technical analysis, the more likely their actions will reflect the interpretations of technical analysis, reinforcing the impact of that analysis. Believe us when we say that professional currency traders who do not practice some form of technical analysis are a rarity.

What technical analysis is not

Despite its name, technical analysis is not some engineer-designed, surefire, guaranteed method of market analysis. There are no such methods, period. Technical analysis involves a high degree of subjectivity where individual interpretations can vary significantly. Two technical traders looking at the same currency chart could reach opposite conclusions about the course of future prices. What's more, they could both be right, depending on their timing and specific strategies.

Technical analysis requires a great deal of patience, practice, and experimentation based on individual preferences and circumstances. Short-term traders focusing on the next few minutes and hours find certain tools and approaches more helpful than long-term traders do. Longer-term traders looking at multiday or multiweek trades use other tools and indicators entirely. Certain technical approaches work better in some currency pairs than others. Overall market conditions of volatility and liquidity also influence which technical approach works best. The key is to develop your own approach based on your particular circumstances — time frame, risk appetite, discipline (see Chapter 10 for more on this).

No single, magical technical indicator or approach always works. Be careful about becoming too reliant on any single indicator. A particular indicator may yield excellent signals in certain market environments but fail when market conditions begin to change. We suggest becoming familiar with several different approaches and indicators, using them to cross-check each other depending on market conditions. (We look at this idea in the "Waiting for confirmation" section, later in this chapter.)

Forms of technical analysis

Technical analysis can be broken down into three main approaches:

- ✔ **Chart analysis:** Visual inspection of price charts to identify price trends, ranges, support, and resistance levels. (We look at chart analysis in "The Art of Technical Analysis," later in this chapter.)

- ✔ **Pattern recognition:** Identifies chart formations or patterns that provide specific predictive signals, such as a reversal or a breakout. (We show you some of the most common traditional chart patterns and candlestick formations in the "Recognizing chart formations" section, later in this chapter.)

- ✔ **Momentum and trend analysis:** Looks at the rate of change of prices for indications of market sentiment regarding the price movement. Trend indicators seek to determine the presence of a trend and its strength. (We look at these indicators in "The Science of Technical Analysis," later in this chapter.)

Finding support and resistance

One of the basic building blocks of technical analysis is the concept of *support and resistance:*

- ✔ **Support:** A price level where buying interest overwhelms selling interest, causing a price decline to stop, bottom out, or pause. Think of support as a floor for prices in a downmove.

- ✔ **Resistance:** The opposite of support. Resistance is where selling interest materializes and slows or overpowers buying interest, causing prices to peak, stall, or pause in a price rally. Think of resistance as the ceiling in a price advance.

Support and resistance levels are identified based on prior price action, such as highs and lows and short-term (minutes to hours) *consolidation* or *congestion zones* (where prices get all stopped up and can't move one way or the other for a period of time). Support and resistance can also be determined by drawing trend lines. Still other forms of support and resistance come from Fibonacci retracement levels, *Ichimoku* lines, and moving averages, which we save for later in this chapter. Figure 11-1 shows some basic support and resistance levels from sloping and horizontal trend lines drawn off key highs and lows.

Sloping trend line support from key highs and lows

Figure 11-1:
Trend lines drawn off key highs and lows can be used to identify important support and resistance levels as well as illuminate unfolding pattern formations.

Horizontal support and resistance from prior lows and highs

One of the key concepts of support and resistance is that after a support or resistance level is broken, it shifts direction. In other words, after a support level is broken in a move to the downside, it becomes resistance in subsequent price attempts to rally. After a resistance level is broken to the upside, it may later act as support for further price gains.

Not all support and resistance are created equal

Support and resistance come in all shapes and sizes. Some support or resistance levels are stronger or weaker than others, and technical analysts typically refer to support as either minor or major. But those terms are subjective and difficult to quantify with any precision.

The best way to get a handle on the relative strength of a support or resistance level is to view it in the context of time and price significance.

- ✔ **The longer the time frame of the price point, the greater its significance.** A weekly high/low is more important than a daily high/low, which is more important than an hourly high/low, and so on, down the time scale.

- ✔ **Trend-line strength is also a function of time frame and durability.** A trend line based on daily charts tends to be stronger than a trend line based on hourly prices. A trend line that dates back six months has greater significance than one that's only a week or two old. Also, the more often a trend line is tested (meaning, prices touch the trend line but do not break through it, or break through it only very briefly and by small amounts), the more valid it is.

- ✔ **The strength of support or resistance levels during a retracement depends on the strength of the support or resistance during the prior directional move.** A retracement refers to a price movement in the opposite direction of a previous price advance or decline. The distance that prices reverse, or retrace, is called a *retracement.* For example, trend lines that were support in a downmove will act as resistance in any retracement higher. The strength of the trend-line support on the way down, such as how many attempts were needed to break below it, will give a good indication of its likely strength as resistance in the retracement.

Support and resistance are made to be broken

We don't want to leave you with the impression that support and resistance levels are immutable forces in the market that are never challenged or broken. Just the opposite: Forex markets spend much of the time testing support or resistance levels, looking for the weak side in which to push prices.

Different trading styles focus on different types of support and resistance:

- ✔ **Tests and breaks of short-term support or resistance levels are the meat and potatoes of intraday trading.** Short-term traders focus on the nearest support or resistance levels (for example, 5- or 15-minute or hourly highs/lows and trend lines) as guides to the immediate direction of prices.

> ✔ **Tests and breaks of longer-term support and resistance levels are the fuel that fires longer-term trends or defines medium-term ranges.** Medium- to longer-term traders typically focus on longer-term support or resistance levels, such as daily/weekly highs/lows, and trend lines drawn off them, to guide their trading.

One of the keys to assessing the significance of a break of support or resistance levels is the strength of follow-through that occurs after the level is broken. *Follow-through* is the price action that takes place after technical support or resistance is broken. After resistance is broken, for example, prices should accelerate higher as shorts who sold in front of the resistance buy back their positions and new buyers enter the market, because resistance has been surpassed. The amount of follow-through buying or selling that materializes, or fails to materialize, after the break of a technical support or resistance level is an important indication of the strength of the underlying move.

Waiting for confirmation

We were tempted to title this section "Looking for confirmation," but we thought that sounded too proactive in the sense that if you go looking for something on a chart, odds are you can find it and rationalize it as confirmation. The more disciplined approach involves *waiting* for confirmation, letting market prices provide you with unambiguous signs of a change in direction or break of a chart pattern.

Confirmation refers to price movements that verify, or confirm, a technical observation that suggests a particular outcome. For example, certain chart patterns are useful predictors of a potential reversal in price direction. But note that the starting point in this case is that prices are moving in a trend or steady direction. Blindly following a pattern that suggests that a trend is about to end is very risky. After all, the trend is your friend, so why would you take the risk of going against the trend?

If you're patient and wait for price action to provide you with confirmation that a directional move or trend is indeed reversing, essentially confirming that the observed chart pattern is playing out as you expected, you're reducing the risks of being wrong-sided or premature in your trade. The trade-off is that you may sacrifice a better entry level for a higher degree of certainty in the overall trade setup. Looked at the other way around, you're reducing the risks of getting into a trade setup too soon and being wrong if the setup doesn't play out as you expected. The difference is not making as much money as possible or losing money outright. Which would you prefer?

Technical-based observations provide you with a heads-up alert that a price shift may soon take place — for example, prices may be stalling in a move higher, potentially setting up a reversal lower. Confirmation comes when prices break an established trend line, prior high or low, or other key technical levels of support or resistance. Be careful about looking for confirmation from multiple technical indicators, because they may be measuring the same thing, just in slightly different formats. *Price* is the key element of confirmation.

The Art of Technical Analysis

Chart analysis is at the heart of technical analysis. Don't become reliant on all the fancy indicators and technical studies on your charting system. The most powerful technical indicators you have are your eyes and what's behind them.

In this section, we show you the basics of drawing trend lines and look at some of the most common, yet significant, price patterns you'll encounter over and over again in your trading. In Chapter 12, we go into greater detail and suggest practical approaches to drawing and applying trend lines on a regular basis, as well as how to trade the chart formations you observe.

Bar charts and candlestick charts

In this section, we introduce the two main types of charts you'll likely be using as you pursue your own technical analysis.

Measuring markets with price bars

Most charting systems are set to default to show *bar charts,* probably the most widely used form of charting among Western traders. Bar charts are composed of price bars, which encompass the key points of each trading *period* — namely, the open, high, low, and close. A period is the time interval you've selected to analyze, such as 5 or 15 minutes for short-term traders, and 1 hour, 4 hours daily, or weekly for longer-term traders (though short-term traders need to be aware of the longer periods, too). Each bar is displayed as a vertical line with a tick mark on each side of the bar. The tick mark on the left side of the price bar represents the open of the period; the tick mark on the right side is the close of the period; and the upper and lower levels of the bar are the period's highs and lows. For example, Figure 11-1 is a bar chart.

You can use bar charts to draw trend lines, measure retracement levels, and gauge overall price volatility. Each bar represents the trading range for the period; the larger the bar, the greater the range and the higher the volatility (and vice versa for smaller bars). Bar charts are best suited to relatively basic analysis, such as getting a handle on an overall trend.

Lighting the way with candlesticks

We put our favoritism right out front for everyone to see: We love using candlestick charts to spot trade setups, especially impending price reversals. We think candlesticks are among the more powerful predictive tools in the trader's arsenal, and we strongly recommend that you study them further. In particular, we highly recommend reading Steve Nison's *Japanese Candlestick Charting Techniques,* 2nd Edition (see Chapter 19 for more on Nison's book).

Candlestick charts are among the earliest known forms of technical analysis, dating back to trading in the Japanese rice markets in the 18th century. Candlestick charts, or just *candles* for short, provide a more visually intuitive representation of price action than you get from simple bar charts. They do this through the use of color and by more clearly breaking out the key price points of each trading day — open, close, high, and low.

Figure 11-2 shows the components of two candlesticks. Immediately, you can see that one candle is light, and the other is dark. What does that mean? Think of yin and yang, good and bad, up and down. The light candlestick indicates that the close was higher than the open — it was an up day. The dark candle indicates that the close was lower than the open — a down day.

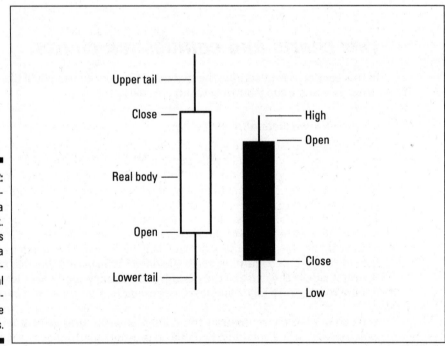

Figure 11-2:
The anatomy of a candlestick. Candlesticks provide a highly intuitive visual representation of price movements.

Source: FOREX.com

The light/dark portion in the middle of the candle is called the *real body* or just *body;* it displays the difference between the open and the close. The lines above and below the body are called *tails* (the term we use going forward), *shadows,* or *wicks;* these lines represent the high and low of the period. (We look more at candlesticks in the "Candlestick patterns" section, later in this chapter.)

Candlestick charts are best analyzed using daily or weekly periods rather than intraday periods like 1 hour or 30 minutes. The philosophy behind candlestick analysis is that a full day or week of trading is needed before the market has rendered a verdict, potentially offering signals about future direction.

Drawing trend lines

Probably no exercise in technical analysis is more individualistic than identifying and drawing trend lines. Very often, it comes down to a matter of beauty being in the eye of the beholder. But in the case of chart analysis, beauty is order, and the trend lines you draw are the outlines of that order. Ultimately, drawing trend lines is not that complicated — with a bit of practice, you'll get the hang of it pretty quickly.

What is a trend line? Basically, a *trend line* is a line that connects significant price points over a defined time period on a price chart. The significant price points are usually the highs and lows of bars or candles, though in the case of candles you can also use the open or close levels of the candle's real body.

Connecting the dots

The starting point in drawing trend lines is looking at the overall price chart in front of you. What do you see? If it's your first time looking at a price chart, it probably looks like a jumble of meaningless bars or candles. The key is to turn that jumble into a meaningful visualization of what's happening to prices. (We offer several graphical representations of trend lines throughout Chapter 12.)

Scan the chart from left to right, starting in the past and looking into the present. What are prices doing? Are they moving up, down, or a little of both? (If you're looking at a currency chart, you can bet they're doing a little bit of both.) Draw your first trend lines to connect the highest highs (you need only two points to form a line) and the lowest lows, to capture the overall range in the observed period. Always use the extreme points of the price bars or candles when connecting price points (lows with lows, highs with highs).

Look at what's happening between those two trend lines. You'll invariably see a number of smaller, distinct price movements making up the whole. You can draw trend lines to connect the highs of price moves down and the lows of price moves up. Be sure to extend your trend lines all the way to the right edge of the chart, regardless of other bars or candles that later break it. Look for evenness, whether it's horizontal, sloping down, shooting steeply higher, or anything in between. Eventually, that evenness will be broken by price moves that break through the trend lines.

Your ultimate focus will be on the prices on the right side of the chart, because that's the most recent price action, and beyond lies future price developments. The idea is to winnow out trend lines from the past that appear to have little relevance (they're frequently broken), and keep the trend lines that have the most relevance (prices reverse course when they're hit, and they're largely unbroken) and extend them into the future. Those trend lines are going to act as support and resistance just as they did in the past and provide you with guidance going forward.

Looking for symmetry

When you're drawing trend lines, be alert for symmetrical patterns, such as parallel channels, sloping up or down, or simply horizontal. Look for horizontal tops and bottoms to be made where prior high and lows were reached. Note that a rising trend line may be heading for a falling trend line, forming a triangle. The two lines are set to intersect at some point in the future, and one of them will be broken, sparking a price reaction.

Charting systems usually have a trend-line function that allows you to draw a line parallel to another line, or copy an existing line and move it to a parallel position. Experiment with that tool, and you'll be surprised how frequently price points match up to it.

Recognizing chart formations

Pattern recognition, or the identification of chart formations, is another form of technical analysis that helps traders get a handle on what's happening in the market. In the following sections, we cover some of the most widely observed chart formations and what they mean from a trading standpoint. While you're looking through them, keep in mind that the formations can occur in different charting time frames (for example, 15 minutes, hourly, daily).

The key to trading on chart formations is to recognize the time period in which they're apparent and to factor that into your trade strategy. A reversal pattern that occurs on an hourly chart, for example, may constitute a reversal that lasts for only a few hours or a day and retrace a relatively smaller pip distance. A reversal pattern on a daily chart, in contrast, could signal a significant multiweek reversal spanning several hundred pips. Keep the formations you observe in the proper time-frame perspective.

Basic chart formations

Chart formations are part and parcel of trends. They're generally grouped into categories that reflect what they mean in the context of a trend. The two most common types of chart patterns are

- ✔ **Reversal patterns:** A reversal pattern indicates that the prior directional price movement is coming to an end. It does not necessarily mean that prices will actually begin to move in the opposite direction, though in many cases they will.

✔ **Consolidation and continuation patterns:** Consolidation and continuation patterns represent pauses in directional price moves, where prices undergo a period of back-and-forth consolidation before the overall trend continues.

Double tops and double bottoms

Double tops and *double bottoms* are typically considered among the most powerful chart formations indicating a reversal in the direction of an overall trend. Double tops form in an uptrend, and double bottoms form in a downtrend. Figure 11-3 shows a double-bottom pattern on a daily AUD/USD chart, and Figure 11-1 shows a double top on a four-hour AUD/USD chart (not labeled, but you can see the two highs).

Figure 11-3:
A double-bottom formation suggests that the prior trend down may reverse.

Double bottoms signal end of declines

Source: eSignal (www.esignal.com)

In terms of market dynamics, the idea behind both is that a directional move (up or down) will make a high or low at some point. After a period of consolidation, the market will frequently test the prior high or low for the trend. If the trend is still intact, the market should be able to make a new high or low beyond the prior one. But if the market is unable to surpass the prior high or low, it's taken as a signal that the trend is over, and trend followers begin to exit, generating the reversal.

As with most chart formations, double tops and bottoms rarely form perfectly. The second high or low may come up short of the prior high/low; that inability even to retest the prior high/low can create a more rapid and volatile reversal. Other times, the first low may be surpassed by a brief amount and for a brief time (possibly due to stops at the prior low being triggered), as in Figure 10-3, only to be rejected, leading to the reversal.

Head and shoulders and inverted head and shoulders

Head-and-shoulders (H&S) formations are another form of reversal pattern, sometimes referred to as a *triple top*. The H&S top formation develops after an uptrend, and an *inverted H&S* comes after a downtrend. Figure 11-4 shows a classic example of an inverted H&S formation, signaling the end of the EUR's decline after the Eurozone debt crisis. In the case of an uptrend, a high is made at some stage followed by a pullback lower, creating the left shoulder. A subsequent new high is made, generating the head, followed by yet another correction lower. A third attempt to move higher fails to reach the second or highest high and may surpass, equal, or fall short of the left shoulder. Failure to reach the prior high typically triggers selling, and confirmation of a reversal is received when prices fall below the *neckline,* which is formed by connecting the lows seen after each pullback from the shoulder and the head.

Figure 11-4:
An inverted head-and-shoulders formation in EUR/USD signals that the euro's declines may be ending after the worst of the Eurozone debt crisis.

Source: eSignal (www.esignal.com)

The standard *measured move objective* (the price move suggested by a chart pattern) in an H&S pattern is the distance from the top of the head to the neckline. When the neckline is broken, prices should subsequently move that distance.

Flags

Flags are consolidation patterns that typically form in a counter-trend direction. For example, if prices have moved higher (the trend is up) and run into resistance above, for a flag to form, prices will begin to consolidate in a downward (counter-trend) channel. The formation suggests that the flag consolidation channel will eventually break out in the direction of the prior trend, and the directional move will resume. Perhaps somewhat confusingly, a *bull flag* actually slopes downward, but it's called a bull flag because after it breaks, the bullish trend resumes. A *bear flag* slopes upward, but after it breaks to the downside, the bearish trend resumes.

If the opposite side of the flag channel is broken (the lower end of a bull flag/upper end of a bear flag), the pattern is invalidated and it may signal a larger reversal.

Flags have a measured move objective based on the *flagpole,* or the distance of the prior move that ultimately stalled, resulting in the formation of the flag. When the flag is broken, the price target is usually equal to the length of the flagpole projected from the flag break, as shown in Figure 11-5.

Figure 11-5: A break of a bear flag consolidation pattern on an hourly chart of NZD/USD signals that the move down is resuming.

Bear flag consolidation pattern break sees downmove continuation measured move objective equal to length of flagpole

Flagpole

Flag projection from channel break gives a price target

Source: eSignal (www.esignal.com)

Triangles

Triangles are another type of consolidation pattern, and they come in a few different forms:

✔ **Symmetrical triangles:** These formations have downward-sloping upper edges and upward-sloping lower edges, resulting in a triangle pointing horizontally. Symmetrical triangles are mostly neutral for the direction of the ultimate breakout, but they have a slightly greater tendency to break out in the direction in which they entered the triangle consolidation, meaning the trend is resuming.

✔ **Ascending triangles:** These formations have a flat or horizontal top and an upward-sloping lower edge (see Figure 11-6). Ascending triangles typically break out to the upside after resistance on the top is overcome. The rising lower edge signifies that buyers keep coming back at ever-higher levels to push through the horizontal top. The minimum measured move objective on a breakout is equal to the distance between the rising bottom and where the flat top is first reached.

✔ **Descending triangles:** These formations are the inverse of ascending triangles, where the horizontal edge and the expected direction of the breakout are to the downside.

Figure 11-6:
The break of the flat top in an ascending-triangle formation signals an upside breakout. Note that the top of the triangle subsequently acted as support.

Ascending triangle signals upmove is resuming when flat top is broken

Source: eSignal (www.esignal.com)

Candlestick patterns

Candlestick patterns are some of the most powerful predictors of future price direction. Candlesticks have little predictive capacity when it comes to the size of future price movements, so you need to look at other forms of technical analysis to gauge the extent of subsequent price moves. But if you can get the direction right, you're more than halfway there. (We look more at using candles to develop trade strategies in Chapter 12.)

Candlestick formations come in two main forms:

- ✔ **Reversal patterns:** Where a preceding directional move stops and changes direction
- ✔ **Continuation patterns:** Where a prior directional move resumes its course after a period of consolidation

We like to look at candlestick patterns primarily for reversal signals because they're among the most reliable of the candlestick patterns.

The key to interpreting a candle formation as a reversal indicator is that there has to be an identifiable directional move in the preceding days. The directional price move may be part of an extended uptrend or downtrend, or simply a day or two of a clear directional move higher or lower, as shown by relatively large real bodies.

Literally dozens of different candlestick reversal patterns exist, but we focus on the most common patterns in the following sections. Keep in mind that some candle reversal formations consist of a single candle, whereas others depend on two or three candles to constitute the pattern. Look closely, and you'll see that many of them are variations on the same theme (namely that a directional move is losing force, increasing the potential for a price reversal). A good source of candlestick reference can be found for free at www. candlesticker.com.

Doji

Doji are among the most significant of the candlestick patterns because their basic shape forms the basis for many other candlestick patterns. A doji occurs when the close is the same as the open, generating a candlestick with no real body — simply a vertical line with a cross on it.

On days when the close is only a few points apart from the open, generating a candle with an extremely small real body, you can take some artistic license and consider it a potential doji depending on the preceding candles. If the prior days' candles were composed of long real bodies, that increases the likelihood that the very small real body should be viewed as a doji (or a spinning top, which we cover later in this section). Figure 11-7 is a good example of this — the open and close were only 5 pips apart. Whenever you spot a doji after a daily close, you should note it and consider that the preceding directional move may be ending or set for a reversal.

A doji signals indecision and may
indicate the prior trend is about to end

Figure 11-7:
After a
move higher
in AUD/
USD, a doji
signals the
gains may
be about to
reverse.

Doji are significant because they represent indecision and uncertainty. When viewing a doji, think of buyers and sellers fighting to a draw. In the case of a preceding decline lower, for example, it signals that sellers are losing power and buyers have emerged. Figure 11-7 shows a classic doji, where the open and close are the same and about in the middle of the day's trading range. The longer the upper and lower tails are in a doji, the greater the sense of uncertainty displayed by the market and the more likely the prior trend is to be ending.

A double doji occurs when two doji appear in successive periods. The increased uncertainty associated with a double doji tends to signal that the subsequent price move will be more significant after the market's indecision is resolved. A long-legged doji, one with larger tails, is another indication that the market's uncertainty may resolve with a more pronounced move.

On its own, a doji is considered neutral. You need to wait for subsequent price action, such as a trend-line break, to confirm that the doji is signaling a reversal.

Hammers and shooting stars

Hammers and *shooting stars* are single-candle formations that indicate a reversal may be in store. Hammers appear after a decline and are notable for a long lower tail (at least twice the height of the real body) and a small real body at the upper end of the candle (akin to a doji or spinning top). A shooting star is the mirror image after a move higher — a long upper tail and a small real body at the bottom of the day's range. The color of the candle can be either light or dark. In both cases the market dynamic is the same:

After a price rise, in the case of a shooting star, buyers attempted to extend the advance, but by the end of the day were beaten back by sellers, and vice versa with hammers.

The size of the tails is an important indication of the strength of the signal — the larger the tail, the greater the opposing force to the prior move and the more likely prices are to reverse course. Figure 11-8 shows a shooting star signaling recent gains may be set to reverse. (See Figure 11-10 for a hammer as part of another candle pattern.)

Hammers and shooting stars are one of our major alerts for price reversals. They're a signal to exit or at least reduce positions in the direction of the prior trend, and a good basis to establish a position in the opposite direction. If the high of a shooting star or the low of a hammer is exceeded, then the signal is negated and you have to get out. (See more in Chapter 12 for trading tactics using candles.)

Figure 11-8:
A shooting star signals a price peak and potential for a downside reversal. The bullish engulfing line suggests a decline is over and a rebound may follow. Note the white candle's body completely engulfs the prior candle's body.

Source: eSignal (www.esignal.com)

Spinning tops

A *spinning top* (see Figure 11-9) is a single-candle formation that has a small real body and typically short tails, sort of like a fatter version of a doji, but with larger tails. (Larger tails may signify a greater potential price move;

however, the size of the tails is secondary.) The formation gets its name because it resembles a child's toy top. A spinning top frequently appears in pairs, similar to a double doji. The significance of a spinning top is that it has a small real body, which represents a drop in directional momentum after a series of up or down candles, which may signal a directional move is stalling and is ripe for a correction. Spinning tops require confirmation by subsequent candles, but be on alert for potential reversals if you spot a spinning top.

Figure 11-9:
Spinning tops are similar to doji both in shape and in that they suggest uncertainty and a potential reversal of the prior directional move.

Source: eSignal (www.esignal.com)

Engulfing lines

Engulfing lines are two-candlestick patterns that can be either bullish or bearish, depending on whether they come after a downmove or an upmove:

- ✔ **Bullish engulfing line:** The first candle is dark, followed by a large light candle, the body of which completely engulfs the body of the dark candle, seen in Figure 11-8. The smaller the body of the first candle (think spinning top — see the preceding section), the more significant the reversal signals.

- ✔ **Bearish engulfing line:** The first candle is light, followed by a long dark-colored candle that engulfs the body of the first candle, as shown in Figure 11-10 as part of another candle pattern.

Engulfing lines also rank among our favorite candlestick patterns and are a sufficient basis to establish a position in the opposite direction of the preceding price move. If the high/low of the candle preceding the engulfing candle is exceeded, the pattern is negated and you need to exit.

Tweezer tops and tweezer bottoms

Tweezers formations are two-candlestick patterns that get their name because they resemble the pincer end of a pair of tweezers. Tweezer tops and bottoms (shown in Figure 11-10) correspond to double tops and bottoms in traditional chart analysis, and they mean the same thing — a reversal after failing to make new highs or lows. Tweezer tops and bottoms are characterized by long tails on the bottom after a move down, similar to a hammer, and long tails above after a move higher, like shooting stars. The extremes of the tails should ideally be equal, but if the tails are sufficiently long, we'd take notice.

Figure 11-10: A tweezer top and bottom formation signals that an upmove is set to reverse and that a decline may be ending. Note the doji in the days prior to the tweezer top suggesting that upside sentiment was already uncertain.

Source: eSignal (www.esignal.com)

Hopefully you noticed that many of the candlestick patterns we discuss have two things in common — long tails and small bodies. As part of your technical analysis routine (see Chapter 12), we strongly suggest reviewing daily candle charts after each day's close (5 p.m. ET), and on the weekends for weekly candles, to see if any patterns are evident. They can be powerful signals about where prices are heading in the next trading day or week.

Fibonacci retracements

A *retracement* is a price movement in the opposite direction of the preceding price move. For instance, if EUR/USD rises by 150 pips over the course of two days and declines by 75 pips on the third day, prices are said to have retraced half the move higher, or made a 50 percent retracement of the move up. (Fifty percent is not technically a Fibonacci retracement, but we include it here because many traders watch it, too, because of its clean, halfway demarcation.)

Fibonacci retracements come from the ratios between the numbers in the Fibonacci sequence, a nearly magical numerical series that appears in the natural world and mathematics with regularity. The most important Fibonacci retracement percentages are 38.2 percent and 61.8 percent, with 76.4 percent as a secondary, but still important, level.

Most charting systems contain an automatic Fibonacci retracement drawing tool. All you need to do is click the starting point of a directional price move (the low for an upmove; the high for a downmove) and drag the cursor to the finishing point of the movement. The charting system will then display lines that correspond to 38.2 percent, 50 percent, 61.8 percent, 76.4 percent, and 100 percent.

Currency traders routinely calculate Fibonacci retracement levels to determine support and resistance levels, and Fibonacci retracement levels are strong examples of self-fulfilling prophecies in technical analysis. Figure 11-11 provides a good illustration of how Fibonacci retracement levels can act as resistance in a correction higher following a price decline. You can see the 38.2 percent retracement level put up a pretty good fight for a while, but after it broke above, prices blew right past the 50 percent point and quickly moved to the 61.8 percent level, even exceeding it briefly before a pullback. That pullback was nicely contained by the 38.2 percent level. Prices went on to surpass the 61.8 percent level and then tested 76.4 percent, which also held for a time and sent prices back to the 61.8 percent point. From there they rallied higher and finally broke the 76.4 percent level, setting up potential for a 100 percent retracement of the prior decline.

Figure 11-11:
You can identify future support and resistance levels by drawing Fibonacci retracements of prior directional price moves on your charting system.

Source: eSignal (www.esignal.com)

The Science of Technical Analysis

Relax. Nothing is especially scientific or particularly complicated about technical analysis. Many in the market use the term *science* to describe the mechanics of various technical tools, but in our opinion technical analysis is far more art than science.

Each tool in technical analysis has a number of concrete elements that we need to outline before you can start interpreting what they mean. Unless you're developing your own systematic trading model, you don't need to get too caught up in the math or the calculations behind various indicators. Far more important is understanding what the indicators are measuring and what their signals mean and don't mean.

Momentum oscillators and studies

Momentum refers to the speed at which prices are moving, either up or down. Momentum is an important technical measurement of the strength of the buying or selling interest behind a movement in prices. The higher the momentum in a downmove, for example, the greater the selling interest is thought to be. The slower the momentum, the weaker the selling interest.

Currency traders use momentum indicators to gauge whether a price movement will be sustained, potentially developing into a trend, or whether a directional move has run its course and is now more likely to reverse direction. If momentum is positive and rising, it means prices are advancing, suggesting that active buying is taking place. If momentum begins to slow, it means prices are advancing more slowly, suggesting that buying interest is beginning to weaken. If buying interest is drying up, selling interest may increase.

Momentum takes on added significance in currencies because there's no viable way of assessing trading volume on a real-time basis. In stock and futures markets, volume data is an important indicator of the significance of a price move. For example, a sharp price movement on high volume is considered legitimate and likely to be sustained, while a similarly sharp move on low volume is discounted and viewed as more likely to reverse.

Momentum indicators fall into a group of technical studies known as *oscillators,* because the mathematical representations of momentum are plotted on a scale that sees momentum rise and fall, or oscillate, depending on the relative speed of the price movements. A variety of different momentum oscillators exist, each calculated by various formulas, but they're all based on the relationship of the current price to preceding prices over a defined period of time.

Momentum oscillators are typically displayed in a small window at the bottom of charting systems, with the price chart displayed above, so you can readily compare the price action with its underlying momentum.

Overbought and oversold

Momentum oscillators have extreme levels at the upper and lower ends of the oscillator's scale, where the upper level is referred to as *overbought* and the lower level is referred to *oversold.* No hard definitions of *overbought* and *oversold* exist, because they're relative terms describing how fast prices have changed relative to prior price changes. The best way to think of overbought and oversold is that prices have gone up or down too fast relative to prior periods.

Many momentum indicators suggest trading rules based on the indicator reaching overbought or oversold levels. For example, if a momentum study enters overbought or oversold territory, and subsequently turns down or up and moves out of the overbought or oversold zone, it may be considered a sell or buy signal.

Just because a momentum indicator has reached an overbought or oversold level does not mean that prices have to reverse direction. After all, the essence of a trend is a sustained directional price movement, which could see momentum remain in overbought or oversold territory for a long period of time as prices continue to advance or decline in the trend. Breaking news or data may be behind the price move, lending a fundamental urgency to price adjustments that defy momentum analysis. Momentum is only an indicator. The key is to wait for confirmation from prices that the prior direction or trend has, in fact, changed.

Divergences between price and momentum

Another useful way to interpret momentum indicators is by comparing them to corresponding price changes. In most cases, momentum studies and price changes should move in the same direction. If prices are rising, for example, you would expect to see momentum indicators rising as well. By the same token, if momentum begins to stall and eventually turn down, you would expect to see prices turn lower, too. But relatively frequently, especially in shorter, intraday time frames (15 minutes, 1 hour, or 4 hours), prices *diverge* from momentum (meaning, prices may continue to rise even though momentum has started to move lower).

When prices move in the opposite direction of momentum, it's called a *divergence*. Divergences are relatively easy to spot — new price highs are not matched by new highs in the momentum indicator, or new price lows are not matched by new lows in the momentum study. When a new price high or low is made, and momentum fails to make a similar new high or low, the price action is not confirmed by the momentum, suggesting that the price move is false and will not be sustained. The expectation, then, is that the price will change direction and eventually follow the momentum.

When prices make new highs, and momentum is falling or not making new highs, it's called a *bearish divergence* (meaning, prices are expected to shift lower — move bearishly — in line with the underlying momentum). When prices are making new lows, but momentum is rising or not making new lows, it's called a *bullish divergence* (meaning, prices are expected to turn higher — bullish — in line with momentum). (In Chapter 12, we show an example of a bearish divergence.)

Divergences are great alerts that something may be out of kilter between prices and the underlying strength or momentum of the price move. Whenever you spot a divergence between price and momentum, you should start looking more closely at what's happening to prices. Are stop-loss levels being run in thin liquidity conditions? Or has some important news just come out that has sent prices moving sharply, and momentum will eventually catch up?

In a trending environment, prices may continue to move in the direction of the trend (that's what a trend is), but at a slower pace, causing momentum to diverge. To know for certain, you need to wait for confirmation from prices before you enter a trade based on a divergence.

Using momentum in ranges and trends

Momentum indicators work best in range environments, where price movements are relatively constrained and no trend is evident or has moved into consolidation. As buying drives prices toward the upper end of a range, for example, selling interest comes in, slowing the price advance and turning momentum lower. As the buyers turn around, the selling interest increases and momentum begins to accelerate lower, confirming the change in direction. At the bottom of the range, the same thing happens, but in the opposite direction.

Momentum studies frequently give off incorrect signals during breakouts and trending markets. This is especially the case when using shorter time frames, such as hourly and shorter periods. The key to understanding why this happens is to recognize that momentum studies are backward-looking indicators. All they can do is quantify the change in current prices relative to what has come before. They have little predictive capacity, which is why you always need to wait for confirmation from prices before trading based on a momentum signal.

Some of the most extreme price moves typically occur when momentum readings are in overbought or oversold territory. Divergences in shorter time frames also appear frequently, especially during breakouts, where rapid price moves are not reflected quickly enough in momentum studies. By the time the momentum indicator has caught up with the price breakout, prices may already have peaked or bottomed, again causing momentum to signal a divergence. Just because momentum is overbought or oversold doesn't mean prices can't continue to move higher or lower.

Here are the main momentum oscillators used by currency traders:

- ✔ **Relative Strength Index (RSI):** A single-line oscillator plotted on a scale from 0 to 100, based on closing prices over a user-defined period. Common RSI periods are 9, 14, and 21. RSI compares the strength of up periods to the weakness of down periods — hence, the label *relative strength*. RSI readings over 75 are considered overbought; readings below 25 are considered oversold. RSI signals are given when the indicator leaves overbought or oversold territory and on divergences with price.

- ✔ **Stochastic:** A two-line oscillator plotted on a scale of 0 to 100. The two lines are known as *%K* (fast stochastic) and *%D* (slow stochastic). Stochastics are also based on closing prices of prior periods. The basic theory behind stochastics is that the strength of a directional move can be measured by how near the close is to the extreme of a period. In an uptrend, a close near the highs for the period signifies strong momentum; a close in the middle or below signals that momentum is weakening. In a downtrend, the close of a period should be nearer to the lows for momentum to strengthen. As momentum shifts, the %K line will cross over the slower-moving %D line. Crossovers in overbought or oversold territory are considered sell or buy signals. Overbought is above 80, and oversold is below 20.

- ✔ **Moving Average Convergence/Divergence (MACD):** Not really a momentum oscillator, but a complex series of moving averages. (It functions similarly to momentum studies, so we include it here.) MACD fluctuates on either side of a zero line and has no fixed scale, so overbought or oversold are judged relative to prior extremes. MACD also consists of two lines: the MACD line (based on two moving averages) and the signal line (a moving average of the MACD line). Trading signals are generated if the MACD line crosses up over the signal line while below the zero line (buy) or crosses down below the signal line while above the zero line (sell). MACD tends to generate signals more slowly than RSI or stochastics due to the longer periods typically used and the slower nature of moving averages. The result is that it takes longer for MACD to cross over, generally preventing fewer false signals.

Trend-identifying indicators

One of the market's favorite sayings is "The trend is your friend." The idea is that if you trade in the direction of the prevailing trend, you're more likely to experience success than if you trade against the trend. Now, how can you argue with logic like that?

The hard part for us mortals is to determine whether there's a trend in the first place. The question becomes more complex when you look at multiple time frames, because trends can exist in any time frame. On a daily time frame, the market may be largely range bound. But in a shorter time frame, such as hourly or 30 minutes, there may be a trending movement that presents an opportunity for short-term traders.

Determining whether a trend is in place is also important when it comes to deciding whether to follow the signals given by momentum indicators. Momentum studies are great in relatively range-bound markets, but they tend to give off bad signals during trends and breakouts. The key is to determine whether a trend is in place.

In the following sections, we look at a few technical studies you can use to identify whether a trend is in place and how strong it may be.

Directional Movement Indicator system

The Directional Movement Indicator (DMI) system is a set of quantitative tools designed to determine whether a market is trending. The DMI is based on the idea that when a market is trending, each period's price extremes should exceed the prior price extremes in the direction of the trend. For example, in an uptrend, each successive high should be higher than the prior period's high. In a downtrend, the opposite is the case: Each new low should be lower than the prior period's low. That's the essence of a trend.

The DMI system is comprised of the ADX line (the average directional movement index) and the DI+ and DI– lines (which refer to the directional indicators for up periods [+] and down periods [–]). The ADX is used to determine whether a market is trending (regardless if it's up or down), with a reading over 25 indicating a trending market and a reading below indicating no trend. The ADX is also a measure of the strength of a trend — the higher the ADX, the stronger the trend. Using the ADX, traders can determine whether a trend is operative and decide whether to use a trend-following system or to rely on momentum oscillator signals.

As its name would suggest, the DMI system is best employed using both components. The DI+ and DI– lines are used as trade-entry signals. A buy signal is generated when the DI+ line crosses up through the DI– line; a sell signal is generated when the DI– line crosses up through the DI+ line. Wilder suggests using the *extreme-point rule* to govern the DI+/DI– crossover signal. The rule states that when the DI+/DI– lines cross, you should note the extreme point for that period in the direction of the crossover (the high if DI+ crosses up over DI–; the low if DI– crosses up over DI+). If that extreme point is exceeded in the next period, the DI+/DI– crossover is considered a valid trade signal. If the extreme point is not surpassed, the signal is not confirmed.

The ADX can also be used as an early indicator of the end or pause in a trend. When the ADX begins to move lower from its highest level, the trend is either pausing or ending, signaling that it's time to exit the current position and wait for a fresh signal from the DI+/DI– crossover.

Moving averages

One of the more basic and widely used indicators in technical analysis, moving averages can verify existing trends, identify emerging trends, and generate trading signals. Moving averages are simply an average of prior prices over a user-defined time period displayed as a line overlaid on a price chart. There are two main types of moving averages:

- ✔ **Simple moving average** gives equal weight to each historical price point over the specified period.

- ✔ **Exponential moving average** gives greater weight to more recent price data, with the aim of capturing directional price changes more quickly than the simple moving average.

In terms of defining a trend, when prices are above the moving average, an uptrend is in place; when prices are below the moving average, a downtrend is in place.

Traders like to experiment with different periods for moving averages, but a few are more commonly used in the market than others, and they're worth keeping an eye on. The main moving average periods to focus on are 21, 55, 100, and 200. Shorter-term traders may consider looking at the 9- and 14-period moving averages.

Another way moving averages are used is by combining two or more moving averages and using the crossovers of the moving averages as buy or sell signals based on the direction of the crossover. For example, using a 9- and 21-period moving average, you would buy when the faster-moving 9-period average crosses up over the slower-moving 21-period average, and vice versa for a crossover to the downside.

Trading with clouds — Ichimoku charts

Ichimoku Kinko Hyo, or "one-glance equilibrium," charts are another technical analysis approach imported from Japan that is gaining widespread popularity in forex (and other financial) markets. Often referred to as *cloud charts* because of the central feature of the system (the cloud, or *kumo* in Japanese), Ichimoku is basically a trend-following system. But Ichimoku lines can also define significant support and resistance levels not identified by more traditional technical approaches.

The key components of Ichimoku charts are five lines shown in Figure 11-12:

- ✔ **Tenkan line:** The faster moving average based on the average of the high and low of the prior nine days.

- ✔ **Kijun line:** The slower moving average based on the average of the high and low from the prior 26 days.

- ✔ **Senkou span A (leading span A):** The average of the Tenkan and Kijun lines from the prior 26 days, projected 26 days into the future.

- ✔ **Senkou span B (leading span B):** The average of the high and low of the prior 52 days projected 26 days into the future. The cloud is the space between the two leading spans.

- ✔ **Chikou span (lagging span):** Today's closing price reflected 26 days into the past.

Figure 11-12: Ichimoku charts provide a quick way to identify trend direction and also offer support and resistance levels not found elsewhere.

Source: FOREX.com

A few points to note here: Ichimoku is a daily-based chart approach (weekly views can also be used), making it a tool for longer-term traders. Most importantly, intraday breaks of Ichimoku lines are relatively common, but it's only the daily close that matters, reinforcing it as a medium/longer-term trading tool.

Ichimoku trading signals are based on the position of the current price relative to the lines as well as crossovers of the lines themselves. In the simplest form, the trend is up when prices are above the cloud and down when prices are below. Buying and selling signals also come from crossovers of the Tenkan and Kijun lines, but the strength of the signal depends on the position of price relative to the cloud. A crossover of the Tenkan below the Kijun line (bearish crossover) with price above the cloud is a weak sell signal. If price is inside the cloud, it's a medium strength sell signal. If prices are below the cloud, it's a strong sell signal. The same applies in bullish crossovers, but in reverse. The Chikou span is also used to gauge the validity of the trade signals, based on where current prices are relative to prior periods. The idea is that if an uptrend is in place, for example, current price should be above those of prior periods, as seen by the lagging span.

Earlier we indicate that intraday breaks of Ichimoku lines are common, but they also have an uncanny way of acting as formidable support and resistance, too. In particular, the slower moving Kijun line can be used as a level to re-enter a prevailing trend, buying a downside retracement in an uptrend or selling rebounds higher in a downtrend. We always make a point of noting the Ichimoku levels as part of our daily technical analysis routine.

Chapter 12

Identifying Trade Opportunities

Spotting trade opportunities and applying a trading plan are what it all boils down to. Traders and speculators spend the time and energy to follow the market and know what's going on. They analyze and strategize, persistently scanning the market for trade opportunities, or *setups,* and waiting for the right time to step in and commit their money. And when they step in, they have a well-defined trade plan to guide them through whatever the market throws at them.

There's certainly no shortage of opinions and ideas being voiced by market analysts and commentators, but in the end the trades you make are your decision. In this chapter, we go through the key steps to spotting trade opportunities and putting together a risk-aware trading plan to exploit the setup. In this chapter, we draw on many of the technical analysis concepts we outline in Chapter 11.

Developing a Routine for Market Analysis

The first step is to commit to making time for market analysis. The more regular your analysis, the greater the feel you'll develop for where the market has been and where it's likely to go. Also, the more regularly you update yourself on the market, the less time it'll take to stay up to speed. It's a lot easier updating yourself every day than it is trying to catch up on several days' worth of market news, data, and price developments.

Give some long, hard thought to how much time you can realistically afford to devote to market analysis before committing yourself to a specific routine. You may find you're able to devote only a relatively short amount of time each day, so focus your energies on only one or two currency pairs. If you have the time, you can more effectively follow and analyze multiple currency pairs.

At the minimum, you should be prepared to devote at least an hour every day to looking at the market and keeping tabs on upcoming data and events. We like to follow a routine that focuses on:

- ✔ Multiple-time-frame technical analysis to identify support and resistance levels and to track overall price developments

- ✔ Candlestick and Ichimoku analysis after each daily and weekly close

- ✔ Reading economic data reports that have come out overnight to update our fundamental model (see Chapter 7)

- ✔ Assessing the likely market impact of upcoming data reports and events

- ✔ Reviewing market commentaries to stay on top of major themes and overall market sentiment

This may seem like a lot to squeeze into a single hour, but with time and practice, you'll get your charting and market information sources all lined up so you can streamline the entire routine.

Performing Multiple-Time-Frame Technical Analysis

Look closely at the charts in Figures 12-1, 12-2, and 12-3. Notice anything similar about them? Don't be surprised if you don't — they all look extremely different. But that's the point. They're all charts of the same currency pair, but viewed in three different time frames. As you can see, viewing the forest through the trees takes on a whole new meaning when it comes to chart analysis.

Multiple-time-frame technical analysis is nothing more complicated than looking at charts using different time frames of data. The basic idea is to look at the big picture first to identify the key longer-term features and then drill down into shorter data time frames to pinpoint short-term price levels and trends. Our own preference is to focus on daily, four-hour, and hourly time frames, but you can use whichever time frames you think best match your trading style. Short-term traders, for instance, may want to focus on 2-hour, 30-minute, and 5-minute charts to better reflect the narrower time frames of their trading.

Figure 12-1:
EUR/USD
on a daily
candlestick
chart.

Source: eSignal (www.esignal.com)

Figure 12-2:
EUR/USD on
a four-hour
candlestick
chart.

Source: eSignal (www.esignal.com)

Whichever time frames you end up working with, we strongly recommend that you include longer time frames, like daily and weekly, so you can get a sense of where the most significant price levels are. The strength and significance of support and resistance levels are a function of the time frame in which they're evident, with longer-term technical levels holding greater meaning than shorter ones. You don't want your focus to become so narrow that you lose sight of the big picture and go with a break of short-term resistance, for instance, when major daily or weekly resistance is just beyond.

Figure 12-3: EUR/USD on a one-hour candlestick chart.

Source: eSignal (www.esignal.com)

The good thing about daily and weekly charts is that the technical levels don't change quite as frequently as shorter time frames, so you can probably make do with updating the daily and weekly charts much less often.

In Figures 12-4, 12-5, and 12-6, we reproduce the same charts as the ones shown in Figures 12-1, 12-2, and 12-3, but this time we include our trend lines. We start by looking at the daily chart to identify the big levels and draw in longer-term trend lines. Then we drill down to the four-hour chart, where we take a fresh look based on what we're seeing in that time frame and draw in more trend lines to encapsulate any price patterns or trends. To finish, we go down one more level to the hourly charts for a close-up view of the market's most recent price action.

Make sure the charting system you're using has the capability to save trend lines across time frames, meaning that a trend line you draw on a daily chart should also appear on the four-hour and hourly charts, and vice versa. Also, make sure the charting system has the capability to save the entire chart so you don't have to redraw the trend lines every time you pull up the same chart.

On subsequent updates, keep the trend lines that still appear to be valid (meaning, price action has not broken through them), and erase trend lines that are no longer active or have been broken. But don't be in too great a rush to erase broken trend lines, because they'll often continue to act as support or resistance, but in the opposite direction.

Figure 12-4:
Start out by drawing trend lines on longer-term charts, like weekly and daily (shown here), to identify major technical levels.

Source: eSignal (www.esignal.com)

Figure 12-5:
Drill down from a longer-term view to a medium-term time frame, such as four hours (shown here) or two hours, to identify key medium-term support and resistance levels.

Source: eSignal (www.esignal.com)

Figure 12-6:
Focus in
on shorter
time frames
using 1-hour
(shown
here),
30-minute,
15-minute,
and shorter
time frames
to identify
short-term
support and
resistance.

When support is broken, it becomes resistance, and vice versa.

Over time, you'll get an idea of how good you are at spotting meaningful trend lines by the frequency with which you have to discard old trend lines. The longer the trend line contains price action or the longer prices react substantially when a trend line is broken, the more significant the trend line was. In Figures 12-4, 12-5, and 12-6, we keep in some of our older trend lines to give you an idea of how to draw them, as well as to show that some broken trend lines can still be valid.

Identifying Support and Resistance Levels

Multiple-time-frame technical analysis is your early-warning radar system. It alerts you to key support and resistance levels that, if broken, are likely to lead to larger directional breakouts and potential trading signals. Of course, the flip side is that if the support or resistance levels hold, price direction is likely to reverse course.

Now that you've gone through and analyzed a currency pair with trend lines in multiple time frames, you're well on the way to identifying key technical support and resistance levels. But while trend lines are one of the simpler yet more powerful technical tools, there are still plenty of other sources of support and resistance to take note of. In Figure 12-7, we provide a chart showing support and resistance derived from the methods we outline in the following sections.

Figure 12-7: Identifying short-term support and resistance levels on an hourly chart using trend lines, key price points (highs, lows, breakouts), congestion zones, and retracements.

Source: eSignal (www.esignal.com)

Trend lines

You didn't think you were done with trend lines yet, did you? Believe us when we say that trend lines are the gifts that keep on giving, as long as you keep drawing and redrawing them.

To determine support and resistance levels that correspond to the trend lines you've drawn, you simply need to place the cursor of your charting system on the trend line at the current time period. Your charting system should display the price value of the cursor placement on the right side of the chart; if not, you may have to use the crosshairs tool of the charting system to see the value. Keep in mind that trend-line price values will shift over time based on the slope of the trend line. If you've identified a trend line that's sloping steeply higher, for instance, its price value will be higher in later periods. You can run the cursor up the trend line and note the price level and time interval to gauge how much it will change over time.

Note the price levels of the trend lines you observe and use them for placing orders based on your fundamental or technical view. Breaks of trend lines are signals for short-term traders to go with the break. We suggest using a relatively tight stop loss of 20 to 30 points from the trend line in case the break is not sustained (a false break). You can also use trend lines as entry points in trending moves, buying on pullbacks of up moves and selling on rebounds in downtrends. Depending if any chart pattern is evident, the breakout may have a target, or measured move objective (see Chapter 11), which you can use to establish you're take-profit order. Again, allow for a margin of error in case the target level is not quite reached. It's better to capture 80 percent of something than 100 percent of nothing.

Breaks of sloping trend lines always have an immediate hurdle to climb, namely the prior high of a move up in the case of a break of downward sloping trend lines, or the prior low in the case of upward sloping trend lines. Some technical traders disregard sloping trend lines altogether and focus only on breaks of recent highs or lows, which we discuss next. (By the way, you can probably tell we're not among them. We'll leave it to you to judge the importance of sloping trend lines based on the charts in this book.)

Highs and lows

After trend lines, markets tend to place the greatest amount of emphasis on period highs and lows as points of support and resistance, frequently referred to as *horizontal* support/resistance. You can pinpoint support or resistance levels from highs and lows by simply noting the price high or low, but give yourself a few pips of latitude (5 to 10 pips), because different charting systems have different data feeds, which may have slightly different high/low readings.

When you're looking at a daily chart, you can pretty easily identify the relevant high or low. But when you're looking at charts in shorter time frames, it's not always clear which high/low you should use. A general rule is to look for significant price reactions from recent prior highs and lows.

The more sharply prices move away from a high or low, the more significance that high or low carries as support or resistance. The more slowly or less dramatic the price movement off the high or low, the less significance that high or low usually carries. Look for long tails on shorter-term candlestick charts, like 30-minute or hourly time frames, for indications that a prior high is acting as resistance or a prior low is giving support.

Lots of algorithmic trading systems are based on breaks of period highs and lows. To use such breaks as trade signals, prices need to finish the period beyond the break of the high/low. For example, a short-term system will need to see the break of a recent hourly high sustained on an hourly close basis before going long. A longer-term model will want to see the break of a daily low sustained on a daily close below it before going short. You can use such period closes as confirmation the break is valid, but always have a stop in place in case that level is subsequently breached on another similar period close.

Congestion zones

Congestion zones are price bands in which prior price action gives way to *consolidation,* or a period of sideways price action (see Figure 12-7 for some examples). Most congestion zones are roughly 30 to 50 pips wide, but they may be larger in more volatile pairs, like GBP/USD, or the JPY crosses. Unfortunately, there's no easy recipe when it comes to deciding whether the top or bottom of a congestion zone will act as support or resistance, so you need to factor in the whole zone as a potential source of support/resistance. Prices moving higher, for instance, may stall at the base of a congestion zone, or they may make it all the way to the top. If the zone is cleared, however, prices are likely to move on to the next resistance level.

Fibonacci retracements

Fibonacci retracements should be drawn after significant directional price moves when it's clear (or as clear as it can be) that the directional movement has stopped and reversed direction. (For more on Fibonacci levels, see Chapter 11.) You can draw the retracements by using the Fibonacci retracement drawing tool that's standard in most charting systems. Figure 12-7 contains a Fibonacci retracement based on the most recent decline, and with prices currently above them they serve as potential support levels in any pullbacks.

 Breaks of Fibonacci levels on a daily close basis are considered significant by traders. (See Chapter 11 for a discussion of how breaks of Fibonacci levels can be a trading signal.) You can also use Fibonacci levels as targets for price moves, placing take profits based on them or using them as stop-loss exit levels.

 The 76.4 percent mark is sort of the forgotten Fibonacci level, but it's often the key turning point in more volatile currency pairs, like GBP/USD. Just when you think that the 61.8 percent level failed, and it looks like the market is going for a 100 percent retracement, it pulls up short at 76.4 percent.

 Fibonacci retracements can be drawn for almost any discernible price movement, but their significance is closely related to the size of the main directional move. The larger the primary directional price move, the more significance the support or resistance from the Fibonacci retracements will be. Generally speaking, don't get caught up calculating retracements of moves of less than 200 points. Instead, focus on daily charts to spot the most significant price moves, and calculate the potential retracements based on them.

Ichimoku levels

Ichimoku, or cloud charts, are an important source of support and resistance levels you won't find anywhere else. We discuss the basics of Ichimoku charts in Chapter 11. The key to spotting trade opportunities with Ichimoku charts are daily closes above/below the various Ichimoku lines (Tenkan, Kijun, and the leading spans that make up the top and bottom of the cloud). On an intraday basis, those levels may be exceeded, but it's only on a daily close basis that trading signals should be taken. After a move higher, for instance, a daily close below the Tenkan line should be taken as a cue to exit the prior trend, or potentially to go short.

For intraday trading, Ichimoku levels can provide actionable trading levels, providing seemingly unseen support or resistance levels to buy or sell on in extreme price moves. But if those levels are exceeded on a daily close basis, you should exit the trade. For longer-term traders, those with a wait-and-see attitude, daily closes above/below Ichimoku levels offer a potentially longer-term trading signal. We like to use pullbacks or rebounds to the Kijun line as potential entry opportunities when a trend is evident.

Looking for Symmetry with Channels

If you're new to chart analysis, you may be thinking that the array of bars or candles on a price chart looks like the ultimate in randomness. Sometimes that's true, but more often than not, you'd be surprised how frequently symmetrical formations appear. By *symmetrical formations,* we mostly mean *price channels,* but also other chart patterns that we illustrate and cover in detail in Chapter 11.

Drawing price channels

A *price channel* is nothing more complicated than a series of parallel trend lines that encapsulate price action over a discernible period. Channels will form in all time frames, with long-term channels on a daily chart highlighting multiday or multiweek trading ranges, and short-term channels on an hourly chart revealing steady buying or selling during a trading session. Price channels can also form in any direction, from horizontal to steeply sloping up or down and anything in between.

The way to identify price channels is through visual inspection, using your eyes and imagination, as well as a fair amount of trial and error. Drawing channels is made much easier by the Copy a Line and Parallel Line functions, which are standard in most charting systems. To begin looking for and drawing potential channels, you need only one trend line to start with — the *primary* trend line. (In Figure 12-7, the lower trend line in the primary upchannel is the primary trend line.)

If the primary trend line is below the price bars or candles (support), look up at the tops of the price action to see if there is any parallel symmetry to the primary support trend line. If you're not sure, simply copy the support trend line and drag it to the tops of the price bars to see if it captures the highest highs. If the copied trend line fits neatly onto the tops of the price action, you've found yourself a price channel.

That said, the parallel side (the upper channel line based on upward-sloping primary trend lines, and the lower channel line for downward-sloping primary trend lines) never behaves quite as neatly as the primary side. For example, during an uptrend most people are looking to buy; that's why the price action often goes exactly to the primary channel support and then bounces higher. However, on rallies during an uptrend, there usually aren't as many traders looking to sell and price action frequently exceeds the upper channel line. The same happens with the base of channels during declines, where fewer buyers are involved.

When you're looking for channels, especially if prices have just changed direction and a new move is just beginning, keep in mind that you may have only one or two price points opposite the primary trend line to connect the parallel channel line. When that happens, go ahead and draw the parallel channel line — it'll extend into empty space for the time being — but consider it only a tentative channel top or bottom until more price action confirms its validity.

The whole point of looking for and drawing channel lines, of course, is to highlight additional sources of support or resistance. Directional price moves rarely go from Point A to Point B in a straight line. More typically, for example, prices will move higher for a period of time before short-term buying interest fades or encounters heavier selling interest, sending prices back down to the trend-line support. When this pattern repeats itself several times, a channel is formed.

You can use channels as part of your trading strategy to guide both position entry and exit. Short-term traders in particular like to use channels to trade around a core position, for example, selling short on trend-line resistance and buying a portion of the position back if prices drop to channel support. If the channel continues to hold, they'll resell on gains back toward trend-line resistance, reestablishing their core short position. When channels break, it's also a sign that prices are either accelerating in the direction of the trend, as shown by the channel, or that the trend is reversing and prices break out of the channel in the opposite direction.

Listening to Momentum

In Chapter 11, we look at various momentum indicators, like Relative Strength Index (RSI) and stochastics, and what they mean. As part of your routine of multiple-time-frame technical analysis, we strongly suggest that you incorporate two technical studies into your regimen of analysis.

Factoring momentum analysis into your routine

The first study to include in your analysis is a momentum oscillator like RSI or stochastics. We also recommend Moving Average Convergence/Divergence (MACD) — it's not technically a momentum indicator, but it certainly acts like one. In fact, we prefer MACD over the more traditional momentum studies because MACD tends to change direction and generate crossovers more slowly than the other momentum studies. The result is fewer false signals, but the trade-off is that the signal may be delayed, giving you a less advantageous price entry level. In reality, though, the generally slower MACD signals are well suited to the forex market's tendency to push a directional move as far as it will go for as long as possible.

The second study we recommend that you include in your analysis routine is the Directional Movement Indicator (DMI) system (which we also look at in greater detail in Chapter 11). The DMI serves as a double check on the momentum study. The Average Directional Index (ADX) component of the DMI is a trend identification signal that tells you whether the market is trending, regardless of direction. Relying solely on a momentum study can lead to serious problems when the market sets off on an extended trending movement.

Momentum studies typically register overbought and oversold readings after an extensive directional move, potentially signaling that the market is ripe for a correction in the opposite direction. Worse, shorter-term momentum studies routinely cross over as price movements inevitably slow in the course of a directional, potentially trending movement, giving a signal to trade in the opposite direction. But if a trend is, in fact, taking hold, those momentum readings can be highly misleading.

The key is to double-check momentum readings with the ADX level to see if trending conditions are in place. If the ADX is above 25, you should discount what the momentum studies are indicating. Don't completely ignore what the momentum study is showing — just defer to the ADX reading while it's above 25. When the ADX tops out and turns down, you have a second indicator signaling that the directional move is likely coming to an end. If the ADX is below 25, defer to what the momentum indicators are signaling.

Most charting systems will allow you to save charts including multiple technical studies, such as MACD, RSI, stochastics, and ADX/DMI. We suggest layering the studies so only one is visible at a time, leaving the maximum amount of space to display the price chart, which is always the primary focus. You can then toggle between different studies at your convenience.

Looking at momentum in multiple time frames

Just as you were presented with starkly differing images by looking at the same price chart in different time frames, so will you be confronted with vastly different momentum readings across time frames. At any given moment, daily momentum readings may be negative and moving lower; four-hour momentum may be nearing overbought territory; and hourly momentum may have topped and turned lower.

Which one should you listen to? Simply put, all of them. The trick, however, is to keep each reading in perspective according to its time frame. Daily momentum readings develop over many days and weeks. Shorter-term readings play out in correspondingly shorter time frames.

The key is to view each period's momentum indication in line with the time frame of the study. An hourly reading that has bottomed out and turned higher suggests that prices may stop declining for a few hours and possibly begin to move higher — but it's no sure thing. Look next to the longer time frames to put the shorter-term readings into perspective. For example, if the hourly has bottomed out and started to move higher, and the four-hour reading is bottoming out in oversold territory, you may just have the makings of a larger turnaround to the upside. But if the four-hour reading is still in neutral territory and pointed lower, the hourly reading may suggest just a short-term bounce in a continuing move lower.

We like to focus on four-hour momentum readings as the principal gauge of the durability of a directional price move. Shorter-term studies, such as hourly or 90-minute, are good as early-warning indicators and guides to short-term timing, but they can be quickly overwhelmed by strong directional price moves. Daily studies tend to be too slow to give off timely signals for short- and medium-term trading, generally confirming larger directional shifts well after the fact. The four-hour period is a solid compromise that's long enough to capture intraday and multiday mini-trends without generating too many false signals, while being just short enough to give timely indications of a pending reversal.

Trading on divergences between price and momentum

In Chapter 11, we introduce the idea of bullish/bearish divergences between price and momentum. In a nutshell, a bullish divergence occurs when prices make new lows, but momentum is not making similar new lows; a bearish divergence occurs when prices make new highs, but momentum is not making similar new highs.

Figure 12-8 shows an example of a bullish divergence between price and MACD. Because momentum is an underlying gauge of the speed of a directional move and, therefore, an indication of the level of market interest behind the move, a divergence between price and momentum typically signals that the latest price movement is false or unlikely to be sustained and will eventually reverse course in the direction of the momentum. So a bullish divergence tends to signal a price rebound after fresh selling makes new lows, and a bearish divergence typically signals a price decline after last-ditch buying makes a new high.

Figure 12-8: A bullish divergence is created when new price lows are not matched by new lows in momentum, suggesting that the latest price decline may not be sustained.

Source: eSignal (www.esignal.com)

The key to trading using divergences is to be patient and wait for confirmation. The latest rally in prices, for example, may be the start of a new wave higher, and the momentum study may eventually turn around or catch up and confirm the latest gains, negating the apparent divergence. Also, prices can diverge from momentum for many hours or days. By all means, always take note of divergences when you spot them, but keep them in context:

- ✔ **Has *new* information (data, comments, and so on) come into the market?** If it's new news, it may generate a fresh wave of directional buying or selling and overwhelm the divergence. If it's old news, like reiterated comments or as-expected data that's already been discounted, it could make for an ideal divergence setup.

- ✔ **Are prices making *significant* new highs or lows?** If prices have broken below a key daily low or trend-line support, for example, fresh selling interest may be coming into the market that creates a new wave lower.

But if prices are pushing only below recent hourly lows, and longer-term support is still some distance off, the divergence will tend to correctly reflect that the price move down is invalid.

The safest way to trade off divergences is to wait for confirmation that prices are indeed reversing course in the direction of the momentum divergence. In most cases, there will be a key trend line that is guiding prices higher or lower while prices are diverging with momentum. When that trend line is broken by a price reversal, such as in Figure 12-8, you can consider it confirmation that the divergence is beginning to play out.

Using momentum for timing entry and exit

You can also use momentum studies to refine the timing of your trade entry and exit. If your analysis has led you to conclude that a long position is the way to go, for instance, and you've identified key trend-line support on which to buy, you can look at various time frames of momentum to determine the likelihood of prices actually reaching that support. If hourly momentum has turned up from oversold levels, and four-hour momentum is showing signs of bottoming out, but prices are still 50 pips away from your trend-line entry level, you may consider stepping in ahead of the trend-line support and buying sooner.

Alternatively, if daily and four-hour studies are both solidly negative, and hourly momentum has just gone through a short-term bounce higher but is now turning negative again, you can likely afford to wait for prices to reach your desired price level. (You may even rethink the overall strategy in light of such bearish momentum readings.) You can use momentum studies in the same way to gauge the likelihood of reaching your take-profit targets.

Momentum is only a gauge of the relative speed of price movements and not always a leading indicator of changes in direction. Although you should always listen to what momentum studies are saying, so you can anticipate and prepare for alternative outcomes, you should always wait for confirmation from prices themselves. Even then, markets and events have a way of throwing curve balls at you, but at least you minimized the risks by waiting for price confirmation.

Trading on Candlestick Patterns

Candlestick formations are among our favorite trade identification tools; we highlight some of the most common reversal patterns to look for in Chapter 11. There are lots more patterns where those came from, with others signaling trend continuation or consolidation. Obviously, we like to home in on the reversal patterns because we think they give us the most price bang for our analysis buck.

Most trading books say that you can analyze candles in any time frame, but we like to focus exclusively on daily and weekly candles. Our thinking is that a full day's or week's price action carries more weight than a few hours or other intraday periods. Besides, a candlestick pattern that presents itself on a daily or weekly chart typically portends a larger price movement (hundreds of pips) over the next few days or weeks rather than smaller price moves signaled by intraday candle analysis.

The other neat feature of candlesticks is that most formations offer a clearly defined price level that negates the scenario suggested by the pattern. Clarity is a rare commodity in the forex market, so when you have a tool that offers generally clearly defined scenarios, it's well worth making it a standard part of your analysis routine.

The catch with candlesticks is that the formations offer only a general directional signal, such as a recent price move higher that looks set to reverse. Even the term *reverse* doesn't necessarily mean prices will move lower — only that they're likely to stop going up. But this is the forex market, where prices are always moving, so when they stop going in one direction, they usually start going in the other direction. The other trick with candlestick formations is that they typically don't suggest tactical price levels to enter or exit. As a result, trading based on a candle formation can be a leap of faith, as in "The pattern suggests prices should move lower in coming days but doesn't indicate how high prices may go first."

One way to trade candlestick reversal patterns is to leave orders to sell at higher levels in the case of a bearish reversal pattern, or to buy at lower levels in the case of a bullish reversal formation. The selling level would be on the approach to the highs for the preceding move up, with a stop placed a margin of error above those highs, which should not be surpassed if the pattern is valid. A similar approach could be used to buy on a bullish reversal pattern. The idea is that the market may still try again in the direction of the prior move, providing you better levels at which to enter your position based on the candlestick formation.

Alternatively, or in tandem with the above strategy on an either/or basis, you can identify a key support/resistance level in the direction suggested by the candlestick pattern and place a stop-loss order to enter on the other side, in case the market moves directly as the pattern suggests. We outline a similar strategy in more detail in the following section.

Building a Trade Strategy from Start to Finish

If you've read any other trading books, you've undoubtedly seen numerous chart illustrations where the authors can point to a chart pattern and say, "See, the pattern indicates a price top," and sure as shootin', the rest of the chart shows that prices move lower. Don't you just hate that? Well, hindsight is 20/20. Don't get us wrong; we're guilty of the same thing in this book. It's largely unavoidable to get the point across.

In the real market, you're never going to have the benefit of hindsight in advance. On every chart you look at, the future is going to be blank. And that's the eternal struggle — basing decisions in the here and now on events that have yet to happen, all the while putting your money at risk.

To make amends, we do something a bit strange here and depict a trade opportunity in real time, or as real as we can make it in a book. Who knows? The trade may blow up in our faces, and we'll have a bad trade recommendation preserved in book form for posterity. The point of this exercise, however, is not to show you how good or bad we are at spotting trades. It's to give you an insight into how you may analyze the market and construct a trade strategy on a regular basis, using many of the approaches we outline in this chapter.

Follow along with Figures 12-9 and 12-10, which show some of the key daily and hourly price points we use to define our trade strategy for EUR/USD from March 21, 2011. In Chapter 11, we indicate our preference to use fundamental elements to determine the overall direction a currency pair should move, and then apply technical analysis to refine entry and exit levels.

So, how do the fundamentals for EUR/USD stack up? At the moment, pretty good in our view. European leaders have reached agreement on a long-term debt relief mechanism, and the market seems to find it credible, reducing fears of financial instability. The ECB has strongly indicated it plans to raise rates at its next meeting in a few weeks' time, while the Fed has signaled rates will stay low for the foreseeable future, giving EUR an advantage over the USD on the monetary policy outlook. Also, one week ago the G7 intervened for the first time in more than a decade to support Japanese efforts to restrain JPY strength in the aftermath of the earthquake/tsunami/nuclear disaster earlier in March. That action saw the ECB buy EUR/JPY, giving EUR/USD, and risk assets in general, a boost in the process. And the USD is generally quite weak.

As such, our expectation is to see EUR/USD strengthen further (currently 1.4230) to the 1.4450 to 1.4500 area initially, with potential to around 1.4680 based on the measured move objective of the broken bull flag last month. A look at daily Ichimoku charts shows price well above the cloud and above the Tenkan and Kijun, signs of a solid trend higher.

But we're also wary that EUR/USD has *already* gained ground on the fundamental factors we cite earlier, so we're reluctant to buy at current levels. We also note the highs from November 2010 at about 1.4250/1.4280 as a potentially significant resistance point. We definitely don't want to get long 50 points below a major daily high.

Instead, we'll look to get long at better levels. Looking at the daily chart in Figure 12-9, the break above the 1.4000/50 level stands out as the most recent acceleration in the trend higher. Maybe we'll get a chance to buy a retest of the break?

Source: eSignal (www.esignal.com)

Figure 12-9: Daily EUR/USD analysis suggests potential price targets based on the broken bull flag, but key daily highs loom just above current prices.

The hourly chart in Figure 12-10 shows prices potentially set to drift out of the primary channel, another cautionary sign. The hourly MACD is showing a bearish divergence on the newest highs, but it could also be basing out above the zero line, potentially signaling another move higher. Cross-checking with the ADX, it based out above the 25 trending level, and is currently above, but only barely. All in all, we think we have a reasonable basis to expect a pull-back lower while the 1.4280 highs hold. If they don't, we'll have a strategy for that scenario.

Our strategy then is to buy a pullback at 1.4070 for a single lot of 100,000 EUR/USD, placing our if-done/then-OCO limit buying order just above the key 1.4000/50 break level in case it's not reached. We'll place our stop below that zone, allowing for a 20-pip margin of error, at 1.3980, for a total risk of about 90 pips, or $900. Our take-profit order will be to sell at 1.4420, just below what we think will be key round number resistance in the 1.4450/4500 area, possi-bly on some option-related selling interest, too, for a potential gain of around 350 pips, or $3,500. We'll raise the stop loss to 1.4200 if the 1.4280/85 highs are tested, to lock in some profit in case of a failure.

In case prices move directly higher, we're prepared to step up and buy on a stop-loss basis at 1.4310, which would represent a clear break of both the 1.4280 highs and the 1.4300 level. But if it's triggered, we won't hang on for too long in case the break ultimately fails. We'll leave our stop at 1.4240 for a risk of around 70 pips, or $700. The take profit will be the same at 1.4420 for a potential gain of around 110 pips. Depending on the strength of any follow-through buying above 1.4280, we may opt for a trailing stop loss of 70 pips and see how the 1.4450/4500 area reacts.

Figure 12-10: Hourly EUR/USD shows some signs of a potential stall in recent gains as seen in a bearish divergence in MACD.

Source: eSignal (www.esignal.com)

So how'd the trade turn out? Surprise, surprise, it went well, but we changed what was a medium-term strategy into a short-term trade based on market developments. First, EUR/USD tried higher one more time on Tuesday, but stopped short of 1.4250 with a high at 1.4249, before turning lower. A combination of weaker Eurozone data, better U.S. data, and escalating concerns over Portuguese debt (the government collapsed on Wednesday night) saw EUR/USD drop to as low as 1.4054 (which is where the Ichimoku Tenkan line was on that day), triggering our limit entry order at 1.4070 on Thursday morning in European trading. A disappointing U.S. durable goods report later in the New York morning saw EUR/USD rebound quickly above 1.4120, eventually triggering stop-loss orders at 1.4150/70 and jumping as high as 1.4220.

With the quick bounce from the key 1.4000/50 support area identified earlier, we felt quite confident in the overall strategy. But we were also mindful of the key resistance up at 1.4250/80, which now appeared to be drawing sellers in below it. We decided to protect our profits, so we narrowed our order to a stop loss at 1.4145 (locking in 75 pips profit), just below the break-up level at 1.4150 earlier in the morning and lowering our take profit to 1.4230. The rest of Thursday traded between those levels, and we finished out the day still long one lot from 1.4070. Looking ahead, we considered headlines coming from the EU debt summit could send EUR/USD lower in a flash, and also that the German IFO survey due out on Friday morning was forecast to decline, also potentially sending EUR/USD back down. Shortly after the New York close, we decided to exit the trade and sold at 1.4175, for a gain of 105 pips, or $1,050.

What did we do right and what did we do wrong in the trade? First, we took time to analyze key price levels and identify an opportunistic entry level, placing our order just above key support, in case it wasn't reached. Second, we aggressively protected our profits, adjusting our stop-loss order based on unfolding price movements. Third, we stayed flexible regarding exiting the trade, taking into account technical levels and developing fundamental events. Last and most important, we took profit. EUR/USD could've gone to the moon on Friday (it didn't, but that's another story) and we might've missed out as our ultimate view of a higher EUR was realized. But the bottom line is that we developed a trade strategy, stuck to it, and have something to show for it. You can't go broke taking profit.

What did we do wrong? In hindsight, we could have been more aggressive and sold short above 1.4200, keeping a tight stop over 1.4250 or 1.4280, for a well-defined and relatively minimal risk. But that would have been contrary to our fundamental expectations, and we would have regretted it if it failed. We also may have then become gun-shy and reluctant to get long at even higher levels. So maybe it wasn't such a bad thing after all.

We hope this example gives you a practical idea of how to put it all together, drawing on fundamentals, chart formations, and technical analysis to identify a trade setup and construct the trading plan to exploit it. In Chapters 13, 14, and 15, we look at considerations and strategies for entering positions, managing positions, and exiting trades in much greater detail. See the appendix for a comprehensive list of actionable trading strategies.

Chapter 13

Risk-Management Considerations

. . . .

In This Chapter

▶ Understanding the different types of risk

▶ Managing leverage and inflated expectations

▶ Setting up trade plans in terms of risk

▶ Planning for the unexpected

. . . .

rading is all about risk, yet it's frequently the last thing many individual traders think about. Too often, they're fixated on the expectation of positive trading results, as in "How much can I make?" To a large extent, that's basic human nature. Why would anyone speculate in anything unless he believed he could win?

We think traders should approach the forex market with eyes wide open when it comes to the risks they're taking. And we're not talking about some simple risk formula that comes out to dollars and cents. We're looking at it from the perspective of an overall risk-taking enterprise philosophy. The more aware you are of the risks you face in the forex market, the more likely you'll be able to avoid them — and the more likely your success.

Managing Risk Is More Than Avoiding Losses

On the most basic level, *risk* in currency trading is the same as trading in any other financial market — the risk is that you'll lose money. But risk comes in many different forms and from many different sources. Sometimes the biggest risks are the ones that you never knew existed.

We believe forewarned is forearmed. In this section, we look at some of the main sources of risk that may not be readily apparent or that are easily overlooked.

Leverage amplifies gains and losses — and expectations

Leverage refers to the multiple applied to your available margin collateral, which translates into the maximum size of your market position. Leverage is typically expressed as a multiplier rate (like 10 times or 20 times) or a ratio (like 10:1 or 20:1). If the leverage rate is 10-times/ratio is 10:1, for example, and you have $1,000 of available margin, you're able to hold a maximum position equal to $10,000.

Online currency trading firms typically offer higher leverage ratios than you may be familiar with from trading stocks on margin. Leverage ratios among currency brokers are typically on the order of 100:1 for standard-size accounts (100,000 trade-lot size) and 200:1 for mini-accounts (10,000 trade-lot size). Recent regulatory changes around the world have limited maximum leverage ratios to lower levels, such as 20:1 in Hong Kong or 50:1 in the United States, which we think is more than sufficient for individual traders.

Be wary of forex brokerage firms that offer super-sized leverage. We've seen some offering up to 400-times leverage, or 400:1. We strongly discourage you from employing that much leverage. As well, regulatory limits on leverage have seen some traders go jurisdiction shopping, looking for the highest leverage available, but ending up in dodgy locales that may carry additional risks.

Leverage is a great trading tool, allowing traders with less capital to participate in markets that they couldn't trade otherwise. But leverage is still just a tool. As with any other tool (think of a chainsaw here), if you learn how to use it properly, you'll be able to get the job done faster and easier. But if you don't learn how it works, and respect it, you're asking for trouble.

Most people see only the upside benefits of leverage — the larger the position on a profitable trade, the larger the profit, right? Yes, leverage will magnify your gains, but it'll also magnify your losses — the larger the position on a losing trade, the larger the loss you'll experience. You need to have a healthy respect for the downside risk in trading, or you won't last very long.

Take an example of a $100,000/lot-size account with $10,000 in initial margin deposited at a 50:1 leverage ratio. That margin balance translates into a maximum position size of $500,000, or five lots. If you were to take a position in USD/JPY at 90.00 using the maximum position size available, every pip change in USD/JPY is worth about $55.55 ([$500,000 × 0.01 pips] ÷ 90.00 = $55.55). But USD/JPY is regularly subject to 50- to 100-pip price swings in a single day (or more). If you're positioned the wrong way, you could lose around $2,778 to $5,555 in the course of a normal, run-of-the-mill trading day. That's about 28 percent to 55 percent of your trading capital in just one trade!

The key here is to avoid being seduced by leverage. Just because you're able to get 100:1 leverage doesn't mean you have to use it all. Trading a larger position may seem sexy, but no one ever said prudent, risk-aware trading was supposed to be sexy. Use leverage as a tool to facilitate your trading strategies, not as an ego booster.

Knowing your margin requirements

Online forex brokers require margin posted as collateral to cover any losses on your trading account. To protect themselves from client losses eating up the entire margin (or going negative) in adverse market movements, online brokers typically require you to have 100 percent of available margin for any open positions.

For example, at 50:1 leverage, if you're holding a $100,000 position in USD/CHF, you'll need to have at least $2,000 of available margin to hold the position ([$100,000 ÷ 100] × 0.50 = $500). If your available margin balance falls below $2,000 at any time, even for a second or just by pip, your broker has the right to liquidate your position, which is a fancy way of saying it closes out your position for you. Your losses are locked in, and your available margin balance is reduced.

Margin balances are typically monitored by computer programs based on current market prices. If a price move causes your available margin to fall below the required level, the position will be closed — no margin call, no notification to you, just a liquidated position. You may think that's unfair, but the reality is that brokers need to liquidate losing positions at some point, or your loss will become theirs.

As a trader, it's your responsibility to read the fine print and to know the minimum margin requirements and liquidation policies before you start trading. Regulated forex brokers must disclose their policies in your customer account agreement.

Liquidation policies can vary among brokers with some closing all open positions at once (in the case of multiple open positions) and others closing the largest losing position first until the minimum requirement is met to close remaining open positions.

From a trader's perspective, you never want to be in the situation where your positions are liquidated due to insufficient margin. It means you're trading too large a position for your available margin or you've let the losses run for too long relative to your available margin. Each trade plan needs to factor in the minimum margin requirement, and it should never even come close, or you're better off with a smaller position size. We look at the critical relationship between position size and margin later in this section.

Market liquidity, volatility, and gap risk

The forex market is routinely described as the most liquid financial market in the world, and that's true. But it doesn't mean that currencies are not subject to varying liquidity conditions.

Liquidity refers to the amount of market interest (the number of active traders and the overall volume of trading) present in a particular market at any given time. From an individual trader's perspective, liquidity is usually experienced in terms of the volatility of price movements. A highly liquid market will tend to see prices move very gradually and in smaller increments. A less liquid market will tend to see prices move more abruptly and in larger price increments.

Shifting liquidity conditions can increase volatility

Forex market liquidity will vary throughout each trading day as global financial centers open and close in their respective time zones. Reduced liquidity is first evident during the Asia-Pacific trading session, which accounts for only about 21 percent of global daily trading volume. Japanese, Chinese, or Australian data or comments from regional finance officials may provoke a larger-than-expected or more-persistent reaction simply because there is less trading interest to counteract the directional move suggested by the news.

Peak liquidity conditions are in effect when European and London markets are open, overlapping with Asian sessions in their morning and North American markets in the European afternoon. Following the close of European trading, liquidity drops off sharply in what is commonly referred to as the *New York afternoon market*.

During these periods of reduced liquidity and interest, currency rates are prone to drift in narrow ranges, but are also subject to more sudden and volatile price movements. The catalyst could be a news event or a rumor, and the reduced liquidity sees prices react more abruptly than would be the case during more liquid periods.

Another common source of erratic price moves during less liquid periods is short-term market positioning. A classic example is a strong rally in a currency pair during the North American morning/European afternoon. As Europe heads home, the currency pair typically settles into a consolidation range near the upper end of the day's rally. If sufficient short positions have been established on the rally, further price gains may force some shorts to buy and cover. With reduced liquidity, prices may jump abruptly, provoking a flood of similar buying from other shorts, resulting in a *short squeeze* higher.

The same phenomenon can occur following market declines, where market longs are forced to exit in a rush on further price declines. Still another variation on this theme is sharp price reversals of an earlier rally, where longs take profit in thin conditions and the resulting price dip brings out selling by other longs rushing to preserve profits. After a sell-off, profit-taking on short positions can provoke a sharp *short-covering reversal.*

There's no way to predict with any certainty how price movements will develop in such relatively illiquid periods, and that's the ultimate point in terms of risk. The bottom line is that if you maintain a position in the market during these periods of thin liquidity, you're exposed to an increased risk of more volatile price action.

Liquidity is also reduced by market holidays in various countries and seasonal periods of reduced market interest, such as the late summer and around the Easter and Christmas/New Year holidays.

Typically, holiday sessions result in reduced volatility as markets succumb to inertia and remain confined to ranges. The risks also increase for sudden breakouts and major trend reversals. Aggressive speculators, such as hedge funds, exploit reduced liquidity to push markets past key technical points, which forces other market participants to respond belatedly, propelling the breakout or reversal even further. By the time the holiday is over, the market may have moved several hundred points and established an entirely new direction.

Just because you're enjoying an extended holiday weekend doesn't mean you're not exposed to risk from higher volatility in holiday markets. You are — and you need to factor liquidity conditions into your overall trading plan.

Getting a handle on volatility

Volatility is a statistical term referring to price fluctuations (standard deviation) relative to the average price over a specified period of time. Volatility is what makes the trading world go 'round, and without it, speculators would have a lot of time on their hands.

But not all volatility is created equal, and you need to be aware of two main types of volatility that can alter the currency playing field:

- ✔ **Market volatility:** Market volatility is the overall level of price volatility in various financial markets at any given time. The VIX S&P 500 volatility index is a good overall barometer of market volatility. Market volatility typically increases during periods of uncertainty or unexpected economic data or monetary policy developments. If you're trading on a short-term basis or using a model that relies on relatively low volatility (for example, mean reverting systems, moving averages, or regression channels), you need to be aware that increased volatility can quickly swamp such strategies. Better to stay on the sidelines and sit out the upheavals than jump in with a strategy unsuited to higher volatility.

✔ **Currency-pair volatility:** Different currency pairs trade with different volatility characteristics, both in the short and long term. Before you go with a trade setup in a currency pair you've spotted on a chart, make sure you're aware of the pair's relative volatility. (We discuss individual currency-pair volatility and other trading characteristics in greater detail in Chapters 8 and 9.)

Minding the gap

Gap risk refers to the potential for prices to *gap,* or jump from one price level to another with no tradeable prices in between. Gap risk typically is associated with events such as economic data reports, central bank rate decisions, and other major news events. In that sense, most gap risk is identifiable in advance by looking at data and event calendars. Unexpected news or official comments can also trigger price gaps. Breaks of key technical levels are another source of price gaps.

Gaps vary in size depending on the nature of the news, but price gaps of 20 to 80 pips or more are not uncommon in currencies after major news and data events. Gaps occur because the interbank market reduces its bids and offers in the minutes or so immediately before and after major announcements, leaving online currency trading platforms with no prices to show individual traders.

After the news is out, interbank traders adjust their prices to reflect the news, resulting in a price gap higher or lower. It may be up to 30 seconds (or more depending on the news or event) before normal pricing returns.

If you're holding open positions at the time of major data releases or events, you're subject to gap risk. The same goes for stop-loss orders left with online brokers — stop-loss executions are subject to gap risk. Depending on market circumstances, stop-loss order executions will see *slippage* (meaning, your stop-loss order may not be filled at the rate you specified). In the case of price gaps, brokers are obligated only to fill your order on a "best efforts" basis.

Don't expect to be able to leave a stop-loss order nearby on either side of the market before a major news or data event and have it filled at your order rate. Occasionally, the market will take out both sides of the stop-loss orders before the release ever hits the market, locking in your loss. If that doesn't happen, and the market gaps through one side of your order, you're subject to slippage, and you'll be filled where the market resumes trading, which could be substantially different from where you left your order.

If you're thinking that this is some trick that online brokers cooked up to sock it to individual traders, keep this in mind: The big players in the interbank market are subject to the same gap risk as individuals trading online. Even if you were a prop trader (see Chapter 3) at some big bank, with one of your own bank's traders watching your order, you're going to get filled where your trader is able to execute the order in the market. The same applies to online brokerages. ***Bottom line:*** No market-maker will survive very long if he fills his customers at rates even he can't access.

The other type of gap risk stems from events that occur over weekends, potentially resulting in a substantial gap between Friday's closing level and the Sunday/Monday opening price. Weekend gap risk is typically also identifiable in advance because it most often occurs around scheduled events like a G20 meeting or a Chinese data release.

That said, there's still plenty of potential for unexpected events (earthquakes, terrorism, and currency revaluations or devaluations, to name just a few) to happen over weekends. To judge the risks of a weekend gap, you need to have a good sense of what's going on in the major currency nations and a healthy sense of expecting the unexpected. The safest approach is simply not to hold positions over a weekend.

We have a winner here! Protecting your profits

It's one thing to speculate in the market and get the direction wrong. That's good old-fashioned risk-taking, and it's just part of the business of trading. But it's another result entirely to get the direction right and still lose money, or not make as much as you could have, or not keep as much as you'd already made.

Most traders can readily accept the idea of getting the direction wrong. They shrug it off and get back to work in short order. But take a trader with a winning position in the morning that goes south in the afternoon, and you're suddenly looking at a case study of negative trader emotions. With a wrong-way trade, it's a simple case of not missing what you never had. With a good trade gone bad, it's hard not to feel regret or think the market is out to get you.

Experienced traders know that keeping what you've made is often as hard as making it in the first place, so they guard their profits aggressively. The best way to do that is by adjusting your stop loss in the direction of the trade once it's in the money. You can do this by using either a *trailing stop loss* or manually changing your original stop loss based on specific price levels being surpassed.

A trailing stop loss is a stop-loss order that automatically trails the market at a user-defined distance (say, 40 pips). For example, if you're short at 55, and you have a 40-pip trailing stop loss, the stop starts out at 95. As the market moves lower, the trailing stop will adjust so that it is always 40 pips from the low. If the market trades down to 10, your trailing stop is now at 50, guaranteeing you at least a 5-pip profit. Trailing stops are great for catching longer-term movements, because they rely on a market reversal of *x* pips before being triggered.

If you're more inclined to trade according to technical levels, you may want to consider manually adjusting your stop loss after specific levels are broken. For example, if you're long, you may raise your stop loss from its original level after technical resistance has been broken.

Above all, if the market reverses and your profit starts to decline, don't worry about getting back what you've just lost — worry about keeping what you've still got.

Placing your orders effectively

Currency traders rely on orders to take advantage of price movements when they're not able to personally monitor the market and also to protect themselves from adverse price movements. If you're going to be trading currencies, odds are that you'll be relying on orders as part of your overall trade strategy. We cover the various types of orders in greater detail in Chapter 4.

The two main types of orders are *limit orders,* used to buy or sell at rates more favorable than current market prices, and *stop-loss orders,* which are used to buy or sell at worse rates than prevailing levels. The key difference between the two types is that you generally want your limit orders to get filled, but you don't want your stop-loss orders to be triggered. That's because limit orders are used to take profit and enter positions (which you want), and stop-loss orders are used mainly to exit losing positions (which nobody likes). (The exception is stop-loss entry orders, in which you use a stop-loss order to enter a position — on a breakout, for example [see Chapter 14].)

The risk with using orders is that you miss having your take-profit limit or entry orders filled or that your stop-loss orders are triggered at extreme price points. The catch here is that markets have a penchant for going after stop-loss orders and shying away from limit orders in the routine noise of daily fluctuations.

That makes where you place your orders a critical factor in your overall trading strategy. Deciding where to place orders is definitely more art than science, and even the most experienced currency traders continually grapple with the question of where to place their orders.

Factoring in the dealing spread with orders

Online currency traders face two other complicating factors: the dealing spread of the currency pairs and the order execution policies of online currency trading platforms.

Most online platforms execute on the basis that a limit order to sell is filled when the bid price reaches the order rate and a limit order to buy is filled when the offer price reaches the order rate. In the case of stop losses, a stop-loss order to sell is triggered if the bid price reaches the order rate, and a stop order to buy is executed if the offer price reaches the order rate. In both cases, the dealing spread works against the order, and traders need to take that into account.

For example, you may be long USD/CHF at 1.0250 with a limit, take-profit order, to sell at 1.0330 and a stop-loss order to sell at 1.0200. For your take profit to be executed, the dealing price must print 1.0330/33. If the highest price quoted is 1.2329/32, no cigar. Your stop loss would be triggered if the dealing price ever trades at 1.0200/03; if the lowest quoted price is 1.0201/04, your order is still alive. As you can see, it's frequently a game of inches played out in milliseconds.

Factoring in technical levels when placing orders

Many traders focus on technical levels to decide where to place their orders. Continuing the order example from the last section, if there is resistance from a trend line or hourly highs at the 1.0330 level, many other sell orders could be grouped there. If the selling interest is strong enough, the market may never get that high because sellers step in front of the resistance level, start selling, and stop prices from rising.

In the case of the stop-loss level, it may be placed on Fibonacci retracement support or recent daily lows, which may also attract other technically minded traders to place their stops at the same level. If the market starts to move lower, sellers will frequently try to test key technical-support levels to see if they hold, in the process triggering stop-loss orders left at those levels. The stops may be triggered and the level exceeded briefly, only to see prices rebound and the support ultimately hold.

Getting stopped out at a market top or bottom is a very frustrating experience, but it's happened to everyone at one point or another. **Remember:** Someone has to sell at the low and buy at the high.

Margins of error and market extremes

One way to prevent getting stopped out by market extremes is to factor in a margin of error when placing your orders. Using a margin of error is a fairly sophisticated practice, but the idea is to err on the side of getting your limit order filled — leaving a sell order a few points below key resistance levels or a buy order a few points above support levels. At a minimum, the margin of error should account for the dealing spread of the currency pair you're trading.

For stop losses, the concept is to err on the side of not allowing your stop to be triggered — leaving a stop-loss sell order several points below key support levels and a stop-loss buy order above technical resistance levels.

In both cases, the margin of error will depend on the relative volatility of the currency pair you're trading as well as overall market volatility at the time. Generally speaking, the greater the volatility, the greater the margin of error, and vice versa. (We look at individual currency pair volatility and trading behavior in greater detail in Chapters 8 and 9.) Our own preference for limit orders is for a small margin of error of around 5 to 10 pips. For stop losses, we like to use a wider margin of error of around 20 to 40 pips, allowing for a greater cushion in case others' stops get triggered and the technical level is briefly broken.

Using a margin of error in placing orders will also require you to rethink the overall trade strategy, especially in terms of position size. If you're going to place stops with a margin of error, and the stop ends up getting triggered anyway, your losses will be greater. So you may need to reduce the position size to mitigate the impact on your margin.

Placing stop-loss orders based on technical or financial levels

There are generally two schools of thought when it comes to the basis for deciding where to place stop-loss orders:

- **Technical stops:** Placing a stop-loss order according to price levels identified through technical analysis. Whatever technical approach you choose to follow, you'll be looking to identify key technical points that, if exceeded, will invalidate the trade setup and signal that it's time to get out of the trade.

- **Financial stops:** Based on the amount of money you're prepared to risk on a given trade. You may base the trade on a fundamental view of future developments, but you're willing or able to risk only a certain amount of money on the trade.

Financial stops may be appealing to highly conservative traders who don't want to risk more than a fixed amount on any single trade. If that's your way of maintaining trading discipline, by all means go with it. But we think it's important to note that financial stops are essentially arbitrary and have no relation to the market. They're much more a function of position size and entry price — elements you control — than any objective market measure.

Technical stops, on the other hand, are based on past price action, which is about the only concrete way traders have of gauging future price movements. If GBP/USD has repeatedly failed to trade above 1.6215 in recent weeks, to pick a random price as an example, a move above that level suggests that something has changed. And the market, in its infinite wisdom, has decided that GBP/USD should move higher. We have no way of knowing for sure whether the break will be sustained; we can only go with our best analysis.

Our own preference is to base orders on technical levels rather than financial considerations, but the ultimate limiting factor is the amount of money at risk. That may sound like we're trying to have it both ways — we explain this idea further in the next section.

Applying Risk Management to the Trade

When it comes to trading, risk management is frequently an afterthought — that is, until you take a loss that you weren't expecting. Suddenly, the wisdom of the ages is upon you, and you vow never to let it happen again.

By the way, who in her right mind would ever put on a trade expecting to take a loss, anyway? Sounds crazy, right? But all the experienced traders we know calculate the risk they're facing in every trade before they ever enter it. It's part of their decision-making DNA and goes a long way to determining which trade opportunities they pursue and which ones they skip.

We strongly recommend that traders approach the forex market with risk management as the first thought. It's how you'll be able to get some trades wrong and still survive to get other trades right.

Analyzing the trade setup to determine position size

The starting point for any successful trade is developing a well-conceived trading plan. And the most important element of a trading plan is the size of the position that will be traded. Position size will determine how much money is ultimately at risk, as well as the overall viability of the trade.

But position size is only one half of the equation that determines how much money is at risk. The second half of the equation is the pip distance between the entry price and the stop-loss level. Wait a minute, you may be thinking. Why didn't we mention the upside potential or the pip distance between the entry price and the take profit? Why aren't we looking at how much money we can make on the trade?

Save the rose-colored glasses for buying lottery tickets. When you're plunking down a dollar or two, it's okay to focus only on the upside and dream about winning millions. But when you're trading in any financial market, you have to remember the market is not there to give you money.

We know you're not drawn to currency trading for the chance to lose money. You're interested in making money, and you're prepared to take some risks to do that. The question is how much risk are you prepared to accept. Because you're dealing with finite resources in your trading — the amount of risk capital you've devoted to your trading — you have a definite limiting factor to your trading. If you eat through your trading capital, you're done. So the starting point of a risk-aware trading plan has to focus on the downside risks.

That brings us to the trade setup, which we cover in greater detail in Chapter 12. A *trade setup* is a trade opportunity that you've identified through either fundamental or technical analysis, or a combination of both.

In every trade setup, you need to identify the price point where the setup is invalidated — where the trade is wrong. For example, if you're looking to sell a currency pair based on trend-line resistance above, price gains beyond the trend line would invalidate your rationale for wanting to be short. So the price level of the trend line is the line in the sand for the overall strategy.

Now comes the entry point for the trade. Let's say that current market prices are 50 pips below the trend-line resistance you've identified. That means the market could move higher by 50 pips and your trade setup would still be valid, but you'd be out of the money by 50 pips. You now have a clear delineation of how much risk your trade setup would require you to assume. If you get in now, you're risking at least 50 pips.

Alternatively, you could reduce that risk by waiting and using an order to try selling at better levels — say, 25 pips higher. If the market cooperates and your limit-entry order is filled, you're now risking only 25 pips before your trade setup is negated.

So how large a position should you commit to the trade? From a risk standpoint, it all depends where you're able to enter the trade relative to your stop-out level (see the following section).

Doing the math to put the risk in cash terms

After you've identified where your stop-loss point is — where the trade setup is negated — and where you're able to enter, you're able to calculate the amount of risk posed by the trade. Let's say you're inclined to enter the position at current market levels, and your stop is 50 pips away. For example, if you're trading a standard-size account (100,000 lot size), and the trade is in NZD/USD (where profit and loss accrues in USD), each lot would translate into risking $500 (100,000 × 0.0050 NZD/USD pips = $500).

If your margin balance is $10,000, you're risking 5 percent of your trading capital per lot in this trade, which is frequently cited as the maximum risk in any one trade.

There are no hard and fast rules as to how much you should risk in any single trade, but we recommend limiting your risk to no more than 10 percent of your account balance.

If you're able to enter the position at a better level (say, using the order to sell 25 pips higher), you're now risking only 25 pips on the trade. You could double the position size and still be risking the same amount of trading capital. Or you could stick with the single lot and cut your risk in half.

Devising the trading plan in terms of risk

Risk in the trading plan is not confined simply to losing money on the trade. There are also opportunity risks from trade setups that you're not able to enter. Another old market saying is that some of the best trades are the hardest to get into. You may be eyeing a trade setup that involves buying a dip toward rumored buying orders or significant technical support. But what happens if the dip never comes?

Identifying the trade entry points

Winning or losing on a trade is difficult if you never get into the position in the first place, which makes identifying where to get into the trade one of the most important steps in any trading plan.

We like to use technical analysis as the primary means of identifying entry levels. When looking to identify entry points, we focus on the following technical levels:

- Trend lines in various time frames (daily, four-hour, and hourly)
- Hourly highs and lows for short-term intraday position entries
- Daily highs and lows for medium- to longer-term positions
- Congestion zones
- Fibonacci retracements of prior price movements (38.2 percent, 50 percent, 61.8 percent, and 76.4 percent)
- Spike highs and lows

After you've identified a price point to enter into the trade, double-check the level. Is the entry level realistic? If you're looking to enter a short-term trade, is your entry point likely to be reached in the short-term time frame (minutes to hours)? You can use momentum readings to help gauge the likelihood of an order level being reached. For example, if hourly momentum readings are moving lower, a buy entry to the downside probably stands a better chance of being reached than a sell entry above.

What happens if your entry level is never reached? Do you have a backup plan? If you were planning on selling on further rallies, for example, but the market moves directly lower, is there a price level below that you would consider selling at on a stop-entry basis? What does that backup plan mean for your overall trade stop level? Should you reduce the position size to compensate for the worse entry rate?

Establishing stop losses with foresight

The stop-loss level is the starting point in any trade plan from an overall risk perspective. It's the point where the trade setup is negated and the strategy fails.

When considering where to place the stop level, be aware that the currency market, like most financial markets, has a tendency to try to take out levels where stop losses are likely to be located. Nothing is worse than having the right strategy but being taken out by a short-term, stop-loss-driven price move that eventually reverses and goes in the direction of your outlook.

To guard against the risk of being unnecessarily whipsawed out of a position, you need to approach selecting your stop-loss level from a defensive point of view. Anticipate that the market *will* test the level where the trade setup is invalidated, such as trend-line support or hourly lows. Then consider if the market tests that level, how far must it go through before it's really considered a break.

No set formula exists for this calculation, but allowing for a margin of error can sometimes prevent a stop loss from being triggered unnecessarily. The margin of error you apply will depend on the general volatility of the currency pair you're trading, as well as on the overall market volatility at the time of the trade.

Above all, you need to balance the risk of being taken out on a false move with the larger risk that your overall strategy is wrong. You can be flexible up to a point, but you still need to set your ultimate stop loss and then stick to it.

Setting take-profit objectives dynamically

When it comes to establishing the take-profit objective, a lot of trading books recommend using some sort of risk/reward ratio, like 2:1 (meaning, if you're prepared to risk 50 points on a trade, you should be aiming to make 100 points). That approach is all well and good in theory, but it fails to account for the realities of the market. Just because you've identified a trade opportunity that risks *x* amount, why would the market necessarily "reward" you with twice that amount in profit?

Instead, we suggest using a much more dynamic market-based approach, one that considers where the market is likely to go based on where it's been (technical analysis) and overall market conditions. The idea is to be *realistic* about how much you can take out of the market, not *idealistic* about how much the market will reward you.

We focus on technical support and resistance levels as the primary guide-posts in the progress of market movements. If you're looking to buy based on a Fibonacci retracement level as support, for example, you're going to be looking at technical resistance levels above for your take-profit targets. Chart formations, such as channels and flags, also suggest relatively predictable and attainable price targets.

We look to momentum indicators like Moving Average Convergence/Divergence (MACD) and stochastics as gauges of the underlying speed of the price move-ment. If short-term momentum is accelerating in the direction of the trade, stay with it, and consider revising your take-profit objectives to capture a larger move. But if short-term momentum in the direction of the trade is slowing or stalling, consider scaling back your profit targets and adopting a more defen-sive, profit-protecting stance, like raising your stop loss or taking partial profit.

Time is another important consideration in dynamically managing your profit objectives. You need to be aware of and anticipate upcoming events and market conditions. If you've been long for a rally during the North American morning, what's likely to happen when European markets begin to close up for the day? If you're positioned in USD/JPY in the New York afternoon, and Japanese industrial production is slated to be released in a few hours, what can you expect in the interim? Stay flexible and dynamic, just like the market.

Choosing Your Trading Broker

With the explosion in online currency trading over the past several years, dozens of forex brokerage firms now operate all over the world. Competition among various brokerages is fierce, and there's no shortage of advertising seeking to win you as a client. In this section, we look at some of the differ-ences between forex brokerages from a risk perspective, because where you trade can sometimes influence your trading outcomes.

In case you skipped the introduction to this book, we think it's important in the interest of full disclosure to note that we're affiliated with FOREX.com. Before you choose a broker, we recommend you take a look at the Cheat Sheet, where we provide a list of questions to ask.

Different business models of brokers

Most online forex brokers function as the market-maker for your trading, meaning that the broker is on the other side of every trade — when you buy, you're buying from the broker; when you sell, you're selling to the broker.

Brokerage firms that are market-makers typically provide both consistent liquidity and execution, which allows you to trade your desired amount at all times.

Market-makers typically offer either fixed spreads or variable spreads:

- ✓ **Fixed spreads** remain constant all the time, regardless of what's happening in the market. Because the broker must assume the additional market risk of quoting a fixed spread all day long (including in thinly traded or volatile markets, when interbank spreads tend to widen), fixed spreads tend to be slightly wider than variable spreads.

- ✓ **Variable spreads** fluctuate depending on market interest. In highly liquid periods — such as the overlap between the London and New York sessions — variable spreads will be the tightest (as low as 1 or 2 pips in EUR/USD and the other heavily traded currency pairs). In slower periods (such as 6 p.m. Eastern time [ET], when New York is closed and Asia is not yet fully online), spreads will tend to be wider.

Whether you should choose fixed spreads or variable spreads largely depends on your trading style. If you're a short-term trader looking to make just a few pips on each trade, you're probably better off with variable spreads, which are tightest in liquid markets. If you trade around news, fixed spreads will allow you to avoid the inevitable widening of spreads (sometimes by a significant amount) that typically happens around fundamental announcements.

Another model being promoted by a few brokers is the *nondealing desk* model. The term is meant to differentiate these brokers from market-making brokers — who have trading, or *dealing,* desks — that manage the firm's market exposure. Nondealing desk brokers will tell you that the price you're trading on is coming directly from the interbank market and that they route all your trades directly to the banks. But if that's the case, why is the nondealing desk broker even needed? Online forex brokers have emerged precisely because the large institutional players did not have the capacity to process tens of thousands of individual trades.

More important, if the nondealing desk is commission free and routing every trade to a bank, how does it make any money? A legitimate nondealing desk firm will offer very tight bid/offer spreads and charge commissions for each trade.

Commission-free forex brokers are compensated by the spread between the bid and the offer. If you buy from a broker at 15, for example, and another trader at the same time sells to the broker at 14, 13, or 12, the broker realizes a profit from the spread.

The reality with the nondealing-desk approach is that such trading platforms may display wider prices and sharper price gaps during periods of volatility, all the while claiming no control over the prices being shown. Be careful about promises of dealing in the interbank market — if it sounds too good to be true, it usually is.

Financial risks of brokers

The main financial risk posed by forex brokerages involves the brokerage firm's failing due to mismanagement or fraud, as happened in the case of MF Global in 2011. If a brokerage collapses, your trading account could be frozen and your funds tied up in bankruptcy proceedings for months or lost forever.

To reduce that prospect, you need to make sure your broker is registered with the appropriate financial authorities in the jurisdiction where it operates. In the United States, forex brokers are required to be registered as a Futures Commission Merchant/Retail Foreign Exchange Dealer (FCM/RFED) with the Commodity Futures Trading Commission (CFTC) and are ultimately subject to CFTC rules and regulations. The National Futures Association (NFA) is the self-regulating body for forex brokers, similar to FINRA (formerly known as NASD, or the National Association of Securities Dealers), which oversees stock brokers regulated by the Securities and Exchange Commission (SEC).

You can visit the NFA's website at www.nfa.futures.org to check on the regulatory status of a prospective broker. You should also review the brokerage firm's regulatory history and its overall financial condition. Go with firms that have solid histories and strong financials.

Technology Issues and Contingency Planning

Online currency trading presents its own host of potential technological problems that you need to be prepared for. We cover the primary technology risks originating from the broker's side in the previous section, but plenty of things can go wrong on *your* side of the connection.

Unfortunately, it's the catch-22 of today's technology: Without it, you couldn't access the forex market in the first place — but when there's a problem, it's just another example of modern technology making your life more difficult. The trick is to anticipate what can happen and be prepared for when it does. We talk about the problems with technology in Chapter 4.

Contingency planning is the name of that game, and redundancy is the solution. By *redundancy,* we mean having a backup plan for your backup plan, with a backup plan in case the other backup plan fails. Now try saying that three times fast.

In particular, if your Internet connection is disrupted, make sure you're able to call your brokerage's trading desk; memorize its phone number and any account numbers or passwords you need to verify your identity, in case you need to trade or place orders over the phone.

Above all, make sure to do the following:

✔ **Always have a stop-loss order in place for any open positions.** This is your first and ultimate backup plan for any and all contingencies. Also, make sure your stop-loss order is good until canceled, so it'll never expire while the position is open.

✔ **Write down your open positions and orders.** Keep a hard copy of all your trades and orders in a notebook or trading journal so you can refer to it in the event of an emergency. If you can't access your brokerage's trading platform, you won't be able to see your exposure.

Part IV
Executing a Trading Plan

Source: eSignal (www.esignal.com)

In this part . . .

- ✔ Open up your first trading position.
- ✔ Understand the trade-off between a great trade idea and opening a position at the best price.
- ✔ Find out the most common ways to enter a trade.
- ✔ Monitor the trade while it's active.
- ✔ Discover how to close a position.

Chapter 14

Pulling the Trigger

"**Y**ou gotta be in it to win it" is a favorite saying that currency traders like to throw around. The "in it" part refers to being "in" the market, having the right directional view expressed with an open position (long/short) in a currency pair.

But there's always a trade-off between having the right position and getting into that position at the most advantageous price. For example, being short AUD/USD may be the correct position to have, but if you enter at the wrong price, you may have to endure some pain before the trade moves your way.

In this chapter, we walk you through some of the different ways of entering trades and establishing the position to fit your overall strategy.

Getting into the Position

You can make trades in the forex market one of two ways: You can trade *at the market,* or the current price, using the click-and-deal feature of your broker's platform; or you can employ orders, such as limit orders and if/ then contingent orders. (We discuss order types in Chapter 4.) But there's a lot more to it than that. Certain trade setups suggest a combination of both methods for entering a position, while others rely strictly on orders to capture rapid or unexpected price movements. Then there's the fine art of timing the market to get in at the best price at the moment.

Buying and selling at the current market

Many traders like the idea of opening a position by trading at the market as opposed to leaving an order that may or may not be executed. They prefer the certainty of knowing that they're in the market. Actively buying and selling is also what makes trading as fun and exhilarating as it is hard work.

Deciding whether to enter now (at the market) or wait for better price levels (using orders) depends greatly on the nature of your strategy. If you're aiming to trade short term (minutes/hours) on news or economic data reports, for instance, you're going to be trading mostly at the market. If you're looking to position for a larger price adjustment over the next day(s), you're better off using orders to execute your market entry.

For short-term trade entry at the market, you want a good handle on the recent price action, which means knowing where prices have been over the past several hours. Just because you've settled on a strategy to buy USD/CAD doesn't mean you have to close your chart window, open your trading platform, and pay the offer.

Take a step back and look at shorter-term charts, such as 5 or 15 minutes, to get an idea of where prices have been trading recently. Chances are you'll observe a relatively narrow range of price action, typically between 20 and 30 pips. Unless the situation is urgent, a little patience can go a long way toward improving your entry level. Why buy at 1.0550 when you have a viable chance to buy at 1.0535?

Let the routine price fluctuations work to your advantage by trying to buy on downticks and sell on upticks in line with your overall strategy. Selecting your trade size in advance helps — so when the price gets to your desired level, you need to click only once to execute the trade. You can also use limit orders to buy or sell just a few pips from the current market, letting the broker's platform execute automatically in case the price moves are too quick to click and deal manually.

As you watch the price action, keep a disciplined entry price in mind, both in your favor and in case prices start to move away from your desired entry level. If the market cooperates and moves to your desired trade entry price, stay with your plan and make the trade. If prices move away from you, have a worst-case entry level in mind and be prepared to pull the trigger so you can still execute your overall strategy. You may not be able to enter at better prices every time, but we think you'll be surprised how often you can.

Averaging into a position

Medium- and longer-term trade strategies typically benefit from averaging into a position. *Averaging into a position* refers to the practice of buying/selling at successively lower/higher prices to improve the average rate of the desired long/short position. The idea here is to allow larger market swings to unfold and use them to establish a larger position at better prices than current levels in anticipation that the market will eventually reverse course in line with your strategy.

Take a look at a detailed example of averaging into a position to see how it works. Imagine that the USD/JPY is moving lower from 82.20 on a weak U.S. economic release, but you think USD/JPY is unlikely to decline below 81.00, where the 200-day moving average is located.

One possible strategy would be to buy USD/JPY on the current weakness, spacing your buys so that you can buy as low as possible, but above 81.00 where you don't expect it to trade. (The stop-loss exit in this example would be somewhere below 81.00.) Imagine that you buy one lot of USD/JPY at the market, now at 82.00, just so you have some piece of the position in case the market rebounds abruptly. You decide that 81.20 is another good level to buy at because it's a margin of error above the key 81.00 level. If your order to buy at 81.20 is filled, you'll be long two lots at an average price of 81.60 ([82.00 + 81.20] ÷ 2 = 81.60).

Take a look at what just happened there. To begin with, you were long one lot from 82.00. To add to the position at 81.20 means the market was trading lower, which also means you were looking at an unrealized loss of –80 pips on your initial position from 82.00. After you buy the second lot, your unrealized loss has not changed substantially (assuming that the market is still at 81.20 and excluding the spread, you're still out –80 pips, now –40 pips on 2 lots), but your position size has just doubled, which means your risk has also just doubled.

If the market rebounds from 81.20, your unrealized loss will be reduced. But if the market continues to decline, your losses are going to be twice what they were had you not added on to your position. If your strategy plays out and the market reverses higher, you now have a larger position from a better entry price than if you had entered the two lot position earlier at higher levels.

We've seen the practice referred to as *pyramiding* in other trading books, and the advice is usually to avoid doing it (as in "Don't pyramid into a losing position"). Sometimes "adding on" to winning positions is acceptable, such as after a technical level breaks in the direction of your trade. The result of adding on to winning positions, however, is a worse average rate for the overall position — a higher average long price or a lower average short price. If the market reverses after you add on, any gains in the overall trade can be quickly erased.

So what's the deal? Should you average into positions or not? As with most questions on trading tactics, the answer is a straightforward "It depends." Before deciding whether to average into positions, consider the following:

- ✔ **Time frame of the trade:** Short-term trades seek to exploit the immediate direction of the market. If you're wrong on the direction in the first place, adding to the position at better rates will likely only compound your losses. For medium- and longer-term trades, averaging into a position can make sense if the trade setup anticipates a market reversal. (We talk about this a bit more in the "When averaging into a position makes sense" section, later in this chapter.)

- ✔ **Account size:** Depending on your account size, you may not have the capability to add to positions. You also need to keep in mind that adding to a position will further reduce your available margin, which reduces your cushion against adverse price movements, bringing you closer to liquidation due to insufficient margin. If that means trading smaller position sizes, such as 10,000 mini-lots, go with that.

- ✔ **Volatility:** If the overall market or the currency pair you're trading is experiencing heightened volatility, averaging into trades is probably not a good idea. Increased volatility is usually symptomatic of uncertainty or fresh news hitting the market, both of which are prone to see more extreme directional price moves, in which case averaging is a losing proposition. In contrast, lower volatility conditions tend to favor range-trading environments, where averaging can be successful.

Signs that averaging into a trade is not a good idea

Many trading books recommend avoiding averaging into, or adding on to, a losing position — and with good reason. The tactic can lead to dramatically higher losses on smaller incremental price movements. Also, if you're adding on to a losing position, you're missing out on the current directional move. In other words, not only are you losing money, but you're also not making money, which is the opportunity cost of averaging.

But that still doesn't stop people from averaging into losing trades, even professional traders. Here are some indications that averaging is probably not a good idea:

- ✔ **The market just blew through your stop-loss level.** But you didn't have a stop-loss order in place, so you're still holding onto the losing position. First tactical error: Trading without an active stop-loss order. Second tactical error: Instead of exiting the position in line with your trade plan, you're reluctant to take the larger loss than you initially reckoned with, so you decide to hold on to the position, hoping it will recover. This is usually the first wipeout on the slippery slope of relinquishing trading discipline. Save yourself some money and don't commit a third tactical error by averaging into an even larger position (which you had already planned to be out of by that point anyway).

✔ **The range just broke.** You may have had great success in recent trades playing a range-bound market, and you're in a position again based on that range. But ranges do break, and prices do move to new levels. Remember the basis for your trade — the range is going to hold — and don't hang on, much less add on, to positions beyond your predetermined stop-loss exit level based on the range.

✔ **News is out, but the currency pair is not responding the way it should.** The news or data may be USD-positive, for example, but the dollar is coming under selling pressure anyway. Keep in mind that multiple cross-currents are at work at any given moment in the forex market. Sometimes they're position related (a large hedge fund may be turning around a multibillion-dollar position); other times they're based on news or information that is not widely known in the market, like a mergers-and-acquisitions (M&A) deal or a rumor. *Remember:* The market reaction to a news/data report is more important than the report itself. If you've taken a position based on the news, don't second-guess the market reaction by adding on to the position if the market doesn't respond the way you think the data indicates. Instead, accept that something else is going on and that the news you based your trade on is not it.

When averaging into a position makes sense

Depending on the trade setup, you may be entirely justified in averaging into a position. In fact, with some trade opportunities, you'll be hoping to have the chance to average into the position at better rates, because if the trade setup is correct, you'll want to have on as large a position as possible.

Even though we're suggesting that certain trade opportunities warrant averaging into a position, we want to stress that you still need to identify the ultimate stop-loss exit point in every trade setup. In other words, you can average into a position as much as you want up to a certain point, but after that the trade setup is invalidated, and you need to exit the position.

The trade setups we're referring to are those where a *reversal* is anticipated. Prices frequently move into *counter-trend consolidation ranges,* where prices move in the opposite direction of the primary trend for a time before the trend resumes. You may see signs of an impending reversal from daily candlestick patterns, such as a shooting star/hammer or a tweezers top/bottom. You may begin to suspect a reversal after a significant intraday spike reversal/rejection from key technical levels. The market may also be nearing important long-term trend-line support or resistance that suggests a medium-term bottom or top is close by.

What all these setups have in common is a price difference between current market levels and the ideal entry point based on the setup. For example, major daily trend-line resistance dating back six months may lie above in EUR/USD at 1.2960/70. Current market levels are well below at 1.2890, and there has been a spike rejection from an intraday test to 1.2930/35. Adding up these observations, we may justifiably conclude that the current market price is just below an area of major resistance, suggesting a short position as the overall way to proceed.

But we have no accurate way of predicting how much higher the market might trade, or even if it will, before the anticipated reversal lower takes place. The market could start moving directly lower from current levels. It could retest the spike highs seen earlier in the day, or it could make it all the way to test the key trend-line resistance before stalling. So where might we look to get short?

The answer is in that zone of resistance we just identified between current market levels and the daily trend-line resistance. This is where it makes sense to average into a trade to exploit the trade setup.

As an example of our own approach, we may not know how much higher the market will go, so we may be prepared to short a portion of the over-all position at current market levels, in case the top has already been seen and prices move directly lower. We may also be prepared to sell remaining portion(s) of the position at successively higher levels, if the market allows it. We'll save our last portion of the position for the trend-line resistance level in case it's reached.

When considering where to leave your limit-entry orders to average into a trade, be aware of what your final average rate will be if all your orders are filled. The difference between that average rate and your stop-loss level multiplied by the total position size will give you the total amount you're risking on the trade. (In Chapter 16, we look at the profit/loss implications of closing out a multiple lot position that was averaged into.)

Although there are no 100 percent accurate gauges to tell us how much higher the market is likely to trade, we can use short-term momentum studies — such as stochastic models, the Relative Strength Index (RSI), or Moving Average Convergence/Divergence (MACD) — to make an educated guess as to how much more upside potential there may be.

If hourly momentum studies have already topped out and crossed over to the downside, for example, the upside potential is likely more limited. This may argue for being more aggressive in establishing a short position, such as making the initial sale at current market levels and placing any additional limit orders to sell above at closer levels. But if hourly momentum studies are still moving higher, we can reasonably wait and look to sell at relatively higher levels using limit sell orders.

Averaging into a reversal setup requires that you're able to buy/sell multiple lots over relatively large price zones, sometimes as much as 100 pips or more. Make sure that you have sufficient margin resources available *before* you start averaging into your overall position. Depending on the size of the buy/sell zone and your available margin balance, you may have to space your limit-entry orders farther apart or trade fewer lots overall.

It's always a trade-off between being in the right position to catch the move and getting in at the best price possible. It's quite frustrating to identify a potentially significant market reversal, leave a single limit-entry order, but then see the reversal take place without your order being filled. Averaging into the position starting at current prices is one way to make sure you're on board for at least some of the move.

If the setup works out, you'll have taken advantage of any favorable price moves the market has made, resulting in a better average rate on your position. If the setup fails, averaging into the position at successively better rates will cost less in the end than entering the whole position at the current market level.

Trading breakouts

A *breakout* or *break* refers to a price movement that moves beyond, or breaks out of, recent established trading ranges or price patterns captured with trend lines. Breakouts can occur in all time frames, from weeks and days on down to hours and minutes. The longer the time frame, the more significant the breakout in terms of the overall expected price movement that follows.

In the very short term, prices on a 15-minute chart may establish a trading range of 20 to 30 pips over several hours, for example. A breakout on such a short time scale might result in a 30- to 50-pip movement in a matter of minutes/hours. Daily trading ranges of 300 to 400 pips may see a breakout result in an initial 50- to 150-pip movement in subsequent hours, with more to come in following sessions.

There's no real fixed ratio or scale for range breakouts; we've just given those examples above to give you an idea of the relative scales involved. To be sure, a breakout of a 15-minute range can lead to the break of an hourly range, which can lead to a breakout of a daily range.

Breakouts are important because they represent a shift in market thinking. Most trading theories start with the premise that the current price reflects all the known information on that market at the moment. But rather than settling on one price and stopping, markets tend to consolidate into a zone of prices, or a range, where relatively minor price fluctuations are simply noise in terms of the grand theories of market price behavior.

For a range to break, then, by definition something must have changed in the market's thinking. And there's only one thing that will change the market's thinking: new information. New information can be anything from news and data to rumors or comments, down to the prices themselves. Many traders rely on price information as their primary source of decision-making information. If prices in USD/CHF have been capped by 1.0500 for the past four weeks, a price move above that level is new information and requires adjustments in the market.

The beauty of breakouts from an individual trader's perspective is that you don't necessarily need to know the reason for the breakout — just that prices have broken out. Of course, being aware of what's going on and what news is driving the market always helps give you a leg up in anticipating and preparing for potential breakouts.

In terms of entering a position, breakouts frequently represent important signals to get in or out of positions. In that sense, they take a lot of the guesswork out of deciding where to enter or exit a position.

Identifying potential breakout levels

The first step in trading on a breakout is to identify where breakouts are likely to occur. Pinpointing likely breakout levels is most easily done by drawing trend lines that capture recent high/low price ranges. In many cases, these ranges will form a sideways or horizontal range of prices, where sellers have repeatedly emerged at the same level on the upside and buyers have regularly stepped in at the lower level. Horizontal ranges are mostly neutral in predicting which direction the break will occur.

Other ranges are going to form price patterns with sloping trend lines on the top and bottom, such as flags, pennants, wedges, and triangles. These patterns have more predictive capacity for the direction of the eventual breakout and even the distance of the breakout. (We review the most common patterns and what they imply in greater detail in Chapter 11.)

The time frame that you're looking at will determine the overall significance of the breakout and go a long way toward determining whether you should make a trade based on it. Very short time frames (less than an hour) are going to have much less significance than a break of a four-hour range or a daily price pattern. The length of time that a price range or pattern has endured also gives you an idea of its significance. A break of a range that has formed over the past 48 hours is going to have less significance for price movements than the break of a range that has persisted for the past three weeks.

Trading breaks with stop-loss entry orders

After you've identified a likely breakout point, you can use a resting stop-loss entry order placed just beyond the breakout level to get into a position if a break occurs. To get long for a break to the upside, you would leave a stop-loss entry order to buy at a price just above the upper level of the range or pattern. To get short for a break lower, you would leave a stop-loss entry order to sell at a price just below the lower level of the range or pattern. Figure 14-1 is a chart showing EUR/USD and where stop-loss entry orders could be placed to trade breakouts.

The appeal of using stop-loss entry orders is that you're able to trade the breakout without any further action on your part. Breakouts can occur in the blink of an eye. Just when you thought the upper range level was going to hold and prices started to drift off, for example, they'll come roaring back and blow right through the breakout level.

| 03/22/11 | O: 1.00629 H: 1.01310 L: 1.00380 C: 1.01108 | +0.00479 |

Hourly AUD/USD

Recent range highs–buy a break above

Buying a retest of the break level

Recent range lows–sell a break below

Exit (sell) on break of trend-line support

Copyright © 2011 eSignal ForexCharts™

| 02/14/11 | 02/16/11 - 11:00 | 02/2 | #2532 |

Figure 14-1: Placing stop-loss orders to trade a breakout identified with trend lines.

Price moves like that can leave the most experienced traders caught like deer in the headlights. By the time they react, the break has already seen prices jump well beyond their desired entry level. Worse, by trying to trade at the market in a fast-moving breakout, you may miss your price and have to reenter the trade, by which time prices may have moved even farther in the direction of the break.

When placing a stop-loss entry order to trade a breakout level, be aware of any major data or news events that are coming up. If your stop-loss entry order is triggered as a result of a news event, the execution rate on the order could be subject to slippage, which may reduce much of the gains from getting in on the breakout. (We discuss slippage in Chapter 13.)

Trading the retest of a breakout level

The other way to trade a breakout is after the break has occurred. You may not have noticed the significance of a particular technical level, or you may not have left orders in overnight to exploit a break. You turn on your computer the next morning to discover that prices have jumped higher overnight and feel like you've missed the boat. But you *may* still get a chance to trade the breakout if prices return to re-test the breakout level.

A *retest* refers to prices reversing direction after a break and returning to the breakout level to see if it will hold. In the case of a break to the upside, for example, after the initial wave of buying has run its course, prices may stall and trigger very short-term profit-taking selling. The tendency is for prices to return to the breakout level, which should now act as support and attract buying interest.

You can use these retests to establish a position in the direction of the breakout, in this case getting long on the pullback. Figure 14-1 shows where you could have bought on the retest of the break higher in AUD/USD. Note that prices did not make it exactly back to the breakout level. When trying to get in on a retest, you may consider allowing for a margin of error in case the exact level is not retested. You could also consider using a strategy of averaging into a position, discussed earlier in this chapter, to establish a position on any pullbacks following a breakout. Here the averaging range would be between current prices and the break level.

Earlier we wrote that you *may* get the chance to buy/sell a retest of a breakout level. The reason is that not every breakout sees prices return to retest the break level. Some retests may retrace only a portion of the breakout move, stopping short of retesting the exact break level, which is typically a good sign that the break is for real and will continue. Other breakouts never look back and just keep going.

But to the extent that it's a common-enough phenomenon, you still need to be aware of and anticipate that prices may return to the breakout level. From a technical perspective, if prices do retest the breakout level, and the level holds, it's a strong sign that the breakout is valid, because market interest is entering there in the direction of the break.

Guarding against false breaks

Breakouts are relatively common events in currency trading, especially in the very short-term. But not every breakout is sustained. When prices break through key support or resistance levels, but then stop and reverse course and ultimately move back through the break level, it's called a *false break*.

There's no way to tell whether any given breakout is going to turn out to be a false break except in hindsight. To protect against false breaks (as well as maintaining trading discipline and sound risk management), you also need to follow up your stop-loss entry with a contingent stop-loss exit order to close out the position if the market reverses course.

Although there's no surefire way to tell whether a breakout is a false break or a valid one that you should trade, a few points to keep in mind are:

✓ **Time frame of the breakout level:** The shorter the time frame you're looking at, the greater the potential for a false break. The break of a price range on an hourly chart may trigger stop losses only from short-term intraday traders. But the break of a daily price range dating back several weeks is likely to spark greater interest from the market, especially systematic models.

✔ **Significance of the price level:** The more important the price level that's broken, the more likely it is to provoke a market response and to be sustained. A break of a three-month daily trend line is more likely to trigger a market response than the break of recent hourly highs/lows.

✔ **Duration of the break:** The longer the breakout level is held, the more likely the breakout is to be valid. Many false breaks are reversed in a matter of minutes. An hourly closing price beyond the break level increases confidence that it's a valid breakout, and a daily close beyond confirms it.

✔ **Currency pair volatility:** Relatively volatile currency pairs, such as GBP/USD and USD/CHF, are more prone to false breaks than others, especially in short-term time frames. Look for confirmation in bigger pairs, like EUR/USD and USD/JPY. If they're pressing against similar price levels, the less-liquid pairs could be leading the way.

✔ **Fundamental events and news:** What's the fundamental reason for the breakout? Did someone say something? Have major market expectations on monetary policy, for example, been disappointed or surprised? Sustained breakouts tend to have a fundamental catalyst behind them — a significant piece of news that has altered the market's outlook. If the news is relatively minor or not entirely "new" news, it increases the chances it's a false break.

Trading breakouts is a relatively aggressive trading strategy and is certainly not without risks. Until you've gained some experience in the forex market, you're probably better off focusing only on breaks of levels identified by trend-line analysis in longer time frames, such as daily charts, or breaks of longer-term price levels, like daily or weekly highs/lows. They may not occur as frequently, but they'll tend to be more reliable.

Making the Trade Correctly

When using an online trading platform, entering a position is as easy as making a few simple mouse clicks. At the same time, the simplicity and speed of online trading platforms make those simple mouse clicks a done deal that puts your trading capital at risk.

That's why it's important to understand from the get-go that any action you take on a trading platform is your responsibility. You may have meant to click Buy instead of Sell, but no one knows for sure except you.

If you do make a mistake, correct it as soon as you discover and confirm it. Don't try to trade your way out of it. Don't try to manage it. Don't start rationalizing that it may work out anyway. No trader is error-proof, and you're bound to make a mistake someday. Just cover the error and get your position back to what you want it to be. Covering errors immediately is one of the few hard-and-fast rules we subscribe to in trading any market.

Buying and selling online

We take you through the basic steps of making a trade online in Chapter 4, but here we aim to clue you in to some of the human and technical aspects common to online trading.

Most every online trading brokerage now provides for click-and-deal trade execution. *Click and deal* refers to trading on the current market price by clicking either the Buy button or the Sell button in the trading platform. Before you can click and deal, you have to:

1. **Select the right currency pair.**

   This may sound silly, but make sure you've selected the currency pair that you actually want to make a trade in. When the market gets hectic, and you're switching between your charts and the trading platform, you could easily mistake EUR/USD for EUR/CHF if you're not careful. This can also happen when different currency pairs are trading around similar price levels. If EUR/USD is trading at 30/33 and USD/JPY is trading at 31/34, it's easy to home in on the price and overlook the big figures, which would tell you you're in the wrong pair.

2. **Select the correct trade amount.**

   Make sure you've specified the correct amount you want to trade. Different platforms have different ways of inputting the trade amount. Some use radio buttons, others use scroll-down menus, and others allow you to type the amount manually. When the trading is fast and furious, make sure your selection has been properly registered on the platform. Some trading platforms allow you to customize your default trade sizes in advance, so you're able to simply click and deal on the currency pair of your choice.

3. **Double-check your selections.**

   Remember: This is your money; be certain now or be sorry later. In case you think input errors can't happen to you, think about the equity trader at a New York investment bank who meant to sell 10 million shares of a stock but ended up entering 10 *billion*. By the time the trade was stopped, the system had sold several hundred million shares. Ouch!

4. **Click Buy or Sell.**

   Be sure you know which side of the price you want to deal on. If you want to buy, you'll need to click the higher price — the trading platform's offer. If you want to sell, you'll have to click the lower price — the platform's bid. Most platforms have labeled the sides of the prices from the user's perspective, so the bid side will be labeled Sell, and the offer side will be labeled Buy.

After you've clicked Buy or Sell, the trading platform will confirm whether your trade went through successfully, usually within a second or less. If your trade request went through, you'll receive a confirmation from the platform. Double-check your position, and make sure it's what you want it to be.

If the trading price changed before your request was received, you'll receive a response indicating "trade failed," "rates changed," "price not available," or something along those lines. You then need to repeat the steps to make another trade attempt.

Attempts to trade at the market can sometimes fail in very fast-moving markets when price are adjusting quickly, like after a data release or break of a key technical level or price point. Part of this stems from the *latency effect* of trading over the Internet, which refers to time lags between the platform price reaching your computer and your trade request reaching the platform's server.

If you're continually getting failed trade responses, it may be due to the speed of your Internet connection, which is preventing your trade requests from getting to the brokerage trading platform in a timely way or delaying the incoming prices you're seeing so that they're always behind the real market. For more on how to optimize your trading on your smartphone or tablet, turn to Chapter 4.

Whatever the outcome of your trade request, you need to be sure you've received a response from the trading platform. If you have not gotten a response back after more than a few seconds, you need to call your broker immediately and confirm the status of the trade request. The deal may have gone through, but confirmations may be delayed due to processor slowness. Or the trade may have never been received by the trading platform because your computer lost its Internet connection.

Placing your orders

Orders are critical trading tools in the forex market. Think of them as trades waiting to happen because that's exactly what they are. If you enter an order, and subsequent price action triggers its execution, you're in the market. So you need to be as careful as you are thorough, if not more so, when placing your orders in the market.

We go over the different types of orders and how they're used in Chapter 4, and we look at the finer points of placing orders in Chapter 13. Here are some additional important tips to keep in mind when placing and managing your orders:

✔ **Input your orders correctly.** Make sure you've correctly specified the currency pair, order type, amount, and price. Most trading platforms are designed to reject an order that is obviously wrong, such as a stop-loss order to buy at a price below the current market, and will prompt you to correct it. But other errors, such as a wrong big figure on the order price, can be accepted and end up being your problem. Double-check your order after it has been accepted by the trading platform. If it's wrong, edit it or cancel it and start again.

✔ **Note the expiration of your orders.** Order expirations are typically good-'til-cancelled (GTC), where the order remains active until *you* cancel it, or good until the end of the day (EOD), which means that the order automatically expires at the end of the trading day (5 p.m. Eastern time [ET]). If you had an intraday position with a stop-loss good until EOD, and you later decide to hold the position overnight, you'd need to revise the expiration. GTC orders will expire on some trading platforms after an extended period of time, such as 90 days, so be clear on your broker's policy.

✔ **Cancel unwanted orders.** Some trading platforms allow orders to be *associated with a position,* meaning that the order will remain valid as long as the position is open. Such *position orders* will also usually adjust the order amount if you increase or reduce the associated position. Other orders are *independent of positions,* so even if you close out your position, the independent orders will remain active. Make sure you understand the difference between the two types, and remember to cancel any independent orders if you close the position they were based on, such as take profits, stop losses, or OCO.

Chapter 15

Managing the Trade

So, you've pulled the trigger and opened up the position, and now you're in the market. Time to sit back and let the market do its thing, right? Not so fast, amigo. The forex market isn't a roulette wheel where you place your bets, watch the wheel spin, and simply take the results. It's a dynamic, fluid environment where new information and price developments create new opportunities and alter previous expectations. Actively managing a trade when you're in it is just as important as the decision-making that went into establishing the position in the first place.

We hope you'll take to heart our recommendations about always trading with a plan — identifying in advance where to enter and where to exit every trade, on both a stop-loss and take-profit basis. (We go into more detail about developing trading plans in Chapters 10, 12, and 13.) Bottom line: You improve your overall chances of trading success (and minimize the risks involved) by thoroughly planning each trade before getting caught up in the emotions and noise of the market.

Depending on the style of trading you're pursuing (short term versus medium to long term) and overall market conditions (range-bound versus trending), you'll have either more or less to do when managing an open position. If you're following a medium- to longer-term strategy, with generally wider stop-loss and take-profit parameters, you may prefer to go with the "set it and forget it" trade plan you've developed. But a lot can happen between the time you open a trade and prices hitting one of your order levels, so staying on top of the market is still a good idea, even for longer-term trades.

Shorter-term trading styles looking to capture intraday and even smaller price movements will necessarily have more frequent adjustments to overall trade strategies. We say *necessarily* because short-term price movements can be extremely rapid as well as short lived. If your trade strategy is designed to capture only smaller price shifts — say, on the order of 30 to 50 pips — you'll need to be more proactive in guarding against short-term reversals of 15 to 25 pips, which constitute nearly half of your expected upside.

On top of that, short-term price movements are the market noise that makes up larger price movements. There will be a lot more 30- to 50-point moves than 100- to 200-pip moves. If you're going after the more frequent fluctuations, you'll have to be more nimble when it comes to adjusting to incoming news and price developments.

Monitoring the Market while Your Trade Is Active

No matter which trading style you follow, it'll pay to keep up with market news and price developments while your trade is active. Unexpected news that impacts your position may come into the market at any time. News is news; by definition, you couldn't have accounted for it in your trading plan, so fresh news may require making changes to your trading plan.

The starting point for any trading plan is determining how much you're prepared to risk, which is ultimately the result of the size of the position and the pip distance to the stop-loss point. When we talk about making changes to the trading plan, we're referring only to reducing the overall risk of the trade, by taking profit (full or partial) or moving the stop loss in the direction of the trade. The idea is to be fluid and dynamic in one direction only: taking profit and reducing risk. Keep your ultimate stop-out point where you decided it should go before you entered the trade, when your emotions weren't in play.

Following the market with rate alerts

One way to follow the market from a distance is to set rate alerts from either your charting system or your trading platform. A *rate alert* is an electronic message that alerts you when a price you've specified is touched by the market in a currency pair you specify. Rate alerts are a great way to keep tabs on the market's progress.

Rate alerts on charting systems usually have the capability of alerting you to price developments only while you're logged on to your computer or using your smartphone or tablet and the charting service. With charting systems, you're able to work on other tasks on your computer and keep the charting system minimized or in the background, which means you can use these at your job. If your requested price level is hit by the market, the chart system will typically start beeping or flashing and send a pop-up message.

Some forex brokers, including FOREX.com, can send rate alerts via email and text message direct to your smartphone. Many brokers now also have a large presence on Twitter and Facebook, so it's worth following your broker on social networks as well.

Rate alerts are a convenient way to follow the market remotely, but they don't take the place of live orders and should never be substituted for stop-loss orders. By the time you respond to a rate alert and log on to the trading platform or call your broker's trading desk, prices may have moved well beyond your desired stop-out level, leaving you with a larger loss than you anticipated. Rate alerts are a nice little extra service, but only orders represent obligations on the part of your broker to take an action in the market for your account.

Staying alert for news and data developments

Every trade strategy needs to take into account upcoming news and data events before the position is opened. Ideally, you should be aware of all data reports and events scheduled to occur during the anticipated time horizon of your trade strategy. You should also have a good understanding of what the market is expecting in terms of event outcomes and anticipate how the market is likely to react.

For instance, if the Fed chair is scheduled to deliver remarks on the economy or the monetary policy outlook, find out what her recent comments have been. Is she currently leaning hawkish or dovish? If it's an economic data release, make sure you understand what the report covers and what it means for the market's current expectations. At the minimum, be sure you know what the consensus expectations are for the report and what the data series has been indicating recently.

It's often said that the market's reaction to news and data is more important than the news or data itself. But you can't properly interpret the market's reaction if you don't have a grasp on what the news means in the first place. (See Chapter 7 for a detailed look at economic reports and Chapters 5 and 6 for major fundamental drivers and how the market interprets them.)

The other reason to stay alert for news while your trade is active is that many trade strategies are based on fundamental data and trends. If your trade rationale is reliant on certain data or event expectations, you need to be especially alert for upcoming reports on those themes.

Part of your calculus to go short EUR/USD, for instance, may be based on the view that Eurozone inflation pressures are receding, suggesting lower Eurozone interest rates ahead. If the next day's Eurozone consumer price index (CPI) report confirms your view, the fundamental basis for maintaining the strategy is reinforced. You may then consider whether to increase your take-profit objective depending on the market's reaction. By the same token, if the CPI report comes out unexpectedly high, the fundamental basis for your trade is seriously undermined and serves as a clue to exit the trade earlier than you originally planned. There's no sense hanging on until the bitter end if your trade rationale has already been knocked down. You may even consider reversing your position in light of the new data.

Speculating based on expected event or data outcomes is perfectly okay. It becomes a problem only if you maintain the trade even after the data/event outcome has come out against your expectations and strategy. Always relate incoming news and data back to the original reason for your trade, and be prepared to adapt your trade strategy accordingly.

Keeping an eye on other financial markets

Forex markets function alongside other major financial markets, such as stocks, bonds, and commodities. Although these financial markets have seen higher long-term correlations with forex in recent years, short-term correlations are far less reliable.

But there are still important fundamental and psychological relationships between other markets and currencies, especially the U.S. dollar. In that sense, we look to developments in other financial markets to see whether they confirm or contradict price moves in the dollar pairs. So, even though there may not be a statistically reliable basis on which to trade currencies based on movements in other financial markets, you'll be a step ahead if you keep an eye on the following other markets.

U.S. Treasury yields

U.S. government bond yields are a good indicator of the overall direction of U.S. interest rates and expectations. We focus on the benchmark ten-year Treasury-note yield as the main interest rate to monitor. We also keep an eye on shorter-term rates, like three-month T-bills and two-year notes. Rising yields tend to be dollar positive, and falling yields tend to be negative for the dollar. If yields are rising, but the dollar isn't, it suggests that other factors are at work keeping the dollar down and that dollar bulls should be cautious. If yields are falling and the dollar is falling, too, you're getting confirmation from the bond market of a negative U.S. dollar environment — lower interest rates.

Make sure you understand the reason for the bond yield's movements, because it can suggest different interpretations. If it's based on interest rate expectations — due to data or Fed comments, for instance — it's more likely to reflect overall dollar direction. If it's due to market uncertainty and a flight to quality — due to European debt concerns, for example — the impact on the U.S. dollar may be more positive. The larger the change in yields, the more important is the message that's coming from the bond market. Yield changes of more than 5 basis points (1/100 of a percent) should get your attention.

Gold and silver prices

Precious metals like gold and silver are typically viewed as hedges against inflation and safe-haven investments in times of financial market uncertainty. In recent years, gold and silver have seen heightened demand as alternatives to the major currencies, most especially the U.S. dollar, but also the euro, as the European debt crisis has threatened the single currency. As such, gold and silver prices tend to move in the opposite direction of the U.S. dollar overall (inverse correlation), but the short-term correlations are trickier. Gold and silver are relatively illiquid markets and mostly take their cues from the larger forex market, but the metals are no stranger to their own market-specific gyrations, typically based on breaks of technical levels.

Look for confirmation of the U.S. dollar direction in gold and silver prices. If the dollar is rallying and the metals are falling, for instance, it's a good sign that the dollar's gains are for real. If the dollar is rallying but gold is holding steady or even rising, the dollar's strength looks more suspect.

Oil

Oil is similar to the precious metals and other commodities in that it has a long-term inverse correlation to the U.S. dollar (dollar down/oil up and vice versa). But the same caveat also holds true — shorter-term correlations are less reliable, and oil is especially vulnerable to oil-specific supply/demand shocks. We would also note an *asymmetric bias* to the relationship between oil and the U.S. dollar. What that means is that oil is likely to experience greater strength on a falling dollar than weakness on a rising dollar, if all else is equal.

We also like to look to oil price developments for what they suggest about interest-rate expectations and relative economic growth. Higher oil prices tend to increase inflation pressures, which may lead to higher interest rates. At the same time, higher oil prices tend to reduce economic growth by under-mining personal consumption. Between the two, oil's impact on the growth outlook is more important due to the speed with which consumers react to changes in oil prices. Interest rate changes take longer. The recent surge in emerging market nations' growth has also heightened global demand for oil, so oil increasingly functions as a barometer for overall global growth.

Stocks

Long-term, such as over the last decade, there is very little correlation between stock markets and currencies. However, since the Great Financial Crisis of 2008–2009, there has been a stronger relationship between stocks and forex, especially the U.S. dollar. The relationship is best described as risk on/risk off (see Chapter 5 for more on risk sentiment), where stocks are con-sidered risk-seeking assets and the dollar is viewed as the safe-haven asset, as investors buy USD to buy U.S. Treasury debt, the ultimate safe harbor. In recent years, the risk-on/risk-off scenario has typically played out as follows: When the overall market environment is positive, investors embrace risk and buy stocks, reducing the demand for dollars, usually leading to dollar weakness. When the news turns bad, however, investors have dumped stocks and fled to the safety of U.S. Treasuries and the greenback. As long as recent financial travails plague the global economy, this relationship seems set. But when economic and financial conditions begin to improve to something resembling normalcy, we would expect the stocks/forex relationship to return to lower historical correlations.

Updating Your Trade Plan as Time Marches On

If you're like most traders, after you enter a position you're keenly aware of every single pip change in prices, at least as long as you're watching the market. Every little price change, and the attendant change in your unrealized profit and loss (P&L), evokes emotions ranging from joy to despair and everything in between. And that's to be expected. After all, at the end of the day, it's the P&L that matters, and pips are how that's measured.

But one element that tends to receive remarkably little attention from traders, at least on a conscious level, is the passage of time. Prices may seem to stand still for extended periods — when a currency pair may be stuck in a range (that is, it keeps trading back and forth over the same ground) — but time is constantly moving forward.

 Staying aware of time and its passing is an important skill for traders to develop..You know where the market price is now, so the question is really: Where will the market price be in the future? As soon as you think of the future, it becomes a question of time: *When* will it be there? If you consider these questions as you formulate each trade strategy, you'll go a long way toward incorporating time into your overall trade planning. More important, you'll gain an intuitive appreciation of the importance of time in trading, and you'll find yourself asking *when* as often as *why* or *where*.

On the most concrete level, as time progresses, it brings with it routine daily events, such as option expirations and the daily fixings, to name just two. These are specific time periods where traders can reasonably expect a flurry of activity, though it doesn't always materialize. (We run through the series of regular trading-day time events in Chapter 2.)

Time's passing also brings you nearer to scheduled news or data events. The *pricing in* of market expectations for major events occurs in the hours and days ahead of the event or data release. As the release time draws closer, anticipative speculation generally declines, and price movements can become more erratic as traders take to the sidelines ahead of the release. Prices may chop around more, but ultimately not go anywhere. All these market reactions are as much the result of time as they are of the event itself.

On a more objective level, as time progresses, it can add significance to, or detract significance from, price movements that have already occurred, frequently providing trading signals as a result. For instance, the failure of prices to make an hourly close below a break of trend-line support suggests that it may be a false break and that prices are likely to rebound higher. But if the break occurred at 10:12 ET, for instance, you won't know until the next hourly close in 48 minutes. Potentially more significant trading signals are generated from longer time periods, such as a daily close above long-term trend-line resistance or a prior daily high.

Trend lines move over time

If you're basing your trading strategies on trend-line analysis, you need to be aware that price levels derived from trend lines will change depending on the slope of the trend line. The *slope* of a trend line refers to the angle of a trend line relative to a horizontal line. The steeper the slope of the trend line, the more the relevant price level will change over time; the shallower the slope, the more gradually the price levels will change with time.

Figure 15-1 gives you a good idea of how short-term price levels based on a 15-minute trend line will shift over the course of just a few hours. Note how steeply the trend line is sloping upward. For prices to continue to move higher in line with this trend line, they must stay above the trend line as it rises over time, suggesting price gains of 10 to 15 pips per hour are needed.

Figure 15-1: Trend-line levels can change over time, depending on their slope.

Source: eSignal (www.esignal.com)

Using your charting system, you can pinpoint relatively accurately where prices must be in the future for the trend line to remain active as a support/resistance level. To do this, slide the cursor along the trend line, and note the time that appears on the horizontal axis at the bottom of the chart.

The same applies with longer-term charts, but the price shifts are typically less pronounced, meaning an hourly trend line may see levels adjust by 10 to 15 pips every 6 to 12 hours, and daily charts may see levels shift by 10 to 30 pips over a few days. But there are no concrete rules on this; it all depends on the slope of the trend line.

No matter what time frame you're trading, be sure to factor in the shifting levels of trend lines, if they're part of your trade strategy. You may need to adjust your order levels accordingly. In particular, consider the following:

✔ **Short-term and overnight positions:** Consider where trend-line support or resistance will be over the next 6 to 12 hours, when your position is still active but you may not be able to actively follow the market. You may want to use a trailing stop as a proxy for changes in trend-line-based support/resistance levels.

✔ **Limit-entry orders:** If your limit buying/selling order is based on a sloping trend line, periodically adjust your order so that it's still in play according to changes in the trend line. You may miss a trade entry if the trend line is eventually touched, but, in the meantime, its level has shifted away from where you first placed the order.

✔ **Breakouts:** A significant trend line that looks to be a mile away one week may suddenly be within striking distance in the following week or two weeks, substantially altering the market's outlook. Alternatively, the market may be focused on a price high/low as a breakout trigger, when a sloping trend line touching that high/low may actually be the catalyst for a breakout.

Impending events may require trade plan adjustments

As you develop your trading plan, we strongly recommend that you look ahead to see what data and events are scheduled during the expected life of the trade. If you follow that simple advice, you strongly reduce the chances of having your trade strategy upset by largely predictable events. More important, you'll be able to anticipate likely catalysts for price shifts, which will give you greater insight into subsequent price movements. Forewarned is forearmed.

If you've entered into a trade strategy based on an upcoming event — an expected weak U.S. data report, for instance — and the market has cooperated and priced in a lower U.S. dollar before the report is released, you may be looking at a profitable position before the data is even released. As the release time draws near, you may consider taking some profit off the table and holding on to the remaining partial position.

Consider the possible outcomes. If the data comes in negative for the U.S. dollar, and the market reacts by selling the U.S. dollar, you're still in the partial position to gain from further dollar weakness. But what if the data comes in stronger than expected? Or what if the data comes in weak as expected, but the market takes profit on short-dollar positions made in advance, in a "sell-the-rumor/buy-the-fact" reaction? You've protected your profit and taken some money out of the market before the event ever transpired. Now, that's called playing the market!

In the preceding scenario, we intentionally depict a short trade to remind you that being short is as common as being long in currency trading. You may be more familiar with "Buy the rumor, sell the fact." We just want to make sure you know that it works both ways.

Before major data and events, the market also frequently goes into a sideways holding pattern. The event speculators have all put on their positions, and the rest of the market is waiting for the data to decide how to react. These holding patterns can develop hours or days in advance, depending on what event is coming. Especially if you're trading from a short-term perspective, be prepared for these doldrums and consider whether riding through them is worthwhile.

Updating Order Levels as Prices Progress

Just because you've got a well-developed and considered trade plan doesn't mean it has to be carved in stone. Well, at least the ultimate stop-loss exit should be carved in stone. But when you're in a position, and the market is moving in your favor, it's important to be flexible in adjusting take-profit targets and amending stop-loss orders to protect your profits.

The key to being flexible in this regard is also being prudent — don't adjust your take-profit targets without also adjusting your stop-loss order in the same direction. If you're long, and you raise your take profit, raise your stop loss too. If you're short, and you lower your take profit, lower your stop-loss order as well.

Increasing take-profit targets

You've put together a well-developed trade strategy ahead of your trade, as we've recommended, so now that you're in the trade, why would you change your take-profit objective? That's a very good question, and you'd better make sure you have a very good answer, because we've also touted the virtues of not tampering with a trade plan after the position is opened.

So what constitutes a very good reason to extend your take-profit objective? Keep an eye out for the following events to consider extending your take-profit targets:

✔ **Major new information:** More likely than not, the new information will have to come out of left field. If it was a scheduled event, like a data report or speech, the market speculation surrounding it would have sopped up all the interest and muted its impact. *Major* means it has to come from the very top echelons of decision-making, like the Fed chairman, the European Central Bank (ECB) president, or other central bank chiefs; the U.S. Treasury secretary; or, increasingly, China. Surprise interest rate changes or policy shifts are always candidates. The more at odds the information is with current market expectations, the better the chances that it will generate an extensive price move.

✔ **Thinner-than-usual liquidity:** Reduced liquidity conditions can provoke more extensive price movements than would otherwise occur, because fewer market participants are involved to absorb the price shocks. Reduced liquidity is most evident during national holidays, seasonal periods (late summer, Christmas/New Year's), end of month, end of quarter, and certain Fridays.

✔ **Breaks of major technical levels:** Trend lines dating back several months or years, Fibonacci retracement levels of major recent directional moves, and recent extreme highs and lows are likely to trigger larger-than-normal price movements.

✔ **The currency pair:** The more illiquid and volatile the currency pair you're trading, the greater the chances for an extreme move. GBP and JPY are the most common culprits among the majors, and the commodity currencies (AUD, CAD, NZD, and ZAR) are also candidates.

As you can see, the list is pretty short, and there may be only a dozen or so events in the course of a year that warrant altering your trade plan. Be careful about getting caught up in the day-to-day noise and routinely extending your profit targets — it undermines trading discipline and the basis for your trade strategy.

Tightening stop-loss orders to protect profits

We're generally reluctant to extend our take-profit objectives unless there are significant grounds to do so (see the preceding section) or we're using a trailing stop loss. But when it comes to protecting profits, we're much more comfortable about adjusting stop losses to lock in gains. When you've got a profit in the market, taking steps to protect it is always a smart move.

When formulating your overall trade plan, always consider what price levels need to be surpassed to justify moving your stop loss. If it happens in the market, you'll be ready and know exactly what to do.

We like to focus on hourly and daily trend-line levels, highs/lows, and breaks of Fibonacci retracement levels. When these technical support/resistance points are exceeded, it's an indication that the market has seen fit to move prices into a new level in the overall direction of the trade. When that happens, consider moving your stop-loss order to levels just inside the broken technical level. If the market has second thoughts about sustaining the break, your adjusted stop will then take you out of the trade.

For example, say you're long GBP/USD at 1.5250, your original stop loss is at 1.5180 below, and your take-profit objective is above at 1.5380. Also above is resistance from yesterday's high at 1.5335. If that level is surpassed, consider raising your stop loss to break even (where you entered, at 1.5250) at the minimum. To more aggressively protect profits, you may raise the stop further to 1.5315 or 1.5325, locking in 65 to 75 pips minimum, on the basis that 1.5335 should now act as support.

The risk with adjusting stops too aggressively is that the market may come back to test the break level (1.5335, in this example), triggering your adjusted stop loss if it's too close, and then go on to make fresh gains. But the trade-off in that situation is between something and more of something, or potentially nothing and more of nothing. We prefer to have something to show for our efforts.

Another way to lock in profits in a more dynamic fashion is by using a trailing stop-loss order (see Chapter 4). After a technical level in the direction of your trade is overcome, similar to the preceding example, you may consider instituting a trailing stop to replace your fixed stop-loss order. Set the trailing distance to account for the distance between the current market and the other side of the technical break level, possibly allowing for a margin of error in case the break level is retested.

Chapter 16

Closing the Position and Evaluating Your Results

Deciding how and when to exit, or close out, an open currency position is obviously one of the last steps in any currency strategy, but it's also one of the most important. In our trading experience, no other part of a trading strategy has the potential to stir up greater feelings of self-recrimination by traders.

The classic trader's lament is "coulda, woulda, shoulda." And at no time is that sentiment more palpable than after a trade is closed out because that's when the profit or loss has been registered and you're looking at real money made or lost.

"Coulda, woulda, shoulda" refers to actions you may have taken in the market, but for some reason didn't. In the context of exiting a position, it captures after-the-fact thoughts like "I could've taken profit when it was testing x level," "I would've cut my losses sooner if I'd known it was going to keep going," or "I should've stayed in longer for the big move." The key is to understand beforehand that you're never going to know with 100 percent certainty how the actions you take now will pan out in the future. In currency trading, you make more decisions in an hour or a day than most people make in a month, and that's half the excitement!

In terms of maintaining a positive trading attitude, you have to accept that you won't be right all the time, so why should you kick yourself when a trade doesn't work out? The answer is, you shouldn't — unless you failed to actively plan and monitor your trades. If you didn't do that, you have every reason to blame yourself.

If you ever find yourself thinking "coulda, woulda, shoulda" — and everyone does — you need to look back not at what you failed to do, but at *why* you failed to do it. This chapter covers some of the main considerations you face when it's time to close out a position.

Closing Out the Trade

If you've embraced the idea of always trading with a plan — and we hope you have — you're way ahead of most of the market. Developing a thorough trading plan (trade size; entry levels; and exit levels, both stop-loss and take-profit) while you have a clear head (no open market risk and its attendant emotional distractions) is the first step to actively trading in the currency market.

Taking profit and stopping out

On the most basic level, every trade ends with either a profit or a loss. Sure, some trades finish *flat,* which is when you exit the trade at the same price you entered, producing no gain or loss. Most of the time, though, you'll be dealing with the agony of being stopped out or the ecstasy of taking profit.

Taking profit too soon or not at all

Taking profit is usually a positive experience for most traders. But if the market continues to move in the direction of your trade after you've squared up and taken profit, you may begin to feel as though you're missing out or even losing money. This is where traders may begin to fear they've taken profit too soon. The emotional element can become very strong, and past trading experience can begin to color your current thinking. The alternative is usually not taking profit at all, which ultimately leaves you exposed to continued market risk.

The important factor to remember is that you took profit based on your trade plan, whether it was based on a technical level being reached or an event playing out. You identified a trade opportunity and went with it, so enjoy the fact that you've got something to show for it. And don't get greedy. No trader ever captures 100 percent of any price movement, so keep your gains in perspective and remember: The market is not there to *give* you money. That's why it's called *taking* profit.

Above all, avoid making rash trading decisions after you've taken profit. The market may continue to move in the direction of your earlier position, and you may be tempted to reenter the same position. In some cases, reentering the same position may be the right thing to do, but until you reevaluate the market objectively and without the emotional baggage of previously being right (but not as right as you could've been), you run the risk of overstaying your welcome.

Also, avoid the urge to suddenly take a position in the opposite direction. If you were short and prices moved lower, for example, and your analysis and strategy have led you to buy back that short, you may be tempted to venture into a long position. After all, if you were right that prices would move lower, and you're now buying back your position, it stands to reason that the market may begin to move up — otherwise, why would you be buying now? But this trade is another trade entirely and not the one you identified earlier.

Treat each trade independently, and recognize that the outcome of one trade has no bearing on the next trade. Instead, take a step back and reassess the market after you've regained the objectivity that comes from being square.

Taking partial profits

One way in which traders are able to stay in the market with a profitable position and hang on for a potentially larger move is to take partial profits on the overall position. Of course, taking partial profits requires the capability to trade in multiple lots — at least two. The idea is that as prices move in favor of your trading position, you take profit on just a portion of your total position.

For example, you may have bought 15 mini lots for a total position size of 150,000. If prices begin to move higher, you may sell out pieces of the overall position, realizing profit on a part of your position, but hold on to the rest if prices continue to move in your favor. If prices reverse course, you've reduced your market exposure and you may still have a profit to show for the overall trade. If prices continue to rise, you can continue to take profit until your position is completely closed out.

Whenever you're taking partial profits, you need to modify the size of your stop-loss and other take-profit orders to account for the reduction in your total position size. Some online brokers offer a position-based order-entry system, where your order size automatically adjusts based on any changes to the overall position.

Depending on the jurisdiction in which you're trading, closing partial positions may be treated differently. In the United States, forex providers are required to account for your trades on a first-in, first-out (FIFO) basis. For example, if you buy one lot at 30, one at 20, and one at 10, you're long three lots at an average of 20. When you close out your first lot, you're going to be selling the one you first bought at 30. In most other jurisdictions, you're able to choose which individual lot you want to close.

There's no practical difference on your margin balance between the two, but some traders like the idea of closing out the lots with the most profit. The key here is that you've averaged into a position, and the market needs to reverse beyond your average for you to realize a profit under either system. If you take profit only on those lots that are in the money, you're still exposed to a loss from the ones that remain out of the money. If the market never fully reverses, it means it's still moving against you, and you'll need an exit strategy.

Stopping out before things get worse

As part of any trade strategy and to preserve your trading capital for future trading, you always need to identify where to exit a trade if the market doesn't move in the direction you expect. Devote as much time and energy to pinpointing that level as you need, always keeping in mind that a lot of short-term price action can be stop-loss driven.

Anticipate that key technical and price levels will be tested to see if stop-loss or market orders are there. Testing levels is what trading markets spend a lot of time doing. For this reason, we like to factor in a margin of error in placing our stops, based on the individual currency pair and the current market environment. (We discuss the pros and cons of applying a margin of error for stop-loss orders in more detail in Chapter 13.)

In our experience, no one is ever happy when a stop-loss order gets triggered. The fact of the matter is that stop losses are a necessary evil for every trader, big and small. You never know beforehand where a price movement will stop, but you can control where you exit the market if prices don't move as you expect. Most important, stop losses are an important tool for preventing manageable trading losses from turning into disastrous ones.

No trader is right all the time, so getting stopped out is simply a part of trading reality. Traders who apply intelligent and disciplined stop-loss orders occasionally may suffer setbacks, but they'll avoid getting wiped out, and they'll still be around to trade the next day. Traders who fail to use stops, or who move them to avoid having them triggered, run the risk of getting wiped out if the move is large enough.

Trailing stop losses for larger price movements

The one type of stop loss that traders may actually enjoy seeing triggered is trailing stop-loss orders, which are often used to protect profits and enable traders to capture larger price movements. (We explain how trailing stop-loss orders work in Chapter 4.)

Trailing stops are no surefire guarantee that you'll be able to stay onboard for a larger directional price move, but they do provide an element of flexibility that you should consider in adjusting your trade plan. For example, if your position is in the money and holding beyond a significant technical break level, you may want to consider adjusting your stop loss to a trailing stop that has its starting point on the other side of the technical level. If the break leads to a more sustained move, you'll be able to capture more than you otherwise might. If the break is reversed, the trailing stop will limit the damage.

Setting it and forgetting it: Letting the market trigger your order

When you've identified a trade opportunity and developed a risk-aware trading plan, you're going to have active orders out in the market to cover your position one way or the other (stop-loss or take-profit). Depending on your trading style and the trade setup, you can reasonably follow a set-it-and-forget-it trade strategy where your orders will watch the market and your position for you.

Medium- to longer-term traders are more likely to rely on set, or *resting*, market orders to cover open positions due to the longer time frame of such trade strategies and the burdens of monitoring the market overnight or for longer stretches of time.

Remember to use rate alerts to update you on specific price movements (see Chapter 15). The archetypal picture of the currency trader sleeping with a phone under the pillow is not really that far off. Depending on how your trade is developing, you can make order adjustments typically in a matter of seconds or minutes and get back to sleep (or whatever it was you were doing).

Shorter-term traders are more likely to follow a more dynamic approach, again based on the shorter time frame of such trades. Short-term traders are more apt to be in front of their trading monitors or using their smartphone trading apps while their trades are still open, but they should always still have an ultimate limiting set of orders to cover the trade strategy.

You may want to be flexible with where you leave your take-profit order, but always have a stop-loss order in place to protect you in case of unexpected news or price movements. If you're trading the market from the long side (meaning, you think prices in a currency pair are likely to move higher), you need to pinpoint the ultimate price level on the downside, which negates this short-term view.

Squaring up after events have happened

Depending on the basis of the trade opportunity you've identified, there will be very real hallmarks indicating what, if any, adjustments you should make.

Trades based on fundamental events (like a data report or an expected monetary policy statement) have a very real basis in both time and content. If you've taken a position based on a data release, for example, when the report is issued, you and the rest of the market now have that information.

If you've anticipated various outcomes to the report, you'll have a leg up on the market in interpreting the subsequent price action. If the market is not reacting the way you expected, it's a strong sign that other forces are at work. The market reaction to the data or news is usually more important than the event itself.

Most important, though, is that the basis for your trade strategy — the event — has taken place. If the market doesn't react as you thought it would, you have very little reason to continue to hold onto the position. Always relate your original rationale for holding your position back to the reality on the ground. When events turn out differently from what you expected, start looking for the exit sooner rather than later.

Exiting at the right time

In trading, it's frequently said that timing is everything. Truer words were never spoken. But that line applies to trying to time your entry and exit to capture tops and bottoms in the market — market timing, in other words.

But we're talking about the time on the clock on the wall. The time of day and the day of the week can frequently influence how prices behave and how your ultimate trade strategy plays out. If you're trading ahead of major data releases, for example, you need to be aware that price action is going to be affected in the run-up to the scheduled release, not to mention in its aftermath. There's no set way that prices will behave before data releases, but you still need to be alert to upcoming events that may dictate changes to your trade plan.

Similarly, if you've been positioned correctly for a directional price move in the New York morning, for example, you need to be aware that there may be a price reaction as European traders begin to wind up their trading day. Some London closes may see the price move continue in the direction it was going; other times, the price move may reverse. The question for you as a trader, though, is: Do you really want to find out which way it plays out?

At the minimum, you may want to make adjustments to your trade strategy to limit any negative impact from session closes, such as reducing your position size, tightening stop losses, or squaring up altogether.

Depending on the day of the week, you may be looking at different liquidity conditions (such as a holiday, a month end, or a quarter end, which frequently see lower liquidity and the chance for outsize volatility). If it's a Friday, the market will be closing for the weekend in a matter of hours. If you hold on to your position, you run the risk of being exposed to weekend gap risk. Do you want to wait until the last minute and expose yourself to the uncertain price action?

Staying on top of the time of day is as important a trading consideration as having the right position. When it comes to adjusting your trading plan or closing out your position, it frequently pays to be a clock-watcher.

Getting out when the price is right

When it comes to market information, the most reliable information is always the prices themselves. Sharp price reactions are usually strong indicators of significant market interest — interest that is either pushing prices faster in the same direction or repelling them in the opposite direction.

As you're monitoring your position in the market, you need to be closely attuned to significant price reactions, such as spike reversals or price gaps, with a good benchmark being typically more than 20 points over a few minutes. The sharp move in prices may be due to news or rumors, or it may just be a pocket of illiquidity. Either way, the sharp price move carries its own significance that is information to you. There's no set way such moves always play out, but if you're alert for them, you've got one more piece of information to help you decide when and how to exit your position.

If the rapid price movement was in your favor, you can look at it as a new high-water mark, or as a new support or resistance level. If the move is reversed, the tide is reversing, and you should consider exiting sooner rather than later. If the tide doesn't reverse, you've got a solid short-term price level on which to base your decisions going forward. If the price move was against you, you may want to consider that the market is not cooperating and adopt a more defensive strategy, such as tightening stop losses, reducing your position, or exiting altogether.

Assessing Your Trading Strategy

Active currency trading is as much a learning process as it is a speculative endeavor. Good traders learn from their mistakes and try to avoid repeating them in the future. Bad traders keep making the same mistakes over and over again until they give up in frustration or are forced to give up for financial reasons.

Successful trades also represent excellent learning opportunities, both about how different trading strategies work best and about your own personal response to them. Successful traders remember what they did right and try to emulate it in the future, knowing full well that no two trades are ever the same. Bad traders only remember that they won, but they fail to take the lessons of why they won to heart.

The best way to learn from each trading experience — both good and bad — is to make post-trade analysis part of your regular trading routine.

Identifying what you did right and wrong

Regardless of the outcome of any trade, you want to look back over the whole process to understand what you did right and wrong. In particular, ask yourself the following questions:

- ✔ **How did you identify the trade opportunity?** Was it based on technical analysis, a fundamental view, or some combination of the two? Looking at your trade this way will help identify your strengths and weaknesses as either a fundamental or technical trader. If more of your winning trades are being generated by technical analysis, you'll probably want to devote more energy to that approach. If more of your winning trades are coming from the fundamental approach, you're probably better off concentrating on a fundamental style.

- ✔ **How well did your trade plan work out?** Was the position size sufficient to match the risk and reward scenarios, or was it too large or too small? Could you have entered at a better level? What tools might you have used to improve your entry timing? Were you patient enough, or did you rush in thinking you'd never have the chance again? Was your take profit realistic or pie in the sky? Did the market pay any respect to your choice of take-profit levels, such as stopping short of it, or did prices blow right through it? Ask yourself the same questions about your stop-loss level. Use the answers to refine your position size, entry level, and order placement going forward.

- ✔ **How well did you manage the trade after it was open?** Were you able to effectively monitor the market while your trade was active? If so, how? If not, why not? The answers to those questions will reveal a lot about how much time and dedication you're able to devote to your trading. Did you modify your trade plan along the way? Did you adjust stop-loss orders to protect profits? Did you take partial profit at all? Did you close out the trade based on your trading plan, or did the market surprise you somehow? Based on your answers, you'll learn what role your emotions may have played and how disciplined a trader you are.

There are no right or wrong answers in this review process. Just be as honest with yourself as you can. No one else will ever know your answers, so you have nothing to lose by being candid. On the contrary, you have everything to gain by identifying what you're good at, identifying what you're not so good at, and understanding how you should best approach the market.

Updating your trading record

Recollections of individual trades can be hazy sometimes. Some traders may tend to favor remembering winning trades, whereas others may remember only the losing trades. The only way to get to the heart of the matter is to look at the numbers — the results of your trades over a specific time period, such as a month.

A trading record doesn't lie, but you still have to interpret it properly to glean any useful lessons from it. We find that depending on your trading style, it's best to approach analyzing your trading record from two different angles, each with a common denominator — average wins and average losses.

- ✔ **Long-term and medium-term traders:** Tend to have fewer overall trades because they're more likely to be looking at the market from a more strategic perspective, picking trade opportunities more selectively. If that's you, you'll want to tally your results on a per-trade basis, totaling up separately the number of winning trades and the number of losing trades, along with the total amount of profits and the total amount of losses. Divide the number of profits by the number of winning trades to find your average winning trade amount. Do the same with your losing trades.

- ✔ **Short-term traders:** Tend to have a larger number of trades due to their short-term trading style. If that's you, you're going to want to measure your results on a per-day basis. Tally up your daily profit and loss (P/L) and note the number of winning/losing days in a month, along with the average win/loss per day.

Your results can be very helpful in allowing you to further identify your strengths and weaknesses as a trader. The main focus is to evaluate how good you are at spotting trades and how your financial successes compare to your financial losses.

If you have more winning trades or trading days per month than losing ones, you're on the right track and you're likely adept at spotting trading opportunities or actively trading in and out in the market. If your losing days or trades outnumber your winners, you probably need to take a good hard look at how you're identifying your trades or making your short-term decisions.

Next, you want to look at the size of your average win and average loss. Again, if your average win is larger than your average loss, you're doing something right, and that bodes well. When you're right, you're right for a larger amount than when you're wrong — and that's just the way you want it to be.

Focus on what you're doing right, but also figure out what you're doing wrong. Refine your analysis of your trading results by breaking them down to smaller categories, such as day of the week and currency pair or even trade size. Are your losing days or trades concentrated on certain days of the week, such as Fridays or Mondays? For example, in our own experience, trading on the last day of a month was a losing proposition. Are your losing trades concentrated in certain currency pairs? Does the position size of each trade have any relationship to wins and losses? Are you winning more on large trades, for example, or are you giving up larger losses on smaller trade sizes?

Look at your results as dispassionately as possible. They're the real reflection of your currency trading. Learn from them, and use them to do the following:

- **Keep yourself honest.** You may remember only the winning trades and not realize you're developing bad risk-management habits.

- **Spot dangerous habits or lapses.** Over time, you'll develop and refine your trading style. If you're successful, you'll want to stay that way, and monitoring your trading results on a regular basis is the way to do that. If you lose more than you normally do on a losing trade, you may want to consider scaling back. If you're winning on more days or trades than normal, you'll also want to do a reality check and make sure you aren't overextending it.

- **Be your own best teacher.** Identify your strengths and weaknesses, as well as trading styles and market conditions that fit your temperament and discipline best. Focus on those where you experience the greatest success, and avoid those with bad results.

- **Identify market sessions and currency pairs that suit you best.** Interpret your trading results to help pinpoint currency pairs where you've had the most success and avoid those where you don't. You may need to adapt your trading schedule and concentrate on only a portion of a particular trading session.

Currency trading is all about getting out of it what you put into it. Evaluating your trading results on a regular basis is an essential step in improving your trading skills, refining your trading styles, maximizing your trading strengths, and minimizing your trading weaknesses.

Part V
The Part of Tens

Find ten beginner trading mistakes in an article at www.dummies.com/extras/currencytrading.

In this part . . .

✔ Discover the positive habits of the most successful traders.

✔ Manage risk effectively.

✔ Find resources for more information.

Chapter 17

Ten Habits of Successful Currency Traders

Here are ten rules we think define the best currency traders we've ever seen. Many of these rules apply to traders in any market, but some of them are unique to the currency market. The important idea to keep in mind: No one is born with all these habits. The only way to acquire them is the way other successful currency traders have — through patience, discipline, and experience.

Trading with a Plan

No successful trader will last very long without a well-conceived game plan for each trade. Sure, you may have some short-run success winging it, but the day of reckoning will surely come. Successful currency traders have a specific plan of attack for each position, including position size, entry point, stop-loss exit, and take-profit exit.

They stay flexible with their take profits, sometimes settling for less if they judge that that's all they can take out of the market at the moment, other times extending their profit targets if market developments are shifting in their favor. But they never move their stop-loss orders from the original setting unless it's in favor of the position to lock in profits.

Anticipating Event Outcomes

Trading is very similar to chess, in which the best players are thinking several moves ahead of their opponents. Successful forex traders look ahead to future events and consider how much the market has (or has not) priced in an expected outcome. They also consider the likely reactions if the event matches, or fails to match, those expectations. Then they construct trading strategies based on those alternative outcomes. While the rest of the market is trying to figure out what to make of the event, checking charts and redrawing trend lines, the forward-looking trader has a game plan already in place and is ready to trade.

Staying Flexible

Successful currency traders resist getting emotionally attached to positions. They recognize that it's not about being right or wrong — it's about making money. They adapt to incoming news and information, and quickly abandon an open position if events run counter to it instead of waiting for price action to take them out of their trade. At the same time, they're alert to fresh opportunities that may develop in the market and are prepared to react. To be prepared, they must keep sufficient margin available for additional positions. Also, they need an ongoing mental model of other major pairs so they can factor in fresh news and events. They may not be actively trading AUD/USD, but they still know the lay of the land for Aussie.

Being Prepared for Trading

Successful currency traders are always prepared, at least as much as possible in a market that's open 24 hours a day and subject to random events from half a world away. To stay on top of their game, successful currency traders are prepared for the following:

- **Upcoming economic data releases in the next week to two weeks:** Know what the prior report indicated and what's expected in the upcoming report.

- **Scheduled speakers:** Find out who's speaking (central bankers or finance officials), what they've said in the past, and what they're likely to say this time.

- **Central bank interest rate setting meetings and announcement times:** Know when they're scheduled and what decision the market is expecting.

✔ **Important gatherings of financial leaders, such as G20 meetings or monthly get-togethers of Eurozone finance ministers:** Get a sense of whether currencies are on the agenda and what actions are expected.

✔ **Liquidity conditions:** Stay aware of time periods — such as end of month, market closings or holidays, and time of day (for example, European close, option expirations, or daily fixings) — when market liquidity may be affected.

✔ **Unexpected events:** Use rate alerts to stay on top of price movements outside expected ranges. Follow up on alerts to check for significant news and to assess potential trading opportunities.

Keeping Technically Alert

Even if they're not pursuing a technical-based trading strategy themselves, successful currency traders are still aware of important technical levels in the currency pairs they're trading. For instance, they know the key Fibonacci retracement levels, where various moving averages are, important short- and long-term trend lines, and major recent highs and lows (see Chapter 11).

You may be trading based on price behavior or momentum analysis, but be sure to keep abreast of key technical levels as part of your overall strategy.

Going with the Flow/Trading the Range

Successful currency traders are able to assess whether the market is trending or likely to remain confined to ranges. If they think the market is trending, they aim to go with the flow more often than against it. When the short-term trend is higher, they're looking for levels to get long at, and vice versa when the direction is down. At the same time, they're aware that trends pause and frequently correct, so they're also actively taking profit at key technical points as the larger trend unfolds.

If the environment favors range trading, successful currency traders are able to switch gears and become contrarians, selling near the top of the range when everyone else is buying, or buying near the bottom of the range when everyone else is selling. Just as important, when they're in range-trading mode, they've defined an ultimate point when the range is broken. If that point is hit, they throw in the towel without any remorse, possibly even reversing direction and jumping on the breakout.

Focusing on a Few Pairs

Many successful forex traders focus on only one or two currency pairs for most of their trading. Doing so enables them to get a better feel for those markets in terms of price levels and price behavior. It also narrows the amount of information and data they need to monitor. Above all, they recognize that different currency pairs have different trading characteristics, and they're able to adjust their tactics from one pair to the next.

Focus on gaining experience and success in just one or two major pairs before trying to broaden out and take on the whole market. Look at other pairs only when they're trending or trading at key levels.

Protecting Profits

There are numerous market aphorisms on the benefits of taking profits, such as "You can't go broke taking profit." One of our favorites is "Bulls and bears each get a seat at the table, but pigs get slaughtered."

Successful traders take profit regularly, whether it's a partial take profit (reducing the size of a winning position) or squaring up completely and stepping back after a profitable market movement. Above all, when a trade is in the money, successful traders focus on keeping what they've made and not giving it up for the chance to make a little more.

If you don't take some money off the table from time to time, the market will do it for you.

Trading with Stop Losses

All successful traders lose money from time to time. What makes them successful in the long run is that their losses are relatively small compared to their average winning trades. The absolute key is to have a stop loss in place at all times to prevent an everyday losing trade from becoming an account killer.

No one likes to lose money, but the best traders are able to accept it as part of the cost of doing business. And the only way they can regularly accept losses is by keeping them small in the first place. Master this habit, and you're halfway there.

Watching Other Markets

Currencies don't trade in a vacuum, and smart traders keep an eye on other major financial markets as a matter of routine. The primary markets they focus on are benchmark bond yields of the major currencies (U.S., German, U.K. and Japanese ten-year government notes), oil, gold, and major global stock indexes.

On an intraday basis, they look to these other markets for confirmation of short-term U.S. dollar directional bias. For example, if the dollar is moving higher, U.S. ten-year yields are rising, and gold is falling, it's confirmation from other markets in favor of the dollar's move higher. If yields are flat or down, and gold is higher, the dollar's move up may be only short lived. On a longer-term basis, currency traders analyze those other markets for significant technical levels and overall directional trends, just as they do the currencies.

Spend the extra money for charting services that include live rate feeds for those other markets.

Chapter 18

Ten Rules of Risk Management

. . . .

In This Chapter

▶ Limiting the financial downside

▶ Getting a handle on human nature

▶ Managing your market exposure

. . . .

*W*hen people think about risk management in the context of currency trading, the natural tendency is to zero in on the risk of losing money. No two ways about it, that's the ultimate risk. But traders can head down many different streets before they get to their final realized profit or loss address.

Throughout this book, we stress that risk management is a multifaceted process that ends only with the final trading tally. In case you skipped it, check out Chapter 13 for more detailed ideas on the various forms of risk. Sometimes, what you don't know *can* hurt you.

How you navigate the avenues of risk has as much to with trading outcomes as it does with whether you ever reach the final destination. In this chapter, we group ten practical rules of risk management to guide you in your forex trading.

Trade with Stop-Loss Orders

Stop-loss orders are the ultimate risk-limiting tools. (The exception is data/ events where stop-loss order executions may be subject to substantial slippage. Avoid that risk by not carrying positions into news releases.) If you trade without stop-loss orders, you're exposed to virtually unlimited risk. Always have a stop-loss order in place for every open position, and don't move the stop-loss order except to protect profits. Do your analysis and risk calculations before you enter the trade, and then stick to your trading plan.

Leverage to a Minimum

Position size will ultimately determine how much financial risk you're exposed to — the larger the position, the greater the risk. Don't be seduced by high leverage ratios and take too large a position. Trading too large a position relative to your available margin reduces your cushion against routine, adverse price movements. Keep your use of leverage to the minimum needed to trade your strategy.

You can request a lower leverage ratio from most forex brokerages to systemically limit your leverage utilization. Just because they offer 50:1 or 100:1 leverage doesn't mean you have to use it all.

Trade with a Plan

The best way to limit the inevitable emotional reactions that come with trading is to develop a complete trading plan from entry to exit (stop loss and take profit) before you ever open a position. (We devote most of Part III to the merits of trading with a plan.) Committing yourself to having a trade plan for every strategy will also keep you from speculating on a whim or *overtrading* (always having an open position). Of course, no trading plan will work if you don't follow it, which brings us back to the human risks in trading. You stand a much better chance of sticking to a trading plan if you've drawn one up in the first place.

Stay on Top of the Market

Make sure you have a firm grasp of what's happening in the market and the currency pair you're trading. Know what data and events are scheduled in the days and weeks ahead. Consider liquidity conditions during your trade plan's time horizon. What has the market priced in and priced out? Anticipating market events and conditions won't guarantee a winning trade, but it will alert you to potentially disruptive circumstances that you can factor into your trading plan to limit overall risk.

Trade with an Edge

The currency market trades around the clock, but that doesn't mean you have to be in it all the time. Pick your spots, and choose your timing; don't get pulled in by the noise. Keep your ammunition dry, and look for trade setups with a clearly defined risk/reward scenario. Be opportunistic, and spend your time and efforts looking for trading opportunities still to come instead of getting caught up in the market move of the moment. Other opportunities will surely develop, and you'll be ready for them.

Step Back from the Market

When you're not involved in the market, a funny thing happens: Your perspective is clearer; your objectivity is at its peak; you're not emotionally invested in a market position. Make it a point to square up and step back from the market on a regular basis. Use the downtime to catch up on your charting and fundamental analysis. Take time off completely, and just forget about the markets for a while. When you return, you'll be refreshed and thinking more clearly, ready for new trading opportunities.

Take Profit Regularly

Taking profit regularly is the surest way to limit risk. By definition, if you take profit — even partial profit — you're reducing your exposure to market risk. Your trade plan may have a more aggressive profit target, but if market events play out in your favor, it pays to protect what you've gained by taking partial profit or adjusting your stop-loss orders to lock in some of the gains. It may be a fluke that the market jumped 40 pips in your favor on a data release, or it may be a fluke that the market dropped back by 50 pips ten minutes later. The only way to be sure is to take some profit. You can't go broke taking profit.

Understand Currency-Pair Selection

Market risk varies significantly from one currency pair to the next, based on volatility, liquidity, data sensitivity, and many other factors. Each currency pair brings its own idiosyncrasies to the table, requiring different analytical tools or strategic approaches. Different currency pairs also carry higher or lower margin utilizations and pip values. Make sure that you understand what currency pair you're trading and that your trading plan reflects that pair's characteristics. (Chapters 8 and 9 look at the trading behavior and drivers of the most heavily traded currency pairs and crosses. Not all currency pairs are the same.)

Double-Check for Accuracy

Currency trading is a fast-paced environment made even faster by electronic trading. The risk of human error in inputting trades and orders is ever present and requires diligence on your part to avoid costly errors. A stop-loss order won't help if it's entered for the wrong currency pair or the wrong amount. Make it part of your routine to double-check every trade and order entry you make, ideally before you submit it but at least immediately after you make it. Mistakes happen to everyone, but only careless traders let minor errors slip through and become big disasters.

Take Money out of Your Trading Account

Here's one you won't see in many trading books: If you've made some money in the market, make periodic withdrawals from your trading account. We call it *taking money off the table*. If your profit stays in your margin account, it's subject to future trading decisions, which represents an unknown risk. Keep your margin balance at a level that allows you to trade in sizes you're comfortable with. Also, remember why you're trading — it's not just about the money, but what you can do with it. Withdraw your profits, and spend or invest them the way you always said you would.

Chapter 19

Ten Great Resources

This book gives you a solid foundation for understanding the ins and outs of currency trading, but it can't cover all the subdisciplines of trading, such as technical analysis, market psychology, and strategy development. Those subjects are deep enough and rich enough to warrant further study on their own as you develop your own trading style and favorite techniques. We think you'll find the following suggested additional resources very helpful in gaining a deeper understanding of the technical tools, economic data reports, and practical applications of strategy and psychology.

Technical Analysis of the Financial Markets

Technical Analysis of the Financial Markets: A Comprehensive Guide to Trading Methods and Applications, by John Murphy (New York Institute of Finance), is *the* encyclopedia of technical analysis, written by perhaps the most prominent technical practitioner in the market. Murphy covers all the tools and all the rules in depth, from both a theoretical and a practical standpoint. Murphy also lays out one of the most comprehensive reviews of chart patterns you'll find anywhere. If you're going to have only one book on technical analysis in your library, make it this one.

Japanese Candlestick Charting Techniques

We're huge proponents of candlestick charting, and for our money, *Japanese Candlestick Charting Techniques: A Contemporary Guide to the Ancient Investment Techniques of the Far East,* 2nd Edition, by Steve Nison (Prentice Hall), is the best book on candlesticks out there. Nison takes you inside the linguistic and cultural meanings behind the myriad candle patterns, which leaves you with a more intuitive understanding of the patterns. With that greater understanding, you're more likely to spot viable candlestick patterns and understand what they're telling you. We keep this book handy and refer to it frequently in our own candlestick observations. (We look at several key candlestick patterns in Chapter 11.)

Elliott Wave Principle

Elliott Wave Principle: Key to Market Behavior, by A. J. Frost and Robert R. Prechter, Jr. (Wiley), is the go-to guide if you're interested in learning more about the Elliott wave principle. Elliott wave patterns are an important part of currency price movements, especially if you're intending to trade from a medium- to longer-term perspective. This book explains the philosophy behind Ralph Nelson Elliott's theories of price patterns and provides practical examples of how to apply those theories to all financial markets.

Technical Analysis For Dummies

Technical Analysis For Dummies, 3rd Edition, by Barbara Rockefeller (Wiley), is an excellent introduction to the many and varied tools and methods of technical analysis, all delivered in the easy-to-read *For Dummies* style. Rockefeller takes you through all the important tools and approaches, and provides plenty of real-life do's and don'ts that you can apply to your own trading.

The Book of Five Rings

The Book of Five Rings, by Miyamoto Musashi and translated by William Scott Wilson (Shambhala), is known as *Go Rin No Sho* in Japanese. This relatively short book (about 150 pages) is a fascinating exposition on the philosophy of strategy and rules of tactical warfare. Musashi was the greatest samurai ever to live, and this book is his end-of-life distillation of all the rules of strategy and swordsmanship gained in his lifetime.

Musashi's exhortations on timing and staying calm in the midst of chaos are as applicable to successful trading today as they were to martial artists in the mid-17th century, when the book first appeared. This book is not for a single reading only. Pull it out and reread it often. Not only does it contain advice on strategy and mental discipline, but it also offers lessons on personal fulfillment and finding a spiritual, focused, and balanced existence.

Market Wizards: Interviews with Top Traders

In *Market Wizards: Interviews with Top Traders* (Wiley), Jack D. Schwager, a veteran trader himself, interviews the legends of the trading world for their insights and philosophies of trading. *Wizards* is not confined strictly to the forex market; it offers a wider-ranging discussion of stocks, futures, and currency trading. In it, you learn how the likes of Richard Dennis, Bruce Kovener, and Paul Tudor Jones, to name just a few, approach trading. These traders are living legends today, but they all started out relatively modestly and succeeded through discipline, strategy, and diligence while managing intense psychological pressures. If you're in search of a trading style, these guys have plenty to offer.

Come into My Trading Room

Come into My Trading Room: A Complete Guide to Trading, by Dr. Alexander Elder (Wiley), was written by a practicing psychiatrist and trader. Elder's observations on the personal psychology and emotions of trading are especially insightful if you're new to the markets. His book is a well-rounded overview of all aspects of individual trading, from understanding emotions to managing money and risk to following the habits of an organized trader.

Zero Hedge

Zero Hedge (www.zerohedge.com) is a news website and content aggregator that reports on economics and the goings-on of Wall Street. This is one of the first websites we check each day due to its contrarian analysis. It often takes the opposite side of what the market thinks, which can be a refreshing, and much-needed, change in perspective. The blog also posts the most interesting and relevant research from some of the world's most prominent analysts. The posts are signed under a pseudonym, Tyler Durden, a character from the film *Fight Club.* There is a lot of speculation over who Tyler Durden actually is; at the time of writing, it is still unconfirmed. Be sure to check our Zero Hedge on Twitter at @zerohedge.

BabyPips.com

BabyPips.com (www.babypips.com) says it's a "beginner's guide to forex trading," but some of the posts are fairly sophisticated, so we recommend it for the beginner to intermediate trader who is trying to up his game. One of the best things about this site is that some of the contributors talk you through their trades. They go through the reason for their trades, the setup, and the execution. They often post after the trades are closed out to let you know what went well and what didn't, and why. This site is a good place to learn market dynamics and market discipline.

Forex Factory

Forex Factory (www.forexfactory.com) may not be as pretty as some other site, but it's an extremely useful resource. Here's why:

- ✔ It has one of the most-trusted economic calendars out there, which is extremely useful if your broker doesn't provide you with one.

- ✔ It includes market news and has a trade feed with its members' latest positions; the feed is updated in real-time.

- ✔ Perhaps the most useful thing about Forex Factory is its trader forums. These forums have different threads of conversation that offer you the chance to join a community of retail traders and talk through your ideas, problems, and so on.

- ✔ It's free!

Twitter accounts worth following

For breaking news, we like @bloombergnews and @reuters. These two wire services tend to break news extremely fast, so it's worth following them. In some shameless self-promotion, we also recommend @FOREXcom, which is updated by FOREX.com's award-winning research team. You can get access to their latest research reports and their technical and fundamental observations throughout the day, along with their latest actionable trade ideas. For other trade ideas and all forex-related news, check out @FXStreetNews and @FXStreetReports.

Appendix

Trading Strategies

. . . .

. . . .

*T*he forex market is the largest financial market in the world. A market with more than $5 trillion a day in turnover presents plenty of opportunities for the retail trader, but those opportunities won't be handed to you on a silver platter — you have to work hard to ensure you're successful in the forex market. In this appendix, we set you up to do exactly that by helping you choose the right trading strategy for you and giving you tips on implementing that strategy.

What's Your Sign? Determining Your Trader Type

There are thousands of forex strategies, but you need to choose the one that works best for *you*. At FOREX.com, we've grouped traders based on personality types and developed specific strategies for each. We've identified three trader types:

✔ **The scalper:** A scalper is a trader who looks for short, minimally profitable opportunities in the market that can add up over time. If you're a scalper, you don't have the patience to hold a position for a lengthy period and you grow bored easily when keeping trades active for too long. You're motivated by the excitement of seeing fast-moving markets, sometimes trading around major news events to realize the vast potential of a large move in a very short period of time. You aren't happy about placing a losing trade, but you're typically less impacted both financially and emotionally due to the small nature and frequency of trades that you place.

✔ **The swing trader:** A swing trader is someone who typically enjoys staying in a trade for as little as a few hours to potentially days. If you're a swing trader, you like the analysis aspect of trading — finding patterns that develop and exploiting them like a cunning strategist. Because you place fewer trades on a daily and weekly basis, losing trades could have more of an impact on your psyche, so keeping your longer-term goals in mind and sticking to the plan are imperative.

✔ **The position trader:** A position trader has a much longer time frame in mind than most other traders. If you're a position trader, you could be in a trade for months or even years if your conviction is strong enough. Usually based on a fundamental perspective of political, sentimental, or supply/demand reasoning, you brush off the fear of short-term movements. You're much more tolerant of drawdowns and could take losses for a very long time before finally admitting defeat.

To more precisely determine what type of trader you are, take the quiz at www.dummies.com/extras/currencytrading. *Note:* You can move between trader types. At the start, you may feel more comfortable as a scalper, but as you become more confident, you may prefer to be a swing trader and hold trades for a slightly longer period of time.

There's no "right" or "wrong" trader type — you just need to identify the type of trader *you* are and trade accordingly.

Looking at Trading Strategies Based on Trader Type

In this section, we offer some actionable trade ideas for each trader type. These strategies have been developed by FOREX.com's research team. We're grateful for input from Matt Weller, Neal Gilbert, Fawad Razaqzada, Chris Tedder, and our former colleague Chris Tevere.

Strategies for the scalper

In this section, we provide two strategies for the scalper. We call them the Red Zone strategy and the Opening Range Breakout strategy.

The Red Zone strategy

News trading (buying and selling around high-impact economic data) is notoriously difficult, to the point that many traders intentionally close all their trades ahead of major news reports like nonfarm payrolls (NFP) or central bank meetings. To be successful with this style of trading, you need to have a predetermined, disciplined structure — you don't want to haphazardly place emotional trades.

One potentially effective strategy is to take advantage of markets' tendency to gravitate toward round numbers, like 1.3200 in a currency pair like EUR/USD. These levels are significant for two primary reasons:

- ✔ Newer traders often set stop losses at or around these levels.
- ✔ Option strike prices are overwhelmingly set at round handles.

With a large swath of traders focusing on these areas, it's no wonder that they exert a strong influence on the market. The difficulty is determining how to design a trading strategy to take advantage of this tendency.

To describe the Red Zone strategy, we like to evoke the analogy of a football game. The final 20 yards before the end zone, where good teams have historically scored a touchdown 50 percent to 70 percent of the time, is referred to as the "red zone." (For our non-American friends, this area is analogous to the penalty area in your version of football [which Americans call soccer], where a team is more likely to score a goal on any open shot.)

Note that in both of these examples (football and soccer, er, football), a score is not guaranteed — it's just more likely.

The same idea can be applied to trading. When an instrument comes within 20 points of a round number (the "red zone"), a continuation to that round number becomes more likely, particularly following a supportive news event.

How it works

Here are the Red Zone strategy buy rules:

- ✔ Wait for a news-driven move.
- ✔ Set a buy-stop order at 0.*xx*80 ($*xx*8.00 for gold, $*xx*.80 for oil).
- ✔ Set a target at 0.*xx*98 ($*xx*9.80 for gold, $*xx*.98 for oil).
- ✔ Set a stop loss at 0.*xx*60 ($*xx*6.00 for gold, $*xx*.60 for oil).

Here are the Red Zone strategy sell rules:

- ✔ Wait for a news-driven move.
- ✔ Set a sell-stop order at 0.*xx*20 ($*xx*2.00 for gold, $*xx*.20 for oil).
- ✔ Set a target at 0.*xx*02 ($*xx*0.20 for gold, $*xx*.02 for oil).
- ✔ Set a stop loss at 0.*xx*40 ($*xx*4.00 for gold, $*xx*.40 for oil).

Because this is a short-term trading strategy, you want to trade heavily traded markets, such as major currency pairs, gold, oil, and widely followed indices, with low spreads. You may also want to focus on trading only during times of *high liquidity* (when many different traders are buying and selling) to improve the speed of entries and exits.

The Red Zone strategy in action

Example 1: EUR/USD Buy

This first example (see Figure A-1) shows the ideal execution of the strategy. Following the release of weak U.S. housing data, the EUR/USD rallied strongly toward 1.2700. In anticipation of a continuation to that level, the strategy suggested placing a buy-stop order at 1.2680 with a stop loss at 1.2660 and a target at 1.2698. When the buy order was triggered, the EUR/USD went on to hit the target within 15 minutes for a winning trade. Although the EUR/USD eventually rallied another 20 pips, the highest-probability trade was the initial run to 1.2700.

Figure A-1: EUR/USD short-term chart.

Example 2: EUR/USD Buy

A few weeks later, the EUR/USD was making another run for the 1.2700 handle after the announcement of a new European Stability Mechanism (ESM) for supporting the European banking sector. As in the preceding example, a buy-stop order was set at 1.2680 with a stop loss at 1.2660 and a target at 1.2698. In this case, though, rates lost momentum before reaching 1.2700 and hit the stop about an hour after entry for a 20-pip loss. As Figure A-2 shows, the failure to continue up to 1.2700 foreshadowed further consolidation, and prices eventually rolled over. When the currency pair reverses 20 pips from the entry, the probability of a move up to the round number decreases.

Figure A-2:
EUR/USD
short-term
chart.

EUR/USD: fx O = 1.26564 H = 1.26619 L = 1.26502 C = 1.26600

EUR/USD 15MIN CHART

TARGET 1.27000

STOP BUY 1.26800

STOP 1.26600

EU SUMMIT STATEMENT
OUTLINES PLAN FOR ESM
RECAPITALIZATION OF BANKS

1.25948

© John Wiley & Sons, Inc.

Example 3: AUD/USD Sell

Our final example (see Figure A-3) is a sell scalp on the AUD/USD. After dovish Reserve Bank of Australia (RBA) minutes, rates were approaching the 0.9300 level from the topside, and the strategy suggested setting a sell-stop order at 0.9320 with a stop loss at 0.9340 and a target at 0.9302. Following entry, the pair sold off to hit the target for an 18-pip gain within an hour. Although the AUD/USD did continue to drop from there, the Red Zone strategy is only concerned with taking a small, higher-probability slice out of news-driven moves.

15MIN CHART

AUD/USD. f x 0 = 0.92536 H = 0.92539 L = 0.92536 C = 0.92537

RBA MINUTES SHOW CONCERN
WITH AUSTRALIAN ECONOMY

STOP 0.93400

STOP SELL 0.93200

TARGET 0.93020

07:15   09:15   11:15   13:15   15:15   17:15   19:15   19th   23:15   01:15   03:15   05:15   07:15

Figure A-3:
AUD/USD
short-term
chart.

© *John Wiley & Sons, Inc.*

The Opening Range Breakout strategy

Let's face it: The whole purpose of doing any form of analysis — whether it's technical, fundamental, or statistical — is to try to identify higher-probability trading opportunities. One such strategy is to use a European opening range. This strategy will typically focus on EUR/USD, but it could be applied to any of the European majors.

The forex market is open 24 hours a day (Sunday evening through Friday evening Eastern time), but market activity in a given pair is not necessarily consistent throughout. The forex market is typically divided into three major sessions:

- ✔ **London:** Open 3 a.m. Eastern time, close 12 p.m. (noon) Eastern time
- ✔ **New York:** Open 8 a.m. local time, close 5 p.m. local time
- ✔ **Tokyo:** Open 6 p.m. Eastern time, close 3 a.m. Eastern time during the winter months; open 5 p.m. Eastern time, close 2 a.m. Eastern time during the summer months

How it works

Here are the basics:

- ✔ Identify the high and low during the half-hour just prior to the London open (2:30 a.m. to 3 a.m. Eastern time), and then look for a breakout of this range +/–10 pips or 1/10 of the daily Average True Range (ATR) and maintain above/below this level for 10 to 15 minutes. You're trying to detect a direction of the "flow" for the remainder of the day.

- ✔ From there, look to manage this bullish or bearish bias by focusing on one-, two-, or five-minute charts and using a combination of moving averages (13-SMA, 144-EMA, and 169-EMA) and oscillators (RSI, stochastics, and CCI).

- ✔ Other factors to include are major news announcements (usually in efforts of avoidance) and the time of day (when major markets open/ close, option expirations, fixings, and so on).

Noteworthy times to be aware of include the following:

- ✔ **Major option expirations:**
  - New York expiry: 10 a.m. local time
  - Japan expiry: 3 p.m. local time

- ✔ **Currency fixings:**
  - London fix: 4 p.m. local time
  - Tokyo fix: 8:55 a.m. local time

- ✔ **Currency futures:** International Monetary Market (IMM) closes 3 p.m. Eastern time

- ✔ **U.S. equity markets:** Open 9:30 a.m. Eastern time, close 4 p.m. Eastern time

Ideally, if price is struggling near these events (typically spotted by a bullish/ bearish divergence with an oscillator), it could be prudent to reduce the position size ahead of time. Additionally, this type of approach may help to minimize the emotional aspect to trading, because there's an identifiable area to know where you're wrong (the opposite side of the breakout's high/low).

The Opening Range Breakout strategy in action

In this example, EUR/USD made an important low during the 2:30 a.m. to 3 a.m. Eastern time time frame (which was preceded by an RSI bullish divergence with price) and shot higher shortly thereafter (as shown in Figure A-4). EUR/ USD appeared comfortable above the two-minute 144/169-EMAs, while the 13-period simple moving average (SMA) remained above the EMAs, and RSI continued to find support into the key 40/45 zone. Consequently, there was no reason to divert from the intraday bullish bias.

Plus, as highlighted earlier, another factor to keep in mind is the time of day. In the forex market, most London traders tend to close their positioning between 11 a.m. and noon Eastern time, while traders in New York close between 4 p.m. and 5 p.m. Eastern time. Accordingly, price often sees a final end-of-day push, followed by profit taking (typically spotted by a bullish/bearish divergence with an oscillator) near these times of the day.

Sure enough, just after 11 a.m. Eastern time in our example, EUR/USD pushed higher once again to finally reach the intraday ATR target of 1.2927, which was then followed by a bearish divergence with RSI just ahead of noon Eastern time.

Figure A-4:
EUR/USD
two-minute
chart.

Here are some general observations regarding potential opening range scenarios per week (these are just overall findings — they should *not* be expected):

> ✔ **Two days of the week:** Won't do much (finish roughly flat)
>
> ✔ **Once a week:** False break and potential reversal
>
> ✔ **One day a week:** Respectable movement (50 to 70 pips from highs/lows)
>
> ✔ **One day a week:** Reaches ATR target (pip amount generally equal to Average True Range using a 14-day period)

Note: If the ATR is achieved earlier in the week, the likelihood of it occurring twice in the same week is dramatically reduced. If it does occur, it's typically in opposing directions.

As a forex trader, when volatility begins to pick up, it's usually a time that you want to be trading currencies, not sitting on the sidelines. As a result, if this strategy has yet to achieve the ATR target on Monday, Tuesday, or Wednesday of a particular week, it may be sensible to pay close attention to this tactic on Thursday and Friday. Conversely, if the ATR is reached earlier in the week, it may be prudent to be on the lookout for potential market failures in the latter half of the week because they could be the marking of a false break and/or possible outright reversal.

Most important, the goal is not for you to think, "Wow, I need implement this strategy right away," but rather to analyze the way that you approach the market on a day-to-day or week-to-week basis and think about whether you're adequately taking into account time — because time may actually be more significant to a trader than price!

Strategies for the swing trader

In this section, we provide two strategies for the swing trader. We call them the Favorite Fib strategy and the Moving Average Crossover strategy.

The Favorite Fib strategy

The Favorite Fib is a Fibonacci-based strategy that takes advantage of momentum. It can be used on various time frames and markets, including forex majors, stock indices, and commodities, providing the trader with endless opportunities. The strategy could be used, for example, after some major economic news — ideally, at the earlier stages of the move following the news. But if the news merely causes a corrective rally or sell-off inside an established trend, then this strategy won't work as well. It's best suited for markets that are in a clear strong trend — for example, when the price is making fresh all-time, multiyear, or multi-month highs or lows.

The higher the time frame, the more effective the Favorite Fib strategy works. It's typically used on one- or four-hour time frames, although sometimes it can be applied to the daily time frame, too. The shortest time frame on which you can use this strategy is about 15 minutes.

A Fibonacci refresher

In the 13th century, Leonardo Fibonacci developed a sequence of numbers called the *Fibonacci sequence,* where each number in the series is the equivalent of the sum of the two numbers previous to it. (We could get really mathematical here, but we'll spare you the algebraic details.) This is the Fibonacci sequence: 0, 1, 1, 2, 3, 5, 8, 13, 21, 34, 55, 89, 144, and so on, out to infinity.

From this number sequence, we get Fibonacci ratios, which are important for traders. The math involved behind the Fibonacci ratios is pretty simple. All you have to do is take certain numbers from the Fibonacci sequence and follow a pattern of division throughout it. As an example, let's take a number in the sequence and divide it by the number that follows it:

$0 \div 1 = 0$

$1 \div 1 = 1$

$1 \div 2 = 0.5$

$2 \div 3 = 0.667$

$3 \div 5 = 0.6$

$5 \div 8 = 0.625$

$8 \div 13 = 0.615$

$13 \div 21 = 0.619$

$21 \div 34 = 0.618$

$34 \div 55 = 0.618$

$55 \div 89 = 0.618$

Notice a pattern developing here? Starting at $21 \div 34$ going out to infinity, you will *always* get 0.618! Other important ratios derived from Fibonacci numbers include 38.2 percent and 23.6 percent. (***Note:*** 50 percent isn't a Fibonacci ratio, but it's often used when looking at Fibonacci ratios.)

So, how do we use Fibonacci for trading? The relationship between these numbers gives us the common Fibonacci retracements pattern that is used in technical analysis. During a trend, currencies will often pull back or retrace a certain percentage of a previous move, before continuing in the previous trend. We use Fibonacci ratios to determine key support and resistance levels during this retracement process. You can also use Fibonacci extensions to see where prices may go in the future, based on the same Fibonacci ratios.

If the trade is based on a higher time frame, it's a good idea to zoom in to a five-minute chart in order to refine entry.

How it works

The Favorite Fib strategy is based on some Fibonacci retracement and extension levels: the 38.2 percent and 50 percent retracement levels (the latter is not technically a Fibonacci level; see the nearby sidebar for more information), and the 127.2 percent, 161.8 percent, and 261.8 percent Fibonacci extension levels.

To understand how the strategy works, let's say that following a strong upward move (for example, from point A to point B), the market retraces a little (to point C) because of profit taking and/or top picking, before continuing in the original direction (beyond point B). The strategy requires three price swings — the move from point A to point B, from point B to point C (correction), and from point C to point D (extension). Figure A-5 shows what a Favorite Fib buy strategy would typically look like.

2nd Target: 161.8% of BC

1st Target: 127.2% of BC

Entry: above B

Stop: below B (discretion required)

< 50% retracement of AB

© John Wiley & Sons, Inc.

Figure A-5: An example of a Fibonacci buy strategy.

In the Favorite Fib strategy, you're interested in some part of the CD leg of the move — the bit beyond point B, where entry is based. The profit target would be determined by a Fibonacci extension level of the BC move (more on this later).

One condition for this strategy to work well is that you need momentum. By definition, this implies that point C should represent a shallow retracement of AB, and then a continuation in the original direction, beyond point B. So, if price retraces more than 50 percent, or too much time elapses before it breaks point B, then the entry signal would not be valid.

In other words, for optimal entry signal, you need a strong move from point A to point B; a relatively quick and shallow retracement of less than 50 percent to point C; and then a continuation toward point D.

When point C is established, all the strategy's parameters can be determined.

Entry

The entry would be based on break of point B, and the objective is to ride the move toward point D, which would be a Fibonacci level, determined by the BC swing.

For a buy (sell) trade, the entry could be via a buy-stop (sell-stop) order a few pips/points above (below) point B, or it could be via a market/limit buy order after point B is broken.

Entry via a stop order ensures the trade would be triggered. However, in the case of a false breakout, it could mean buying (selling) right at the high (low). What's more, if the market gaps, the entry may not be at the same level as the one the trader had chosen.

Entry via a market or limit order allows the trader some time to determine whether the breakout above (below) point B is genuine or false. If price holds above (below) point B for, say, a few minutes, then the trader may want to buy (sell) at the best available price. However, the risk is that the market moves quickly toward the target without a pullback, and the trader misses the opportunity.

If the entry is based on a higher time frame — like the four-hour chart — the trader may want to hold fire and zoom into a five- or ten-minute chart and wait until price closes above (below) point B on the lower time frame before buying (selling).

Targets

The Favorite Fib strategy has two targets:

- The 127.2 percent level of BC, at which point the stop loss would be adjusted to break even to eliminate risk
- The 161.8 percent extension level of BC (or sometimes the 261.8 percent), at which point the position should be closed

One way to estimate which level price would most likely extend to is by looking at the retracement of the AB swing (that is, point C). If the retracement is around 38.2 percent or lower, point D could be at the 161.8 percent or sometimes 261.8 percent extension of BC. However, if price achieves a deeper retracement — say, to the 61.8 percent or 78.6 percent Fibonacci level of AB, then you should expect point D to complete around the 127.2 percent extension of BC. Of course, this would *not* be a valid Favorite Fib entry, because the retracement is greater than 50 percent.

Stop loss

For a buy (sell) trade, the stop loss would be some distance below (above) point B, ideally below (above) a small fractal within the larger swing. The maximum distance between the stop loss and entry should be less than the distance between entry and the profit target. In other words, the risk-to-reward ratio should be better than 1:1 (ideally, 1:2 or better).

Final notes

- For a higher probability trade, the entry should be in the direction of the underlying long- or medium-term trend.

- The speculator should be aware of other, longer-term, technical levels when trading the Favorite Fib strategy. For example, if the 200-day moving average is at 1.8560 and the target for the long position is at 1.8580, this trade should not have been taken. In this situation, it may be better to take profit at around the 200-day average rather than hope for price to reach the 161.8 percent extension (the original profit target that was based on a smaller time frame).

  The minute you notice yourself *hoping* for something to happen is when you know the trade is in trouble — get out as soon as possible.

- The trader should avoid taking on opposing simultaneous trades in similar markets (for example, going long on DAX and short on FTSE, or long on NZD/USD and short on AUD/USD, and so on). If the trader is feeling bearish about the AUD and at the same time bullish about NZD, she should look for a short trade on the AUD/NZD pair instead.

- If price breaks point B, triggers the entry order, and then loses momentum prior to reaching the first target (127.2 percent), the trader should close the trade at the best available price (even if it's worse than the entry price — why wait until being stopped out?). After all, the whole objective of the entry was based on expectation of a generous continuation move, which hasn't happened.

You can't force the market to give you what you desire. Never blame the market for getting it wrong — it all comes down to your own ability (or lack thereof) to respond to changing dynamics or conditions of the market.

The Favorite Fib strategy in action
Example 1: Buy NZD/USD

Figure A-6 shows you what NZD/USD looks like before it has reached its Favorite Fib target.

Figure A-6:
NZD/USD
hourly chart.

NXD/USD 1HR

0.80597 — 161.8%
Target 0.80590
0.80383 — 127.2%
Stop to B/E 0.80380
0.80215 / 0.80215 — Buy stop 0.80240
Stop 0.79970
0.79577 — 0.79597 — 38.2%
0.78546

4th 13.00 22.00 5th 16.00 6th 10.00 19.00 9th 13.00

© John Wiley & Sons, Inc.

Figure A-7 shows you how NZD/USD managed to reach its target Fibonacci resistance level. Fibonacci can seem a bit like magic — the support and resistance levels really do work!

Example 2: Buy GBP/USD ahead of a key economic release

As you can see in Figure A-8, GBP/USD was trading higher ahead of a key economic release.

After the economic data release, the pound reached its target (see Figure A-9). This is another example, of how Fibonacci extensions can work in practice.

Figure A-7:
NZD/USD hit
the target.

© John Wiley & Sons, Inc.

The Moving Average Crossover strategy

Moving averages are one of the most commonly used technical indicators across a wide range of markets. They have become a staple part of many trading strategies because they're simple to use and apply. Although moving averages have been around for a long time, their capability to be easily measured, tested, and applied makes them an ideal foundation for modern trading strategies, which can incorporate both technical and fundamental analyses.

The two main types of moving averages are simple moving averages and exponential moving averages; both are averages of a particular amount of data over a predetermined period of time. While simple moving averages aren't weighted toward any particular point in time, exponential moving averages put greater emphasis on more recent data. In this trading strategy, we focus on simple moving averages; the goal is to help determine entry and exit signals, as well as support and resistance levels.

Figure A-8:
GBP/USD
hourly chart.

How it works

Most trading platforms plot simple moving averages for you, but it's important to understand how they're calculated so you can better comprehend what's happening with price action. For example, a ten-day SMA is calculated by getting the closing price over the last ten days and dividing it by ten. When plotted on a chart, the SMA appears as a line that approximately follows price action — the shorter the time period of the SMA, the closer it will follow price action.

A favorite trading strategy of ours involves 4-period, 9-period, and 18-period moving averages, helping to ascertain which direction the market is trending. The use of these three moving averages has been a favorite of many investors and gained notoriety in the futures market for stocks. We retain the basic concepts of this strategy but put our own spin on them and apply them to numerous markets.

Figure A-9:
GBP/USD
hourly chart
after the
economic
data.

© John Wiley & Sons, Inc.

First, it's important to remember that shorter moving averages will hug price action more closely than longer ones because they're focused more on recent prices. From this, we can deduce that shorter moving averages will be the first to react to a movement in price action. In this case, we look at simple moving averages crossing over, which may signal a buy or sell opportunity, as well as when to exit the position (we use simple moving averages because they provide clearer signals in this case). It's important to note that this strategy should be used in conjunction with the overall trend of the market.

Entry

A buy/sell signal is given when the 4-period SMA crosses over the 9-period SMA *and* they both then cross over the 18-period SMA. Generally, the sharper the push from all moving averages, the stronger the buy/sell signal is, unless it's following a substantial move higher or lower. So, if price action is wandering sideways and the 4-period and 8-period SMAs just drift over the 18-period, then the buy/sell signal is weak, in which case we keep an eye on price to ensure it remains below/above the 18-period SMA. Whereas if the first two moving averages shoot above/below the 18-period SMA with a purpose, then the buy/sell signal is stronger. (In this case, a confirmation of a strong upward/downward trend can come from an aggressive push higher/lower from the 18-period SMA.)

Aggressive traders can enter the position if they see a strong crossover of the 4-period and the 9-period SMAs in anticipation of both crossing the 18-period SMA. In this case, we recommend ensuring that all moving averages are running in the direction of the break and that you keep a close eye on momentum. If momentum starts to dwindle early, it can be an indication of a weak trend.

Keep an eye on the overall trend by using medium-term and long-term time frames. If the market is trending in either direction, then investors have to be watchful of retracements in the opposite direction. Sometimes price action can retrace sharply, which causes the 4-period and 9-period SMAs to cross over the 18-period quickly, but because it's a retracement and not part of the overall trend, price action can run out of steam fairly quickly. A trend that's losing momentum will become evident sooner in the short-term SMAs.

Exit

This is where the strategy becomes more subjective. Our favored path of attack from here is to judge the strength of the trend and proceed accordingly. You can wait for the aforementioned moving averages to recross each other or you can use your own judgment to determine when to exit the position. In a strong trend, it's sometimes worth exiting the trend when it starts to head in the wrong direction over a few time periods, because sharp pushes in either direction can be subject to retracements. In weak trends, we tend to favor trailing stops. In any case, a big warning sign is when the 4-period and 9-period SMAs cross back over the 18-period SMA, especially if the trade isn't working out as planned (that is, it's a good time to get out to prevent possible further losses).

Stop

Ideally, a stop should be placed far enough away that it isn't triggered prematurely but close enough to minimize losses. It's basically there in case of a sharp spike in the wrong direction. In many cases, the 4-period and 8-period SMAs will cross over the 18-period SMA before a stop is triggered, which should be a signal to cut your losses.

Final notes

- We highly recommend using stop orders for all trades; however, placing such orders will not necessarily limit your losses.
- Look at short and multiple time frames; for instance, look at both the 10- and 15-minute charts simultaneously.
- Center your trading strategy on an effective risk-reward ratio.
- Keep an eye on the overall trend. Cautious traders should avoid going against the grain.
- Have an exit strategy before you enter the trade and wait for the signals. Don't let emotions cloud your judgment as the market starts to move.

Investors may improve their odds of identifying trading by using this strategy in conjunction with other analysis, which can help to determine the overall trend of price action and why the market is reacting the way it is. Did price action just break a key resistance/support zone? Was there an event that caused price action to spike in either direction?

The Moving Average Crossover strategy in action
Buy example: USD/JPY ten-minute chart

Notice that there is a strong push higher in price action after the crossover and then are a few opportunities to exit the trade (see Figure A-10). It's also interesting to note that when the 4-period and 8-period SMAs cross back under the 18-period SMA, it's a very uninteresting crossover (price action and the SMAs are very flat), so it wouldn't entice us to get short.

Figure A-10: Using moving averages to make a trade.

© John Wiley & Sons, Inc.

Sell example: NZD/USD 15-minute chart

Here there isn't a strong sell signal, but the overall trend of the pair is lower, so we're comfortable getting short (see Figure A-11). We would obviously set a stop, which is largely discretionary, just in case price action suddenly shoots higher.

Sell: 4-period SMA crosses over the 8-period SMA and then both cross over the 18-period SMA

Two exit signals: price is starting to retrace and the 4-period and 8-period SMAs crossover the 18-period SMA

Figure A-11: NZD/USD short-term chart.

© John Wiley & Sons, Inc.

Strategies for the position trader

In this section, we provide a strategy for the position trader. We call it trading the Ichimoku cloud.

How it works

You may hear people talk about trading the cloud. They're referring to Ichimoku clouds (short for Ichimoku Kinko Hyo, which translates to "one-glance equilibrium chart"). It's a moving average–based trend identification system composed of five different lines, two of which form the system's main component, the cloud. Ichimoku analysis is primarily longer term and best utilized on daily or weekly charts. In addition to assisting in detecting trends, the components of the system are also very useful in identifying key levels of support and resistance. A unique feature of the cloud is that it factors in time as well as price, because the cloud is projected several periods outs.

The Ichimoku approach was developed in the 1930s in Japan by Goichi Hosoda, a Japanese journalist. Hosoda spent 30 years developing his idea before releasing his findings to the public in the 1960s. Despite the numerous components of the system, the approach is easy to understand and follow (there is a reason why it's named the "one-glance" chart). Furthermore, Ichimoku can be used for all liquid financial markets. In this section, we cover the components and derivations of the Ichimoku system and explain how signals of varying degrees of strength are formed.

The Ichimoku chart contains five different lines with both a Japanese name and an English name that can be used interchangeably. The lines are modified moving averages because they're calculated by using highs and lows rather than closing prices. These lines are overlaid on a price chart so that prices can be viewed in relation to the Ichimoku chart, allowing you to quickly and easily identify a trend, as well as key support and resistance levels.

The five lines of the Ichimoku chart and derivations are as follows:

- **Conversion (tenkan) line:** (Highest high + lowest low)/2 from prior 9 days

- **Base (kijun) line:** (Highest high + lowest low)/2 from prior 26 days

- **Leading span 1 (senkou span A):** Average of tenkan/kijun lines from prior 26 days projected 26 days ahead

- **Leading span 2 (senkou span B):** Daily average from prior 52 days projected 26 days ahead

- **Lagging span (chikou):** Today's close projected 26 days backward

The numbers 9, 26, and 52 are used in the traditional approach. In the past, a trading week in Japan was six days (one week minus Saturday). So, 9 represents a week and a half, 26 is the typical number of trading days in a month (30 days minus 4 Saturdays), and 52 is used to represent two months of trading days.

Ichimoku's most prominent feature, the cloud (kumo), is formed by leading spans 1 and 2. The space between the two lines creates the Ichimoku cloud.

There are a number of ways that signals can be formed using an Ichimoku chart. The most common method is to look at the price position relative to the cloud, also referred to as the *simple form*. A break above the cloud is viewed as a bullish signal, and a break below is seen as bearish. Price movement that is contained within the cloud shows a consolidation and, therefore, no clear trend.

Crossovers of the conversion (tenkan) and base (kijun) lines generate what are referred to as *main form signals.* This is similar to the typical moving average crossover where a faster moving average (the conversion line) crosses a slower moving average (the base line). When the faster moving average rises above the slower moving average, a bullish signal is generated. Likewise, when the faster moving average crosses below the slower one, a bearish signal is formed. The difference with the Ichimoku chart is that not all signals are equal. Signal strength depends on the location of prices relative to the cloud:

- ✔ **Strong signal:** Price above/below the cloud in the direction of the crossover

- ✔ **Medium signal:** Price inside the cloud

- ✔ **Weak signal:** Price above the cloud when a bearish crossover occurs, or price below the cloud when a bullish crossover is made

The strategy in action

Figure A-12 shows you how to trade EUR/USD using Ichimoku clouds. As you can see, this is a slightly longer-term chart — it's a daily chart, because this strategy can favor traders who prefer a slightly longer time frame.

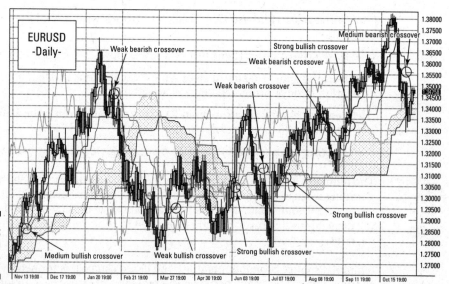

Figure A-12: EUR/USD daily chart.

Index

• E •

• *F* •

About the Authors

Kathleen Brooks: Kathleen is the research director at FOREX.com and has over eight years of experience in financial markets. FX is her specialty. She has worked in the institutional and retail side of forex trading, starting out as a trading analyst with BP. Kathleen produces research on G10 and emerging-market currencies using both fundamental and technical analysis methods. She focuses on providing FOREX.com clients with actionable trading ideas on a daily basis, alongside producing longer-term strategic pieces of research.

Kathleen has spearheaded FOREX.com's award-winning research offering since she joined Gain Capital in 2010. She also led the development of its social media presence; the @FOREXcom Twitter account that she contributes to has more than 50,000 followers.

Her views on financial markets, economics, and politics are regularly quoted in the global financial press. She is a familiar face to many as a regular on business TV, including Bloomberg, BBC, Sky News, and Fox Business, both in the UK and farther afield. She also presents weekly webinars for FOREX.com and FXStreet and has spoken at forex and finance conferences around the world, including in London, the Middle East, and Australia.

As of 2013, Kathleen is also a published author, having penned *Kathleen Brooks on Forex* (Harriman House). Kathleen and her team at FOREX.com won Best Analysis at the 2014 FXStreet Forex Best Awards. She is a graduate of both Trinity College Dublin and Columbia University.

Brian Dolan is a 20-plus-year veteran of the currency market. He has analyzed the G10 currency markets with a blend of fundamental and technical analysis to provide actionable trading strategies.

Brian has also been a frequent commentator on currency-market developments for major news media, including *The Wall Street Journal*, Reuters, Bloomberg, Dow Jones, CNN Money, and MarketWatch. Prior to his time at GAIN Capital, Brian was a vice president at Bank Julius Bär, where he advised hedge funds and high-net-worth individuals on currencies. He spent the first 12 years of his forex career trading major currency pairs in the interbank market in New York at some of the world's largest banks, including Credit Suisse, Dai-Ichi Kangyo Bank, and American Express Bank, as well as two years in Bermuda as a proprietary trader at Butterfield Bank. Brian is a graduate of Dartmouth College.

Dedication

This book is dedicated to all the clients at FOREX.com who have made our jobs so rewarding and interesting. Without their enthusiasm for learning about the complex world of forex, this book would not exist.

Authors' Acknowledgments

Readers of this book will benefit from the experience we've gained from our time at GAIN Capital. From the trading team to marketing and client services, there are so many people who have helped to guide the research team and make it what it is today. A special mention to Samantha Roady, for setting the whole process in motion and encouraging us to go the full distance. How could we forget the rest of FOREX.com's award-wining research team: Chris Tedder, Matt Weller, Fawad Razaqzada, and Neal Gilbert. You can thank them for contributing their superb forex-trading strategies to the appendix of this book. Finally, thanks to all the editors and staff at John Wiley & Sons, Inc., who have helped with this third edition, especially Stacy Kennedy, for organizing the book in the first place.

Publisher's Acknowledgments

Acquisitions Editor: Stacy Kennedy

Project Editor: Elizabeth Kuball

Copy Editor: Elizabeth Kuball

Technical Editor: McLean D. Giles

Project Coordinator: Erin Zeltner

Cover Image: © iStock.com/nicky39

pple & Mac

ad For Dummies,
th Edition
78-1-118-72306-7

hone For Dummies,
th Edition
78-1-118-69083-3

lacs All-in-One
or Dummies, 4th Edition
78-1-118-82210-4

S X Mavericks
or Dummies
78-1-118-69188-5

logging & Social Media

acebook For Dummies,
th Edition
78-1-118-63312-0

ocial Media Engagement
or Dummies
78-1-118-53019-1

ordPress For Dummies,
th Edition
78-1-118-79161-5

usiness

tock Investing
or Dummies, 4th Edition
78-1-118-37678-2

nvesting For Dummies,
th Edition
78-0-470-90545-6

Personal Finance
For Dummies, 7th Edition
978-1-118-11785-9

QuickBooks 2014
For Dummies
978-1-118-72005-9

Small Business Marketing
Kit For Dummies,
3rd Edition
978-1-118-31183-7

Careers

Job Interviews
For Dummies, 4th Edition
978-1-118-11290-8

Job Searching with Social
Media For Dummies,
2nd Edition
978-1-118-67856-5

Personal Branding
For Dummies
978-1-118-11792-7

Resumes For Dummies,
6th Edition
978-0-470-87361-8

Starting an Etsy Business
For Dummies, 2nd Edition
978-1-118-59024-9

Diet & Nutrition

Belly Fat Diet For Dummies
978-1-118-34585-6

Mediterranean Diet
For Dummies
978-1-118-71525-3

Nutrition For Dummies,
5th Edition
978-0-470-93231-5

Digital Photography

Digital SLR Photography
All-in-One For Dummies,
2nd Edition
978-1-118-59082-9

Digital SLR Video &
Filmmaking For Dummies
978-1-118-36598-4

Photoshop Elements 12
For Dummies
978-1-118-72714-0

Gardening

Herb Gardening
For Dummies, 2nd Edition
978-0-470-61778-6

Gardening with Free-Range
Chickens For Dummies
978-1-118-54754-0

Health

Boosting Your Immunity
For Dummies
978-1-118-40200-9

Diabetes For Dummies,
4th Edition
978-1-118-29447-5

Living Paleo For Dummies
978-1-118-29405-5

Big Data

Big Data For Dummies
978-1-118-50422-2

Data Visualization
For Dummies
978-1-118-50289-1

Hadoop For Dummies
978-1-118-60755-8

Language &
Foreign Language

500 Spanish Verbs
For Dummies
978-1-118-02382-2

English Grammar
For Dummies, 2nd Edition
978-0-470-54664-2

French All-in-One
For Dummies
978-1-118-22815-9

German Essentials
For Dummies
978-1-118-18422-6

Italian For Dummies,
2nd Edition
978-1-118-00465-4

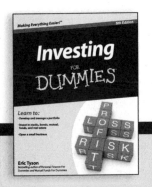 **Available in print and e-book formats.**

Available wherever books are sold. **For more information or to order direct visit www.dummies.com**

Math & Science

Algebra I For Dummies,
2nd Edition
978-0-470-55964-2

Anatomy and Physiology
For Dummies, 2nd Edition
978-0-470-92326-9

Astronomy For Dummies,
3rd Edition
978-1-118-37697-3

Biology For Dummies,
2nd Edition
978-0-470-59875-7

Chemistry For Dummies,
2nd Edition
978-1-118-00730-3

1001 Algebra II Practice
Problems For Dummies
978-1-118-44662-1

Microsoft Office

Excel 2013 For Dummies
978-1-118-51012-4

Office 2013 All-in-One
For Dummies
978-1-118-51636-2

PowerPoint 2013
For Dummies
978-1-118-50253-2

Word 2013 For Dummies
978-1-118-49123-2

Music

Blues Harmonica
For Dummies
978-1-118-25269-7

Guitar For Dummies,
3rd Edition
978-1-118-11554-1

iPod & iTunes
For Dummies, 10th Edition
978-1-118-50864-0

Programming

Beginning Programming
with C For Dummies
978-1-118-73763-7

Excel VBA Programming
For Dummies, 3rd Edition
978-1-118-49037-2

Java For Dummies,
6th Edition
978-1-118-40780-6

Religion & Inspiration

The Bible For Dummies
978-0-7645-5296-0

Buddhism For Dummies,
2nd Edition
978-1-118-02379-2

Catholicism For Dummies,
2nd Edition
978-1-118-07778-8

Self-Help & Relationships

Beating Sugar Addiction
For Dummies
978-1-118-54645-1

Meditation For Dummies,
3rd Edition
978-1-118-29144-3

Seniors

Laptops For Seniors
For Dummies, 3rd Edition
978-1-118-71105-7

Computers For Seniors
For Dummies, 3rd Edition
978-1-118-11553-4

iPad For Seniors
For Dummies, 6th Edition
978-1-118-72826-0

Social Security
For Dummies
978-1-118-20573-0

Smartphones & Tablets

Android Phones
For Dummies, 2nd Edition
978-1-118-72030-1

Nexus Tablets
For Dummies
978-1-118-77243-0

Samsung Galaxy S 4
For Dummies
978-1-118-64222-1

Samsung Galaxy Tabs
For Dummies
978-1-118-77294-2

Test Prep

ACT For Dummies,
5th Edition
978-1-118-01259-8

ASVAB For Dummies,
3rd Edition
978-0-470-63760-9

GRE For Dummies,
7th Edition
978-0-470-88921-3

Officer Candidate Tests
For Dummies
978-0-470-59876-4

Physician's Assistant Exam
For Dummies
978-1-118-11556-5

Series 7 Exam For Dummies
978-0-470-09932-2

Windows 8

Windows 8.1 All-in-One
For Dummies
978-1-118-82087-2

Windows 8.1 For Dummies
978-1-118-82121-3

Windows 8.1 For Dummies
Book + DVD Bundle
978-1-118-82107-7

Available in print and e-book formats.

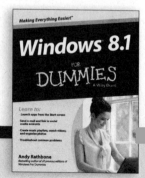

Available wherever books are sold. **For more information or to order direct visit www.dummies.com**

Take Dummies with you everywhere you go!

Whether you are excited about e-books, want more from the web, must have your mobile apps, or are swept up in social media, Dummies makes everything easier.

For Dummies is the global leader in the reference category and one of the most trusted and highly regarded brands in the world. No longer just focused on books, customers now have access to the For Dummies content they need in the format they want. Let us help you develop a solution that will fit your brand and help you connect with your customers.

Advertising & Sponsorships

Connect with an engaged audience on a powerful multimedia site, and position your message alongside expert how-to content.

Targeted ads • Video • Email marketing • Microsites • Sweepstakes sponsorship

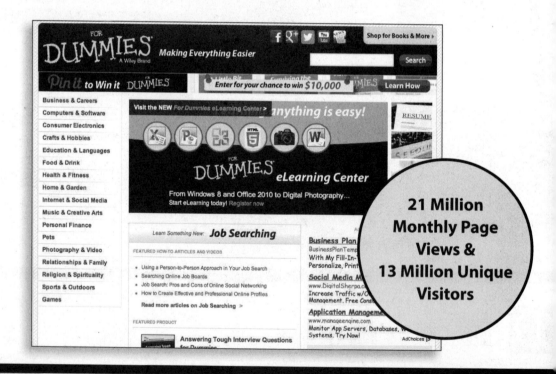

Custom Publishing

Reach a global audience in any language by creating a solution that will differentiate you from competitors, amplify your message, and encourage customers to make a buying decision.

Apps • Books • eBooks • Video • Audio • Webinars

   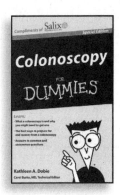

Brand Licensing & Content

Leverage the strength of the world's most popular reference brand to reach new audiences and channels of distribution.

For more information, visit www.Dummies.com/biz